Communicating Science: Contexts and Channels

Communicating Science: Contexts and Channels is a collection of articles that consider the communication between scientists and the public.

The first part of the reader includes material about what the public needs to know about science and why. It includes discussion of case studies of the public use of scientific information. The second part looks at the variety of ways in which scientific ideas are communicated to the public, either in formal education or by informal means. The informal sources of scientific knowledge considered include popular science books (non-fiction, fiction and science fiction), museums and science centres, and television programmes. Chapters include discussion of the role of museum visits in promoting scientific literacy, development of museum special exhibits, visitor behaviour and new trends in communicating science in museums, and a discussion of science in popular science books and on television.

To communicate science one must have an idea of what people think science is and how it works, but also how the mass media work and how they represent science. Therefore the third part of this reader includes material on the relationship between scientists and the media and covers representations of science (as an activity) in the media and representations of scientific issues or controversies in the media. For example, one chapter is an empirical investigation of the coverage of the 'Life on Mars' story which occurred in the summer of 1996, and another is a discussion of the media coverage of food scares.

Written with scientists in mind, this book is also eminently suitable for and accessible to students of science policy, media or communications courses.

Eileen Scanlon, **Elizabeth Whitelegg** and **Simeon Yates** are all members of the Open University MSc in Science team.

Companion volume

The companion volume in this series is:

Communicating Science: Professional Contexts edited by Eileen Scanlon, Roger Hill and Kirk Junker.

Both of these Readers are part of a course, Communicating Science, that is itself part of the Open University MSc in Science Programme.

The Open University MSc in Science

The Open University MSc in Science is a new 'distance-taught' programme which has been designed for students who want to explore broad scientific topics at postgraduate level. It provides opportunities to pursue some of contemporary science's most pressing issues using innovative teaching methods pioneered by the Open University.

Structure of the MSc

The MSc is a modular degree and students are therefore free to select from a range of options the programme that best fits with their interests and professional goals. The programme will deal in a topic-led way with two main themes or 'strands': *Studies of Science* and *Frontiers in Medical Science*.

Courses currently available

Science and the Public
Imaging and Molecules in Medicine
Communicating Science
Issues in Brain and Behaviour
The Project Module

It is also possible to count study of other Master's modules towards the MSc in Science.

OU supported learning

The MSc in Science programme provides great flexibility. Students study at their own pace, in their own time, anywhere in the European Union. They receive specially prepared course materials, and benefit from tutorial support (both electronically and via Day Schools), thus offering them the chance to work with other students.

How to apply

If you would like to register for this programme, or simply find out more information, please write for the MSc in Science prospectus to the Course Reservation Centre, PO Box 724, The Open University, Walton Hall, Milton Keynes, MK7 6ZS, UK. (Telephone 0(0 44) 1908 653231.) Details can also be viewed on our Web page http://watt.open. ac.uk/SciMSc/mscsci.html

Communicating Science: Contexts and Channels

Reader 2

Edited by Eileen Scanlon, Elizabeth Whitelegg and Simeon Yates

London and New York
in association with
The Open University

First published 1999
by Routledge
11 New Fetter Lane, London EC4P 4EE

Simultaneously published in the USA and Canada
by Routledge
29 West 35th Street, New York, NY 10001

Typeset in Galliard by
J&L Composition Ltd, Filey, North Yorkshire
Printed and bound in Great Britain by
TJ International Ltd, Padstow, Cornwall

British Library Cataloguing in Publication Data
A catalogue record for this book is available from the British Library

Library of Congress Cataloging in Publication Data
Communicating science.
    p. cm.
    Includes bibliographical references and index.
    Contents: Reader 1. Professional contexts/edited by Eileen Scanlon,
    Roger Hill, and Kirk Junker. – Reader 2. Contexts and channels/
    edited by Eileen Scanlon, Elizabeth Whitelegg and Simeon Yates.
    1. Communication in science. 2. Science news. I. Scanlon, Eileen.
    Q223.C6542   1998
    501'.4–dc21   98-22290
                                                                    CIP

ISBN 0–415–19752–X (hbk)
ISBN 0–415–19753–8 (pbk)

Contents

Figures

Tables

Preface

This reader is a collection of articles dealing with the communication between scientists and the public – one of two readers which form the key part of the readings in the course. The other reader deals with communication between scientists and between scientists and other professionals.

These two volumes of readings form a small part of the Master's module on *Communicating Science* which is part of a Master's course in Science being produced by the Science Faculty of the Open University. It is being studied by students aiming for a qualification in the Studies of Science, but it also acts as a subsidiary course for students aiming for a Master's degree in the Frontiers of Medical Science. The course aims to help students to develop skills in communicating scientific ideas to a variety of audiences, to develop skills in the study of communication, and to consider ways in which the contemporary mass media influence the communication of scientific information and understanding. Study materials provided by the University also include a study commentary, set texts and a CD-ROM, with a library of selected papers and video material produced by the BBC. Our students also have access to the Internet and receive tutorials using computer conferencing.

Some of the material in this reader is totally new, commissioned by the editors for use in our course; some has been adapted and edited from previously published papers in journals, conference proceedings or books. As a result, a range of styles have been used by the authors, which were appropriate for their original contexts, and also a range of referencing styles are in use in the volume; students of our course may notice that they do not all conform to our course referencing style.

The first part of this reader includes material on what the public needs to know about science and why. It includes some discussion of case studies of the public use of scientific information. The second part looks at the variety of ways in which scientific ideas are communicated to the public, either in formal education or by informal means. The informal sources of scientific knowledge include popular science books, science fiction, and museums and science centres. Chapters include discussion of the role of museum visits in promoting scientific literacy, analysis of museum special exhibits and visitor behaviour, new trends in communicating science in museums, and a discussion of science on television. Science writing for the public is also discussed.

To communicate science it is necessary to have an idea about what people think science is and how it works, and also how the mass media work, and how they represent science. Therefore the third part of this reader includes material on the relationship between scientists and the media and covers representations of science (as an activity) in the media and representations of scientific issues or controversies in the media. For example, we include an empirical investigation of the coverage of the 'Life on Mars' story that occurred in the summer of 1996, and a discussion of media coverage of food scares.

This is a book that encourages scientists to consider these issues but is also suitable for students in the area of science policy, media and communications courses.

The editors would like to thank the other members of the course team for their help in selecting the articles. Opinions expressed in the articles are not necessarily those of the course team or of the Open University.

The editors also wish to thank the authors who produced newly commissioned material: Ben Gammon, Science Museum, London, UK; Jo Graham, Science Museum, London, UK; Jannette Griffin, University of Technology, Sydney, Australia; Jon Turney, University College London, UK; Russell Stannard, Open University, UK; Robert Lambourne, Open University, UK; David Miller, University of Stirling, UK; Richard Holliman, Open University, UK.

Eileen Scanlon

Part I

What the public needs to know and why

Introduction

Eileen Scanlon

The first part of this reader includes material which investigates what the public needs to know about science and why. The first paper, by Brian Wynne, reviews relationships between members of the public and science, 'that diverse body of institutions, knowledges and disciplinary scientists' in local settings and reviews a number of ongoing research projects. It also argues against a simplistic view of the public understanding of science and moving towards locating issues of the public understanding of science within a specific practical social context. It highlights the importance of moving away from large-scale samples and standardized questions to participant observation and in-depth interviews. The projects covered include hill farmers in Cumbria after the Chernobyl crisis and the public involved in familial hypercholesterolemia.

The second paper, by Alan Irwin, discusses the relationship between science, technical knowledge and the wider population, critiquing the notion that 'the future belongs to science and those who are friends with science' and reviewing past and current pressures on scientists to communicate with the public in terms of a number of case studies.

Chapter 1

Knowledges in context*

B. Wynne

Our projects begin by exploring the relationships between 'citizens' and 'sources' – between members and groups of the public and that diverse body of institutions, knowledges and disciplinary specialists that we term *science*. We ask questions such as: What do people mean by science? Where do they turn for scientific information and advice? What motivates them to do so? How do they relate this information or advice to everyday experience and to other forms of knowledge? We focus on the diverse encounters with science and expertise that typify everyday experience, a central analytical issue being the construction of authority.

Some important prior points must be emphasized:

1   Although our *empirical* focus has usually been *local* settings, the common patterns emerging from our findings – and indeed their consistency with those of the group studying formal communication settings[1] – indicate their more *universal* significance and validity, both conceptually and in terms of practical policy implications. The projects were set up and planned separately from one another, making their convergence over findings all the more striking.

2   The findings distilled here for policy consideration are only part of a further range of conceptual issues investigated in these projects. Some of these investigations have produced surprises and falsified initial hypotheses, which we will follow up in forthcoming publications.

3   Just like other social institutions, policy institutions tend to take themselves for granted and recognize 'relevant' or 'feasible' policy proposals only if they fit within the 'natural' framework of existing institutional structures. Our research indicates that the current institutional structures within which science is organized and projected may be part of the problem in public understanding and uptake of science. We feel it is therefore necessary to develop a wider *conceptual* framework clarifying the integration of what are defined as natural knowledges and natural institutional frameworks. Only

*Previously published in *Science, Technology, & Human Values* (1991) Vol. 16, No. 1, pp. 111–21.

with such a conceptual basis can we understand the full dimensions of public uptake and lack of uptake of science. It is only from such a conceptual basis that constructive development and redesign of institutional structures concerning science and policy can take place in a measured and self-aware way, rather than as *ad hoc* piecemeal and blind reaction to political forces and events. The full conceptual structure of this more complex policy-oriented output cannot be articulated here, though we hope the grounds for it can be recognized in this outline of our research findings.

4   As a corollary to the previous observation, we should note as an object of curiosity the science-centered basis of the whole research program on the public understanding of science. In this, it reflects a wider belief in scientific and policy circles that this is *naturally* how the world is. The assumption appears natural that science is unitary and coherent, and that it should be central to everyday beliefs and practices. This allows us not only to measure how far people fall short of some level of scientific understanding – that is, their 'ignorance' – but also to assume that such ignorance indicates a deficit of democratic capability.

In sharp contrast with this common perspective, our research begins from the now everyday insight in sociology of science that there is no clear consensus even among scientists themselves as to what is 'science' or 'scientific knowledge' in any specific context. This question should not be ignored in our enthusiasm to explore people's attitudes toward or understanding of 'it', as if it is unproblematic. We wish to stress, therefore, that studying the public understanding of science requires us to devote equal attention to the various ways in which scientists themselves understand, interpret and represent 'science'. Otherwise, we tacitly consolidate the false view that all the problems have to do with the public's understandings rather than also with scientists and scientific institutions.

In light of this, it should not be surprising, and the fact should not be obscured, that 'science' means different things to different people in different situations. Science is an icon of modern society, and such a pervasive one that asking questions about it phrased in abstract and general terms is not likely to elicit the same responses as would specific encounters with specific bits of science. Thus we should not be puzzled by the ordinary fact that 'science' (in general) enjoys high public esteem and interest in surveys yet suffers apathy and worse in many *specific* encounters. The problem here is not so much public inconsistency but lack of analytical control of what is meant by 'science' in general, and simplistic over-interpretation of large-scale surveys. We return to this point later, in our discussion of methodology.

While maintaining a critical perspective on the meaning and representation of science as part and parcel of the proper public understanding of science research agenda, it is also worth emphasizing the dangers of over-generalization about 'the public' and its levels of understanding/ignorance. Once we move outside a simple 'cognitive deficit' model of the public understanding of science, we become increasingly aware of the range and variety of possible interactions between people's existing understandings of particular situations and those that emanate from science. In order to pursue this, our research has attempted to locate issues of the public understanding of science within specific practical social contexts. Examples include a study of those who have inherited a gene that raises blood cholesterol levels (familial hypercholesterolemia), an investigation into two communities living close to hazardous industry, and an analysis of the role played by scientists in environmental organizations.

These contextual studies do not merely add color or interesting embellishments to the data derived from national quiz-type surveys, but they represent in themselves a point of entry to the real-world encounters within which scientific knowledge is reconstructed to make it fit real situations in all their rich complexity (or rejected if it cannot). Understanding this general process of contextualization is crucial to understanding the social authority (or lack of authority) of science.

Our research has used small-scale and interpretive approaches rather than large-scale samples and standardized questions. The main methods of obtaining data have been participant observation, longitudinal panel interviews, structured in-depth interviews, and some local use of questionnaires on specific issues. In this way, we have attempted to form a picture of the conflicting accounts and interpretations available to specific publics, and to the individual and collective negotiation of everyday practical meanings.

An example of the difficulty of measuring understanding in a standardized way arose from the Bradford project on familial hypercholesterolemia. The standard question, used in a national public understanding of science survey, asked whether eating a lot of animal fats can *contribute* to heart disease. The public involved with familial hypercholesterolemia operates with a more sophisticated distinction of saturated, mono- and polyunsaturated fats. Thus the binary animal/nonanimal-fat distinction was insufficient for this part of the public. The *qualitative* and *interpretive* approaches thus allow insights that are excluded by standardized questions and analytical methods, especially concerning the complexities of beliefs, understandings and responses.

Findings

One of the projects discussed here (at Bristol Polytechnic) has tackled issues of 'science' and its multiple representations as a central focus of investigation. The findings correspond strongly with those of other projects, in which these issues have been approached less directly. Differing – sometimes contradictory – accounts of science are expressed by the experts themselves. No unified concept of science emerged from a series of interviews with scientists, research managers, research council officials and environmentalists. Instead, a series of 'scientific understandings of science' seem to coexist within groups engaged in scientific research. What is more, these different models of science may be associated with specific social roles and positions in institutional networks. A similar picture of diverse models of science among those who were claiming to communicate science was found in all our projects. Thus, for example, our research on scientists' involvement in legal settings in environmental conflicts demonstrates disagreement not only about 'facts' and interpretations but also about what is 'proper' science. This is consistent with broader sociology of science research.

The research from our group shows that people do not use, assimilate or experience science separate from other elements of knowledge, judgment or advice. Rarely, if at all, does a practical situation not need *supplementary knowledge* in order to make scientific understanding valid and useful in that context. This supplementary knowledge may be highly specialist and 'expert', even if it is not recognized widely as such.

Thus a sheep farmer may understand that radio-caesium is flushed from lambs more quickly on improved valley grass than on the high fells. But he may also know what the scientist does not – that valley grass is a precious and fragile resource whose loss by intensive grazing can have damaging consequences for future breeding cycles. The scientific account is valuable, but the situation requires more than scientific understanding. Other kinds of judgment are needed – including an assessment of the uncertainties involved and of the previous accuracy of scientific accounts. In cases such as familial hypercholesterolemia, patients over time acquire knowledge about their condition that may be less generally authoritative but more specifically accurate than that held by their physician. Communities close to hazardous installations will similarly compile information and understanding about pollution within which technical data will play only one small part. In all these cases (and others), the public understanding of science represents an *interactive* process between lay people and technical experts rather than a narrowly didactic or one-way transmission of information packages.

The extent to which the public is collectively organized, or individualized (as in many medical situations), is an important social variable, we find. Organization allows more comparison of experiences and expert accounts, more accumulation of alternative perspectives and questions, and more confidence to negotiate with or challenge imposed frameworks.

One obvious practical implication is that scientific and policy institutions that want to integrate science into lay public lives must be organized so as to understand and relate to public agendas and knowledges better, rather than appear to wish to impose a scientific (which often means standardized) framework of understanding as if that on its own were adequate.

It is also important to recognize that people judge whether or not they can use or *trust* expert knowledge partly by measuring it against elements of their own already-tested knowledge and direct experience. For example, predictions based on average figures for environmental contamination may not be credible to farmers who know in detail the variability of their own micro-environment;

medical advice based upon standard metabolisms or dietary habits may be treated with very great skepticism by people who are well aware of their own or others' variability. In the Lake District post-Chernobyl crisis, many hill farmers reasoned that at least a large proportion of the contamination must be from Sellafield when they saw from Ministry of Agriculture, Fisheries and Food maps a persistent 'crescent' of high contamination near the Sellafield plant. The scientific statement that Sellafield and Chernobyl contamination could be clearly distinguished by the typical Cs-137/Cs-134 isotope ratio was questioned by referring to the scientists' earlier mistake over Cs mobility in acid mountain soils and to unacknowledged uncertainties that the farmers had seen for themselves lay behind public scientific statements about environmental contamination. So (they reasoned) perhaps similar unrecognized uncertainties pervaded the so-called clear Sellafield–Chernobyl Cs isotope distinction.

The supplementary knowledge needed in order to contextualize science embodies not only extra, perhaps situation-specific, physical knowledge (say about a local environment, a particular occupation or hobby, or a personal illness); it also involves institutional or *social* knowledge or judgment. Thus, for example, people never experience scientific knowledge of genetics relating to familial hypercholesterolemia as pure knowledge. They experience it indirectly, as part of their concrete experience of and position in particular institutional processes. Thus it comes clothed in social and institutional forms and cannot easily be divorced from those associated social prescriptions, interests or orientations. It is normal (and rational) for people to respond not to scientific knowledge *per se* but to the whole complex of knowledge plus its particular social 'body language' – the interests people think lie within it, the social values and relationships it is thought to imply, and so on. These may not be deliberately chosen by scientists but may nevertheless be structured into the knowledge, for example via the questions it emphasizes, the degree of standardization it imposes, or the extent to which uncertainties are withheld (even for the best of reasons).

While – from an outsider's perspective – science and technical information are central to everyday life, the closer one gets to everyday discussion of apparently technical issues such as those examined in these projects, the more science seems to 'disappear'. This is not to deny the importance of science in such contexts but to note the extent (and variety) to which it needs translation, or 'reframing'. However, it is also clear that even in areas where technical assessment might be of value (e.g., in seeking action to reduce the hazards of local industry), there is often a sharp contrast between the high salience of the issues and the small number of information requests actually made. Once again, other considerations are likely to be seen as more significant than science – particularly that of which institutions are both trustworthy and competent. In research on the public understanding of radiation hazards, we were surprised to discover that Sellafield apprentices knew little about basic radioactive processes, such as the different properties of alpha, beta and gamma radiation. More significantly, however, they did not feel the need to know. We eventually realized that this was an entirely functional response, in that all this scientific understanding had already been encapsulated by various scientific experts within the design of the plant and its operating procedures; that is, into *organizational* norms and relationships. The workers simply learned the organizational procedures, not the science (which could have made life more difficult for them), and they placed their confidence in the institution. (Scientists themselves also do this to an extent not adequately recognized in the public domain.)

Thus the main insight here is that public uptake (or not) of science is not based upon *intellectual capability* as much as social-institutional factors having to do with social access, trust and negotiation as opposed to imposed authority. When these motivational factors are positive, people show a remarkable capability to assimilate and use science or other knowledge derived (*inter alia*) from science.

People may appear to be unresponsive or incapable of digesting scientific knowledge (which experts consider to be important to them) when they are rejecting the scientists' agenda. Our research shows that public nonreceptivity to scientific information is often based on judgment that it is not *useful* or does not match public or personal experience. Thus advice and emergency-procedure information to people living around chemical plants may well be ignored in a manner that appears quite irrational. However, when the reasoning behind information is not made plain (often because of concern about 'alarming' the public); when it contradicts local experience (reassurances about safety when incidents have previously occurred); when it is conveyed in unreasonably categorical terms (e.g., concerning the precise course of the envisaged emergency); or when it seems to deny accepted social norms (staying indoors rather than seeking out children who are elsewhere), it may be a fine balance whether to ignore the information or follow its rules slavishly as an imposed, inflexible authority.

As a related example, hill farmers in Cumbria refused offers to undergo whole-body radioactivity scans on the grounds that they could do nothing but worry if they discovered high levels. At the same time, their requests for water analysis were ignored, although the supplies could actually have been changed. Thus, from this group's perspective, useless knowledge was offered, while useful knowledge was denied. In the familial hypercholesterolemia case, we found food labeling often offered unhelpful information, such as 'vegetable fat' with no indication of saturation or cholesterol content. Such experiences have a wider negative effect on the credibility of scientific institutions. They point out the need for sensitivity and the ability to listen when devising and communicating not only scientific information but scientific research agendas. This is a matter of the institutional organization of science, not only of individual scientific attitudes.

A more positive corollary of this argument about 'useful knowledge' and the institutional dimensions of access and motivation (at least for a scientific audience) is that when people do see a personal or practical use for scientific understanding and are sufficiently motivated, they often show a remarkable capability to learn and to find relevant sources of scientific knowledge. This is true of medical self-help organizations (for example, in the area of AIDS/HIV), but also of birdwatchers, amateur astronomers and many other groups.

An important discovery from our research has been the enormous amount of sheer *effort* needed for members of the public to monitor sources of scientific information, judge between them, keep up with shifting scientific understandings, distinguish consensus from isolated scientific opinion, and decide how expert knowledge needs qualifying for use in *their* particular situation. They must also judge what level of knowledge is *good enough* for them. This is not necessarily the same level as scientists have assumed; the threshold may be looser, or tighter.

All this public understanding of science is extremely demanding, and unless the motivation is very high, as it is, for instance, with the example of familial hypercholesterolemia, it may well be reasonable for lay people to decide not to be drawn into this open-ended and socially uncertain activism and to opt instead for 'apathy' or a seemingly uncritical trust in a particular source of advice, even if it is partial in some way. The judgment whether or not to show an interest in science is therefore a social one, tied to judgments of one's own power (or powerlessness) to act in one's social environment.

We have found that those who do have or develop the motivation often show great alacrity in seeking out sources and assimilating science. Situations can then arise where these informal expertises confound formal scientific authorities, and local (possibly idiosyncratic) knowledges come into conflict with the generalized claims of more remote technical specialists. We have found frequent examples of this kind from the environmental and medical fields, for example when scientists performed experiments on grazing sheep on contaminated vegetation at stocking levels that farmers immediately realized (correctly, as the scientists discovered) would 'waste' the sheep. Often, also, amateur ornithologists' knowledge about birds' habits may be critical in challenging more general expertise at public inquiries.

The ease with which people can acquire scientific (and para-scientific) competence if sufficiently motivated has implications for the institutional arrangements that serve at present to either encourage or inhibit the growth of public understanding. Are we doing enough at present to increase 'access' to information sources and the motivation to use them?

All of this indicates that, in general, practical policy should be less concerned with feeding people a controlled, 'single correct' scientific understanding and more concerned with providing flexible social access to diverse sources of scientific information. Scientists or policy makers alone cannot prescribe, for example, the degree of scientific uncertainty that people need or how they fit information with other legitimate perspectives and agendas. To enhance public capacity and uptake of science, diverse and accessible sources need to be developed, ones that emphasize advice, negotiation and support rather than control of people's interpretations.

It must also be recognized as part of science 'disappearing' that individuals exhibit a number of ways of 'bracketing off' science from themselves; these may have positive, negative or neutral evaluative connotations and may depend upon perceived power structures and one's own degree of powerlessness within these. There may be a kind of collaborative division of labor, as with the Sellafield apprentices or the majority of interviewees among those having home radon surveys. (To paraphrase them: 'We are helping the scientists, so we don't need to know about what is going on scientifically'.) Or there may be a more clearly defensive social stance, brought about by people's assessment of the institutional interests behind particular scientific statements or by personal experience. Thus skepticism about a company's pollution record will also be applied to any scientific advice that is offered. ('Well, they would say that, wouldn't they?')

Quite commonly, negative attitudes toward science may have developed at school (often linked to identification as an 'educational failure', after which explicitly scientific questions can be met with a strongly emotional and extremely anxious response). The general point here is that these often unseen structures of bracketing and coping are an integral part of the processes of contextualizing science, and of positioning oneself or one's group socially with respect to its institutions. In many cases, they represent solid structural obstacles to the public dissemination of science. Ignorance about science is far more than just a vacuum. It may, as it were, be actively constructed and maintained. These unseen structures need to be understood in their own terms and responded to at that level if an adequate basis for future policy making is to be established.

General conclusions

We have already emphasized the importance of the point that in everyday life people have to interpret and negotiate scientific knowledge in conjunction with other forms of knowledge. We have also stressed the fact that science is itself far from unproblematic but is instead often partial, temporally contingent, conflicting and uncertain to a degree that public statements rarely acknowledge. In these circumstances, people will quite reasonably survey and evaluate many potential sources of advice and assistance. Thus they may well consult sources that they nevertheless regard with some caution; in the Manchester study around hazardous installations, local industry figured prominently as a source of information – yet it was also considered to be by far the least trustworthy.

Scientific communication is normally ignorant of its own tacit 'body languages' of institutional interests, which nevertheless constitute an essential part of people's interpretations of and response to that knowledge. Of course, this lack of self-awareness of the institutional context itself conveys a tacit message to audiences and may encourage a search for alternative sources of advice.

We have created a distinction in our research between three levels of public understanding of science: its intellectual contents, its research methods, and its organizational forms of ownership and control. All of these are necessary in some degree for a rounded public ability to use and act maturely in relation to science and technology. However, the third level may be as important as the first. Indeed, given that, as we have found, the social basis of trust and credibility is a crucial (yet largely neglected) question affecting public uptake of science, neglect of any public discussion of the third factor undermines attempts to improve the other two. One could say that what is often treated as public *mis*understanding of science (in the first sense) may actually be public understanding of science (in the third sense).

It is also necessary to stress that ordinary social life, which often takes contingency and uncertainty as normal and adaptation to uncontrolled factors as a routine necessity, is in fundamental tension with the basic culture of science, which is premised on assumptions of manipulability and control. It follows that scientific sources of advice may tend generally to compare unfavorably with informal sources in terms of flexibility and responsiveness to people's needs. Thus, while science may be judged highly in terms of competence and general credibility, it can appear somewhat low in terms of immediate relevance, *specific* applicability, accessibility and comprehensibility.

Even in apparently 'science-intensive' domains, lay understanding or mis-understanding of science seen as a cognitive issue is not the central point. The institutional forms in which scientific knowledge is clothed, and the social processes of interpretation and integration into other frameworks of knowledge and commitment, should be brought more into research and policy focus.

A general practical conclusion from this is that to advance public under-standing of science we need to encourage more awareness and debate about the institutional forms in which scientific knowledge is both presented and created. Our research shows people to be astute at taking up science as a *means* (when the right social conditions prevail) but wary about its *ends* and *interests*. Thus enhancement of public uptake of science would appear to require the development of multiple institutional forms of science, with correspondingly diverse audiences, patrons, interests and objectives. This would also meet the need for more diverse, independent and context-sensitive sources of scientific information.

However, we need to be aware that the *overall* trend in the structure and control of science is currently running in the opposite direction to the one indicated here. Indeed, it is worth asking whether the current concern about the public understanding of science does not reflect a deeper anxiety about the further intensification of the centralized ownership and control of science as a private resource rather than a public good. While many commentators portray a lack of public understanding of science as an obstacle to democratic vitality, it may be that the reverse is also true: that impoverished democracy and intensifying hegemony around science is a major obstacle to the enhanced public understanding of science.

Note

1 See Silverstone, R. 'Communicating Science to the Public', *Science, Technology, & Human Values*, 16(1), 106–10.

Author's note: This article is condensed from a presentation to the conference 'Policies and Publics for Science and Technology,' London, April 1990. It summarizes early results from five projects, led by Hilary Rose and Helen Lambert (Bradford University); Steve Yearley (Belfast University); Harry Rothman, Peter Glesner, and Cameron Adams (Bristol Polytechnic); and Brian Wynne, Frances Price, John Wakeford, Mike Michael, and Ros McKechnie (Lancaster University). See also Alan Irwin and Brian Wynne (1996) *Misunderstanding Science?* Cambridge, Cambridge University Press.

Chapter 2

Science and citizenship*

A. Irwin

> Now, what I want is, Facts . . . Facts alone are wanted in life. Plant nothing else, and root out everything else. You can only form the minds of reasoning animals upon Facts: nothing else will ever be of any service to them.
>
> (Thomas Gradgrind, Esq.)[1]

> I wish I could collect all the Facts we hear so much about . . . and all the Figures, and all the people who found them out; and I wish I could put a thousand barrels of gunpowder under them, and blow them all up together!
>
> (Thomas Gradgrind, Jun.)[2]

Concern over the relationship between citizens, science and technology seems to be characteristic of contemporary society. Right now, for example, various political and social groups (industry, government, environmentalists, scientific organizations, campaigning bodies) are attempting to educate, propagandize or cajole the general public into accepting their own evaluation of a series of technical – or at least technically related – questions (over the best means of tackling environmental issues, the desirability of new consumer products, the dangers of AIDS, the merits of various energy policies and an endless array of social questions such as genetic screening, transport safety and the implementation of new technology). In that sense, we are all barraged with new 'information' about developments in science and technology that might affect our lives and also, of course, with exhortations about what different social groups would like us to do about those developments.

In such a situation, it is unsurprising that many accounts have been put forward by scientists and others which describe (or, more usually, lament) the linkage between science, technical knowledge and the wider population. At present, the topic of 'public understanding of science' – as defined by, for example, the British Royal Society – has once again focused attention on these issues.

*Chapter 1 in *Citizen Science*, Routledge (1995), pp. 9–36.

As the first section of this chapter will discuss, there have been certain recurrent elements within these more general accounts – a concern at the 'scientific ignorance' of the populace, a consequent desire to create a 'better-informed' citizenry, an enthusiasm for making science 'more accessible' (but with strict limitations on the extent of this accessibility). Notably also, and as we will discuss, these accounts have represented a commitment to 'science as progress' and offer a decidedly 'science-centred' (or 'enlightenment') view of society. Frequently, the accounts offered by scientists and others reveal an anxiety lest public ignorance should get in the way of scientific/technological progress. Thus, one senior British scientist entitles his book on this subject *Is Science Necessary?* but provides the answer – before the text even begins – by citing Nehru's exhortation that the 'future belongs to science and those who make friends with science'.[3]

As this chapter will outline, the notion that the 'future belongs to science' has underpinned most accounts of the relationship between citizens and science. However, there have also been a number of more critical accounts which draw upon the 'tragedy of technology' theme and on a notion of 'science as ideology' in order to ask starker questions about the impact of scientific dissemination on everyday life. It is also possible to portray concerns over the public under-standing of science as an indicator of anxiety amongst the scientific community lest it should become marginalized in the post-Enlightenment era. This chapter will begin with a brief historical excursion into these differing accounts of the 'public understanding of science' before presenting three case studies of the contemporary interaction between citizens, science and technology.

Discussion of the role of 'ordinary citizens' in 'technical progress' extends back to the beginnings of the Industrial Revolution. In nineteenth-century Britain, for example, there was a lively debate about the general level of science education – which was seen by many as holding back industrial and technical development.[4] Just as in the late twentieth century, public indifference was viewed as an obstacle to scientific progress. Of special relevance to these themes was the establishment of institutions such as the Mechanics Institutes, which represented one attempt to build a bridge between formalized scientific know-ledge and working-class people (although, as we shall see, there are differing interpretations of whether the Mechanics Institutes were an attempt to enlighten – or to indoctrinate – the working classes). The Mechanics Institute movement spread across Britain in the 1820s and 1830s and offered a training in science and technology to the skilled working classes.

In the twentieth century, the need for a greater awareness of science became a major theme of the 'visible college' of scientists and writers who adopted a socialist perspective on scientific progress.[5] As J.B.S. Haldane put it in the preface to his 1939 book, *Science and Everyday Life*:

> I am convinced that it is the duty of those scientists who have a gift for writing to make their subject intelligible to the ordinary man and woman.

> Without a much broader knowledge of science, democracy cannot be effective in an age when science affects all our lives continually.[6]

Writing immediately after the Second World War, the Association of Scientific Workers expressed similar sentiments. In so doing, it outlined the three most regular justifications – both of that time and since – for an enhanced 'public understanding':

- that a technically literate population is essential for future workforce requirements ('the present inadequate standards of the available labour').[7] This argument had also been important within nineteenth-century debates over working-class technical education;
- that science is now an essential part of our cultural understanding ('In this age no man can be considered to be cultured who makes no serious attempt to understand and appreciate the broad principles of science');[8]
- that, as Haldane argued above, greater public understanding of science is essential for democratic reasons.

The Association of Scientific Workers made various recommendations for improving public understanding through further education classes and also such media as exhibitions and museums, film, the press, and the radio. It also stressed the need for working scientists to become more involved in public activities and in the dissemination of science – a challenge to which scientists such as Haldane and Hogben had already responded through popular publications on science and mathematics.[9]

The Association of Scientific Workers thus offered a model of 'progress through science' which resonates strongly with many contemporary statements of the need for both greater public understanding and public acceptance of science: 'Science offers means to use unprecedented powers with which a finer, more beautiful and happier world than ever before can be built. With mankind using a vigorously developing science for social ends, the future can be bright and inspiring'.[10]

However, unusually for a group of scientists, the Association recognized that this new world would require scientists to adopt an explicitly *political* role in society. The Association was highly critical of those who simply stood on the sidelines of social change. Important decisions needed to be made about the social control of science and industry – it was the responsibility of every citizen to get involved. Meanwhile, science itself is 'neither good nor bad; it is organized knowledge and a method, a tool or weapon, which society can use for good or evil. It can confer the highest benefits and it can be used to destroy'.[11] Again, this notion of science as value-free has been a regular feature of scientific statements concerning the relationship between citizens and technical change.

Some forty years later, the prestigious Royal Society was to revive these debates in its 1985 report on the 'public understanding of science' – suggesting the durability of these concerns but also a perceived absence of real progress. The Royal Society took a distinctly less 'political' perspective than the Association of Scientific Workers – its recommendations emanate from a more liberal concern with the well-being of both science and society (and perhaps also from a concern that the value of scientific understanding might be neglected by society – the mid-1980s were a time of great anxiety about the future of public support for science).

Despite this difference in political perspective, the 1985 report of the Royal Society presents an argument which many members of the Association of Scientific Workers would readily have endorsed:

> better public understanding of science can be a major element in promoting national prosperity, in raising the quality of public and private decision making and in enriching the life of the individual. . . . Improving the public understanding of science is an investment in the future, not a luxury to be indulged in if and when resources allow.[12]

The report goes on to cite a number of specific areas where an 'improved understanding' would be of personal and national value:

- in terms of *national prosperity*, a better-informed citizenry could appreciate the opportunities offered by new technologies and could provide a better trained workforce;
- in terms of *economic performance*, wider scientific awareness would reduce 'hostility, or even indifference' to science and technology and so aid in the rapid innovation of such product and process changes. There would also be a 'considerable competitive advantage' if those in 'positions of responsibility' were better-informed;
- in terms of *public policy*, science and technology should be major considerations – for the Royal Society there is a strong case that these decisions would be improved by 'better understanding';
- in terms of *personal decisions*, for example regarding diet, smoking, vaccination safety – 'an uninformed public is very vulnerable to misleading ideas';
- in terms of *everyday life*, a basic scientific literacy is needed just to understand what goes on around us (e.g., how a ball-point pen or a television functions);
- in terms of *risk and uncertainty* (e.g., concerning nuclear power or seat-belt wearing), it is important that the public has a better appreciation of the nature of risks and of how to interpret and balance them: 'Once again it must be argued that better understanding fosters better public and personal decisions'.[13]
- in terms of *contemporary thought and culture*, any citizen without an

understanding of science is cut off from the richness of this important area of human enquiry and discovery.

So far, we have briefly examined two major arguments – from the Association of Scientific Workers and from the Royal Society – for greater efforts to be made by scientists and citizens in the dissemination of technical information and understanding. A typical justification for such efforts has also emerged – generally based on a mixture of economic, political, personal and cultural arguments.

Certain assumptions about the relationship between citizens, science and technology have also started to become clear – assumptions which are implicit in the very concept of the 'public understanding of science'. Such assumptions include:

- the notion of contemporary 'public ignorance' in matters of science and technology;
- the notion that a better understanding of science will lead to better 'public and personal decisions';
- the notion that science is a force for human improvement;
- an explicit or implicit notion that science is itself value-free – although there are moral and political choices to be made about its *direction*;
- the notion that the life of citizens is somehow impoverished by an exclusion from scientific thought;
- the notion that wider exposure to scientific thinking will lead to greater acceptance and support for science and technology.

Of course, there are differences between the accounts offered by these two groups of concerned scientists – with the Association of Scientific Workers offering, for example, a more 'political' programme (linked to the aspirations of the postwar Labour government). However, what the two accounts share is a fundamental belief in the centrality of scientific development to the future of society – and a belief (whether as part of a social democratic or more vaguely liberal ideology) that a better-informed citizenry can play a crucial (but essentially reactive) role in this development. The future should indeed belong to science.

There is no suggestion in the Royal Society report that the organization of science is open to change or that it should incorporate citizen views within research policy. The goal is to make the public better-informed about science but not to encourage a critical evaluation of scientific institutions. For the Royal Society and most of the contemporary apologists of science, *science* itself is not the problem – the problem is gaining public understanding and hence *acceptance* of science.

This world view can be characterized as 'science-centred' or (perhaps more accurately) 'enlightened' in its assumptions about science, technology and the wider public. This is not to suggest that all working scientists hold this world view. However, it does provide a powerful and frequently reiterated case for the centrality of scientific reasoning to social development. Within such a world view, any problematic relationship between science and citizens must be a consequence of either public ignorance or public irritationality.

A critical perspective on these issues is required and there are new developments and ways of thinking which suggest that *change* is indeed occurring. We can begin by contrasting the notions expressed so far of 'science as progress' with one account of a nineteenth-century experiment in the 'public understanding of science' – the Mechanics Institute movement as discussed by Maxine Berg and others.[14] Berg's more critical analysis of this movement sets the debates so far concerning citizens and science into a much-needed social and political context.

As already suggested, the Mechanics Institutes appear to offer an excellent example of a highly localized and responsive 'continuing education' (to use the modern jargon) for one section of the working-class community. Institutes were established across Britain and offered technical training at a time when demand seemed to be high – this demand linked, of course, to the rapid progress of industrialization. Berg's account suggests, however, a less attractive ideological purpose for this movement – essentially the institutes were not philanthropic in orientation but were instead one part of the legitimation of the emerging capitalist order. The underlying philosophy of 'self improvement' was designed to divide working-class communities by creating a 'labour aristocracy'. The basis of the movement was to evangelize the harmony between science and industry. The Institutes were largely dominated by the middle classes, whose main purpose was to create a more ordered society and to prevent social unrest. Science was, therefore, an important legitimation of the social order rather than a force for liberation or active citizenship.

The discussion of Mechanics Institutes is important here not for its specific conclusions but for the wider questions which it raises about the relationship between science and citizens. The 'enlightenment' approach – as exemplified by the Royal Society – would argue that the provision of scientific information to public groups will in itself be beneficial – if only in allowing a better appreciation of the scientific changes which are influencing society and in clarifying citizen choices. The analysis provided by Berg suggests that science can present an ideological face to citizens – so that it can be used to obstruct rather than assist understanding. In particular, the control of Mechanics Institutes by middle-class forces meant that training in science was also a propagandizing of a particular political ideology (in this case that known as 'political economy'). At this point, we could add to our discussion a number of Marxist accounts of science which generalize this point about capitalist ideology and its relationship to contemporary science.[15] Thus, for example, Marcuse has argued that: 'The industrial society which makes technology and science its own is organised for the ever more effective domination of man and nature, for the ever more effective utilization of its resources'.[16]

Marx himself expressed such notions of 'technology as domination' with particular clarity:

> Labour [is] . . . subsumed under the total process of the machinery itself, as itself only a link of the system, whose unity exists not in the living work-force, but rather in the living (active) machinery, which confronts his individual, insignificant doings as a mighty organism.[17]

Hill has developed such themes (particularly with reference to the work of Foucault) in *The Tragedy of Technology*:

> Employees generally see technology . . . as an alienated force that stands somewhere behind their left shoulder, and which, with one new breath of change, may extinguish their means of livelihood. The aesthetic is one of externally imposed order rather than human harmony; the words of know-ledge are opaque, controlled by the masters of the technological system and the variety of specialists who inform them. The technological aesthetic is unreadable to the layman, but is embodied in words of knowledge that say 'you shall adjust'.[18]

Of course, the argument here is that this relationship to technology is found also *outside* the workplace – so that people's general experience of technology fits this pattern of 'unreadability' and 'adjustment'.

It would appear, therefore, that we have reached the point of incommensur-ability between those accounts of science which stress its empowering and enabling role and those – drawing broadly on a notion of science as a source of legitimation (Habermas), alienation (Marx) or disenchantment (Weber) – which stress its role as a form of social control and dehumanization. One should nevertheless be wary of splitting debate in a conventionally political fashion (the 'establishment view' versus the 'radical opposition'). Certainly, left-wing and environmental groups have been as eager to adopt a scientific mantle ('if only people knew the facts of ozone depletion, acid deposition or factory farming then they'd support us') as have the political establishment – although such groups have typically had far fewer scientific resources at their disposal. What should also be noted at this stage is that, despite the apparent incommensur-ability over whether science represents progress or disenchantment, all of these approaches stress the centrality of scientific rationality to the modern world. Whilst [. . .] some would argue that the modern world is being radically transformed into late (or post) modernity, the substantial influence of science over the life of citizens seems undeniable and likely to remain so.

[. . .] Rather than pursuing these themes through a general debate, we should begin to look a little closer at actual examples of the contemporary citizen–science interaction. Is there any evidence that science is being used within society as a legitimatory rather than an empowering device? Can the lack of communication between 'science and its publics' be successfully explained by public ignorance or instead by some deeper-rooted set of causes? In order to tackle this, we need to examine questions of science and technology as they occur within people's lives. As a start to this project, we can consider the lessons from three examples of the relationship between science, technology and everyday life. These examples make no claim to representativeness. They are designed simply to illustrate and explore the issues of contemporary citizen– science relations. [. . .]

Three stories of our time

2,4,5-T and the farmworkers

> We shall continue to examine any soundly based new evidence or information. For the present, this Enquiry has strengthened us in our previous view that 2,4,5-T herbicides can safely be used in the UK in the recommended way and for the recommended purposes.
>
> (Advisory Committee on Pesticides)[19]

> It is the NUAAW's conviction, distilled from the experience of thousands of members working in forests and on farms, that the conditions envisaged by members of the [advisory committee] (presumably used to the controlled conditions of the laboratory) are impossible to reproduce in the field.
>
> This single fact must be sufficient to demolish the supposition that the herbicide is safe to use.[20]

In 1980, the National Union of Agricultural and Allied Workers (NUAAW – from here on 'the farmworkers') was engaged in a highly public dispute with the British regulatory authorities over the herbicide 2,4,5-T. By that date, 2,4,5-T had already been controversial for some time because of its allegedly hazardous [effects] (chloracne, birth defects, spontaneous abortion, cancer) and also for its overall impact on the natural environment. Although the herbicide had been produced since the 1940s, perhaps its best-known application was during the Vietnam War, when it was sprayed by US aircraft as a defoliant (and thus as a means of removing ground cover). However, 2,4,5-T has also been used in a number of agricultural, industrial and domestic situations (e.g., by railway workers to keep lines clear of weeds, by forestry workers to clear undergrowth, or by members of the public keeping their gardens free of brambles and nettles).

Given international attention to the hazards of 2,4,5-T, a number of countries had at that time either banned or severely restricted the use of the herbicide, among them the United States, Canada and the then Soviet Union.

There had also been a number of national and international campaigns against 2,4,5-T – with concern being expressed particularly about the usage of this and the other 'dirty dozen'[21] pesticides in developing countries. In Britain, a number of groups had argued for the banning or strict control of 2,4,5-T.

This campaign had some success; many local authorities had by 1980 agreed to cease spraying, as also had major users such as British Rail, the National Coal Board and the electricity generators. However, the British regulatory authorities had historically been resistant to a ban on 2,4,5-T. In this section, and as an illustration of one interlinkage between citizens, science and technical decision making, we will look briefly at one episode in the history of 2,4,5-T: the confrontation between the farmworkers and the regulatory authorities (or, more precisely, their advisory body – the Advisory Committee on Pesticides (ACP)) in just one year – 1980.

Of course, there are a number of ways in which such a story could be told: as a review of the technical evidence (i.e., the 'facts' of the case), as a clash between 'expertise' and 'trade union pressure', as an example of the 'uncaring' nature of modern agro-business or of the use of science as an ideology to oppose workers' rights. For now, it is enough to look at the *kinds* of argument which the farmworkers and the ACP put forward to support their case and to consider the immediate lessons concerning the uses of 'scientific expertise' in such social and technical decision making. Most specifically, does this case suggest any disparity between 'scientific' (as represented by the advisory committee) and 'citizen' (i.e., in this case farmworker) perspectives?

In 1980, the farmworkers presented the ACP with their latest 'dossier' on the herbicide.[22] By that date, the question of the pesticide's safety had been referred to the ACP no fewer than eight times – with the committee standing firm on its contention that 2,4,5-T 'offers no hazard' to users or the general environment 'provided that the product is used as directed'. In their evidence to the ACP, the farmworkers discuss what they consider to be the 'realities' of pesticide use, they present the alternatives to the pesticide, they criticize previous ACP reports, and they offer a number of cases where health damage is allegedly linked to 2,4,5-T exposure.

These cases – which largely represented the 'new' evidence to the ACP – were drawn from a questionnaire which the NUAAW had circulated to its members through its newspaper, *Landworker*.[23] Questions in the survey covered the usage of 'weedkiller 2,4,5-T' (When did you last use a weedkiller containing 2,4,5-T? Are you ever given instructions on how to use protective gear? Are you given any information about the hazards relating to weedkillers containing 2,4,5-T?) but also sought out medical information (Have you ever had any of the following symptoms after using weedkillers containing 2,4,5-T? Do you suffer from any of the following . . . ? Have you or your partner ever had a spontaneous (unplanned) abortion or a miscarriage?). In all, forty questions were asked on a 'voluntary response' basis.

The questionnaire eventually provided a series of case studies (involving fourteen individuals) for submission to the ACP. To take a typical case, one 'victim' is described as having had 'a miscarriage in 1977 and later the same year gave birth to a daughter . . . who has a cleft palate and a hare lip.Her husband had been using 2,4,5-T when he worked for the Forestry Commission'.

This information was then presented to the ACP. The overall conclusion of the farmworkers' submission was that:

> Considering the additional evidence which has not been evaluated by the ACP, the existence of alternative weed killers and the overall lack of information about the effects on users of 2,4,5-T . . . it becomes absolutely incomprehensible that workers, their families and the general public can remain subject to the risks for one minute longer.[24]

The advisory committee's published response to this evidence appeared later in 1980 as the *Further Review of the Safety for Use in the UK of Herbicide 2,4,5-T*.[25] This review is considerably longer than the farmworker dossier – it presented, for example, a thorough review of major scientific developments since the ACP's previous report. It appraised all the evidence in some detail and included a series of appendices on topics ranging from environmental effects and operator exposure to the consideration of alternative pesticides.

As regards the specific matters raised by the farmworkers, the ACP devoted one section of its report to a consideration of the case studies put forward by the NUAAW. For each case the committee concluded that insufficient evidence existed to correlate the medical condition with 2,4,5-T – or at least that it seemed highly improbable that such a correlation could exist. In the above case of miscarriage/birth deformity, for example, the employment records of the father were first of all checked. Following this, the parents and the family doctor were interviewed in order to establish the level of exposure involved and the scale of alleged effects. The ACP's specific conclusion was:

> The type of deformity occurring in this case is common genetically. Mrs K's only possible contact with 2,4,5-T was through handling her husband's working clothes; and the likelihood of her having absorbed sufficient to have produced any toxic effect is remote in the extreme.[26]

In overall conclusion, the ACP argued forcefully that 'there are no grounds to suggest a causal relationship with the stated effects'. The argument is further elaborated during a discussion of the linkage between 2,4,5-T and miscarriage/ birth deformity. The committee suggested that the farmworker cases 'neither implicate nor absolve' the pesticide:

> The reality is that some women who have been in contact with such an agent are likely to miscarry, and that some are likely to bear malformed children; but this in itself does not add up to cause and effect. Indeed,

statistically it would be remarkable if families in contact with particular products such as 2,4,5-T were spared from these misfortunes.[27]

Not surprisingly perhaps, this scientific rationale did not serve to change the opinion of the farmworkers – and during at least one stormy meeting the two sides struggled to communicate their concerns about the issue. As the leader of the farmworkers stated after the meeting:

> We are alarmed at the approach taken by the Committee. In their eyes scientific evidence proving the hazards of a chemical has to be absolutely watertight. In our view the decision has to be made on the balance of probabilities . . . where lives are at stake a responsible body cannot wait, as was the case with asbestos, until there is a sufficiently impressive death toll.[28]

The farmworkers vowed to fight on – both to get a ban on the chemical and to change the regulatory structure for future decisions.

Mad cows and the consumers

> As the Chief Medical Officer has confirmed, British beef can continue to be eaten safely by everyone, adults and children.
> (John Gummer, Minister of Agriculture, Fisheries and Food)[29]

> Eating British beef is completely safe. There is no evidence of any threat to human health caused by this animal health problem [BSE].
> This is the view of the independent British and European scientists and not just the meat industry.
> This view has been endorsed by the Department of Health.[30]
> (Advertisement placed by the Meat and Livestock Commission)

> Scientists do not automatically command public trust.
> (House of Commons Agriculture Select Committee)[31]

In 1990, one technical issue held an especially prominent place in the British mass media: do cows make you mad? The Ministry of Agriculture, Fisheries and Food (MAFF) – and especially its minister, John Gummer – was under widespread attack for its handling of the issue. The meat industry was greatly concerned at the impact of the scare on meat sales. Consumer groups such as the Consumers' Association and Parents for Safe Food registered their low confidence in both the meat industry and MAFF. British newspapers featured photographs of Gummer feeding a beefburger to his daughter – apparently in an attempt to reassure the public. Various scientific groups stated their concern over the issue – Professor Richard Lacey was quoted as fearing that 'a whole generation would be lost' if the worst anxieties over BSE (bovine spongiform encephalopathy) came true. Other scientific figures dismissed 'public hysteria' over the issue. Professor Sir Richard Southwood claimed that 'we have more reason to be concerned about being struck by lightning than catching BSE from eating beef and other products from cattle'.[32]

Quite clearly, therefore, the 'mad cow' issue represented a major public controversy. BSE is a fatal disease which causes degeneration of the brain. It develops over several years and infected cattle, mostly dairy cows, show no symptoms until the final weeks, when they become nervous and uncoordinated. The first case of BSE was reported in Britain in 1985 – by April 1990, 290 cases a week were being confirmed. The issue that exercised the public was, of course, whether BSE – or 'mad cow disease' as it became more dramatically known – could be a threat to the human population.

As with 2,4,5-T, there are a number of ways in which this story can be told (and, indeed, already has been told) – as a struggle between scientists armed with 'the facts' and an irrational group of citizens (in this case, not farmworkers but consumers), as an example of industrial corruption of both regulatory authorities and scientists, as a use of scientific authority to legitimize an exploitative and inherently dangerous mode of food production. However, as with the 2,4,5-T story, it is instructive to look at the broad characteristics of the arguments made by both sides.

If we take those consumer and allied groups which were most critical of government action and the activities of the meat industry, then a number of features of their argument can be identified. First of all, critical groups tended to highlight certain meat industry practices – particularly the feeding of offal to animals. Second, critical groups took the line of emphasizing the uncertainties concerning BSE transmission – so that, for example, when a Siamese cat developed BSE in 1990 this was seized upon as yet more evidence that the disease could travel across species boundaries. Third, these groups could take advantage of the divided scientific opinion over the issue; Professor Lacey became a particularly public figure on this basis. Accordingly, oppositional groups could make it clear that there was no scientific consensus. Fourth, consumer groups found it relatively easy to capitalize on the inconsistencies and weaknesses in MAFF's handling of the debate. As one report put it: 'Knowledge of BSE is as full of holes as an infected cow's brain . . . while the science of BSE is arguable, much more is known about the handling of crisis to contain risk, limit damage and maintain public confidence'.[33]

However, this report argued that the government had succeeded in breaking every rule of public relations. Between them, MAFF and its minister had:

- failed to err on the side of caution;
- acted slowly at every stage;
- attempted to score debating points rather than enlisting support (Gummer, for example, was widely quoted as labelling vegetarians 'wholly unnatural');

- created confusion by refusing to speak openly – thus also losing the confidence of both consumers and the food industry;
- opted for publicity gimmicks (e.g., the photo opportunities with Gummer's daughter and a beefburger) rather than discussing the issues;
- failed to establish a system for dealing with public inquiries.

As the report concluded: 'The grotesque image of the tottering cow thus brands not only an incompetent bureaucracy but a rickety and self-serving information regime'.[34]

Quite clearly, therefore, the BSE issue became the focus for a whole series of criticisms and concerns – about food industry practices, about the independence and competence of the government ministry, about the limits to scientific understanding in such a complex and under-researched area. Despite this broad critique, the typical 'official' response was to present the issue as a challenge to the 'facts'. In statement after statement, the minister repeated his claim that: 'We have taken action to deal with the public health concerns and the animal health aspect of BSE on the basis of the best independent scientific advice'.[35]

In April 1990, the Royal Society and the Association of British Science Writers called their own press conference on the grounds that 'the public remains confused about its [BSE's] dangers'.[36]

The meeting was designed to 'enable journalists to write and broadcast accurately' and heard testimony from five 'experts'. The views of these experts differed slightly – from there is a 'very low risk' to the human population to the 'risks of humans contracting the disease through eating beef are non-existent'. Overall, however, the opinion seemed to be that the dangers of BSE were not great. Nevertheless, public anxiety continued – suggesting, as the House of Commons Agriculture Select Committee concluded in July 1990, that expert statements alone were unlikely to reassure the public.[37]

As 1990 progressed, BSE slowly slipped away from popular concern, only to be revived periodically as new reports emerged. For example, 1994 brought another peak of concern with the action this time focusing on European attempts to control the import of British beef. Meanwhile, the divisions over the governmental response to the issue showed no signs of disappearing. Instead, many consumer groups are set for further battles with the authorities over food safety issues.

Major hazards and the residents

> Your premises are situated in an area that could possibly be affected if a major accident should occur. . . . The Control of Industrial Major Accident Hazards Regulations (1984) requires [sic] to inform you of the emergency procedures that you should follow in the unlikely event of a major accident.[38]

> The industry recognizes . . . that accidents are inevitable . . . In recognizing this, the industry is moving more towards crisis communications, crisis management and evacuation planning. At the same time it increases reassurance operations, beefs up its risk analyses and induces the wider community to share not only in the experience of risk, but also in its management.[39]

In 1982, due to accidents at chemical sites in Europe during the preceding decade – notably at Flixborough in 1974 and Seveso in 1976 – the European Community adopted a directive for the control of major hazard installations.[40] This is commonly known as the 'Seveso Directive'.

Simultaneously, the EC took the then unprecedented step of building into the directive a 'public information' requirement. Article 8 thus specifies that members of the public liable to be affected by a major accident be informed of safety measures and of how they should behave in the event of a major accident. This requirement was then translated into national legislation so that, for example, Regulation 12 of the Control of Industrial Major Accident Hazards (CIMAH) Regulations of 1984 represents the British version of the EC directive. The CIMAH regulations required that this information be provided around a fixed number of major hazard sites by January 1986.

In effect, therefore, the EEC legislation was obliging the petrochemical industry to give to the local community advice and information about the operation of hazardous installations (at least at a very limited number of sites). In contrast to the previous examples of 'citizen–science interaction', here we have technical information being given out largely *in advance* of public concern. By way of contrast also, rather than being a *workplace* (2,4,5-T) or *consumer* (BSE) interaction, this case allows us to look at a *community* matter. As before, however, this interaction is open to a number of interpretations – of communities being totally uninterested in 'technical' matters, of communities being 'co-opted' by industry (as the second quotation at the beginning of this section suggests), of a more complex pattern of local and technical knowledges in juxtaposition.

The information provision requirement of the new legislation certainly caused British industry great concern (greater apparently than the other, more engineering-oriented, requirements). The fear was that the public would react with alarm and hysteria to the information that there were hazards associated with the local chemical works. Debate also centred on the number of sites at which information should be distributed, the extent of information distribution at each site, what information route should be followed (leaflet, newspaper announcement, public meetings) and the amount of detail which should be provided.

The 'information', when it eventually appeared in Britain, generally took the form of a simple leaflet giving very brief information about:

- activities undertaken on site;
- names of the hazardous substances used and their principal harmful properties;

- details of emergency warning systems;
- reference to emergency planning and/or advice on what action to take in the event of an emergency.

Despite the prior industrial concern that this would create an emotional public reaction, there is very little evidence of any outcry – with anecdotal evidence suggesting that certain companies which had been braced for public criticism actually received no phone calls at all from local residents. A more systematic social survey of one information site found no evidence of local anxiety and only a small proportion of residents claiming that the leaflet had changed their opinion of the site. Less reassuringly, however, the same survey suggested that the leaflet had only a small impact in terms of informing residents about the 'correct' emergency procedures.[41] Thus, many residents anticipated that their response to an emergency would be to 'get out of the area' – despite the leaflet's specific advice to 'stay indoors'.

It would appear, therefore, that whilst the information distribution exercise may have been successful in avoiding public outcry, it had only limited success as a preparation for a real emergency. Accordingly, the linkage between this information exercise and 'active and informed citizenship' seems somewhat less than satisfactory. More particularly, this example seems to reinforce the notion of public indifference to technical advice. Here we have specific, carefully prepared and well-distributed advice to an 'at risk' group, which is then apparently ignored. Why should any further efforts be made at dissemination? [. . .]

Science, technology and everyday life

In many ways, these three 'stories' have very little in common – a sustained trade union campaign to outlaw a pesticide, a sudden consumer outcry about the hazards of British beef, a public information campaign that was successful in avoiding backlash but less satisfactory as preparation for a petrochemical disaster. What themes and concerns underlie these apparently disparate cases? If we, first of all, return to the 'science-centred' world view with which this chaper began, several characteristic notions have already been identified. These concerned the notion of *public ignorance*, that science improves the *decision-making process*, that science is a *force for human improvement*, that it is *value-free*, that citizens are impoverished by their *exclusion*, and that *greater scientific understanding* amongst the public will lead to *greater acceptance and support* for science and technology. To what extent can evidence be found in the three case studies to substantiate this general conceptualization?

From the 'science-centred' perspective, all three cases represent the problems of public ignorance – with each case demonstrating the resistance of public groups to the well-balanced testimony of expert bodies (whether the Advisory Committee on Pesticides, MAFF or the chemical industry and local planning authority backed up by the Health and Safety Executive). Of course, whilst the major hazard case seems to represent a kind of dumb apathy among residents (and, in that sense, a sin of omission [. . .]), the other two cases represent a more active form of resistance to technical advice (and, therefore, the much greater sin of *co*mmission). Discussions in the science-centred mode tend to move from this analysis to a discussion of either how to enact decision making apart from the ignorant/irrational public [. . .] or how to be more energetic in disseminating technical information (e.g., the recommendations of the Royal Society). Either way, the view is that the public forms a barrier to intelligent and constructive debate.

These representations of the public became most visible in the BSE case – with numerous references to 'public hysteria' and 'media hype'. For the 'science-centred' view, continued public concern *after* scientifically based re-assurances had been given could only be the product of an emotional and badly informed public.

Equally, the three cases suggest something of the notion that science can be an impartial and 'value-free' agent in such public cases – certainly, the 'official' parties involved would reject vehemently (and be highly offended by) any suggestion that the information that they were presenting was in some way 'biased'. Their claim to authority was based precisely upon the impartiality and neutrality of the expertise which they proffered (and also upon the 'good will' and 'fair play' of the decision-making structures within which they operate). This became an issue especially in the BSE case, with numerous allegations of 'false experts' on the 'opposing' side. Thus John Gummer was quoted in the House of Commons as stressing the significance of 'true' expertise:

> He hoped the BBC, ITV and others would ask before interviewing people as 'experts' whether they had published in journals which their peers could check or if they had submitted evidence to the Tyrrel Committee. If they had not, he hoped they would not be introduced as experts but merely as people with an idea or two.[42]

Particular criticism was made of Professor Richard Lacey, the Leeds University microbiologist, who repeatedly expressed great anxiety over the human implications of BSE. One Commons report stated that his views 'seemed to lose touch with reality'. Lacey replied to these charges with equal vehemence: 'From a medical point of view . . . it is normal to assume the worst and act accordingly. That is the difference between farmers and doctors'.[43]

This disputed territory over expertise was also manifest in the 2,4,5-T case, where the farmworkers' 'dossier' was dismissed by the advisory committee for its anecdotal and unscientific methodology. From the viewpoint of a working scientist (especially, but not solely, in areas such as toxicology and epidemiology), this certainty over risk and safety may seem quite perplexing – the science is typically open to major doubt and uncertainty. The 'official' message filtered out the inevitable technical uncertainties so as to offer an apparently authoritative and self-confident message – suggesting an important difference between 'doing science' (with all its messiness, conjecture and tacit assumptions) and 'the public face of science' (where such provisionality has apparently been lost so as to offer a 'clear' voice). However, this 'filtering' may no longer enjoy easy success as the official presentations of scientific evidence become open to challenge.

Throughout these challenges, nevertheless, official bodies in both the 2,4,5-T and BSE cases have clung to the notion of their own superior understanding. Their task has been to cope with the peculiarities of 'public perception' (meaning *mis*perception) rather than to reconsider their own authority in these matters. In the case of major hazards (the low profile of which may be more typical of citizen–science encounters), that authority has been able to rest unchallenged when no critical voices or counter-expertises have emerged.

If we turn now to those accounts of science that stress its *ideological and legitimatory* nature, then a very different picture emerges. Such an analysis can be conducted at two important levels: first, in terms of the *use* of science to defend certain industrial and political practices; second, in terms of the relationship between the *development* of scientific thinking and underlying social assumptions. This distinction is open to question, since the two levels are inseparable. Nevertheless, their presentation in this form assists discussion at this stage.

A broad line of argument can be proposed which links the official use of scientific argument to the defence of the prevailing social order. Thus, the technical language of the public information over major hazards aims to reassure the public and to avoid any larger social debate over the location of hazardous industry. It permits the *appearance* of openness (and so helps to 'incorporate' local people in the *status quo*) but without engaging in discussion over competing assessments of the risk of major accident. Science thus serves to reinforce one social standpoint and to put local groups at a disadvantage – feelings of anxiety and concerns over safety seem trivial when contrasted with the powerful argumentation of quantitative risk analysis. In Habermas' term, debates over community safety are subjected to a process of 'scientization'.[44] Thus, for Jones, debates over 'risk assessment' are an obscuring of the real (i.e., class) issues:

> there is nothing natural about the fact that those who face the immediate risks of chemical production are generally poor, working class and marginal. Chemical executives do not generally live next door to their plants . . . Risk may be seen as a mystification which attempts to hide the reality of risk as a class relation, another example of the power of capital over our lives.[45]

When local concerns *do* become a focus of attention, e.g., during a planning inquiry, citizens often feel alienated from the mixture of technical and legalistic procedure being followed. Similar points could be made with regard to 2,4,5-T or BSE – references to public hysteria and irrationality serve, from this perspective, the distinctly ideological purpose of downgrading public concerns and re-inforcing the authority of existing decision makers. Science is the servant of power – its investigations claim to open up the possibilities for policy making but instead serve to reinforce the existing social order.

At a second level, a tradition has developed in the post-Kuhnian sociology of scientific knowledge,[46] which links the development of scientific understanding to broader social influences. Of particular relevance to this discussion is the work of Wynne. For example, in an analysis of several risk issues Wynne identifies a series of social assumptions which underpin scientific risk analyses. In the case of 2,4,5-T, he draws attention to the disagreement between the farmworkers and the advisory committee surrounding what constitutes 'normal conditions of use':

> different parties – the scientists and the workers – defined different actual risk systems . . . because they built upon different models of the social practices creating or controlling the risks. The scientists' implicit assump-tions were of idealised worlds of herbicide production and use; and the validity and credibility of their 'objective' risk analysis was committed to this naive sociology embedded in their technical analysis. Conversely the workers, whose risk perceptions were for a long time dismissed as over-active imaginings of side effects, had real empirical experience, indeed expertise, that was directly relevant to an objective risk analysis.[47]

Analysis of this kind stresses the judgemental and unavoidably *social* nature of expertise as offered within the decision-making process. Certainly, Wynne's analysis could readily be extended to the area of major hazards (where the risk analytical techniques employed inevitably involve 'professional judgement') and to the BSE case (how much fallibility do we assume in abattoir methods or BSE identification when establishing new regulations?). In both areas, assump-tions must be made about whether the world of everyday practice will differ from the controlled world of the laboratory. Equally, of course, the 'sociology' discussed by Wynne may not always be naive. There is also, as Bauman has noted, a potential for deliberate manipulation in this area.[48]

Science from this perspective cannot remain aloof from external concerns but must itself offer a reflection of certain social assumptions and taken-for-granted practices – including, of course, those of science itself: 'The assumptions which analysts make are often an unconsciously expressed function of their own social values and relationships within the system'.[49] Despite the rhetoric to the contrary, therefore, scientific analyses must reflect the ideological and institu-tional assumptions of the 'experts' who conduct them – although these assump-tions are not necessarily made consciously and indeed their existence may be strongly denied by those who hold them. In the case of 2,4,5-T, it is also possible to see certain institutional assumptions at work with regard to the 'burden of proof' required by the advisory committee and the farmworkers.

Thus, whilst the farmworkers felt that there were sufficient doubts about the pesticide to justify its withdrawal, the advisory committee argued that it was inappropriate to act until the case was proven 'beyond all reasonable doubt'. As one trade union participant put it:

> Here a crucial difference between our two approaches emerges. 'We will rescind its clearance if the union can prove to us that 2,4,5-T is harmful' was in effect what the ACP told the union delegation. 'No', we responded, we cannot supply proof 'beyond all reasonable doubt'. Our yardstick is to estimate the hazard on the basis of what we know, and if 'on the balance of probabilities', the substance appears dangerous, then it should clearly be taken off the market.[50]

One important dimension of these assumptions will relate to the credibility and legitimacy of the institutions within which scientists operate. External criticisms of key institutions are likely to be met by those within them with incomprehension, anger and (very often) allegations of public hysteria and media irresponsibility. The powerful image of science as 'value-free' serves, of course, to reinforce these notions. Such a process can, in turn, exacerbate the problems of communication between scientists and the wider public – encouraging further the idea that the public are irrational but also fostering public doubts about the value of scientific assessments and damaging the credibility of scientific institutions. When scientists then find themselves in public *disagreement* (as appears such a regular feature of policy debates),[51] the science-centred model struggles to maintain its credibility whilst more critical voices seize upon the apparent confusion in order to stress the limitations and uncertainties of scientific analysis. In such situations, scientific institutions tend to become victims of their own over-inflated promises. Equally, important policy decisions must be made on a poorly understood foundation.

Towards a citizen science?

So far in this chapter, I have offered a polarization between 'enlightened' and 'critical' views of the relationship between science and the general public. Whilst the former emphasizes the positive contribution of science to everyday life and defines the problem as being how to carry (or push) the public towards 'scientific enlightenment',[52] the latter approach is distinctly wary of such an ideology and stresses the negative consequences of much of contemporary science for everyday life. In making this argument, the critical account closely links the physical manifestations of science and technology (production systems, products, environmental impacts) with the intellectual processes of scientific production. Meanwhile, the 'enlightened' approach stresses those manifestations which it sees as progressive and argues that the best antidote to any negative elements is further support for science. Of course, both of these approaches acknowledge the centrality of science and technology within every-day existence. They highlight the 'success' of the scientific world view – but profoundly disagree about the consequences of this for our happiness and social progress.

These matters take on special significance, given the current high level of environmental concern. Can science lead us out of the current crisis or is it the very rationality that creates an exploitative and short-sighted approach to the natural world? Should we be blaming science for environmental problems or looking to it for salvation? One other response to this apparent impasse is to dismiss the application of science in this area and to turn to more romantic (or obscurantist) alternatives – for example, the *pot-pourri* of beliefs, rationalities and self-improvement techniques which together form the 'New Age'. Whilst the science-centred approach would, inevitably, criticize such belief structures as a 'retreat from the rational', there is no doubt that they can provide a sense of order and understanding that, for whatever reason, the scientific world view does not provide to all of society. Once again, accusations of 'irrationality' seem to compound rather than resolve the problems.

Phrased in this manner, the prognosis for science, democracy and citizenship seems extremely gloomy. Whilst the 'enlightened' perspective hopes to re-educate a sceptical public, the critics of science and technology view attempts at 'improved public understanding' as a defensive and self-serving reaction to growing hostility and distrust. However, whilst this argument about the 'disenchantment of the world' is at least as old as the Industrial Revolution, we also need to be aware of new possibilities for renegotiation and change. Might the social and intellectual conditions of our time – where knowledge claims are increasingly challenged and authority is less readily accepted – also create new possibilities in this area?

In particular, and given these emerging social and technical conditions, we need to explore whether it is possible to build constructively rather than remain entangled in a sterile 'science versus anti-science' debate.

In these circumstances, it is clearly important that we should consider the possibilities for an approach to science and expertise which offers at least the potential for a dialogue between scientific and citizen groups. Is it possible for a 'citizen-oriented science' (or '*citizen science*' in that sense) to emerge from these debates over the relationship between science, technology and wider society? Indeed, can the basis for such an approach be found in the three case studies presented above?

We can begin this task by considering the range of expertise and under-standing possessed by citizens but which are at present downgraded by decision-making processes. Both the 'enlightened' approach and many of the more critical accounts discussed in this paper offer a very one-dimensional view of citizens. Typically, they present the 'public' as homogeneous in character and also as essentially *passive* in the face of these contested technical messages. And yet, as we have already suggested, there is both a considerable diversity in public responses (and in the nature of the publics themselves) and a rich pattern of knowledges and understandings. As we shift to a citizen-oriented perspective in these questions, we will also consider a radically different perspective on the perceived *need for* and *relevance* of science and technology within everyday life.

The notion of bringing closer together the concerns of citizens and the understandings of science is not in itself new – many of the same preoccupations can be discerned in the 'science for the people' movement of the 1960s and 1970s, and in various attempts at 'public participation' such as the Dutch 'broad energy debate' of the 1980s. Nevertheless, both our practical experience and our understanding of science and technology have 'moved on' in such a way as to make a re-evaluation especially timely. Two further developments add to the significance of these themes:

- the special importance given to these issues by the current will to tackle environmental problems and to achieve some form of 'sustainable development';
- the availability of fresh research into these issues which attempts not to reaffirm the 'public ignorance' model but instead to capture the needs and understandings of lay groups.

[. . .]

Notes

1 Dickens, C., *Hard Times* (Harmondsworth: Penguin, 1985 reprint) p.47.
2 *ibid.*, p.92.
3 Nehru, J., quoted in Perutz, M., *Is Science Necessary? Essays on Science and Scientists* (Oxford and New York: Oxford University Press, 1991) p.vii.
4 See, for example, Charles Babbage, *Reflections on the Decline of Science in England and on Some of its Causes* (London, 1830).
5 Werskey, G., *The Visible College* (London: Allen Lane, 1978).
6 Haldane, J.B.S., *Science and Everyday Life* (Harmondsworth: Pelican Books, 1939 – reprinted 1943) p.8.
7 Members of the Association of Scientific Workers, *Science and the Nation* (Harmondsworth: Penguin, 1947) p.30.
8 *ibid.*, p.205.
9 For example, Haldane produced a stream of articles for the *Daily Worker* on such topics as 'Why bananas have no pips', 'Is there life on the planets?', 'Occupational mortality' or 'How British science is organised'. Typically, these articles had a political orientation towards the critique of contemporary capitalism.
10 Association of Scientific Workers, *op.cit.*, p.249.
11 *ibid.*, p.16.
12 Royal Society, *The Public Understanding of Science* (London: Royal Society, 1985) p.9.
13 *ibid*.
14 Berg, M., *The Machinery Question and the Making of Political Economy 1815–1848* (Cambridge: Cambridge University Press, 1980).
15 For example, Habermas, J., *Towards a Rational Society: Student Protest, Science and Politics* (London: Heinemann, 1971) Chapter 6.

16 Marcuse, H., *One Dimensional Man* (London: Sphere Books, 1970) p.46.

17 Marx, K., *The Grundrisse* (Harmondsworth: Penguin, 1983) p.693, quoted in Hill, S., *The Tragedy of Technology* (London: Pluto, 1988) p.52.

18 Hill, S., *op.cit.*, p.38.

19 Advisory Committee on Pesticides, *Further Review of the Safety for Use in the UK of Herbicide 2,4,5-T* (London: MAFF, 1980) p.26.

20 National Union of Agricultural and Allied Workers, *Not One Minute Longer!* Submission to Minister of Agriculture, Fisheries and Food, July 1980, p.3.

21 According to the Pesticide Action Network, the 'dirty dozen' campaign identifies twelve 'extremely hazardous pesticides that should be banned, phased out, or carefully controlled everywhere in the world'.

22 NUAAW, *op.cit.*

23 *Landworker*, June 1980, pp.6–7.

24 NUAAW, *op.cit.*, p.20.

25 Advisory Committee on Pesticides, *op.cit.*

26 *ibid.*, p.35.

27 *ibid.*, p.13.

28 Boddy, J., quoted in Cook, J. and Kaufman, C., *Portrait of a Poison – The 2,4,5-T Story* (London: Pluto Press, 1982) p.71.

29 Gummer, J., quoted in *The Times*, May 18, 1990.

30 Advertisement in *The Times*, May 18, 1990.

31 Quoted in *The Guardian*, July 13, 1990.

32 Southwood, R., quoted in Food Safety Advisory Centre leaflet, *The Facts about BSE*. The Food Safety Advisory Centre is sponsored by Asda, Gateway, Morrisons, Safeway, Sainsbury and Tesco.

33 *The Guardian*, July 16, 1990.

34 *ibid.*

35 Gummer, J., quoted in *The Times*, May 18, 1990.

36 The Royal Society and The Association of British Science Writers, *Bovine Spongiform Encephalopathy: A Briefing Document*, April 1990.

37 *The Guardian*, July 13, 1991.

38 Leaflet distributed to the residents of Carrington and Partington, Greater Manchester.

39 Jones, T., *Corporate Killing: Bhopals will Happen* (London: Free Association Books, 1988) p.246.

40 Council Directive, June 24, 1982 on the major accident hazards of certain industrial activities, 82/501/EC, *Official Journal of the European Communities* L230, 25, August 5, 1982.

41 See Jupp, A. and Irwin, A., 'Emergency response and the provision of public information under CIMAH – a case study', *Disaster Management* 1: 4 (1989), 33–7. For a more complete account, see Jupp, A., 'The provision of public information on major hazards'. Dissertation submitted to the Department of Science and Technology Policy, University of Manchester, January 1988.

42 *The Times*, May 18, 1990.

43 Quoted in *The Guardian*, July 13, 1990.

44 Habermas, J., *op.cit.*, Chapter 5.

45 Jones, T., *op.cit.*, pp.245–6.

46 For a starting point to this influential literature, see: Barnes, B. and Edge, D. (eds), *Science in Context* (Milton Keynes: Open University Press, 1982); Latour, B. and Woolgar, S., *Laboratory Life* (Beverly Hills and London: Sage, 1979); Mulkay, M., *Science and the Sociology of Knowledge* (London: Allen & Unwin, 1979); *idem, Sociology of Science* (Milton Keynes and Philadelphia: Open University Press, 1991); Woolgar, S., *Science: The Very Idea* (Chichester and London: Ellis Horwood and Tavistock, 1988).

47 Wynne, B., 'Frameworks of rationality in risk management: towards the testing of naive sociology' in Brown, J. (ed.) *Environmental Threats: Perception Analysis and Management* (London and New York: Belhaven Press, 1989) p.37.
48 Bauman, Z., *Postmodern Ethics* (Oxford and Cambridge, Mass.: Blackwell, 1993) p. 203.
49 Wynne, B., *op.cit.*, p.43.
50 Kauffman, C., '2,4,5-T: Britain out on a limb', in Goldsmith, E. and Hildyard, N. (eds) *Green Britain or Industrial Wasteland?* (Cambridge: Polity Press, 1986) p.169.
51 On this issue, see: Collingridge, D. and Reeve, C., *Science Speaks to Power: The Role of Experts in Policy Making* (London: Frances Pinter, 1986); Jasanoff, S., *The Fifth Branch: Science Advisers as Policy Makers* (Cambridge, Mass. and London: Harvard University Press, 1990).
52 As I write this, one newspaper is running a science-writing competition under the slogan 'Enlighten the public with science'.

Part II

Alternative contexts for communicating science

Introduction

Elizabeth Whitelegg

This section of the reader considers formal and informal learning in science for both adults and children. It takes the theme of lifelong learning in science as its focus, and although learning some lessons from research into science learning at school level, it does not focus on school-based science education. Instead it examines opportunities for learning science or learning about science and scientists from a wider sphere, one of museums and science centres, popular books and finally, from perhaps the most pervasive influence on modern culture, television.

The first two chapters in this section introduce the notion of science learning beyond the classroom. In the first, Shelagh Ross and Eileen Scanlon introduce the debate between the processes and content of science education using a 'science for all' framework. They consider what research has to tell us about the scientific understanding of the public and suggest reasons for a lack of widespread understanding of science. They describe the efforts of the UK's Open University to open up science to adults who may not have had any previous science training and the challenges that this presents.

This 'science for all' theme is continued in the second chapter in a different context – that of the education system in the United States. Walter Massey charts the evolution of science teaching in US colleges and considers what it means to be an educated person, echoing the process/content debate introduced in the first article. He considers what science a reasonably educated person can be expected to know and proposes that a proper education should at least reduce people's fear of science and technology, enable them to ask appropriate questions about scientific and technological issues and appreciate the excitement of the new discoveries in science. However, in view of all the advances being made in science, there is not enough time during the years in formal education to teach a deep understanding of all these areas and so Massey introduces the notion of learning science outside formal settings and suggests characteristics of an educated person who could become a lifelong learner. He concludes by considering the opportunities that museums and science centres have to play in this by encouraging the development of a sense of wonder of science amongst all citizens.

The rest of this section of the reader examines channels of informal learning in science – ranging from museums and science centres to popular science books, journals, films and finally television. The chapter by Leonie Rennie and Terence McClafferty examines the role of science centres in learning about and understanding science and provides a critical summary of research on outcomes of visits to science centres.

Using some of this and other research, Jo Graham and Ben Gammon, audience advocates for the new Wellcome Wing project at the Science Museum in London, describe how they have developed a strategy to foster science learning among visitors to the wing. Their strategy is underpinned by the learning theories of educationalists and psychologists in both the cognitive and affective domains, and in this chapter they describe the processes that they have introduced to the development teams at the museum to promote visitors' learning.

Whilst the Wellcome Wing is being designed with learning as a central aim, this is a contentious position and a fairly recent development in the museum world. Even if learning is core to a museum's design it cannot be assumed that learning necessarily occurs during museum visits. School groups are one of the most frequent groups to visit museums, and Janette Griffin has examined the behaviour of groups of schoolchildren on museum visits to ascertain whether learning occurs. In her chapter, she looks for evidence of learning and develops a set of indicators for learning to use as evidence.

Moving away from the museum setting, the following two chapters consider science learning via popular science books. First, Jon Turney considers the recent publishing boom in popular non-fiction science books and discusses the motivation of popular writers on science and examines how much science they can actually convey. He catalogues the large range of different types of popular science book, which have a variety of agendas, and considers whether there is a limit to the science understanding that can be conveyed to the lay reader through popular writing.

An example of a popular science writer with a firm educational agenda is given in the next chapter. The author, Russell Stannard, who is also a physics professor, believes passionately in his desire to introduce the physics of relativity to young children. Like many in the physics community, he is dismayed by the physics that school students are taught and wants them to learn some modern (twentieth-century) physics as well as classical physics. His trialing of drafts of his book *The Time and Space of Uncle Albert* with schoolchildren led him to believe that 11–12-year-olds could indeed appreciate certain aspects of relativity, a topic often thought too difficult for many adults. His learning strategy is based on the controversial pedagogical theories of educational psychologist Jean Piaget, who proposed that the mind develops in three discrete stages, and that some people may never pass the second stage.

Moving on from non-fiction, Robert Lambourne considers science fiction as a channel for communicating science. This chapter examines which aspects of science are most commonly communicated by science fiction; where in science fiction this science is communicated; and how it is done. Drawing on a wide range of methods and media, Lambourne charts the evolution of science communication through fictionalised accounts of science and concludes that authors have rarely aimed at communicating science facts through science fiction but rather aim to use science as a story-telling device to make their stories believable.

Finally, the last chapter in this section looks at science on television and asks whether museums can learn from the changes that science programming on television has undergone over the last 30 years. Jana Bennett, a former editor of BBC2's flagship science series, *Horizon*, claims that the key features of science coverage on television are a search for relevance; a focus on the impact of breakthroughs and discoveries; and a concentration on process and narrative. She recommends that museums pay attention to these features in developing successful exhibits.

Chapter 3

Opening up science*

S. Ross and E. Scanlon

[Science should be more than] a reserved compartment in which only
specialists have a right to travel.

(HMSO, Science in Secondary Schools, 1960, p.5)

Introduction

The slogan 'science for all', which first emerged from a UNESCO working
party in 1983, has been seen in many countries as the embodiment of a new
approach to science education aimed at improving the scientific literacy of the
public at large. The National Science Foundation (1983) and the American
Association for the Advancement of Science (1989) both published plans in the
mid-1980s aimed at improving science education in the USA; the Science
Council of Canada and the Curriculum Development Centre (1988) in
Australia produced statements with similar titles and aims. In the UK, The
Royal Society boldly declared in 1985 'Science *is* for everybody'; an organiza-
tion devoted to studying and fostering the public understanding of science
(COPUS) and a journal entitled *Public Understanding of Science* were estab-
lished in the early 1990s.

> The importance of a scientifically and technologically literate population is
> being emphasised in all countries, since it is recognised that specialist
> scientists and technologists cannot operate without a knowledgeable
> supporting society.
>
> (Harlen, 1993: p.126)

Many authors have commented on particular aspects of the 'science for all'
approach; Fensham's reviews (1988, 1992) provide an especially interesting
analysis of the curriculum development that has resulted. Although the 'science
for all' movement has been mainly addressed to the compulsory education
sector (primary and secondary), many of the points on which it is based apply

*Chapter 2 in *Open Science*, Paul Chapman Publishing (1995), pp. 17–24.

equally to the programmes of tertiary, adult and open education institutions. In particular, whatever the level, the choice of curriculum content is crucial. Fensham, for example (1988, 1992), has argued that content in science courses should fulfill two essential criteria: it should have societal meaning and usefulness to the majority of learners, and it should allow learners to share in the wonder and excitement that has made the development of science such a great human and cultural achievement. Other issues that must be addressed relate to the provision of gender-inclusive learning materials (Fensham, 1993; Harlen, 1993), differentiated access for students with special educational needs (Purnell, 1993), and a generally more diversified range of opportunities for potential science learners. The open and distance education sector is well-placed to satisfy all these criteria, and hence to recruit new adult audiences for science courses.

Teaching and learning science

The increasing number and sales of 'popular science' books in the last decade may be taken as evidence of a growing public interest in or at least awareness of science (see, for example, the essay by Rodgers, 1992). Such books, however, tend to concentrate on a rather narrow range of (often curiously 'advanced') topics, and to be largely descriptive in nature. They may spark interest in potential science learners but are in no way a substitute for formal instruction. The following quotation from *Primary Science: Why and How* gives a good working definition of what we mean by 'science' in the phrase 'teaching or learning science'.

> One definition of science is that science is what scientists do. Scientists actively confront nature with questions, seeking patterns in what they observe so they can make predictions and possibly use and control aspects of it. The ways in which scientists proceed with their observations, questions and experiments involve processes aimed at achieving reliable, reproducible and objective answers, with the result that scientific knowledge is verifiable. So science is not only the body of knowledge that scientists have accumulated but also the ways in which they acquire this knowledge. These are the 'content' and 'process' dimensions of science so much debated in the context of appropriate science teaching.
>
> (Open University, 1985: p.8)

[. . .] The distinction [between content and process aspects of science education] is a crucial one for curriculum and instructional designers in deciding whether they want to produce courses *about* science or courses *in* science. Most science educators consider that the process dimension excites the curiosity and attention of learners:

> There is a strong case for arguing that process-based science is likely to be more stimulating . . . than the presently predominating content-based approach. Further, because it conveys an image of science as imaginative and created by the human mind, it is more likely to be seen as interesting and relevant.
>
> (Harlen, 1993: p.127)

On the other hand, there is an obvious tension between the requirement of any technological society to train future scientists and technologists in the details of their subjects and the aim of producing an informed and scientifically literature public. Fensham and Harlen, among others, have pointed to the dangers of separating these two categories of learner. The fact that intending scientists have to learn 'real science' does not lessen their need for an appreciation of either the societal relevance of science or its moral and ethical dimension. Conversely, it is impossible to draw the public into the decision-making process about issues such as pollution, genetic engineering or nuclear power if all knowledge about these areas rests only with a small constituency of elite professional scientists.

Different countries have resolved this tension in different ways. Some have opted for a broad curriculum of integrated science in compulsory schooling up to a certain level. Others have streamed or modular programmes that separate the intending science specialists, usually at some point in their secondary education. Before the advent of the 'open', distance-teaching universities there was very little opportunity for direct entry to science or technology courses at the tertiary level for students who had not completed the necessary selection and preparation in their secondary schooling. And as Fensham has pointed out:

> The two tasks of selection and preparation are usually associated. That is, the content of science education deemed a suitable preparation for the science disciplines in tertiary education has also turned out to be a useful selective device since comparatively few students learn it successfully. Whether this low success is due to inherent difficulty in the content of science, or whether it is due to lack of interest among students, is another issue.
>
> (Fensham, 1993: p.112)

It is this issue that we will explore in the next section.

Why science is difficult to learn

There is a public perception that science, like maths, is hard to learn. Most schoolchildren in the Western world receive at least some exposure to science at school, yet many adults are unable to answer correctly questions relating to basic scientific facts (see, e.g., Lucas, 1987). Public understanding of the history of scientific achievement and processes of science seems equally deficient. In a survey of 2,000 adults undertaken in 1985 by the British magazine *New Scientist*, only 45 percent of the sample thought that science did more good than harm, and a further 38 percent considered that the good and the harm cancelled out. Astonishingly, 27 percent of men and 45 percent of women questioned failed to name correctly even one important scientific achievement that occurred after the Second World War. Although the 'science for all' movement is encouraging more people to learn science, it is doing so in a culture in which science is not consistently highly valued. So why is it that much formal teaching of science apparently fails to put across the basic concepts, methodology and value of science?

Millar (1991) has suggested four main reasons for science being hard to learn:

1   learners do not feel that the efforts they must make to learn science are matched by a sufficiently large payoff;
2   an understanding of science involves continual reconstruction of meaning, and cannot be achieved by rote learning of a fixed body of knowledge;
3   many learners are confused or alienated by certain aspects of the nature of science;
4   science is abstract.

Item (1) on this list relates to the perceived relevance of an understanding of science for people's everyday lives, to which we have already alluded in the two previous sections. Science educators have not on the whole made a good job of identifying or demonstrating what part of science is of value for *all* learners, or why it is of value. In many cases this has led to an overburdening of syllabuses, which is counter-productive in terms of learning outcomes.

[The underlying point of] item (2) – [. . .] the requirement for reconstruction of knowledge – is that, in order to switch from everyday perspectives of phenomena to a scientific understanding of those phenomena, the science learner has to restructure prior conceptions; such changes of gestalt constitute a more demanding form of learning than mere accretion of knowledge.

Millar has suggested that item (3) arises from a discrepancy between the attitude of many science educators, who often present science essentially as an algorithm for obtaining knowledge of how the natural and physical world works, and the true nature of science as a body of understanding consensually accepted within the practising community. He believes that

> Science education needs first to acknowledge and then to address the tension between the 'openness' of science as first-hand investigation and the 'dogmatism' of science as a consensually accepted body of knowledge.
> (Millar, 1991: p.70)

If this tension is not resolved at the instructional level, there is, as Russell (1983) has pointed out, a danger that learners can be required to accept conclusions without appreciating the underlying evidence. This can give them a very distorted picture of the nature of science, presenting it as a collection of often unrelated or useless facts and hiding its overarching purpose. Under such circumstances, it is hardly surprising that many learners are confused, demotivated or alienated.

Item (4) encapsulates an issue to which many commentators refer. For example, Millar points to

> compelling evidence that the basic units of understanding are concrete examplars, not rules or syllogisms. . . . This suggests that the knowledge is stored not as a syllogism (a formal logical rule) but as concrete examples of the successful application of that rule. When we use the abstract rule, we check it against our recall of particular instances and not the other way round.
>
> (Millar, 1991: p.71)

Shayer and Adey (1981) have gone so far as to suggest that attempts to teach real physics to children are doomed to inevitable failure because an understanding of physical principles can only be based on formal operational thinking, which in turn demands that the learner should have reached a certain stage of cognitive development. It has been shown that in fact many students do not reach this stage even by the end of their secondary education, so it is not surprising that they cannot cope with the abstractions in which much science is expressed. Related to this is the requirement to deal with a variety of representations of real situations. Johnstone (1991) has highlighted this problem, drawing particular attention to the difficulties many students experience with multi-level thought; some examples are illustrated in Figure 3.1.

Another very obvious source of difficulty for science learners is the language in which science tends to be couched. For one thing, it is full of technical terms and jargon words. Interestingly however, it has been shown (see, e.g., Cassells and Johnstone, 1983) that new technical terms cause fewer problems for learners than words that are in everyday use in one sense but have a different and precise meaning in the context of science. Johnstone gives the following example:

> 'Volatile' has left the realm of science with its meaning of 'easily vaporized' and gone off into common speech where it is applied to markets, people, countries and hostile situations. It then filters back into science with meanings that [to students] do not seem out of place . . . but which make a nonsense of a science discussion. A 'volatile compound' is understood as a 'flammable, explosive, unstable and dangerous compound'.
>
> (Johnstone, 1991: p.80)

[. . .] Difficulties with language also tie back to the abstract nature of science. The language of science, unlike that of, say, history, is removed from the

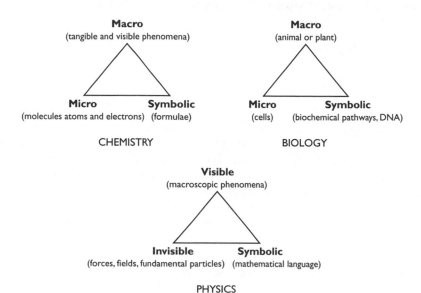

Figure 3.1 Diagrams illustrating 'triangles' of thought levels for three scientific disciplines (adapted from Johnstone, 1991: p. 78). Some good science can be done at one level only (usually the macro), or at two (e.g. classical thermodynamics, which involves only the macro and symbolic levels). However, much science teaching is done 'within the triangles', where all three levels interact. Students' difficulties in juggling the three levels simultaneously may account for many of the problems they have in learning science.

language of everyday intercourse, and this further contributes to its perceived abstraction. This problem is compounded by the fact that in many scientific disciplines the abstract language is coded in symbolic form – the language of mathematics.

The claim that science is hard to learn is really a statement that science educators are not getting the message across. Part of the problem, to which we have alluded several times already, may lie with the very nature of the message; instructors need to pay more attention to demonstrating the significance and relevance of that message. As mentioned briefly in this section, some of the faults may also lie with instructors' failure to appreciate the ways in which science learning is achieved. [. . .] But there may also be major problems with the transmission systems used to convey the message, and these are of particular concern in open and distance education.

The challenge of open or distance education in science

In the early days of the UKOU, Kaye and Pentz – an educational technologist and the original Dean of the Science Faculty, respectively – gave an analysis (Kaye 1973; Kaye and Pentz, 1974) of the specific problems associated with the design of the institution's first science courses. They referred to some of the difficulties already discussed above, which apply across a broad spectrum of science teaching and learning but may be exacerbated in the case of remote students. They also pointed to problems inherent in a system that offered science instruction at undergraduate level to those without prior qualifications. Language issues, some aspects of which have already been mentioned in the previous section, are one example. Any course or institution with open entry policies will have a very heterogeneous body of students, particularly at lower levels. These students need to become comfortable in talking about science, and even comparatively trivial difficulties, such as uncertainty about the pronunciation of a technical term, can create barriers to progress. Students' misunderstandings about the meaning of particular words in a scientific context are also more difficult for instructors to pick up in a remote teaching environment than in conventional classroom or lecture situations.

Another area of language difficulty can arise out of modular systems, in which students can range quite widely across different areas of science. Scientists themselves often have problems communicating with colleagues from other scientific disciplines, as much because of differences in meaning attached to certain terms as because of unfamiliar jargon. The construction of glossaries associated with individual courses can offer partial solutions for learners in such situations, but even this can be difficult in the less 'settled' subject areas, where the meaning of terms is still shifting.

Modular course structures, especially those with open entry systems, present instructors with particular problems in respect of subjects like science that have a strongly sequential or hierarchical knowledge base. An understanding of many concepts in science requires a grasp of a significant number of lower-level concepts. Thus, before physics students can analyse a collision, they need to have understood the concepts of mass, velocity and speed, momentum, energy and conserved quantities, and each of these concepts can be unpacked in their turn to produce an even lower-level list. The syllabus for any science course is in fact an elaborate edifice based on assumed prior knowledge.

In very 'open' modular systems the problem of hierarchies and prerequisites needs to be addressed not only at the level of individual courses but also across the entire spectrum of courses. The UKOU, for example, has always attempted to allow for the diversity in its students' entry behaviours and aspirations by stressing its open policies; these impose no entrance qualifications and permit students an extremely wide freedom of choice in the construction of their degree profiles. Nevertheless, within this free choice system, considerable care is taken to warn students of the pitfalls of eccentric degree profiles and to provide them with advice about sensible combinations and ordering of courses. Although many UKOU students do elect to concentrate mostly on one discipline, a study (Ross and Scanlon, 1989) of UKOU 'science' graduates has shown that the freedom to mix and match courses is widely valued. This diversity of degree profiles is hardly surprising in view of the range of previous experience and aspirations that UKOU students bring to their studies in science: some are updating or upgrading earlier science qualifications; others are embarking on science for the first time, but with intentions of pursuing the field in either teaching or research; still others are doing courses simply for their own interest. One measure of the success of the UKOU's modular system is the extent to which it successfully fulfills the requirements of such a diverse student body.

Another issue highlighted by Kaye and Pentz (1974), and related to the subject of prerequisites for science study, concerns the development of skills, especially mathematical skills. The opportunities afforded by distance education may bring new audiences to science courses, but these audiences seldom come equipped with the necessary mathematical skills for undergraduate-level science; with open entry, this problem is even more severe, particularly at the foundation level. In designing courses, instructors need to be extremely sensitive to the demands on students who may be grappling for the first time with mathematical formulations as well as trying to understand new scientific concepts. Skills development needs to be built into the fabric of courses from the outset, and the weaving in of process-based material must be an integral part of course design.

Constituting a different class of skills and processes, but equally vital to the nature of science, is practical work. The difficulty of providing adequate practical experience has often been seen as one of the chief stumbling blocks for science instruction at a distance.

However, science educators have risen to the challenge of producing open science courses for remote students at undergraduate level. The UKOU, which is an obvious example of this, has had a quarter of a century's experience in science education at a distance. The statistics of this institution certainly indicate that open and distance education in science can be attractive and effective: by the early 1990s a number equal to around 10 percent of full-time British 'fresher' science undergraduates annually began studying science with the UKOU, and it has been estimated (Scanlon et al., 1993) that over the first twenty years of the university's existence a total of 53,000 adults had acquired scientific skills and knowledge by studying its science foundation course. [. . .]

References

American Association for the Advancement of Science (1989) *Science for All Americans*, AAAS, Washington, DC.

Cassells, J.R.T. and Johnstone, A.H. (1983) The meaning of words and the teaching of chemistry, *Education in Chemistry*, Vol. 20, no. 1, pp. 10–11.

Curriculum Development Centre (1988) *Science for Everybody? Towards a National Science Statement*, Curriculum Development Centre, Canberra.

Fensham, P.J. (1988a) Familiar but different: some dilemmas and new directions in science education, in P. Fensham (ed.) (1988b).

Fensham, P. (ed.) (1988b) *Development and Dilemmas in Science Education*, Falmer Press, Lewes.

Fensham, P. (1992) Science and technology, in P. Jackson (ed.) *Handbook of Research on Curriculum*, pp.789–829, Macmillan, New York.

Fensham, P.J. (1993) Reflections on science for all, in E. Whitelegg, J. Thomas and S. Tresman (eds) (1993).

Harlen, W. (1992) Research and the development of science in the primary school, *International Journal of Science Education*, Vol. 14, no. 5, pp.491–503.

Harlen, W. (1993) Education for equal opportunities in a scientifically literate society, in E. Whitelegg, J. Thomas and S. Tresman (eds) (1993).

Johnstone, A.H. (1991) Why is science difficult to learn? Things are seldom what they seem, *Journal of Computer Assisted Learning*, Vol. 7, no. 2, pp. 75–83.

Kaye, A. (1973) Design and evaluation of science courses at the Open University, *Instructional Science*, Vol. 2, pp.119–85.

Kaye, A. and Pentz, M.J. (1974) Integrating multi-media systems for science education which achieve a wide territorial coverage, in *New Trends in the Utilisation of Educational Technology for Science Education*, UNESCO Press, Paris.

Lucas A. (1987) Public knowledge of biology, *Journal of Biological Education*, Vol. 20, pp.41–5.

Millar, R. (1991) Why is science hard to learn? *Journal of Computer Assisted Learning*, Vol. 7, no. 2, pp.66–74.

National Science Foundation (1983) *Educating Americans for the 21st Century*, National Science Foundation, Washington, DC.

Open University (1985) *Primary Science: Why and How* (course code EHP 531), OU, Milton Keynes.

Purnell, R. (1993) Science for special needs, in E. Whitelegg, J. Thomas and S. Tresman (eds) (1993).

Rodgers, M. (1992) The Hawking phenomenon, *Public Understanding of Science*, Vol. 1, no. 2, pp.231–4.

Ross, S. and Scanlon, E. (1989) Conventional wisdom, course choice and student progress in science courses, *Open Learning*, Vol. 4, no. 3, pp.14–22.

Russell, T. (1983) Analysing arguments in science classroom discourse: can teachers' questions distort scientific authority?, *Journal of Research in Science Teaching*, Vol. 20, pp.27–45.

Scanlon, E., Edwards, D. and West, D. (eds) (1993) *Teaching, Learning and Assessment in Science Education*, Paul Chapman Publishing, London.

Shayer, M. and Adey, P.S. (1981) *Towards a Science of Science Teaching*, Heinemann Educational, London.

Whitelegg, E., Thomas, J. and Tresman, S. (eds) (1993) *Challenges and Opportunities for Science Education*, Paul Chapman Publishing, London.

Chapter 4

Science for all citizens
Setting the stage for lifelong learning*

W. Massey

Introduction

Each year at the University of Chicago – and I am sure at other universities – upon presenting the degrees to the graduating class, the president of the university says, 'By the power vested in me, I now declare you graduates and welcome you to the fellowship of educated men and women'. I have always thought this to be a *wonderful* phrase: 'welcome to the fellowship of educated men and women'.

The implication is that after much hard work, dedication and achievement, one is finally being admitted to a well-defined, recognized coterie; and that the passport for entry into that group is the degree, or the diploma. Of course, it does not take a very long time for most graduates to learn that they are not really educated.

The question of what constitutes an educated person is, of course, not new, and is one that has been debated from Plato to Rousseau to our present day. But within the context of American education, this debate is taking on a new vigor, and I believe justifiably so. For the world has grown more complex, our future more uncertain; and some simple assumptions of the past will not necessarily be appropriate for us today – or tomorrow.

Learning from our past: the development of science in the college curriculum

However, the past does set the stage for what education can and ought to be today. According to Frederick Rudolph (1962) in his book *The American College and University*, the past in some ways – at least within American higher education – seemed a lot simpler. For over a hundred years, higher education in America followed a fairly well-prescribed path. The first colleges were almost direct descendants of their European counterparts, as far as curricular structure

*Previously published in *Science Learning in the Informal Setting*, Chicago Academy of Sciences Symposium, 12–15 November 1987, pp. 134–43.

and content were concerned. The curriculum consisted of Latin, Greek and Hebrew in the first two years; logic and rhetoric in the second year; philosophy – natural, moral and mental – in the third year; with mathematics, advanced Greek and Latin in the fourth year. Of course, divinity was spread throughout all four years.

The method of teaching was didactic; that is, it consisted of memorization and recitation. Science entered the curriculum primarily through natural philosophy – the study of mathematics, primarily algebra and geometry. There was some botany; however, science by and large was not viewed as a separate topic of study in earlier American higher education but as part of natural philosophy, and according to Rudolph, 'a handmaiden and servant of the divine'. Instructors during those years (the late 1600s to the mid-1700s) were practically all ministers, or somehow connected to the church. An *educated man* – and I use the phrase deliberately, for women were only rarely admitted to these earlier institutions – was one who had mastered this standard curriculum; and since all colleges had virtually the same course of study, it was relatively easy to define and identify the qualities, attributes and expectations of the educated class.

This pattern of uniformity of curriculum and similarity of institutions continued – with some changes – until the middle of the nineteenth century. According to some scholars, this curriculum was based on the principle that the study of certain subjects led to the learning of certain 'disciplines' or 'faculties of the mind' that were transferable to all aspects of life. One studied Latin and Greek, not to learn Latin and Greek *per se*, but to develop reasoning abilities and memorization. The natural sciences were not seen to be necessary to develop such faculties because of their emphasis on 'mere content'. However, during the late nineteenth century, science and technology became significant forces in society, and this was reflected in the curriculum of the colleges. The teaching of science forced changes, not only in the content of college programs but also in the methodology of teaching. Laboratory work, experiments and open-ended questioning began to replace the strict memorization, recitation format.

It was being recognized that the purpose of college was not simply to learn existing knowledge but to participate in the discovery of new knowledge. This process was greatly accelerated and institutionalized in the late nineteenth and early twentieth centuries by the founding of some of the first true *universities* in America – Johns Hopkins, Clark and the University of Chicago. For unlike colleges, which were student-oriented, these new universities were faculty-oriented and were devoted primarily to the discovery of new knowledge and educating graduate students to become researchers and discoverers themselves.

The establishment of large numbers of universities in America, all with different missions and goals (land grant schools, technical institutions and urban universities), changed college curricula not only directly by providing different models for higher education, but indirectly and more permanently by educating faculty who were to become the teachers of undergraduates and of elementary and secondary school students.

With teachers, students and institutions having such diverse backgrounds and structures, it became very difficult to define simply the characteristics of an educated man or woman – at least in terms of courses taken in the colleges. Scientists became teachers of science and of future scientists; humanists became teachers of humanities, and so on – each group seemingly concerned primarily with perpetuating an image of themselves in their students.

This trend, in many cases, led to a stultification in liberal education and an over-emphasis on professionalization in our colleges, against which many students and faculty rebelled in the 1960s. These rebellious students and faculty – using such words as 'relevance' and 'individuality' almost as battle cries – demanded a change in college curricula. We all had our shares of such demands. Those of us who went through that period, either as students or teachers, remember well those battles (and they were not always on the college greens) and the debates over what should be the nature and content of a college education.

The new (old) debate: what constitutes an educated person?

We seem to have come full circle in this debate. Now many in higher education call for a return to a 'core curriculum', the kind of structured undergraduate educational process that either preceded – or was imagined to have preceded – the 1960s. Many who call for these changes lament the 1960s and look upon that period as one of the most disastrous in the history of higher education. I happen to think that some admirable and worthwhile changes took place in the educational system during that period – many of them being forced by students.

The introduction of new kinds of courses on ecology, the environment, ethnic studies and urban studies comes readily to mind. New methods of teaching – from individual personalized systems of instruction (PSI) to mastery learning – were widely experimented with, and in some cases became regular parts of the educational process. The emphasis on individual achievement in the 1960s had many positive aspects in that it allowed students with natural abilities or strong motivations to progress at a rate and pace that would not have been possible within a tightly structured system. (I use '1960s' as a chronological metaphor for a period that extended well into the 1970s, and for a set of attitudes and points of view that still exist in many places.)

However, I do believe that not even the most optimistic supporters of a 'student-centred' curriculum would argue that all the changes initiated during that period were positive in the long run. Nor do I think that even the strongest advocates of such approaches would argue that an educated person is one who simply declares himself or herself to be such, as was often the case at the time.

Perhaps the most widely discussed, and in some cases the *least read*, book in America today deals with the subject of what it means to be an educated person. I am speaking, of course, of the book by Professor Allan Bloom (1987), *The Closing of the American Mind*. Professor Bloom argues vigorously that the past two decades in higher education have been disastrous, that we have given diplomas or degrees to a generation of students who are woefully under-educated and who do not even recognize their impoverished situation.

Edward Hirsch (1987) has written what is perhaps the second most popular non-fiction book in the country – at least it has been for the past year or so. He agrees with Bloom and argues in *Cultural Literacy* that one can repair some of the damage that colleges and high schools have done in under-educating individuals through the study of sets of facts, which he calls 'things every educated person should know'. This trivial pursuit theory of education is perhaps the best one can expect in the computer age, where access to 'data-bases' is equated with knowledge.

Much of this *new debate* is, of course, not new and revolves around the age-old question: What should be taught, when there is not enough time to teach everything? Or, what should people be encouraged to learn? – which is not quite the same thing. Allan Bloom favors the 'Great Books' approach, although that is a trivialization of his arguments, and I apologize for it. But his thesis is that there are writings that address in a profound way the great questions that face the human race, and by not being familiar with these writings and their authors, one is seriously deprived. By studying them, one at least forms the basis for intellectual growth. Personally, I believe his approach to have a great deal of validity, if only in that it encourages – and presumably creates – an appetite for continued reading and study after formal education.

However, if content mastered (or books read) is to be the basis by which one is judged to be educated, it seems obvious and apparent to me that an educated person ought to have mastered and be capable of understanding the important and complex issues that society faces, and be able to contribute to the solution of some of society's present problems. Using this criterion leads to the conclusion that most people in today's society are woefully under-educated. For I would argue that many – if not most – of the major problems that now confront society – and will continue to confront it for the foreseeable future – are either scientific and technical in nature, or have at their base scientific and technical concerns; and that our educational systems have not adequately addressed these issues. Why our educational instutitions have failed in this regard has been the topic of many studies and analyses. I will not repeat the results of those here; but I would like to dwell just a bit – at the risk of repeating things you may have heard many times before – on the reasons I believe every educated person ought to be knowledgeable in some aspects of science and technology.

Why study science? Who needs to?

The arguments one can give for improving the quality of science, maths and technical education are many. The need to replenish the supply of scientific and technical talent simply to maintain the level of professional participation the nation requires is an obvious argument about which I will say no more. Most individuals will never become professional scientists, engineers or mathematicians, but they will still need to have an understanding of and familiarity with science and technology. Why?

First, jobs in the future will require much more of an understanding of technical issues than they now require. Technical products and processes will permeate the marketplace, requiring managers and executives to have a better appreciation of the role that technology plays in the markets they serve.

This will be important domestically but more important internationally, as the United States is increasingly forced to compete in an international marketplace with many countries (such as Japan) that do recognize the importance of technology to economic growth and that value and support science education. Some argue that even now American industry suffers in its competence because we have lost the ability to focus on long-term results and have become too preoccupied with bottom lines. One reason given for this is that many of the leaders of American history simply do not have the understanding of the role of research and development, or of science and technology, that will allow them to maintain their enterprises at the cutting edge in their fields. This is not true of all companies, of course. The existence and successes of an IBM or an AT&T serve as counter-examples.

Not every individual is destined to be a 'leader of industry', of course, but even for those who will not be such (the average worker), being scientific and technically literate will be equally important. It will not be adequate for workers of the future to be scientifically 'gun shy', as many citizens of our present generation are. We must all become comfortable with science and technology.

Even beyond the marketplace, we now recognize the inherent value of an educated and aware citizenry in a democracy. As many national issues – ranging from the quality of our environment to issues of war and peace and economic productivity – become more and more intertwined with and dependent upon science and technology, it is perhaps more important than ever that the general citizenry be sufficiently literate in these areas to be able to exercise their responsibilities.

An individual who does not understand basic technical issues – and, in fact, has no confidence in his or her ability to understand – will not be able to participate in a meaningful way in decisions involving these issues. The danger is not that such decisions will therefore *not* be made, but that they will be increasingly made either by a small group of educated and informed technocrats or by a large group of uninformed voters who respond to demagoguery and to a sensationalistic press. Neither of these situations is healthy in the long run.

Incidents such as the meltdown of the reactor at Chernobyl; the build-up of fluorocarbons in the atmosphere; acid rain and its effects on the environment, as well as its effects on our relations with our neighbor to the north (Canada); the question of what kind of science can be taught in schools, evolution or a form of pseudoscientific creationism, are all issues currently under debate in the public arena.

What can one expect a reasonably educated citizen to know – or do – about such issues? Although I have always argued – and will continue to do so – that it is critical to have an educated citizenry capable of bringing to bear reasonable judgments through the political process on such issues, this is easier said than done. Certainly no amount of scientific education for nonscientists will allow individuals to judge these issues on a technical basis. When scientists themselves – and in some cases even experts in the same field – disagree, it is an impossible task to try to educate the lay citizen to the point where he or she can be expected to be an expert in any of these areas. So, what can one reasonably expect?

At a minimum, a proper education should at least remove much of the fear people have concerning scientific and technical issues, and their lack of confidence in their ability to comprehend basic scientific and technical principles. A proper education would also allow one to recognize outright demogoguery and chicanery. It would also teach individuals the kinds of questions one should ask when making decisions about the consequences of scientific and technical matters.

Although there are some glaring exceptions, most people – I have found – are actually smarter than they believe themselves to be, and certainly are more capable of comprehending basic principles in science and technology than they believe. Fear of science leads to a distrust of things scientific and technical; this fear is one of the major *learned attitudes* that must be corrected early in life, *before* youngsters develop lack of confidence. I will say more about this later.

But even beyond the need to have an educated and aware citizenry or an educated and competent workforce, science and technology should be learned and appreciated *for its own sake*. The level of general cutlural awareness suffers, and will suffer more in the future, if we as a society do not participate in what is perhaps the most exciting enterprise of our times. No person – even Allan Bloom, perhaps especially Allan Bloom – would call himself or herself educated without at least some understanding of the importance of the great works of art and literature; or who does not appreciate and understand – even at some basic level – the ideas of the great philosophers, or the significant music that has been produced by our civilization. Yet, the majority of people in this country – if not in the world – feel no shame, and in some cases, take a perverse pride in being culturally ignorant when it comes to matters scientific and technical.

I am sure that every scientist in the room has had the experience when people ask, 'What do you do?' You say, 'I am a scientist, or I am a physicist'. And the response is, 'Oh, I was never good at that. I just don't understand anything about science (or physics)'. This is usually said as if it were perfectly natural and expected, and is said with no trace of embarrassment. This failure to participate in the cultural enrichment that science and technology can give means that a large portion of our society is missing out on one of the greatest experiences of being human in our day and age.

So many exciting things are happening now in science and technology that I hesitate to mention any particular ones at all, but just to remind ourselves, let me mention a few.

The new links and understanding between cosmology and elementary particle physics are giving deeper understanding of the most important questions that humankind can address – the origin of the universe and the ultimate fate of the universe. These questions are by no means on the verge of being finally answered; but our understanding is growing, and our appreciation for the kinds of questions that can be asked and answered has increased tremendously.

Chemistry is evolving into a field so far from the test-tube chemistry that many of us learned during our high school days that the field may require a new name. At one time chemists only looked at beginning and end products; they never really understood, and certainly could not observe, the intermediate steps that went from a beginning product to an end product. With new instrumentation, such as fast-pulsed light sources, one is now able to study molecular processes at inter-mediate steps and understand at every point during chemical reactions what is happening at the molecular level. Scientists at Bell Laboratories have recently developed techniques that will allow one to isolate and study individual atoms and perhaps even tailor-make molecules for particular needs.

Perhaps the most exciting scientific area of all has to do with things biological – or the interfaces between physics, chemistry and biology. We will no longer have to rely exclusively on natural products for the benefit of the human race. From drugs to food sources, we are understanding more and more how to engineer genetically the kinds of products we will need. And at the boundary of science and technology, we have superconductivity – the implications of which are truly revolutionary.

I must say that even though I feel we do not give an adequate education in these areas for the nonscientist, things have improved tremendously over the past ten or so years. Increasingly, magazines and newspapers, television, and even radio shows address questions of science and techology. Scientific magazines have proliferated to the point where the competition has forced some of them out of the business. *Scientific American* has been sold; *Science '86* has been sold and combined with *Discover*, and *The New York Times* even has an excellent weekly section on science.

Things are moving in the right direction, but we cannot afford to be complacent. We have witnessed in the past – those of us who have worked in these areas for some time – tremendous enthusiasm on the part of our nation for scientific and technical education, only to see that enthusiasm dissipate as complacency grew. I need not remind all of us over forty that we are having to address these problems anew after all the effort and progress made during the Sputnik era.

To recapitulate, the principal reasons I would give for improving scientific and technical education are (1) to ensure an adequate supply of future profes-sional scientists and engineers, (2) to educate managers and workers for an

increasingly technical marketplace, and (3) to have a scientifically and technically literate populace for social, political and cultural reasons.

Of course, if this were a conference of social scientists, humanists, musicians
or historians, similar arguments could be made by those groups that what the
country really needs is a better appreciation of history and culture, so that we
can recognize our roots and learn from the past how we might face the future.
Or that we need to appreciate more than we do the great writings and works of
art to better understand and realize the full scope of our humanity, and to learn
again how to ask – and try to answer – those questions that continually face the
human race. All of their arguments would be valid, for – as I said earlier – there
is simply not enough time in any *structured* educational system to study all the
things one would like to know or needs to know. Therefore, it seems impossible
that one will ever be able to define an educated person on the basis of content
learned, courses taken or topics studied.

Some key attributes of the lifelong learner

But there are *characteristics* I would attribute to an educated person that go
beyond the bodies of knowledge that one might master. One characteristic or
attribute is the ability, desire and motivation to continue learning once one
leaves the formal educational system. What attributes does a person need to
develop in order to set the stage for lifelong learning? Let me present the
argument for three attributes (or traits or habits): *curiosity*, *confidence* and
skepticism. Individuals possessing these attributes have a high likelihood of
continuing to learn, no matter what setting they find themselves in, and they
are also likely to be motivated to seek out learning experiences for themselves.
My argument is fairly straightforward and simple.

Curiosity is needed in order to want to understand the phenomena encountered
in the world in which one functions and the other human beings with whom
one interacts. A desire to know more about things – to want to know how
things work – becomes a driving force for a continuing desire to learn.

However, curiosity alone will not continue to motivate, unless there is a basic
confidence in one's ability to learn new things and to master new topics.
Curiosity, in fact, is often stifled and driven underground by a lack of
confidence in one's ability to tackle new areas.

Curiosity and confidence will carry one a long way toward developing a
passion and a capacity for lifelong learning, but a healthy degree of *skepticism*
is always needed – perhaps a 'degree of discrimination' may be a better phrase.
Unfocused curiosity and unrealistic over-confidence can lead to gullibility and a
learning and mastery of things either of no importance or simply wrong, and
this can evolve into a fruitless dissipation of mental and physical energy and a
pursuit of activities and subjects that are not worth pursuing. Striving to be
curious and to have confidence is great, but to use this to master astrology – or
to believe that one can learn to communicate with 20,000-year-old beings and

thereby 'channel' spiritual energy into individuals in today's world from ancient civilizations, or rediscover Atlantis – is not what I characterize as fruitful applications of lifelong learning. A healthy degree of skepticism leads one to know that things are not always what they seem to be at first glance, that obvious answers and solutions are not necessarily – or even usually – the correct ones, and that so-called 'authorities and experts' are not always right.

How does one develop these characteristics and/or traits of skepticism, confidence and curiosity? It seems to me that here the study and learning of science can play a second role. These characteristics are exactly the ones that can emerge from the study of science at all levels – from early childhood through college. Science as a discipline and body of knowledge – and as a process – requires curiosity, confidence and skepticism; it nurtures, inculcates and develops curiosity, confidence and skepticism; *and* it is not necessary that such learning be carried out within a formal setting.

I do not mean to encourage a return to the position of pre-twentieth-century educators and argue for the teaching of science because it develops 'certain faculties', and I certainly do not view the value of learning sciences as one mid-nineteenth-century educator viewed Latin. Speaking of the reason one should study Latin, he said: 'The acquisition of a language is educationally of no importance; what is important is the process of acquiring it. . . . The one great merit of Latin as a teaching instrument is its tremendous difficulty'. Unfortunately, too many teachers and students now see science in this vein. Although science can be difficult, it can also be fun; and this is what we often forget.

Confidence can be *taught* to young children; it can be developed through processes by which one masters certain activities and learns certain facts, and through that learning and mastery gains a confidence that other activities can be understood, mastered and learned – even, or especially with, simple experiments and observations that can be made in settings such as museums, zoos and parks.

Skepticism also can be *acquired* by pointing out to youngsters in everyday experiences, or through structured activities and informal settings, that things are not always what they seem. Water that looks as if it flows uphill – as in the famous hanging faucet experiment – does not do so, and can be explained if one looks closely at the situation. Magic performed with magnets and mirrors can be shown to have logical explanations, and can be mastered if one understands the underlying principles.

What about curiosity? Can it be taught? The question is better asked: 'What can one do not to stifle curiosity?' Fortunately for the human race, curiosity is not a characterisic that needs to be taught or acquired, but one which every individual has at birth. Children are naturally curious, but that natural curiosity, unfortunately, is stifled at an early age. Much of youthful curiosity is dimmed at the point when the first questions are asked of parents: 'How is a rainbow made?' Or, 'Why does the moon shine at night, but the sun doesn't?' 'Why do leaves turn from green to brown at certain times of the year?' – and other common questions that all children have asked their parents from time immemorial. The first stifling of curiosity takes place when the answer to the child is 'I don't know'. Or, 'Don't ask such silly questions'. It is the silly questions that are the important ones. As Leon Lederman, Director of Fermilab, has said, 'Those who do not stop asking silly questions become scientists'.

Conclusion

The museums, science centers, and other such institutions can play a tremendous role in the inculcation, development and nurturing of curiosity in youngsters, *old and young*. I use that phrase deliberately, because by youngsters, I mean those who are young in mind and who have managed to maintain their natural curiosity. Such institutions can create the *sense of wonder* about phenomena that is the underlying basis for the desire to understand and learn.

In her book about her father, *The Master of Light*, Dorothy Michaelson Livingston (1973) – reminiscing about the times her father attempted to explain scientific phenomena to her and her sister – says of Albert Michaelson:

> Father's consuming interest in the behavior of light was contagious. We delighted in the double image and brilliant colors produced by a little prism he brought home from the laboratory. On evenings when he was in a mood to talk, he would tell us about rainbows, lightning, or the northern lights.
>
> Sometimes the explanation was longer than a child's span of concentration. Madelyn, my sister, asked him what sounded like a simple question, 'Why is the sky blue?' But as physicists know, the answer could fill a book.
>
> As father explained the propagation of light waves, touched on the scattering of particles, and pointed out the virtues of the undulatory theory as against the corpuscular theory of the motion of light, Madelyn's attention began to wander. Father became so offended when he saw that she was no longer listening; but when she climbed onto his knees and asked to be forgiven, he said, '*It doesn't matter if you don't understand it, as long as you realize the wonder of it*'.
>
> (Emphasis added)

I think that if institutions such as museums and science centers can somehow make youngsters, old and young, appreciate the 'wonder' of science, they will certainly have set the stage for lifelong learning.

References

Bloom, Allan, 1987. *The Closing of the American Mind: How Higher Education has Failed Democracy and Impoverished the Souls of Today's Students*. New York: Simon & Schuster.

Hirsch, Edward, 1987. *Cultural Literacy: What Every American Needs to Know.* New York: Houghton Mifflin.

Livingston, Dorothy Michaelson, 1973. *The Master of Light: A Biography of Albert A. Michaelson.* Chicago: The University of Chicago Press.

Rudolph, Frederick, 1962. *The American College and University: A History.* New York: Random House.

Chapter 5

Science centres and science learning*

L. Rennie and T. McClafferty

In the last 13 years, two excellent reviews [. . .] have drawn attention to the importance of museums and similar institutions in the learning of science. In 1983, when Arthur Lucas focused on scientific literacy and informal learning, museums and science centres formed just one of four sections in his review. More recently, Paulette McManus provided 'an introduction to the field of education in science museums' (1992: p.157). Her review provides a useful historical context to the science museum phenomenon and to the social context of people's behaviour and learning in them. McManus noted, in closing, that science museums 'are still evolving as a communication form and much work needs to be done on the assessment and description of the nature of their communicative activities' (*ibid.*: p.180).

McManus describes the historical development of science museums in three generations, identifying a major change in the 'third generation museums', which are concerned with representing ideas rather than objects. She recognised two strands of museum science communication. The first strand presents thematic exhibitions, with exhibits which portray the big concepts of science, such as evolution and energy. The ecology hall in the Natural History Museum in London is a good example. Around the corner, Launch Pad in the Science Museum is an example of the second strand: a collection of interactive exhibits each representing a specific idea or concept (like the 'Bernoulli Ball', a ball suspended in a current of air), but which as a whole are decontextualised, rather than thematic. Stand-alone science centres, which exemplify the latter strand, are filled with interactive science exhibits, and there are many larger museums, like the Science Museum, which have interactive galleries like Launch Pad. The increasing numbers of both kinds of venue reflect the exponential growth in numbers of interactive science exhibits over the last two decades. In fact, Thomas (1994) reports that the Science Museum has set a target of 25 percent of floor space for interactive exhibits when building extensions are complete.

*Previously published in *Studies in Science Education* 27 (1996), pp. 53–98 (this is an edited version of the original article).

The interactive science centre

This paper is about the purveyor of that second strand of science communication, the interactive science centre. The real growth of science centres has occurred in the last four decades, although the idea of a museum of practical science is attributed to Francis Bacon, nearly four centuries ago (Danilov, 1982; Gregory, 1989). Danilov (1982) traces the development of science centres over the centuries, from their roots in technical museums to their establishment in the 1960s and proliferation in the 1980s. Like McManus, he distinguishes between traditional museums and science centres in terms of their focus: the museum, which emphasises cultural heritage through objects of intrinsic value; and the science and technology centres, which aim to both enlighten and entertain through contemporary, participatory exhibits. Danilov describes the unwillingness of some museum professionals to refer to science centres as museums. Nevertheless, in 1982, he predicted that 'science and technology centres will play a more important role in informal education throughout the world' (1982: p.49).

There is no doubt that interactive science centres are popular. Thomas (1994) estimated that there were 714 visitors per square metre per year to Launch Pad, compared with 44 visitors per square metre per year in the rest of the Science Museum. Science centres are stimulating; they are visually exciting, noisy, active environments. Stevenson (1994) reports that after 60 minutes in Launch Pad, visitors showed little or no reduction in concentration, whereas fatigue typically sets in after 30 minutes during a normal museum visit. But are visitors concentrating because they are learning the science concepts the interactive exhibits portray? Or are they just having fun? And if so, does it matter? After his visit to the Ontario Science Centre two decades ago, Champagne (1975) says his family spent over six hours entertained, but unfulfilled. He gives four reasons why science was 'short-changed' in his visit: the real meaning of science was obscured; some of the demonstrations involved 'sloppy science'; science and technology were presented as ethics-free; and science was dishonestly presented as easy and unproblematic. Similar criticisms of science centres are common today (Fara, 1994; Parkyn, 1993; Ravest, 1993). More than one writer has used the term 'edutainment' to described science centres, politely suggesting that perhaps the entertainment dimension is more successful than the educational one. There is no doubt that enjoyment is a planned part of the science centre experience. Shortland (1987) quotes Beetlestone, honorary Director of Techniquest, as saying that they were serious about education, but first and foremost they were part of the leisure and entertainment industry. Shortland (*ibid.*: p.213) was blunt: 'When education and entertainment are brought together under the same roof, education will be the loser'. Parkyn (1993: p.31) writes of science centres: 'scientific phenomena are presented not within a conceptual framework but as an endless series of unconnected, entertaining magical events'. Soren (1991) describes the scientists and designers of exhibits in the Hall of Technology at the Ontario Science Centre as having 'shied away from instructional objectives, favouring development of hot ideas into visual magnets. Developers overtly intended to excite, engage, move, puzzle, anger and enlighten their visitors . . .' (p.436). The interaction was intended to have visitors make 'conceptual links', but Soren points out that 'playing with the technological device is generally much more compelling than learning about the idea which the device is ostensibly demonstrating' (p.437).

Soren's comments are interesting because Wilson (1986) attributes the development of Launch Pad to the stimulus of the 1981 visit of the Ontario Science Circus to the Science Museum. Wilson states that from that visit three things were learned: the importance of having staff (now generically called explainers) mingling with the visitors; the opinion of the circus staff that educational objectives were counter-productive – one chose exhibits which were fun and educational merit might follow; and successful interactive exhibits were those which gave some sort of reward in the first few seconds. Gillies (1981: p.26) notes in her evaluation of the Science Circus visit that 'the Education Officer . . . explained, the deliniation [sic] of educational objectives was inconsistent with the overall aim of the Science Circus. This aim was the promotion of enjoyment and interest'. Some time later, after working briefly at the Science Museum, Wymer (1991: p.49) was critical of Launch Pad on just this point:

> Didacticism is a dirty word among the interactive science fraternity, the emphasis being on exploration and enjoyment. Thus, in Launch Pad, there is almost no interpretation of the exhibits, and the role of the Explainers, however helpful and enthusiastic, is anything other than the name implies.

Several issues have been raised so far. First, the character of science centres is to exhibit ideas and concepts, rather than objects. As a consequence, the exhibits tend to be self-contained and decontextualised, with reference to their real-world application peripheral to the body of the exhibit. Second, the exhibits are both interactive and participatory in nature. Visitors are meant to handle and explore them, and they are meant to enjoy the experience. Third, although science centres are very popular with the public, there are accusations that the learning of science is a goal jeopardised, even trivialised, by giving primary concern to visitor enjoyment. The continual proliferation of science centres attests to their ability to draw visitors, but the entertainment dimension is perceived by some to overshadow the education dimension.

In this paper, we examine the role of science centres and their interactive exhibits in learning about and understanding science. We begin by defining what we mean by interactive exhibits, and consider their attractiveness to visitors and their potential for learning. We examine the outcomes of the visit experience and problems relating to research in science centres. Following a summary of research on visit outcomes, we suggest directions for research at science centres and their role in the wider community.

In presenting our review, we use the generic term 'science centre' to refer to collections of interactive science exhibits, each of which is designed to represent an idea or concept. We made three other decisions about our approach. First, we do not differentiate between technology and science in our descriptions. Some centres may prefer to consider themselves as technology centres. For example, in its formative stage, Launch Pad consciously opted to be a technology centre by 'concentrating on ideas in action, rather than ideas in the abstract' (Wilson, 1986: p.3). However, it makes little sense to distinguish between science and technology in a review paper such as this, because typically centres contain exhibits which concern both science and technology and the research carried out within them usually fails to consider possible differences. Second, we are cognisant of the heterogeneity of science centres, in both content and audience (Lucas, 1991), and the risks involved in referring to them as a single category. Much of our paper will refer to aspects relating to the interactive science exhibits, rather than the centre itself. Where possible and appropriate, centres are referred to by name. Third, although we draw primarily from literature relating to science centres, some research refers to interactive exhibits in galleries or exhibitions at more traditional museums, and some theoretical papers refer to contexts which are broader than science centres. Discussion of this literature is included where the salient points or the findings are relevant to science centres.

What are interactive science exhibits?

The terms 'interactive' and 'hands-on' are often used interchangeably in talking about exhibits, but they are not the same thing. Hands-on exhibits clearly require some physical involvement of the visitor with the exhibit. This may be in order to experience the touch of animal fur, or it may be that a button is pressed to begin an audio message about the exhibit. In the first example, the exhibit is passive, in the second it is reactive. Interactive exhibits are those which respond to action from the visitor and also invite a further response; there is a dependency between the visitor and the exhibit (Screven, 1974). Interactive exhibits may be hands-on because they rely on physical involvement, or they may require other senses to perceive their message. The important difference is that they offer feedback to the visitor, which provokes further interaction. McLean (1993: p.93) described interactive exhibits as 'those in which visitors can conduct activities, gather evidence, select options, form conclusions, test skills, provide input, and actually alter a situation based on input'. In this way, a good interactive exhibit can personalise the experience for a visitor.

An important reason for distinguishing between hands-on and interactive is that hands-on does not necessarily mean 'minds-on'. As Lucas (1983: p.9) pointed out: 'It is false to assume that any physical manipulation of an exhibit provokes intellectual engagement'. But this does not mean that the hands-on aspect is not important. Many traditional museums are introducing hands-on displays, or have an area set aside where visitors are encouraged to handle objects, and they report heightened interest and understanding from visitors (see, for example, Curtis and Goolnik, 1995; Kirrane and Hayes, 1993; Stevenson and Bryden, 1991). In the context of interactive science centres and learning science, Gregory (1989) equates the term 'hands-on' with the perceptual explorations which are a prerequisite to, but not sufficient for, the process of understanding. Gregory argues that for the perceptual experience to become meaningful, it must be interpreted. He suggests two directions which subsequent understanding might take. 'Hand-waving' is the term he uses for the intuitive, commonsense understandings we develop on the basis of our experiences; they may be wrong and are often misleading. In contrast, he uses the term 'handle-turning' for the formal, mathematical accounts and explanations which are much preferred by scientists. He suggests that:

> the major aim of interactive science centres, after stimulating interest and curiosity, should be setting up hand-waving explanations giving useful intuitive accounts. They are vital for meaningful seeing, and for going on to rigorous handle-turning mathematics which is so important for much – though not all – science and technology.
>
> (Gregory, 1989: p.5)

The importance of interaction with exhibits as a prerequisite for understanding was a fundamental consideration in the development of the Exploratorium, the world's largest and most famous science centre. Its founder, Frank Oppenheimer (1968a: p.175), believed 'It is almost impossible to learn how anything works unless one can repeat each step in its operation at will; furthermore, it is usually necessary to make small changes which impair its operation'. According to Hein (1987), and this is exemplified in his own writing (Oppenheimer, 1968a; 1968b; 1972), it was the pedagogical effectiveness of interaction rather than its public appeal which attracted Oppenheimer to the hands-on approach and exhibit construction which promote active participation. Duensing (1987) notes that many of the Exploratorium exhibits have nothing to do with touch, and she prefers to use the term active participation. The Exploratorium opened in 1969 with the theme of human sensory perception as its overall rationale (Oppenheimer, 1972). There were links with Gregory in the early days (Duensing, 1987; Gregory, 1989; Oppenheimer, 1972) and Hein (1987) describes how the section devoted to human vision was designed using Gregory's perceptual theory as the basis for the theory of vision that the exhibits portray. The Exploratorium opened with one explainer, and the Explainer Program began in the same year (Hein, 1990). Mostly students, explainers are the sole floor staff. They are hired for their ability to interact with people and engage them in conversation about the exhibits, thus enhancing the likelihood of understanding by promoting the visitors' interpretation of the science concepts portrayed in the exhibit.

The attractiveness and learning potential of interactive exhibits

From a theoretical or pedagogical point of view, the attractiveness of interactive exhibits can be explained from a number of positions. Semper (1990: p.5) suggests four positions, which relate to curiosity and intrinsic motivation, multiple modes of learning, play and exploration in the learning process, and self-developed world views and models among people who learn science. Curiosity and intrinsic motivation are frequently mentioned to explain visitors' enjoyment in their participation with all kinds of museum exhibits. Semper refers to Csiksentmihályi's theoretical position on intrinsic motivation and the concept of flow. Recently, Csiksentmihályi and Hermanson (1995) examined intrinsic motivation in the context of museums. They regard visitors' curiosity and interest as the first step towards a rewarding experience in the interaction with an exhibit, but, to become rewarding, the visitor must find that the interaction becomes intrinsically motivating. Csiksentmihályi and Hermanson refer to the 'flow experience', a state of mind which is spontaneous, almost automatic, which maintains engagement in activities that have no extrinsic reward. To produce flow, exhibits must have clear goals and appropriate rules, unambiguous feedback, and provide a challenge to match the skill of the visitor. Because visitors come with a broad range of interests and backgrounds, exhibits which can provide a range of opportunities to engage, at a variety of levels, are more likely to be those which offer the conditions necessary for intrinsic motivation to learn. Csiksentmihályi and Hermanson (1995: p.59) suggest that since 'when we are intrinsically motivated to learn, emotions and feelings are involved, as well as thoughts', then, rather than fleeting attention, the visitor gives the exhibit the deep absorption that leads to learning.

Semper's second educational theme refers to multiple modes of learning. Gardner's idea of multiple intelligences (1983, 1993a) has become a popular reference in the literature relating to museums, particularly science museums, and his seminar in the Capitol Hill Science and Public Policy Seminar Series in 1993 was jointly sponsored by the Association of Science-Technology Centres (Gardner, 1993b). He suggests a pluralistic view of the mind, with seven intelligences rather than the single kind of intelligence traditionally implied by a single IQ score. He describes linguistic and logico-mathematical intelligences, which have been given greatest value in our society; spatial, musical and bodily-kinaesthetic intelligences; and two personal forms of intelligence, interpersonal and intrapersonal. Interactive exhibits in science centres usually require some kind of spatial or kinaesthetic experience and often work better with more than one person. Thus they can appeal to a range of intelligences, promoting the likelihood of engagement by people with different strengths or preferences for learning. Watson (1995) gives examples of exhibits from other kinds of museum which demonstrate appeal to each of Gardner's seven intelligences. If, as Gardner suggests, we all have these intelligences, but they are developed to different levels, the variety of experiences available in science centres provides opportunities for us to interact and learn in multiple modes.

Semper (1990) points out that play and exploration in the learning process are important in the process of learning, but are often overlooked. Piaget's view that learning is based on interaction between the learner and the environment has influenced the development of participatory exhibits (Black, 1989; Thier and Linn, 1975). Bagchi *et al.* (1992) describe the development of the Birla Children's Museum in Calcutta based on Piaget's learning theories. In her exploration of how play and its relationship to learning could be useful in a museum context, Watson (1995) has distilled from a number of theoretical positions, including those of Bruner and Moyles, some of the characteristics of playing. She describes her successful attempts to promote children's involvement by introducing more elements of play in her museum sessions on living history. In science education, play leads to the development of observational skills and experimentation. Hawkins' (1965) classic paper 'Messing about in Science' describes how play (he calls it unguided exploratory work) is the beginning of real learning. Interactive science exhibits invite play and experimentation, and this is a strong component of their success in engaging visitors of all ages. Oppenheimer (1972: p.982) believed that the flexibility of the Exploratorium's exhibits to allow play had a pedagogical advantage: 'Only a limited amount of understanding can come from watching something behave; one must also watch what happens as one varies the parameters that alter the behaviour'.

Semper's last pedagogical theme refers to the background knowledge and understanding about science which visitors bring with them to the science centre. He uses the example of a six-year old child and a person with a PhD in physics, who may both attend the centre in the same family group. How can they obtain satisfaction from the same exhibit? Duensing (1987) emphasises the importance of providing many choices at an exhibit so that visitors can ask their own questions about it and choose their own experiments to perform. Semper (1990, p.6) notes that

> science museums are uniquely able to respond to the highly variable baseline scientific knowledge of the visitors . . . [because] exhibits can be designed to challenge widely held self-developed knowledge by creating cognitive dissonance between an internal theory and an external example.

A programme of research into people's learning from exhibits at the Franklin Institute Science Museum by Borun and her colleagues has taken this approach (Borun *et al.*, 1993).

Semper's four pedagogical positions are not mutually exclusive; each can contribute something towards an explanation of why a particular exhibit is, or is not, successful in attracting visitors and providing a learning experience. Perry (1989) addressed the question of why an exhibit is successful by stating two conditions for success: visitors had to enjoy themselves and they had to learn something. She reviewed the literature in educational psychology, cognitive psychology, motivational theory and instructional design to develop a preliminary model which could be used for the design of intrinsically motivating exhibits. Her six summary criteria are curiosity – the visitor is surprised and intrigued; confidence – the visitor has a sense of personal competence by experiencing success; challenge – the visitor perceives that there is something to work towards; control – the visitor has a sense of self-determination and control; play – the visitor experiences enjoyment and playfulness; and communication – the visitor engages in meaningful social interaction (Perry, 1992). Perry tested and refined her model as she modified an exhibit about colour at the Indianapolis Children's Museum. She included thirteen sub-criteria in the full description of her model (1989, Ch.5) and described how the model could be applied to improving exhibits to promote visitor engagement and the likelihood of their learning. Recently, Peiffer (1995) retested Perry's model during the redesigning of some exhibits at SciTrek in Atlanta. Although the redesigning process had mixed success, her results confirmed the validity of Perry's six criteria. Perry's work can be viewed as a practical encapsulation of a number of the theoretical positions describing how exhibits attract visitors.

What are the outcomes of a successful science centre visit?

It is a short step to change the focus of the discussion from the interactive exhibit to the visitor who uses (or chooses not to use) it. Well-designed exhibits can promote and prolong visitor engagement, but the outcomes of the inter-action have much to do with the characteristics and agenda of the visitor. Perry (1993) extended her model for successful exhibits to a successful museum visit, that is, one in which the visitor's agenda is met (i.e. to have a good time) and also the visitor learns something new, or becomes more aware of, or interested in, something. Perry was able to use her six criteria to describe the psychological needs of visitors as one component of the successful museum visit. She suggests that the successful visit also involves participation of the visitor in intellectual, social and physical interactions, and has outcomes which include cognition, affect and motor skills. The important issue here is that visitor learning is not uni-dimensional. The successful museum experience can include learning in the cognitive sense, but it can also concern affective, or social, or psychomotor skills.

Wellington (1989, p.30) recognised the same issue. 'If hands-on centres are to serve educational functions', he wrote, 'they must lie in one of three domains'. He provided his own 'potted' summary of the cognitive, psychomotor and affective domains. In terms of the cognitive domain, he distinguished between 'knowledge that', 'knowledge how' and 'knowledge why'. He suggests that, in practice, hands-on science centres contribute almost exclusively to 'knowledge that', but they do contribute indirectly to higher-order knowledge and understanding when visit experiences result in understanding when similar phenomena are experienced at a later time. Wellington believes that science centres can contribute to all three areas. In his opinion, the fundamental educational aim is the affective domain, and he points out that by achieving this aim, science centres are more likely to make their indirect contribution to higher-order cognitive learning.

In the general context of museum studies, Falk and Dierking (1992) provide a useful framework that helps to describe and understand the visit experience. Based on their own extensive experience and other research in the field, Falk and Dierking's interactive experience model represents the visit experience as an interaction between three contexts: the physical, social and personal. The physical context is embodied in the exhibits and the physical setting in which they are displayed, and the social context refers to interactions between the visitor and others at the museum. The personal context is important in terms of the visitor's age, sex and personal characteristics and preferences. The model is viewed as dynamic, with the contexts being constructed and reconstructed by visitors from their own perspective.

The interactive experience model appears deceptively simple, but its three contexts are useful reminders that the outcomes from a visit to a science centre are the result of many variables. In terms of the personal context, visitors have their own interests, expectations and reason for visiting. They also bring widely divergent background knowledge and experience, which may include ideas and conceptions that contribute to how they interpret the phenomena they observe and which may interfere with learning (Borun et al., 1993; Feher and Meyer, 1992). This personal context interacts with both the physical and social contexts, playing a major role in selecting what is noticed and what is remembered. Visitors also have choice. They choose what to do, when, and for how long, another factor which contributes to variety in their experience. Aspects relating to the physical context have already been discussed in terms of the nature of interactive exhibits. The fact that they depend on visitor interaction re-emphasises the visitor's role in determining possible outcomes. The social context of the visit is important because the visit provides opportunities for social interaction and cooperative experiences. For example, family visits and visits with friends offer opportunities for group learning in which discussion, experimentation and one visitor 'tutoring' another are frequently observed (Carlisle, 1985; Diamond, 1986; Gottfried, 1980; Tuckey, 1992).

The interactive experience model revisits several of the positions previously discussed and underscores the notion that the visit must be considered as a total experience. Museum researchers agree that it is not just a cognitive, affective or social experience, but all three (McManus, 1993; Roberts, 1993; Uzzell, 1993).

It is, as Bitgood *et al.* (1994) point out, a case of education and recreation happening at the same time. All of these things combine to make each person's visit a unique experience and its outcomes complex.

Research into learning: methodological issues

It is evident that research into learning at science centres is very challenging. Crane (1994: p.9) notes that one reason summative and impact studies are not common in the museum literature is that they are difficult and complicated to design and execute. For example, any attempt to measure learning from a visit must allow for the fact that each visitor has a unique experience. This is the antithesis of the classic pre-test – post-test research design, which assumes that all subjects experience the same treatment. There is also a problem of finding a meaningful placebo treatment for the control group. Twenty years ago Linn (1976) identified the need for research designs which did not depend upon group comparisons, and her group at the Lawrence Hall of Science was already using evidence from many different sources in its evaluation programs.

It is no coincidence that, in science centres, some of the best research into learning has used the exhibit as merely a prop in the learning process rather than as a tool to promote learning (for example, Feher, 1990; Feher and Diamond, 1990). Nevertheless, many effective studies have been done in the wider museum context. In the 1970s and 1980s, these studies were mostly experimental in design and focused on measuring specific outcomes. For example, a series of studies by Falk and his colleagues (Balling and Falk, 1980; Balling *et al.*, undated; Falk and Balling, 1979; Falk *et al.*, 1978) demonstrate clearly the effects that a novel setting can have on students' behaviour and learning on school field trips. Although research such as this provided some valuable findings, it was limited by the need to define, in an *a priori* way, the outcomes of the visit experience, so unanticipated outcomes could be missed.

Falk and Dierking (1992) contend that much research in museums has suffered from 'the misguided notion that learning is primarily the acquisition of new ideas, facts, or information, rather than the consolidation and slow, incremental growth of existing ideas and information' (p.98) When researchers think about learning as the acquisition of knowledge and understanding, they usually design before and after measures of narrowly defined learning outcomes, and employ pre-test–post-test control-group designs. Unfortunately, the tightly controlled studies made possible by this approach increase the artificiality of the research situation, decontextualise the learning experience and decrease the generalisability of the findings. Lucas *et al.* (1986: p.344) note that 'the context of informal learning must be preserved if the results are to have validity' and explore a variety of difficulties inherent in using unobtrusive measures, not the least of which relates to the ethics associated with the techniques of data collection.

Despite the assertion of one researcher that 'If we want people to carry away something, we ought to be able to define what that is and measure it' (Miller, 1987: p.125), it no longer seems to be a realistic option to try to separate the outcomes of museum visits into uni-dimensional fragments that can be measured in well-controlled studies. A broader approach is needed. Koran and Ellis (1991) thoughtfully reviewed four experimental studies (but none with interactive exhibits) and concluded that all would have been enriched by the collection of other 'naturalistic data', an admission that the complexity of the visit outcomes had not been captured. Certainly, more naturalistic studies have been called for (Bonner, 1989; Dierking and Falk, 1994). Lawrence (1993) urges that museum evaluation recognise the changes in research methodology in sociology and psychology, changes from positivistic methods based on behaviourist models of learning to more interpretative methods. There have been major changes over the last decade. Uzzell (1993) describes how, over the last 15 years, summative evaluation research at his institution has moved from a behavioural to a cognitive, then to a socio-cognitive focus, in order to stress the significance of the social context in determining how visitors interact with exhibits. This change in focus recognises that it is not interaction with the exhibit or the display alone which determines learning, but the context in which that interaction occurs. Roberts (1993: p.99) puts it this way: 'The important point is that what we know – regardless of who is doing the knowing – is based less on the nature of the object than on the manner and context in which it is experienced'.

Two anecdotes make the point about context clear. Tulley and Lucas (1991) relate an incident in which a young woman explained to Tulley how she had taken more than 15 minutes to assemble a lock and key exhibit at Launch Pad, and then, a week later, had both the confidence and ability to fix a broken lock on her sister's door. Rennie (1995) describes a woman's interaction with an exhibit which required pulling ropes with one, two or three pulleys to lift a 15 kg weight. She was delighted to find that this gave her the sensory experience she needed to make cognitive sense of a conversation she had heard previously about how 'it was easier to lift things when you used pulleys and the more pulleys you had, the easier it was to lift'. In both cases, visitors were able to place their interaction with an exhibit into the context of outside experience, in the first case demonstrating learning after the visit, the indirect effect to which Wellington (1989) referred, and in the second case, achieving an 'aha!' experience during the visit to the science centre. We suggest that both of these anecdotes provide examples of cognitive, affective and psychomotor learning as a result of the visit experience, but point out that it would be difficult to measure such learning in an objective way.

Review of research into learning in science centres

Nearly 20 years ago, Kimche (1978) described the learning potential of science centres, citing the interaction between 'the predisposition on the part of visitors to be receptive to the museum's message, and the capability of the museum to transmit the message in a multisensory and yet authentic manner' (p.273). However, she also noted that research had concentrated on demographics and exhibit popularity rather than on what visitors had learned from their experiences. She urged that new models for measurement be devised to assess whether visitors' experiences are educational. Kimche may well be disappointed with the advances made on these fronts, but there has been some progress.

A range of methods investigating learning in museums and science centres has had varied but sufficient success to conclude that some cognitive learning occurs some of the time. There is overwhelming agreement among researchers that people enjoy the visit experience but, perhaps surprisingly, comparatively few attempts have been made to measure specific affective outcomes. For example, in a review of research over 50 years into the effect of field trips and visits, Koran et al. (1989) list 27 studies, less than a third of which included measurement of any kind of attitudes. In the following section, we examine a range of methods and issues relating to learning outcomes from visits to science centres.

Approaches to measuring learning

Measuring learning in science centres is difficult (Lucas, 1983; Lucas et al., 1986). Ideally, data collection during a visit to a science centre is unobtrusive, so that the researcher does not affect the behaviour of the visitor. But un-obtrusive data collection can pose problems of ethics (such as using hidden microphones or video cameras) and interpretation (such as trying to interpret what people are saying without seeing what they are doing, or vice versa). With visitors' permission, videotapes have been used successfully (for example, Martin et al., 1991), but they are an expensive means of data collection and time-consuming to transcribe. Observation is also time-consuming and labour-intensive. Further, although these data reveal what visitors do, it is important to note that trying to assess what learning has occurred requires a considerable degree of inference. Some research has used observation only. For example, Carlisle (1985) observed the behaviour of fifth-grade children in science centres. Russell (1989) describes a comprehensive tracking procedure used at Technology Testbed in Liverpool and Techniquest in Cardiff. Visitors are observed and their activities noted using a checklist. The purpose of observational tracking was to document visitor interaction, not their learning, but Russell's team also interviewed visitors informally about their interaction with exhibits to find out what sense they made of them. More detailed still were Diamond's ethological studies at the Lawrence Hall of Science and the Exploratorium (Diamond, 1980; 1986). With permission, Diamond followed family groups, recording a running narrative of all activity, interaction and speech of the subjects. Diamond may have been the first to document the highly social nature of the visit experience and its importance in stimulating learning. Other methods, or a combination of methods, have been tried.

Written measures

Researchers have successfully measured cognitive outcomes using formal written tests (Dymond *et al.*, 1990; Flexer and Borun, 1984; Javlekar, 1989; Schibeci, 1992) and prepared questions answered in interview (Blud, 1990a; Eason and Linn, 1976). These measures must refer specifically to what the visitor did, so they can only be effective when the visit is highly structured, or when they relate to particular exhibits. For example, at Scitech Discovery Centre in Australia, Dymond *et al.* (1990) employed a pre-test–post-test control group design using intact school groups, but they needed to ensure that all students had a similar visit experience by completing a particular pathway of exhibits. Their instruments also included an observational schedule to record students' behaviour, and questionnaires relating to exhibit popularity, students' attitudes and learning. They found enhanced attitudes and evidence of learning, but no differences between exhibits. In his study, also at Scitech, Schibeci (1992) investigated the success of a series of interactive exhibits about the science of sport. Both school groups and adults were included, but only schoolchildren showed a measurable increase in knowledge as measured by the pre-test–post-test design. One problem of using non-intact groups was highlighted by Schibeci. He found it difficult to obtain both pre-test and post-test responses from the adults.

Open-ended questions

Some researchers have asked children to report something they learned or found out from their visit using an open-ended question as part of an interview (Martin *et al.*, 1991; Tuckey, 1992) or a written questionnaire (Gottfried, 1980). Martin *et al.* (1991) found that 86 percent of the young people (aged between seven and eighteen) whom they interviewed immediately after a visit to an activity room at the Liverpool Museum could make some comment about what they found out. A week after their visit to Satrosphere (an interactive science centre in Scotland), Tuckey (1992) asked eight- to twelve-year-old children to think of one thing they had found out from their visit. About half of the students could not think of anything, about a quarter made attitudinal statements, and about a quarter mentioned specific science learning. Gottfried (1980) asked children via a questionnaire what they did during their visit to Biolab at the Lawrence Hall of Science and what they had discovered. Children's responses were given validity by Gottfried's observations of them during the visit. The 400 questionnaires resulted in a total of 600 'discoveries' by the children, and Gottfried grouped them into five categories relating to animal behaviour, animal anatomy, how to . . . (e.g. pick up a snake), about myself, and miscellaneous. Such self-report measures accommodate the unstructured nature of the visit, and they provide information about a range of cognitive, affective and other aspects of the visit, but they can give only limited information about the depth of learning. More information can be obtained by using interviews to probe understanding. Russell (1989) and Medved and Oatley (1995) report the use of interviews of this kind. Russell's purpose was related to exhibit evaluation at three science centres (Technology Testbed, Techniquest and Jodrell Bank) and the research team gained considerable information for exhibit improvement as well as visitor misunderstandings. Medved and Oatley (1995) used interviews about exhibits at the Ontario Science Centre that visitors said they liked best, with a follow-up interview by telephone one month later. They found that most visitors retained memories of the exhibits, and three-quarters of their 39 subjects had some increased awareness of scientific phenomena.

Stimulated recall

Visitors' recollections and reactions to visits to centres with interactive exhibits have been elicited using stimulated recall with videotapes (Stevenson and Bryden, 1991) or photographs (Stevenson, 1991) of the exhibits. Stevenson and Bryden, whose purpose was to obtain visitors' reactions to a discovery room in a Scottish museum, found that a mixture of structured and open-ended questions was more effective in getting a variety of information than open-ended questions alone. Stevenson (1991) used photographs in follow-up group interviews of families six months after their visit to Launch Pad. Not only were the photographs helpful in stimulating memories of the visit, but the group format for the interview allowed family members to be stimulated by each other's comments. Stevenson categorised elements of visitors' memories according to whether they were descriptions, feelings or thoughts about the exhibits. It was clear that the visit had had a long-term impact on the interviewees.

Investigating thinking

Studies of children's thinking need to find ways of examining students' thought processes. Boram and Marek (1991) used pre-tests to determine children's Piagetian cognitive level and after exploration of some exhibits, employed follow-up interviews asking children to explain how the exhibits worked. Their results demonstrated that learning was least at exhibits that required thinking above the child's cognitive level. Feher and Rice (1985) investigated the development of scientific concepts through the use of interactive exhibits at the Ruben Fleet Science Center in San Diego. They used a Piagetian task-based clinical interview technique that probed children's understanding while they interacted with exhibits and mock-ups. Feher and Rice's purpose was to uncover the conceptual frameworks with which the naive learner approaches natural phenomena, in this case persistence of vision. The research exploited the exhibits as part of a laboratory for studying learning, but their findings also have valuable implications for improving the effectiveness of exhibit design.

A series of studies into the 'naive notions' that visitors have about the concept of gravity were undertaken by Borun and her colleagues at the Franklin Institute Science Museum (Borun *et al.*, 1993). Over a period, interview techniques were honed to test for the presence of particular concepts, and standardised follow-up probes were developed. Interviews were videotaped and transcribed. Borun *et al.* used the findings to modify exhibit prototypes in ways that would challenge misconceptions and promote understanding. The work of Feher and Borun and their colleagues represents some of the most valuable research in this area because it contributes to both understanding about learning and understanding about how interactive exhibits communicate their messages.

A phenomenographic approach to investigating learning of sound concepts at a Brisbane science centre was undertaken by Beiers and McRobbie (1992). Prior to the visit, students took part in a structured interview and a concept map exercise, a sequence which was repeated after the visit. The results indicated the importance of prior learning; students who already had a concept of sound as a vibration or wave were most likely to have made major changes in their understanding about amplitude and wavelength. Beiers and McRobbie also found that some exhibits were more likely than others to promote learning.

Comparison studies

Pre-test–post-test designs have been used to compare the outcomes of visiting a science centre with some other learning experience. For example, learning in science centres compared with learning in school classrooms was investigated by Javlekar (1989) at the Nehru Science Centre. A questionnaire based on the cognitive content of the exhibits was used in a pre-test–post-test design, and it indicated superior learning by the students who visited the science centre, particularly on questions testing understanding. Lam-Kan (1985) used general tests to compare the science achievement and interest of girls who visited the Singapore Science Centre and those who went on other educational trips. The groups who went to the science centre achieved gains on these general instruments. Finson and Enochs (1987) used some scales from the Attitude to Science Inventory in an attempt to measure attitude change in students who visited the Kansas Cosmosphere and Discovery Center. Students who visited had higher post-test scores than those who did not, and of the visitors, those who received related instruction had higher scores.

The findings for cognitive and affective change are not always consistent. For example, on the basis of cognitive and affective tests, Flexer and Borun (1984) concluded that a well-structured class lesson was more effective in promoting learning than a visit to a cluster of interactive exhibits at the Franklin Institute Science Museum, but the visit was perceived by students to be more enjoyable and interesting. The students in Flexer and Borun's study considered themselves to be learning during their visit and some thought they learned more than in the classroom lesson.

An issue of concern relates to how the tests employed to measure learning are constructed. Javlekar (1989), Dymond *et al.* (1990), Flexer and Borun (1984) and Schibeci (1992) all constructed cognitive scales that related specifically to the exhibits which were visited. It seems more likely that targeted tests such as these are more likely to detect learning than a general or standardised achievement test.

The importance of context

Donald (1991) pointed out that, because learning with interactive exhibits takes place in a particular context, knowledge gain may be 'stored' in the context in which it was learned and not released unless it can be demonstrated in a similar context. Three examples of research into learning at the Lawrence Hall of Science have taken this into account. Eason and Linn (1976) used a multiple-choice questionnaire and a five-minute interview during which children manipulated mirrors as a way of demonstrating their learning on particular exhibits. Sneider *et al.* (1979) used a picture format for a multiple-choice test about an astronomy exhibit (some of the instructions were pictorial; see Friedman *et al.*, 1979) and asked students to focus a telescope to determine whether they had learned to do this. These two studies are among the very few that have examined psychomotor skills. Gottfried (1980) brought animals from the Biolab to school for children to teach their peers about what they had learned during a recent visit. These methods demonstrated that learning had occurred.

A study by McClafferty (1995) focused on visitor learning relating to a specific exhibit, the Whispering Dishes, which demonstrates the principles of sound reflection and focusing. In a study at Scitech Discovery Centre, he questioned visitors about their understanding of the exhibit, and, if they used it successfully, he asked them how they knew how to make it work. Very few visitors did understand the Whispering Dishes fully, but those that did often linked that understanding with previous knowledge. In a follow-up study at Questacon – the National Science and Technology Centre in Australia, McClafferty tested whether visitors understood the relevant sound principles before they used the exhibit. He found that some visitors did learn from the exhibit, but also that some visitors who previously knew about reflection and focusing in a different context were unable to transfer that knowledge to explain how the Whispering Dishes operated. McClafferty's study demonstrates that visitors do not always link relevant prior knowledge to exhibits they use. Further, even when visitors learn from an exhibit, we cannot be certain that they will be able to link that knowledge to situations beyond their visit. If they do not, can we say that learning has occurred? If we take the Falk and Dierking (1992) position that learning is a slow, cumulative process, then, provided knowledge can be retrieved and linked with other knowledge later, learning has occurred. Unfortunately, the museum researcher may never know whether this linking occurs, which contributes to both the intrigue and frustration of visitor studies.

School visits

School groups form a major part of the weekday audience during school term, and science centre staff are cognisant of their needs. Science centres usually plan the physical resources needed to cater for visiting school groups, such as reception areas and withdrawal rooms, and offer special programmes and resources associated with particular exhibitions. Staff of Her Majesty's Inspectorate indirectly reviewed the use of science centres during surveys of schools' use of museum resources (Moffat, 1993) and have encouraged schools to complement their teaching programmes with visits to science centres. Science centre staff have assisted teachers with this task by linking particular exhibits to sections of the National Curriculum. For example, Tomlin (1990) describes how a popular interactive exhibit, the bicycle generator, displayed at Launch Pad, Science Factory and other science centres, relates to the attainment targets in the English National Curriculum. As a service to teachers, the interactive exhibits at Scitech Discovery Centre in Perth, Australia, routinely have their objectives linked to the science and technology outcome statements of the Australian National Curriculum. Most science centres also provide guidance for teachers organising their visit, and often resource materials as well.
[. . .]

The role of explainers

The important role of explainers in science centres is well-recognised, but very little research has focused on their contribution to visitor learning. In a pedagogical sense, their importance can be explained in terms of their ability to help visitors to focus on the appropriate use of exhibits and to answer questions about their operation. Because students and other visitors have different combinations of background experiences, interests and skills, they will interact differently with exhibits, and explainers can provide cues by asking questions to help visitors to attend to the salient aspects of the exhibits (Bennett and Thompson, 1990; Wanless, 1990). There is also evidence that the presence of explainers increases time spent at an exhibit (Martin *et al.*, 1991). Most importantly, the skilled explainer can assist visitors to structure their own learning experience, opening up their thinking rather than simply directing them to the right answer (Price and Hein, 1991). Busque (1991) found that the mostly adult visitors to the Museum of Science (Ottawa) and science centres in Sudbury and Toronto were more interested in exhibits which had a high potential for interaction but a weak potential for investigation. Busque suggested that explainers could play a role in assisting visitors to interact with exhibits which required investigation to find answers to problems posed.

The experience of being an explainer can be a learning experience as well. Diamond *et al.* (1987) mailed a survey to over 400 people who had been student explainers at the Exploratorium, and interviewed 32 of them at length, including one from each year from 1969 to 1985. The results indicate that even a brief period working as an explainer had influenced the teenagers' interest in learning, and learning science in particular. A different kind of study was carried out by Johnston and Rennie (1995). Explainers are a source of data rarely used in research about outcomes from visits to science centres. Johnston and Rennie used two focus groups of explainers, first to identify and then to validate what were called 'general perceptions' of visitors, including their purposes and outcomes related to a visit to a science centre. Subsequently, two focus groups of visitors themselves were interviewed and found to support the six general perceptions identified by the explainers. The perceptions are first, members of the visiting public have fun at the centre; second, learning is not the main purpose of their visit; third, the role of an explainer is to facilitate understanding of the exhibits, not to teach; fourth, learning occurs when visitors relate experiences at the centre to experiences in the outside world; fifth, the use of analogies to explain exhibits facilitates understanding; and sixth, incidental learning, unrelated to the intention of an exhibit, often occurs. Notice that learning is central to five of the six statements, even though both explainers and visitors themselves perceive that people come to science centres to have fun, not to learn. This points to the importance of both cognitive and affective aspects of learning from visits to science centres.

Family behaviour and learning

In her review, McManus (1992) paid particular attention to family behaviour in museums. As groups with children comprise around 60 percent of all visitors to museum settings (Dierking and Falk, 1994; McManus, 1992), behaviour within family groups is likely to be an important factor in determining the outcome of science centre visits. In fact, audience surveys by Korn (1995) suggest that family groups are more likely to visit science centres than natural history museums. Based on a considerable body of her own research in the United Kingdom, and classic studies by Diamond (1980; 1986) and by Hilke and Balling (1985) in the United States, McManus (1992; 1994) constructed a model of family museum visiting behaviour. She likened the family to a 'coordinated hunter–gatherer team actively foraging in the museum to satisfy their curiosity about topics and objects which interest them' (1992: p.176). Their behaviour is described as 'forage, broadcast and comment' activity, with the more harmonious family unit more likely to be successful in engaging with the messages offered by the museum. McManus summarised the kinds of teaching–learning behaviours typically engaged in by families, with parents acting as interpreters for their children, being the ones more likely to read labels, for example.

In our experience, this model is as apt for science centres as it is for traditional museums, but there is evidence that different kinds of exhibit are likely to promote different kinds of family interaction. For example, McManus (1989) analysed the social discourse at different exhibits at the British Museum (Natural History) and demonstrated that the style of exhibit presentation deeply affects the kinds of thinking engaged in by visitors. Research by Blud (1990a; 1990b) provides further insights here. She investigated family behaviour by comparing interactions between parents and children at three different exhibits, but all relating to gears, at Launch Pad and other galleries in the Science Museum. She found that more exhibit-related interaction occurred at an interactive exhibit than at a push-button and a static exhibit, and that learning seemed to be greater (although not significantly so) at the interactive exhibit compared with the others. She concluded that the interactive exhibit was more likely to promote constructive discussion and debate and hence increase the educational effectiveness of an exhibit.

Although the potential for family learning-related behaviour may be greater at interactive exhibits, that potential is not always fulfilled. It has already been noted that science centres are active, noisy places and it is not uncommon to witness children roaming freely while their adult companions relax on the few available seats. Parents engage in different ways, and a thoughtful study in an unnamed hands-on gallery by Brown (1995) identified eight kinds of parental involvement with their children. Parents performed roles ranging from 'caretakers', who kept children under surveillance but gave them free rein, to 'demonstrators', who carried out the activity while the children watched. The nature of the activity had an effect on the parents' role, as some exhibits required more than one person to operate them. The majority of parents acted as passive helpers or supporters of the children. Brown's study was small (40 parents), the ages of the children are not reported, and no measure of learning was used. However, she felt able to conclude that the type and extent of parental involvement may be a major influence on what children gain from their visit to the centre, and that parent involvement is not sufficiently harnessed through exhibit design.

Recently, Dierking and Falk (1994) reviewed family learning and behaviour in informal settings, and their conclusions were consistent with those of McManus. Although many of the studies that Dierking and Falk quoted were not carried out in science centres, most of the findings seem to be generalisable. For example, children are more likely to interact with hands-on exhibits than adults, and the family agenda is likely to influence learning. The different kinds of exhibit interaction available at a science centre compared with a museum, and the higher incidence of explainers, are additional factors to be considered. Greenfield's (1995) study at an interactive gallery at the Bishop Museum in Honolulu found that most adults watched as their children interacted with the exhibits, and that most adult–child interactions were between explainers and children. She also noted that unaccompanied children, especially older children, demonstrated less learning-related behaviour at exhibits. Given the active and stimulating environment of the science centre, it is not surprising that some families may 'hunt and gather' less closely together than McManus found that they do in the less interactive galleries of the museum. Nevertheless, there remains a high potential for learning among the members of a family who interact together.

Gender effects

In terms of gender effects, McManus (1992) reported in her review that whole-visit studies of family behaviours in museums produced inconclusive evidence with respect to mothers' and fathers' interactions with their sons and daughters. Diamond (1994) reviewed sex differences in science museums and described some sex-related differences in family behaviour, based on her own studies at the Exploratorium and the Lawrence Hall of Science, which suggest that mothers are more likely to manipulate exhibits with their children, and daughters' interactions were more complex when with another person than when by themselves. Diamond also pointed out the inconsistency of findings across institutions. Dierking and Falk (1994) concluded as part of their review of family behaviour that, in most situations, mothers are least likely to choose what exhibits to view, but other gender-based interactions are more complex than originally thought and deserve further investigation.

Even within science centres, a factor which seems to contribute to the inconsistent findings is the different nature of the exhibits. McManus (1992) drew attention to the study by Blud (1990b), which found that more inter-action occurred at the interactive exhibit than at the others, and that, here, girls were favoured by parents and both boys and girls paid more attention to fathers. In her research, Brown (1995) found that men were more active participants than women in their children's interactions. Women were more passive observers but more likely to take an active role with girls. Brown found that her results varied between exhibits, consistent with McManus's (1992) sugges-tion that gender-specific behaviours may be determined more by the nature of the exhibits than by family composition. McManus recognised the potentially confounding effects of family composition, and concluded that definitive results could be obtained only by investigating the behaviour of groups comprising mother, father and children of both sexes. We have found no reports of such studies carried out in science centres.

Apart from family research, studies of gender behaviour in interactive centres are few. Most studies simply ignore gender, although sometimes it is declared implicitly as a control variable by matching groups on sex or by choosing equal numbers of males and females. Some studies analyse their results by gender, although it is not central to their research purpose. For example, Erätuuli and Sneider (1990) found that the only significant gender difference on a series of observations of visitors to the Wizard's Lab at the Lawrence Hall of Science was that girls were more likely to take notice of instructions. Busque (1991) found sex differences in interest for some exhibits. Boisvert and Slez (1994) found that gender was unrelated to engagement, holding power and attracting power in a human body discovery space in the Boston Museum of Science. In further analysis of their data (Boisvert and Slez, 1995), which focused on different types of exhibit, they chose not to report on gender. This is unfortunate because, like McManus, we believe that gender differences are more likely to be found in interactions with specific exhibits, and that possible gender-related behaviours found on individual exhibits are masked when results are averaged over all exhibits.

Carlisle (1985) noted that boys and girls spend different amounts of time at different exhibits, and this has been examined more closely by Kremer and Mullins (1992) and Greenfield (1995). Both studies revealed that children tended to behave in gender-stereotyped ways, especially when they were un-accompanied (Greenfield, 1995). Kremer and Mullins observed children's behaviour on five exhibits at the Centre of Science and Industry, Columbus, Ohio, and found that the attractiveness of the exhibits to boys and girls was related to gender-stereotyped play. For example, 1.7 times as many boys as girls were attracted to the Water Jets exhibit, and twice as many girls were attracted to the face painting exhibit. Boys were more likely to behave in an aggressive or destructive way by using exhibits as weapons, or by kicking blocks, whereas girls spent more time painting their faces and exhibiting nurturing behaviour with baby chicks. Kremer and Mullins report that the behaviour of fathers and mothers tended to support their children's sex-stereotyped activities. For example, mothers more than fathers appeared to teach nurturing skills towards the chicks, and predominantly with girls. Greenfield (1995) observed children and adults at a large number of interactive exhibits in a display at the Bishop Museum in Honolulu. She found that children, but not adults, showed sex differences in their choice of exhibits. Boys and girls tried all exhibits, but boys spent more time on physical science and computer exhibits than girls, who spent more time working on puzzles. Boys tended to stay longer at competitive activities, such as computer games and tests of strength, giving girls less opportunities to use them.

In a detailed study of one exhibit at Launch Pad, where visitors could assemble a model lock and key without instructions, Tulley and Lucas (1991) found that females took almost twice as long to assemble the exhibit as did the males, but there was little difference in the time required for reassembly. Video recordings showed that females spent 58 percent of their assembly time reflecting on the exhibit, compared with 29 percent for males. Learning was clearly evident, as reassembly took just over one-fifth of the time of the initial effort. There were no gender differences in visitors' explanations of how the exhibit worked.

A study by Kubota and Olstad (1991) examined the effect of using a slide show as a novelty-reducing treatment prior to a visit to the Science Playground at the Pacific Science Centre. For boys, time spent in on-task exploratory behaviour was significantly greater for the treatment group, and cognitive learning measured by a post-test was higher for this group. Girls' exploratory behaviour and learning were similar in both the treatment and the control groups. This finding was interpreted by Kubota and Olstad and by Diamond (1994) as demonstrating that novelty-reducing treatment does not work for girls. However, the results demonstrate that girls' exploratory behaviour and learning were higher than for boys in the control group, and this may indicate that girls orient themselves more quickly than boys. More research is needed on this point.

Taken together, the findings about gender suggest that overall, science centres are equally attractive to boys and girls, but that many children are attracted to exhibits that allow them to play and interact in ways that are stereotyped with respect to gender. Given the well-publicised concern that girls and women are less represented in physical science and mathematics at the upper secondary school levels and in science-related careers, and that this can be related to the gendered nature of science in society (Parker et al., 1996), science centres have a role to play in the communication of science to all young people as well as adults. Most science centres have both male and female explainers and generally offer activities attractive to both sexes. Diamond (1994) and Kremer and Mullins (1992) both recommend that museums be proactive in ensuring that they maintain a gender-inclusive learning environment.

Beyond the gallery doors

[In 1993,] the Association of Science–Technology Centers (ASTC) announced that science museums be urged to rethink their role. In a report commissioned by the ASTC, St John and Perry (1993a) encouraged science centres to

> see themselves as institutional resources that, like schools and libraries, are part of the nation's infrastructure. In providing exhibits and programs, they provide resources that in a broad, cumulative, and long-term fashion, help people not only to 'learn' science, but also, more broadly, to develop a long-term (cognitive and affective) relationship with the content, phenomena, and issues of science.
>
> (St John and Perry, 1993a: p.6)

St John and Perry (1993b) expand this position with respect to evaluation and research. Regarding science centres as infrastructure renders the question 'Do people learn science from a visit to a science centre?' impossibly narrow. The question must be rephrased in terms of 'Do science centres help people to develop a more positive relationship with science?' This sensible broadening of focus draws attention to the diversity of means by which many science centres provide the public with opportunities to 'form relationships' with science. These are the educational programmes which extend beyond the gallery doors.

In addition to the exhibition programmes residing in their halls and galleries, science centres engage in a range of activities to achieve their mission statement, which, for many centres, is to increase the public's understanding and appreciation of science, mathematics and technology. These other public activities use a variety of media to inform, even proselytise, under the umbrella of their mission statement, aimed at increasing public access and participation. These kinds of programme are not new; an extensive listing of US public programmes was published [. . .] by the ASTC (Bannerman and Kendall, 1981), and other examples are given by the Committee on the Public Understanding of Science (Quin, 1989). [. . .]

Concluding comments

At the outset of this paper, we established that, although science centres are popular and their educational potential is recognised, there is criticism that education is sacrificed for entertainment, that getting people in through the door to have an enjoyable experience is given priority over ensuring that they go away educationally enlightened. In his discussion of this issue, Friedman (1996) emphasises that science–technology centres must differentiate themselves from other commercial theme parks and the like. He regards this differentiation as essential for the survival of science centres. In our discussion, we tried to demonstrate the complexity of the visit experience, and the juxtapositioning of the physical and social environments constructed and interpreted by visitors through their own personal context (Falk and Dierking, 1992). We examined approaches to research in science centres and reviewed the findings. There emerged a picture consistent at only the most general level, which suggests that some cognitive, affective and psychomotor learning occurs most of the time, but there is considerable variation across science centres and also across exhibits within centres. In our opening paragraph, we quoted McManus's conclusion to her review (McManus, 1992: p.180) that much work needs to be done on the assessment and description of the nature of the communicative activities of science museums and science centres. Our findings indicate that there is still far to go.

Much of the research concerning science centres that reaches the science education and museum literature has been completed by science educators rather than museum researchers. To fulfil their mission more effectively, science centres must become more involved in their own research. In the past, such research has been limited, but as science centres seek new audiences and to maintain their present ones, research is one important aspect they need to consider. The nature of the exhibits presented, the questions they provoke in the visitor and the ambience of the centre all present an image of science to the public. Critics (even from within) say 'Science centres must be more than toys and fun, and ingenuity, and unexpected experiences. . . . Is it too radical to suggest that science centres should say something about science?' (Ravest, 1993: p.11). Research is needed to describe what kinds of images of science are presented by science centres to their visitors and the public, and how those images are communicated.

The success of exhibits, in terms of the kinds of engagement they provoke, is a critical aspect of the effectiveness of a science centre in promoting learning about science. We know what makes a good exhibit (Alt and Shaw, 1984) and how to make a good hands-on exhibit (Kennedy, 1990), yet the quality of exhibits is not uniformly good. What can be wrong? Many interactive science exhibits were pioneered by the Exploratorium. Hein (1987) described the philosophy underlying the development of exhibits in the Vision Section there.

> The Exploratorium was meant to make the processes and practices of science widely accessible. Exhibits were to be constructed that would permit visitors to draw inferences from their own observation, to experience alternative hypothetical models, and to arrive at an understanding of the underlying theory.
>
> (p.30)

Hein recounts how the scientific principles were chosen first, exhibit design followed, and the exhibit evolved through use and trial and error. There are many exhibits within the same theme, often several for the same concept and a planned 'redundancy', which promotes learning by giving different perspectives in different contexts. This care in design and the advantage of redundancy is sometimes not recognised by people from other prospective science centres. Duensing (1993: p.78) describes how 'Hands-on becomes a goal in itself, rather than a means of communicating or teaching about a particular idea'. Much of the criticism directed towards science centres concerns exhibits seen to be hands-on at the expense of 'minds-on'. Of course, visitors are free agents: they can choose how involved they want their minds to be, but poorly designed (and in some cases, poorly copied) exhibits are unlikely to promote the kind of thoughtful interaction and reflection which can result in meaning-making.

Exhibit evaluation is well-developed (see, for example, Screven, 1990) and can not only improve the quality of the exhibits but also give valuable information about what visitors do and think while using them (see, for example, Diamond, 1991). Seagram *et al.* (1993) advocate a transaction approach to audience research and exhibit development, a balance between the traditional, mandate-driven approach in which exhibits are developed according to the values of the curators, down-playing the need for evaluation according to the audience's preference, and the market-driven approach, which assumes that audience needs are paramount. While the traditional approach can result in alienating exhibits, the market-driven approach can result in enjoyable, but not educational, exhibits. A systematic approach to evaluation is essential to find the balance. This will not be easy. Hilke (1993) describes how, even when the need for research and evaluation is recognised, competing pressures interfere with the implementation of an effective research programme, and Linn (1983) discusses the challenges that evaluators face when serving different audiences. Nevertheless, for accountability purposes alone, there remains a compelling argument for the integration of systematic programmes of evaluation into the operations of science centres.

Research must become more cohesive and informative. The tools are available. Crane *et al.* (1994) produced a summary and annotated bibliography on informal science learning, including a section on research challenges. A new book from the Science Museum, *Museum Visitor Studies in the '90s* (Bicknell and Farmelo, 1993), canvasses a wide range of issues relating to research. A broadening of the research base has been slow in coming. The outcomes of research will be more meaningful and useful with a wider range of research designs that recognise and take account of the complexity of the variables under study.

A more complete picture of science centre outcomes can be built up by employing cross-site studies and studies of travelling exhibitions at different locations. These will also provide information about how well different audiences are served by science centres. In a call to promote gender equity in museum programmes, Curran (1992) referred to the American Association of Museums report *Excellence and Equity: Education and the Public Dimension of Museums*, which was more explicitly concerned with racial and cultural equity. Research in science centres which focuses on equitable environments with respect to diversity in the race and culture of its visitors is hard to find. Dierking and Falk (1994) refer to a study in which the 'modest' labelling of an exhibit in both English and Spanish dramatically increased exhibit holding time, correct use and conceptual understanding. Vytrhlik (1994) described how one science museum has approached the task of bringing people from a variety of ethnic backgrounds into the museum. More studies relating to the inclusiveness of the science centre environment are needed.

Finally, science centres provide laboratories for research in science education. Feher (1990) argues that 'interactive exhibits are powerful learning tools of a dual kind: for the user they constitute an independent, teacher-free learning device; for the researcher they are the means for rendering explicit the user's conceptions and studying the learning process' (p.46). This kind of research has value for science educators well beyond the development of excellent exhibits. For example, Ault and Herrick (1991) describe how interactive exhibits were used in a pre-service teacher education programme to assist prospective teachers to learn about visitor misconceptions and how exhibits can contribute to or challenge them.

Some years ago, Danilov (1982) described science centres and their potential in a way which is still befitting.

> Science and technology centres are far from being perfect creations. They cannot possibly cover everything; they may look favourably upon science and industry; they may not present exhibits and programs that please everyone at all times; they may occasionally overlook or misinterpret a subject; and they undoubtedly have other real or imagined faults. However, there is nothing as effective as a contemporary science centre in stimulating

interest, communicating information, and entertaining the public in the fields of science, technology, industry and health. They have achieved this position by focussing on the present and future rather than the past; by emphasising enjoyable participatory techniques; and by being imaginative, flexible, and persistent in the furtherance of public science education. They will continue to evolve, improve, and develop new approaches as they respond to society's changing needs.

(p.12)

Gardner (1993a) regards present-day schooling as having little significance for the majority of young people. He says

schools have become increasingly anachronistic, while museums have retained the potential to engage students, to teach them, to stimulate their understanding, and, most important, to help them assume responsibility for their own future learning.

(p.199)

Our conclusion is that with regard to science centres, that potential remains. Science educators should be among those who help to see that it is fulfilled.

References

Alt, M.B. and Shaw, K.M. (1984). 'Characteristics of ideal museum exhibits'. *British Journal of Psychology*, 75, 25–36.

Ault, C.R. and Herrick, J. (1991). 'Integrating teacher education about science learning with evaluation studies of science museum exhibits'. *Journal of Science Teacher Education*, 2, (4), 101–5.

Bagchi, S.K., Yahya, I. and Cole, P.R. (1992). 'The Piagetian children's science gallery'. *Curator*, 35, (2), 95–104.

Balling, J.D., Falk, J.H. and Aronson, R. (undated). *Pre-trip programs: An exploration of their effects on learning from a single-visit field trip to a zoological park.* Unpublished manuscript, Smithsonian Institution, Office of Educational Research, Washington, DC.

Balling, J.D. and Falk, J.H. (1980). 'A perspective on field trips: Environmental effects on learning'. *Curator*, 23, (4), 229–40.

Bannerman, C. and Kendall, A. (eds) (1981). *Museums, magic and children: Youth education in museums.* Washington, Association of Science-Technology Centers.

Beiers, R.J. and McRobbie, C.J. (1992). 'Learning in interactive science centres'. *Research in Science Education*, 22, 38–44.

Bennett, E.M. and Thompson, E. (1990, April). 'The exhibit interpreter: An attention focuser in science museums'. Paper presented at the National Association for Research in Science Teaching Conference, Atlanta, USA (ERIC Document Reproduction Service No. ED 319 616).

Bicknell, S. and Farmelo, G. (eds) (1993). *Museum visitor studies in the '90s.* London: Science Museum.

Bitgood, S., Serrell, B. and Thompson, D. (1994). 'The impact of informal education on visitors to museums'. In V. Crane, H. Nicholson, M. Chen and S. Bitgood (eds), *Informal science learning: what research says about television, science museums, and community based projects* (pp.61–106). Dedham, Mass., Research Communication Ltd.

Black, L. (1989). 'What research says about learning in science museums: Applying a learning theory in the development of a museum learning environment'. *ASTC Newsletters*, November/December, 7–8.

Blud, L. (1990a). 'Social interaction and learning among family groups visiting a museum'. *Museum Management and Curatorship*, 9, 43–51.

Blud, L.M. (1990b). 'Sons and daughters: Observation on the way families interact during a museum visit'. *Museum Management and Curatorship*, 9, 257–64.

Boisvert, D.L. and Slez, B.J. (1994). 'The relationship between visitor characteristics and learning-associated behaviours in a science museum discovery space'. *Science Education*, 78, (2), 137–48.

Boisvert, D.L. and Slez, B.J. (1995). 'The relationship between exhibit characteristics and learning-associated behaviours in a science museum discovery space'. *Science Education*, 79, (5), 503–18.

Bonner, J. (1989). 'Formal versus naturalistic evaluation in the museum context'. *Visitor Studies: Theory, Research and Practice*, 2, 211–24.

Boram, R. and Marek, E.A. (1991, April). 'The effects of free exploration from hands-on science center exhibits'. Paper presented at the annual meeting of the National Association for Research in Science Teaching, Lake Geneva, Wisconsin, USA (ERIC Document Reproduction Service No. ED 337 354).

Borun, M., Massey, C. and Lutter, T. (1993). 'Naive knowledge and the design of science museum exhibits'. *Curator*, 36, (3), 201–19.

Brown, C. (1995). 'Making the most of family visits: Some observations of parents with children in a museum science centre'. *Museum Management and Curatorship*, 14, (1), 65–71.

Busque, L. (1991). 'Potential interaction and potential investigation of science centre exhibits and visitors' interest'. *Journal of Research in Science Teaching*, 28, (5), 411–21.

Carlisle, R.W. (1985). 'What do school children do at a science centre?' *Curator*, 28, (1), 27–33.

Champagne, D.W. (1975). 'The Ontario Science Centre in Toronto: Some impressions and some questions'. *Educational Technology*, 15, (8), 36–9.

Crane, V. (1994). 'An introduction to informal science learning and research'. In V. Crane, H. Nicholson, M. Chen and S. Bitgood (eds), *Informal science learning: What research says about television, science museums, and community-based projects* (pp.1–14). Dedham, Mass., Research Communication.

Crane, V., Nicholson, H., Chen, M. and Bitgood, S. (eds) (1994). *Informal science learning: What research says about television, science museums and community-based projects*. Dedham, Mass., Research Communication.

Csiksentmihályi, M. and Hermanson, K. (1995). 'Intrinsic motivation in museums: What makes visitors want to learn?' *Museum News*, 74, (3), 36–42.

Curran, E. (1992). 'Half the students in your museum are females: Gender equity and museum programs'. *Journal of Museum Education*, 17, (2), 14–17.

Curtis, N. and Goolnik, J. (1995). 'Hands on!' *Journal of Education in Museums*, 16, 11–12.

Danilov, V.J. (1982). *Science and technology centres*. Cambridge, Mass., The MIT Press.

Diamond, J. (1980). *The ethology of teaching: A perspective from the observation of families in science centres.* Unpublished doctoral thesis, University of California, Berkeley.

Diamond, J. (1986). 'The behaviour of family groups in science museums'. *Curator*, 29, (2), 139–54.

Diamond, J. (1991). 'Prototyping interactive exhibits on rocks and minerals'. *Curator*, 34, (1), 5–17.

Diamond, J. (1994). 'Sex differences in science museums: A review'. *Curator*, 37, (1), 17–24.

Diamond, J., St John, M., Cleary, B. and Librero, D. (1987). 'The Exploratorium's explainer program: The long term impacts of teenagers teaching science to the public.' *Science Education*, 71, (5), 643–56.

Dierking, L. and Falk, J. (1994). 'Family behaviour and learning in informal science settings: A review of research'. *Science Education*, 78, (1), 57–72.

Donald, J. (1991). 'The measurement of learning in the museum'. *Canadian Journal of Education*, 16, (3), 371–82.

Duensing, S. (1987). 'Science centres and exploratories: A look at active participation'. In D. Evered and M. O'Connor (eds), *Communicating science to the public* (pp.131–42). London, J. Wiley & Sons (CIBA Conference Foundation).

Duensing, S. (1993). 'The integration of mission with methods'. In J. Bradburne and I. Janousek (eds), *Planning science museums for the new Europe: Proceedings of a seminar held at the Národní Techniké Muzeum, Prague* (pp.73–80). Prague, UNESCO/Národní Techniké Muzeum, Prague.

Dymond, F., Goodrum, D. and Kerr, I. (1990). *Evaluation of Scitech exhibits.* Perth, Western Australia, MASTEC, Western Australian College of Advanced Education.

Eason, L.P. and Linn, M. (1976). 'Evaluation of effectiveness of a participatory exhibits'. *Curator*, 19, (1), 45–63.

Erätuuli, M. and Sneider, C. (1990). 'The experiences of visitors in a physics discovery room'. *Science Education*, 74, (4), 481–93.

Falk, J.H. and Balling, J.D. (1979). *Setting a neglected variable in science education: Investigations in outdoor field trips.* (Final Report). Edgewater, Md., Smithsonian Institution, Chesapeake Bay Centre for Environmental Studies (ERIC Document Reproduction Service No. ED 195 441).

Falk, J.H. and Dierking, L.D. (1992). *The museum experience.* Washington, Whalesback Books.

Falk, J.H., Martin, W. and Balling, J.D. (1978). 'The novel field trip phenomenon: Adjustment to novel settings interferes with task learning'. *Journal of Research in Science Teaching*, 15, (2), 127–34.

Fara, P. (1994). 'Understanding science museums'. *Museums Journal*, 94, (12), 25.

Feher, E. (1990). 'Interactive museum exhibits as tools for learning: Exploration with light'. *International Journal of Science Education*, 12, (1), 35–9.

Feher, E. and Diamond, J. (1990). 'Science centres as research laboratories'. In B. Serrell (ed.), *What research says about learning in science museums* (pp.26–8). Washington, Association of Science–Technology Centers.

Feher, E. and Meyer, K.R. (1992). 'Children's concept of colour'. *Journal of Research in Science Teaching*, 29, (5), 505–20.

Feher, E. and Rice, K. (1985). 'Development of scientific concepts through the use of interactive exhibits in a museum'. *Curator*, 28, (1), 35–46.

Finson, K.D. and Enochs, L. (1987). 'Student attitudes toward science–technology–

society resulting from a visit to a science–technology museum'. *Journal of Research in Science Teaching*, 24, (7), 593–609.

Flexer, B. and Borun, M. (1984). 'The impact of a class visit to a participatory science museum exhibit and a classroom science lesson'. *Journal of Research in Science Teaching*, 21, (9), 863–873.

Friedman, A.J. (1996). 'Vive la différence: Differentiating science–technology centres from other leisure-time enterprises'. *ASTC Newsletter*, 24 (1), 7–10.

Friedman, A., Eason, L.P. and Sneider, C.I. (1979). 'Star games: A participatory astronomy exhibit'. *Planetarian*, 8, (3), 3–7.

Gardner, H. (1983). *Frames of mind: The theory of multiple intelligences.* New York, Basic Books.

Gardner, H. (1993a). *Multiple intelligences: The theory in practice.* New York, Basic Books.

Gardner, H. (1993b). *Educating the unschooled child.* Washington, DC, Federation of Behavioural, Psychological and Cognitive Sciences. Available from ASTC.

Gillies, P. (1981). *Participatory science exhibits in action: The evaluation of the visist of the Ontario 'Science Circus' to the Science Museum.* London, Science Museum.

Gottfried, J. (1980). 'Do children learn on field trips?' *Curator*, 23, (3), 165–74.

Greenfield, T.A. (1995). 'Girls' and boys' use of interactive science museums'. *Journal of Research in Science Teaching*, 32, (9), 925–38.

Gregory, R. (1989). 'Turning minds on to science by hands-on exploration: The nature and potential of the hands-on medium'. In M. Quin (ed.), *Sharing science: Issues in the development of interactive science and technology centres* (pp.1–9). London, Nuffield Foundation on behalf of the Committee on the Public Understanding of Science (COPUS).

Hawkins, D. (1965). 'Messing about in science'. *Science and Children*, 2, (5), 5–9.

Hein, H. (1987). 'The museum as teacher of theory: A case history of the Exploratorium vision section'. *Museum Studies Journal*, 2, (4), 30–40.

Hein, H. (1990). *The museum as a laboratory.* Washington, Smithsonian Institution Press.

Hilke, D.D. (1993). 'Quest for the perfect methodology: a tragi-comedy in four acts'. In S. Bicknell and G. Farmelo (eds), *Museum visitor studies in the '90s* (pp.67–74). London, Science Museum.

Hilke, D.D. and Balling, J.D. (1985). 'The family as a learning system: An observational study of families in museums'. In J. Balling, D. Hilke, J. Liversidge, E. Cornell and N. Perry (eds), *Role of the family in the promotion of science literacy* (Final Report for NSF Grant, SED-8112927), Washington, DC.

Honeyman, B. (1994, December). 'Science centres: Building bridges with teachers'. Paper presented at the 9th ICASE-Asian Symposium, Bangkok, Thailand.

Javlekar, V.D. (1989). 'Learning scientific concepts in science centres'. *Visitor Studies: Theory, Research and Practice*, 2, 168–79.

Johnston, J. and Rennie, L.J. (1995). 'Perceptions of visitors' learning at an interactive science and technology centre in Australia'. *Museum Management and Curatorship*, 14, (3), 317–25.

Kennedy, J. (1990). *User friendly: Hands-On exhibits that work.* Washington, Association of Science–Technology Centres.

Kimche, L. (1978). 'Science centres: A potential for learning'. *Science*, 199, 270–3.

Kirrane, S. and Hayes, F. (1993). 'Do it yourself'. *Museums Journal*, 93, (2), 28 –30.

Koran, J. and Ellis, J. (1991). 'Research in informal settings: Some reflections on designs and methodology'. *ILVS Review*, 2, (1), 67–86.

Koran, J.J., Koran, M.L. and Ellis, J. (1989). 'Evaluating the effectiveness of field experiences 1939–1989'. *Visitor Behaviour*, 4, (2), 7–10.

Korn, R. (1995). 'An analysis of differences between visitors at natural history museums and science centers'. *Curator*, 38, (3), 150–60.

Kremer, K.B. and Mullins, G.W. (1992). 'Children's gender behaviour at science museum exhibits'. *Curator*, 35, (1), 39–48.

Kubota, C. and Olstad, R. (1991). 'Effects of novelty-reducing preparation on exploratory behavior and cognitive learning in a science museum'. *Journal of Research in Science Teaching*, 28, (3), 225 34.

Lam-Kan, K.S. (1985). *The contributions of enrichment activities towards science interest and science achievement*. Unpublished master's thesis, National University of Singapore.

Lawrence, G. (1993). 'Remembering rats, considering culture: Perspectives on museum evaluation'. In S. Bicknell and G. Farmelo (eds), *Museum visitor studies in the '90s* (pp.117–24). London, Science Museum.

Lewis, J. (1995). 'Shell Questacon Science Circus: 1994 Report'. *Questacon Magazine*, 4, (2), insert.

Linn, M. (1976). *Uses of evaluation in science and technology centers: Informed decision making*. Berkeley, Lawrence Hall of Science, University of California (ERIC Document Reproduction Service No. ED 182 159).

Linn, M.C. (1983). 'Evaluation in the museum setting: Focus on expectations'. *Educational Evaluation and Policy Analysis*, 5, (1), 119–227.

Lucas, A.M. (1983). 'Scientific literacy and informal learning'. *Studies in Science Education*, 10, 1–36.

Lucas, A.M. (1991). '"Info-tainment" and informal sources for learning science'. *International Journal of Science Education*, 13, (5), 495–504.

Lucas, A.M., McManus, P. and Thomas, G. (1986). 'Investigating learning from informal sources: Listening to conversations and observing play in science museums'. *European Journal of Science Education*, 8, (4), 341–52.

Martin, M., Brown, S. and Russell, T. (1991). 'A Study of child–adult interaction at a natural history centre'. *Studies in Educational Evaluation*, 17, (2), 355–69.

McClafferty, T.P. (1995). 'Did you hear Grandad? Children's and adults' use and understanding of a sound exhibit at interactive science centres'. *Journal of Education in Museums*, 16, 12–16.

McLean, K. (1993). *Planning for people in museum exhibitions*. Washington, Association of Science–Technology Centers.

McManus, P.M. (1989). 'What people say and how they think in a science museum'. In D. Uzzell (ed.), *Heritage interpretation: Vol. 2. The visitor experience* (pp.156–65). London, Belhaven Press.

McManus, P.M. (1992). 'Topics in museums and science education'. *Studies in Science Education*, 20, 157–82.

McManus, P.M. (1993). 'Thinking about the visitor's thinking'. In S. Bicknell and G. Farmelo (eds), *Museum visitor studies in the '90s* (pp.108–13). London, Science Museum.

McManus, P.M. (1994). 'Families in museums'. In R. Miles and L. Zavala (eds), *Towards the museum of the future: New European perspectives*. London, Routledge.

Medved, M. and Oatley, K. (1995, April). 'Education or entertainment. Memories and behavioural effects of a visit to a science museum'. Paper presented at the Annual Conference of the American Education Research Association, San Francisco, USA.

Miller, J.D. (1987). Discussion following 'Role of museums in communicating science'. In D. Evered and M. O'Connor (eds), *Communicating science to the public* (pp.123–30). London, J. Wiley (CIBA Foundation).

Moffat, H. (1993). 'Museums and the National Curriculum'. *Museums Journal*, 91, (5), 32–8.

Oppenheimer, F. (1968a). 'A rationale for a science museum'. *Curator*, 11, (3), 206–9.

Oppenheimer, F. (1968b). 'The role of science museums'. In E. Larrabee (ed.), *Museums and education* (pp.167–78). Washington, Smithsonian Institution Press.

Oppenheimer, F. (1972). 'The Exploratorium: A playful museum combines perception and art in science education'. *American Journal of Physics*, 40, 978–84.

Parker, L.H., Rennie, L.J. and Fraser, B.J. (1996). *Gender, science and mathematics: Shortening the shadow*. Dordrecht, Kluwer Academic Publishers.

Parkyn, M. (1993). 'Scientific imaging'. *Museums Journal*, 93, (10), 29–34.

Peiffer, B. (1995, April). 'Interactive science exhibits on color concepts. Testing an educational design model'. Paper presented at the Annual Conference of the National Association for Research in Science Teaching, San Fransisco, USA.

Perry, D.L. (1992). 'Designing exhibits that motivate'. *Assocition of Science–Technology Centers Newsletter*, March/April, 9–12.

Perry, D.L. (1993). 'Beyond cognition and affect: The anatomy of a museum visit'. *Visitor studies: Theory, Research and Practice*, 6, 43–7.

Perry, D.L. (1989). 'The creation and verification of a development model for the design of a museum exhibit'. (Doctoral dissertation, Indiana University, 1989) *Dissertations Abstracts International*, 50, (12), 3926. (University Microfilms Inc. No. 9012186)

Price, S. and Hein, G.E. (1991). 'More than a field trip: Science programmes for elementary school groups at museums'. *International Journal of Science Education*, 13, (5), 505–19.

Quin, M. (ed.) (1989). *Sharing science: Issues in the development of interactive science and technology centres*. London, Nuffield Foundation on behalf of COPUS.

Ravest, J. (1993). 'Where is the science in science centres?' *ECSITE Newsletter*, (Summer), 10–11.

Rennie, L.J. (1995). 'Learning in science centres: What do we know and what do we need to know?' *Proceedings of the 20th Annual Conference of the Western Australian Science Education Association* (pp.69–74). Edith Cowan University, Churchlands, WA.

Roberts, L.C. (1993). 'Analysing (and intuiting) the affective domain'. In S. Bicknell and G. Farmelo (eds), *Museum visitor studies in the '90s* (pp.97–101). London, Science Museum.

Russell, T. (1989). 'The formative evaluation of interactive science and technology centres: Some lessons learned'. In D. Uzzell (ed.), *Heritage interpretation: Vol. 2. The visitor experience* (pp.192–202). London, Bellhaven Press.

Schibeci, R. (1992). *Evaluation of the educational benefit of the 'Sports Works' exhibition at Scitech Discovery Centre* (Final Report). Murdoch University, Perth, WA.

Screven, C.G. (1974). *The measurement and facilities of learning in the museum environment: An experimental analysis*. Washington, DC, Smithsonian Institution Press.

Screven, C.G. (1990). 'Uses of evaluation before, during and after exhibit design'. *International Laboratory of Visitor Studies Review*, 1, (2), 36–66.

Seagram, B.C., Patten, L.H. and Lockett, C.W. (1993). 'Audience research and exhibit development: A framework'. *Museum Management and Curatorship*, 12, 29–41.

Semper, R.J. (1990). 'Science museums as environments for learning'. *Physics Today*, (November, 1990), 2–8.

Shortland, M. (1987). 'No business like show business'. *Nature*, 328, 213–14.

Sneider, C.I., Eason, L.P. and Friedman, A.J. (1979). 'Summative evaluation of a participatory science exhibit'. *Science Education*, 63, (1), 25–36.

Soren, B.J. (1991). 'Education: Curriculum-makers across museums'. *Journal of Museum Management and Curatorship*, 10, (4), 435–8.

St John, M. and Perry, D. (1993a). 'A framework for evaluation and research: science, infrastructure and relationships'. In S. Bicknell and G. Farmelo (eds), *Museum visitor studies in the '90s* (pp.59–66). London, Science Museum.

St John, M. and Perry, D. (1993b). 'Rethink role, science museums urged'. *ASTC Newsletter*, 1, 6–7.

Stevenson, A. and Bryden, M. (1991). 'The National Museums of Scotland's 1990 Discovery Room: An evaluation'. *Museum Management and Curatorship*, 10, 24–36.

Stevenson, J. (1991). 'The long-term impact of interactive exhibits'. *International Journal of Science Education*, 13, (5), 521–31.

Stevenson, J. (1994). 'Getting to grips'. *Museums Journal*, 94, (5), 30–1.

Thier, H.D. and Linn, M.C. (1975). *The value of interactive learning experiences in a museum*. Berkeley, Lawrence Hall of Science, University of California (ERIC Document Reproduction Service No. ED 182156).

Thomas, G. (1994). 'The age of interaction'. *Museums Journal*, 94, (5), 33–4.

Tomlin, N. (1990). 'Interactive science centres and the national curriculum'. *Journal of Education in Museums*, 11, 12–15.

Tuckey, C.J. (1992). 'Schoolchildren's reactions to an interactive science center'. *Curator*, 35, (1), 28–38.

Tulley, A. and Lucas, A.M. (1991). 'Interacting with a science museum: Vicarious and direct experience and subsequent understanding'. *International Journal of Science Education*, 13, (5), 533–42.

Uzzell, D. (1993). 'Contrasting psychological perspectives on exhibition evaluation'. In S. Bicknell and G. Farmelo (eds), *Museum visitor studies in the '90s* (pp.125–9). London, Science Museum.

Vytrhlik, J. (1994, November). 'Let's bring the parents first'. Paper presented at the Inaugural Museums Australia Conference: Identify, Icons and Artefacts, Fremantle, Australia.

Wanless, J.H. (1990). *The Questacon Explainers: A study of the role of explainers at Questacon Science Centre, Canberra*. Unpublished master's thesis, University of Canberra.

Watson, S. (1995). 'Experiments in putting learning theory into practice'. *Journal of Education in Museums*, 16, 8–10.

Wellington, J. (1989). 'Attitudes before understanding: The contribution of interactive centres to science education'. In M. Quin (ed.), *Sharing science: Issues in the development of interactive science and technology centres* (pp.30–2). London, Nuffield Foundation on behalf of the Committe on the Public Understanding of Science (COPUS).

Wilson, A. (1986) *Launch Pad. Project Profile*. London Science Museum.

Wymer, P. (1991, 5 October). 'Never mind the science, feel the experience'. *New Scientist*, p.49.

Chapter 6

Putting learning at the heart of exhibition development

A case study of the Wellcome Wing project*

J. Graham and B. Gammon

This chapter is a study of how the Science Museum, London, is seeking to plan for learning within the exhibition development process. Focusing on the Wellcome Wing project, the museum's most ambitious to date, this chapter will show how the exhibition development team has put visitors' learning at the heart of their work.

The Wellcome Wing (WW) is the museum's contemporary science and technology centre, due to open in the spring of 2000. The new wing will provide the museum with 3,000 square metres of new exhibition space. Four exhibition development teams have been established to create a series of separate, but interrelated, displays with a common theme of contemporary science and technology.

The WW team members have varying degrees of experience in exhibition project work. They bring expertise from a range of backgrounds, including curatorial, temporary exhibition and exhibit design, education, visitor programming, and visitor studies. Most of the team have a science background, and the museum has also appointed science subject specialists to act as advisors.

Whilst contemporary science and technology forms the unifying theme across the exhibitions of the wing, there are many other common strands, the strongest of which is a desire, evident from the conception of the project, to be 'visitor-centred'.

Initially, the teams struggled with what this meant but now, halfway into the five-year project, being 'visitor-centred' has achieved some clarity in relation to the content development. Taking account of visitors' needs, wants, expectations, interests and understandings is now an integral part of the way we work. The project has also appointed a team of audience advocates to provide advice and act as guardians of the visitor-centred approach. The authors of this article have been appointed as the first two of three audience advocates to the Wellcome Wing project. Ben Gammon has substantial expertise in the field of evaluation and visitor studies, and Jo Graham has both education and exhibition management experience and expertise in early years learning. The third

*Newly Commissioned.

audience advocate, Karen Davies, was the Education Advisor for the Challenge of Materials exhibition and has secondary science education experience.

The size of the overall Wellcome Wing team meant that we had to devise a strategy for developing the exhibitions that would enable each exhibition team to work independently and yet create a coherent whole. The museum has no set method for developing exhibitions – different teams tend to work in distinct ways. The key determinant for the development process within the Science Museum to date had been the experience of particular staff involved in any one project.

The Wellcome Wing project is different from most of its predecessors at the museum, primarily due to the scale of the development and the fact that the content is being designed for new exhibition space. This gives unrivalled opportunities for creativity and almost endless possibilities, both a strength and a potential weakness of the project. Developing content, like all other aspects of a project, has to run to a tight schedule. The development process is therefore essentially one of definition, of constantly narrowing the parameters until what the team has is a well-defined, coherent and intellectually balanced 'story'. To achieve this we needed to decide how we would structure the process. This would be based on experiences we had of what had been successful in former exhibition projects and experience of colleagues at other institutions (McLean 1996).

The museum wants to encourage the maximum possible creativity and innovation, but it also needs to deliver a visitor-friendly exhibition on time and to budget. There are many elements to keep in tension: imaginative creativity, educational value, academic credibility, visitor understanding and interest, the sponsors' agenda, and the desire for objectivity. We needed to create a development process that allowed us to mix in all these ingredients in optimum amounts.

The role of the audience advocates

The idea of audience advocacy is not new. In previous projects, audience advocates were seen as a counterbalance to the advocates for the content (lead curator) and of design (head designer).

However, we felt that there were flaws in this model. We were unwilling to be perceived by the team in an essentially confrontational role. We also felt that the model did not build on trust and respect and did not define certain key responsibilities, e.g. who is responsible for ensuring that recommendations from evaluation are acted upon? In reshaping the idea of an audience advocate we began by mapping out the different roles we would need to perform.

Advisor Providing on-the-spot advice on any aspect of the audience – their needs, wants, expectations, likes, dislikes and prior knowledge. We must be familiar with the latest theories in educational research, museum studies, and cognitive and social psychology.

Evaluator   Assessing what is and is not known about the museum's audience. Where there are gaps in our understanding that may affect the development of the exhibition we must ensure that evaluation is undertaken to fill them.

Communicator   Facilitating the development of clear objectives for the content – what does the team want to say to the visitors through the exhibition and how will visitors interpret this?

Strategist   Guiding the team in making key decisions that will affect the target audience. Ensuring that all members of the team and other relevant stakeholders are fully aware that these choices need to be made and the implications of them. The audience advocate must get the team to address issues such as:

- who are the target audience?
- how will each section of the target audience be catered for?
- what prior knowledge, interests and motivations are being assumed?
- how should objects, text, graphics and audio-visuals be used?
- suitability of content as an exhibition – would it make a better TV programme, CD-ROM, book, lecture?
- what are the key messages of the exhibition?
- what are the learning goals of the exhibition?

Trainer   Ensuring that the team learns from previous experience of exhibition development and inspiring the team to think and learn about their target audience.

We then identified a series of tasks that would need to be completed. The principal tasks were establishing a training programme; identifying a target audience for the wing; clarifying what the teams wanted to say; detailing realisable visitor outcomes; considering all the tools we had to communicate with our visitors; and assessing what our visitors already knew and how they preferred to learn.

Visitor awareness training

We have established a visitor awareness training programme that involves all team members and covers both cognitive and affective training. Through cognitive training we are seeking to ensure that the teams learn from past experience both internal to the museum and from external sources. We have organised a programme of weekly meetings that deal with issues ranging from 'what is genetics?' to 'how do children under seven use the museum?' Through affective training we are seeking to change people's attitudes towards the importance of learning, evaluation and considering the needs and wants of visitors. In addition, we are aiming to provide the team with memorable experiences of visitor behaviour and give people first-hand experience of the issues that we are raising.

Each member of the team from the project director downwards has been required to take part in a series of exercises, as outlined below. Full descriptions of these exercises can be found in Gammon and Graham (in press).

- Accompanied visits – where the team member joins a group of visitors (families, groups of adults or school parties) and shadows them as they move through the museum, observing what they do and where they go, and listening to what they say.
- Horrible visits – an attempt to provide our colleagues with the experience of being a reluctant museum visitor. Each team member is asked to select a friend or relative who has an interest or hobby that they themselves do not share. They are then asked to find an exhibition on this topic and visit it with their friend or relative. Participants complete a pre-visit questionnaire, which asks them to examine their hopes, fears and expectations, and a post-visit questionnaire, which explores how their experiences matched their expectations.
- Observation exercises – since many of the team only see visitors as they rush through the exhibitions on their way to a meeting, we wanted to provide them with the chance to spend time just sitting and watching how visitors behave. In these exercises, participants observe visitors at different types of exhibit, in different locations around the museum, at different times. The team members have to note details such as who the visitors are with, how they use the exhibit and for how long, what information is exchanged and any social interaction that occurs.
- Assisting with the data collection in visitor surveys and observation studies so that they can hear and see at first-hand the information we are collecting about our visitors.
- Attending focus groups of visitors as silent observers.

Identifying a target audience

Defining a target audience is not a universally accepted thing to do in exhibition development. Many consider that exhibitions should be aimed at everyone. However, in reality most people have a subconscious vision of a target audience and within a team there are likely to be as many target audiences as there are team members. It has been part of our role to make the teams aware of the consequences of targeting certain groups rather than others. Without targeting, it is difficult to be clear about specific aims and intentions for an exhibition and almost impossible to evaluate the ideas meaningfully, either formatively (as part of the planning process) or summatively.

The Wellcome Wing team took a decision on its target audience in March 1996 and has subsequently been refining that decision for each exhibition. The wing itself, and some of the exhibitions, have main and secondary target audiences reflecting the priority they ascribe to these groups and often also the relevance and potential attraction of the subject matter to them. In practice, this means that for the main target audience each part of the exhibition must be accessible to some extent. However, for a secondary audience only certain elements may be relevant and comprehensible.

How did we choose our target audience?

Discussions of who should constitute the audience of the Wellcome Wing revolved around what the wing would be like, assumptions of the likely appeal of the subject matter and whether to take account of our current audience.

We sought to inform the decision-making process in a variety of ways. We identified key decisions and suggested implications that these decisions might have. Teenagers (not in school groups), for example, were discounted as a target audience as it was realised that to cater effectively for them would risk alienating virtually all other sectors of our audience.

We provided information about the make-up of our current audience and also about people who do not currently visit the museum. As well as finding relevant research that considered how non-visitors perceive museums in general (Trevelyan 1991), we commissioned focus groups with, amongst others, pre-family women aged 20–35, independent adults aged 50+ and non-graduate parents from the C2D socio-economic grouping.

What was the result of these discussions?

The front-end evaluation described above showed that it would be difficult to attract the groups mentioned above to the museum. The museum took the decision that the new wing would be part of the existing museum. It would not be marketed as a separate entity; nor could visitors simply come to the wing on its own. The wing therefore had to appeal to the museum's current audience, and it was felt that there was challenge enough in encouraging more people within the profile of our current audience to visit without radically altering the overall profile. We also decided that the new wing would give us an opportunity to try to increase the number of visits (per visitor) as well as the number of visitors.

The target audience of the Wellcome Wing was therefore defined as:

- family groups with children aged up to 12;
- school groups from Key Stages 2–4 (ages 7 to 16);
- independent adults aged 20–50;
- people from socio-economic groups A, B and C1.

In addition, because the team still wished to broaden the museum's appeal, it was agreed that independent adults should primarily be assumed to be nonscience specialists, i.e. visitors who do not necessarily have degree- or postgraduate-level science.

Since the target audience was so broad we recommended that individual exhibitions should not necessarily aim to accommodate all these audiences but that there should be something substantial for all these groups in the wing as a whole. The inclusion of families with children under 12 as part of the core audience for exhibitions on contemporary science and technology was a bold one, since the subject matter is not intrinsically child-friendly. That single decision has had a profound influence on both the content matter that the wing will cover and how that content will be presented.

Clarifying the messages

In order for the teams to communicate effectively with their target audiences they needed to know what they wanted to say. Based on ideas developed in Roger Miles's book *The Design of Educational Exhibits* (Miles, 1988, in particular Chapter 6) and Deborah Perry's work on learning hierarchies (Perry, 1993: pp.73–7), previous projects had successfully used systems of cascading messages to frame their content. We decided to recommend a messages system for the Wellcome Wing.

Messages begin at level 1, an 'in a nutshell' sentence that sums up the whole exhibition, and run through to level 5, which details individual exhibit ideas. The messages document is not written in stone, but is rather a snapshot of the team's thinking. Working through the hierarchy involves the teams in an increasingly detailed definition of what is *not* going to be in the exhibition. It is, however, an iterative process: define the messages, research them, refine them and so on. In this way, level 1 messages are decided relatively early on in a project, with level 5 messages not being defined until perhaps a few months before opening.

In association with a set of aims, these messages serve a number of purposes:

• to clarify the thinking of the team and allow them to decide which parts of the subject matter should and should not be covered;
• to establish priority of content, which allows content to be cut without compromising coherence;
• to show progression of ideas within a coherent framework;
• to avoid omissions or overlaps;
• to establish a clear common understanding between team members;
• to communicate clearly to others outside the team, e.g. designers, senior management, sponsors;
• to allow comparison across modules, within an exhibition and between exhibitions.

Since the messages document is shorter and more diagrammatic than a traditional script it is easier to read and gives a better impression of what the ideas may look like in three dimensions. Messages imply a didactic one-way communication seen from the exhibition team's point of view, which leaves out ideas for developing skills and affective learning such as changing attitudes, affecting feelings or raising enthusiasm.

The messages work is therefore a transitional stage, a clear and simple content skeleton that will subsequently be translated into a visitor outcomes document embodying all outcomes, cognitive, skills-based and affective. This document would be asking a subtly different question: 'What do we think visitors will get from this exhibition?'

Communicating with our visitors

Once the teams had begun to clarify what they wanted to say, we needed to consider how we might get those messages across. We are urging the teams to think strategically about how they might use a broad range of exhibition media from objects to interactive exhibits, text panels to programmes of events. The value of having defined a target audience becomes apparent as the teams consider the merits of a variety of media not only for different types of message but also for different audiences.

Each team is currently working on communication strategies which will give a clear statement on not only which media will be used in their exhibitions but to what extent, how and why. It will also consider interrelationships between media in the exhibitions.

Defining a strategy for learning

The above work is necessary for, but does not guarantee, planning for learning. We needed to encourage the teams to recognise that learning should be planned for in exhibitions. We began by holding discussions on the nature of learning in a museum context. Some colleagues had very different interpretations of the word 'learning'. Connotations of school days and a perception that education and fun were poles apart meant that we needed a lot of discussion before everyone felt comfortable talking about learning in its broadest sense.

Nonetheless, agreement was reached that learning was at the heart of what we are about and that we needed to plan for it. Thus was born the learning strategy. The learning strategy is not a strategic document, more a way of working. It is not a highly academic approach but takes the elements of visitor learning that we feel are most practical to introduce to the teams.

The exhibition development process is not a linear route from conception to delivery, with readily identifiable stages. In trying to structure the process, we have sought to provide landmarks that show that a certain distance has been covered and that point the way forward. The learning strategy, however, is not a landmark. It is rather a thread that weaves its way throughout the development process, allowing the teams to revisit and revise as often as they create and innovate. Our learning strategy takes the form of a checklist, which teams can use to audit their work at any stage.

What do visitors already know?

We used the learning strategy to ask the teams to identify what prior knowledge and attitudes visitors bring with them to the museum. Most modern educational theories are based upon the idea of prior knowledge and it is our role to interpret these for the teams and distil what we consider useful to them.

We began with constructivism (Hein, 1996). Constructivism is often taken to mean that not only should one identify the learner's current stage of thinking but that one should challenge that stage to achieve learning. Our use of this theory is not so much about challenging 'naive notions' and inserting 'correct' scientific explanations, but rather looking for entry points to the subject. In this way our use of prior knowledge reflects Roschelle's assertion that prior knowledge is not a positive or negative thing but 'rather than rejecting prior knowledge and accepting instructed knowledge, learners must gradually refine and re-structure their prior knowledge' to bring about conceptual change (Roschelle, 1995: p.43).

We also considered other theories, including those developed by Dewey, Bruner and Vygotsky, most of which deal with children's learning. Dewey places prior knowledge at the core of learning but does not suggest that it is incompatible with a curriculum. 'By designing appropriate experiences, an educator should be able to move from children's interest and capabilities toward the more stable, definite, and structured content of organised subject matter' (*ibid.*: p.45). Bruner suggests that through connecting to prior knowledge, and presenting even difficult ideas in accessible ways, children can be taught things that would normally be considered far too complex for them (Wood, 1988).

Vygotsky (Smith and Cowie, 1991) also refers to prior knowledge. He maintains that children can learn up to a certain level based on their own experiences and abilities (prior knowledge), but that with adult help they can be helped to a higher level of understanding. In his view, learning is a social experience with adults bringing children into culturally defined explanations. Bruner, inspired by Vygotsky, introduced the idea of 'scaffolding' as a way of achieving this. By providing content linked into prior knowledge we are attempting to put in place these scaffolds to make the learning leaps that we want people to make into achievable steps.

What about how visitors feel?

Affective learning is as important to exhibition developers as cognitive learning. As well as framing cognitive messages, we have advised the teams to produce affective messages covering both attitudes and feelings. These messages have then been woven into the cognitive ones so that the message document reflects both the affective and cognitive domains of learning. Once this has been done, the messages can be referred to as learning outcomes, and the teams will need to consider prior attitudes in the same way as they consider prior knowledge.

How can we discover what visitors already feel and know?

Each of the teams has produced a detailed table (see Table 6.1 for an extract) that maps the messages defined so far for each of the age ranges covered in our target audience onto their previous knowledge or attitudes.

In certain areas, it has been relatively easy to find published sources of information; for example, much work has been done on children's and adults' ideas in genetics and there has been a large study looking at public attitudes towards biotechnology. In other subjects, attitudes have been less well documented and we have had to make assumptions. Where possible we will test these assumptions through evaluation; for example, we have already carried out a study looking at how teachers feel about IT and a survey with museum visitors on what they know about science in the news.

How do visitors learn?

The next section of the learning strategy asks the teams to consider what thinking skills they want to promote. Displays often require observation and aesthetic appreciation. These skills are usually linked to assimilating additional experience into current theories rather than promoting shifts in conceptual thinking. Museums can create activities that call for a greater range of skills, including classification, creative thinking, prediction, deduction and problem solving. Exhibits can also promote different kinds of talk, a crucial element in learning (Blud 1990). As exhibit developers, we need to consider how visitors of all ages will use the exhibits we design, not only what they will physically do but for how long, who with, what they will be thinking and what they will talk about.

This section of the learning strategy has been designed to be used as part of a spiral process. Initially, the list of skills can be used to encourage the creation of a wider range of exhibit ideas. Once refined, the ideas can be audited to check that the exhibition provides visitors with opportunities to think in different ways. After the final evaluation, and subsequent modification, of exhibits, they can again be audited to ensure breadth of approach.

We also felt that the teams should take account of different ways in which people prefer to learn, so the learning strategy also looks at ways of learning. We have prepared the ground by running training and discussion sessions on Gardner's (1993) theory of multiple intelligences to challenge team members' perceptions of the way visitors think.

The teams have used the idea of catering for different learning preferences in generating ideas for exhibits, and this has helped to broaden the approach and range of media suggested. It has also encouraged the teams to think about ways

Table 6.1 An example of part of a table for 11–16-year-old students

Topic	What do they know?	What do they have problems with?
Brains and behaviour	Know response to stimuli (touch, taste, smell, etc.) and how the eye receives information.	Often do not recognise light, vibration or chemicals as stimuli to which we respond, rather that body actively sensing the environment, i.e. initiates hearing, seeing, smelling.
	At KS4 have an idea of nerves carrying messages and controlling activities and simple CNS reflex arc.	Some aware that the brain is helping the body to function but not until 14 is a brain thought of as necessary for all behaviour.
	Know about hormones, particularly insulin and sex hormones; the medical uses of hormones (e.g. fertility, diabetes).	68% of children aged 14–16 had heard of schizophrenia, but many described it as 'split personalities' or Jekyll and Hyde.
	Among 14–16-year-olds most were familiar with and correctly interpreted depression. About one-third had heard of senile dementia, while nearly all had heard of anorexia nervosa and alcoholism.	The term mania was not understood in its clinical sense, but rather as an extreme form of interest, e.g. Beatle-mania.
		Confusion among 14–16-year-olds between mental illness and disabilities.

General comment: children aged around 16 years are likely to have a similar to if not greater knowledge of genetics than many adults. However, it should be noted that even though the National Curriculum may state that certain biomedical topics be covered at KS3 and KS4, pupils' knowledge and understanding is often far lower than expected. Such topics seem to present teachers with problems (they may be science teachers but have training in chemistry and physics rather than biology) and these topics are often covered at the very end of the final year. This means that there s little, if any, reinforcement of the messages – taught once and only once. Problems may also arise since cell biology, inheritance and genetics are taught separately and pupils may never assimilate knowledge into a complete picture. Nonetheless, most pupils should have been taught some basic genetics by the end of KS4.

in which exhibits would be used and which types of learning might be being promoted. Gardner's work is not an easy read for busy exhibition developers, however, and we are considering further training sessions based on the Kolb/ McCarthy model of types of learning and types of learner (see Durbin, 1996: p.39).

The model shown in Figures 6.1 and 6.2 suggests that there are four main ways of learning. These four ways make up the axes of the model, with sensing and feeling being opposed to thinking, and watching opposed to doing. The ground between the axes gives four types of learning: the dynamic, the imaginative, the analytical and the common-sense problem solving. So learners who like to stand back, watch and think through their observations would be characterised as 'analytical', whilst those who like to dive straight in, actively trying things out without reference to others or to thinking the problem through first would be called 'dynamic'.

These learning types are extreme examples, and in reality all learners combine these types to differing degrees. We feel that many exhibitions have traditionally catered almost exclusively for the analytical type of learning and that all types of learning should be accommodated.

What motivates visitors?

It is impossible to plan for learning without taking account of motivation. Much of the work outlined above, if successful, should contribute to high motivation of the visitor. Presenting content that is accessible and allows visitors to succeed in building understanding is a powerful motivator, increasing their sense of self-efficacy. Catering for different ways of learning and thus allowing visitors to learn in their own preferred style can also motivate.

Other elements that can increase motivation include surprise and novelty, challenge, choice and control, physical exertion, immediate feedback, sensory experience, social interactivity, and perceived value of the end-result.

What will they remember?

The last section of our learning strategy considers memorability. What is it about the experiences we are planning that will make them memorable or unique for our visitors?

At one level, we may be satisfied if visitors leave the Wellcome Wing having had 'a nice time'. However, for the wing to fulfil its potential as a place of learning this is not enough. In order for there to have been any learning in a meaningful sense we must also have provided a memorable experience for the visitors. Museums have the potential to create unique memories, what Herrman and Plude term 'museum memories'. They characterise these as memories, whose 'content necessarily includes some sense of rarity or uniqueness with associated feelings of reverence and a philosophical content regarding the relationship between the visitor and the museum exhibits' (1995: p.55).

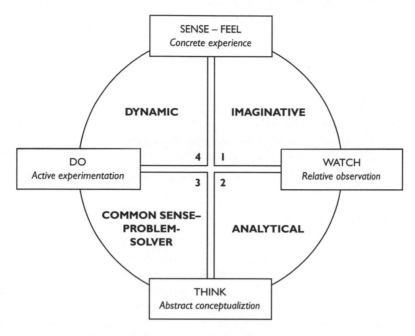

Figure 6.1 Types of learning (from McCarthy and Pitman-Gelles, 1989).

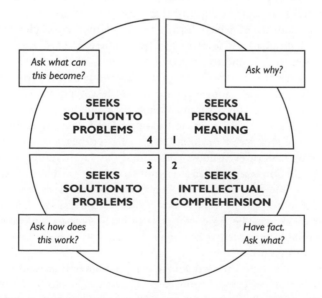

Figure 6.2 Some characteristics of different types of learner (from McCarthy and Pitman-Gelles, 1989).

Experiences in an informal setting can form part of long-term learning, in which understanding comes months or years after the (initial) museum experience. Memory is a vital component of this. There are many elements that affect the formation and retrieval of memories. We have chosen to highlight a few to the teams, including the importance of

- emotions
- the physical environment
- actively engaging the brain in mental manipulations
- providing explicit links between information
- providing a clear overview of the exhibition subject.

Evaluating visitor needs

Underpinning the learning strategy and shaping the messages and target audience is a process of evaluation that provides information on the needs, wants, expectations, prior knowledge, interests and behaviour of visitors. In some situations this information can be gleaned from published data or previous studies. However, in many other instances the questions to be addressed will be specific for that particular exhibit or target audience and no reliable data will be available. In these cases, the audience advocate must ensure that a relevant and focused study is conducted to fill in the gap in the team's knowledge. This may involve commissioning an outside research consultant to conduct the work, or conducting the study using museum staff. This is often referred to as evaluation, which uses a range of methodologies from social science, including quantitative and qualitative surveys, participant and non-participant observations, and focus groups.

Despite similarities in the methods used, evaluation (in our terms) is not the same as research. Research aims to generate and test hypotheses, is conducted over a period of months or years and ultimately results in the production of a report, thesis or paper. Evaluation, on the other hand, aims to assess the actual or probable success of specific exhibits in specific settings, is conducted over a period of weeks, days or even hours and should ultimately result in an effective exhibition. Evaluation is a pragmatic attempt to identify problems in design and content and to suggest possible solutions. The information generated is for immediate use, and usually few if any general conclusions can be drawn. Although a report may be produced it is unlikely ever to appear in a peer-reviewed journal (see Miles, 1993, and Hilke, 1993, for a more detailed discussion of this issue).

However, we rely upon the academic research conducted around the world in the fields of educational and cognitive psychology, sociology, anthropology, public understanding of science, etc. to underpin our data and provide a framework to interpret it.

Stages of evaluation

Evaluation can be broken down into three stages: front-end, formative and summative, depending upon the point in the project at which it is conducted.

Front-end evaluation is conducted at the earliest stages of a project and aims to assess the target audiences' needs, wants, expectations, prior knowledge and attitudes. This information helps the team to refine its definition of the target audience, set realistic objectives for the exhibition, highlight potentially appealing and relevant avenues into the subject matter for the target audience and identify areas of the content that will need particular attention because of the audience's lack of interest and/or knowledge.

Formative evaluation is conducted during the development phase of a project and aims to improve the effectiveness of the different elements of the exhibition by testing prototype versions on samples of the target audience. Formative evaluation focuses upon three questions:

- *Ergonomics* Can visitors operate the exhibit effectively, e.g. can they find the relevant instructions and controls? Do they notice and correctly interpret the feedback from the exhibit?
- *Comprehension* Can they identify the key messages of the exhibit, i.e. does their interpretation of the exhibit broadly match the aims of the project team?
- *Motivation* How successfully does the exhibit attract and hold visitors' attention and what can be done to improve this?

Formative evaluation involves qualitative surveys and observation studies on samples of around 30 to 40 visitors. It aims to assess the range and seriousness of the problems that visitors encounter when using the exhibit, rather than trying to measure the frequency of their occurrence. The other important aspect of successful formative evaluation is that it should be an iterative process whereby a prototype is tested, modified and then re-tested at least two or three times.

The final stage of the process is summative evaluation, conducted once the project has been completed. At its most effective, summative evaluation can provide an invaluable way for the museum to learn from its successes and mistakes and how to apply these lessons to future projects. Ideally, one stage of evaluation would merge seamlessly into the next with the summative evaluation of one project becoming the front-end evaluation of the next.

What have we achieved so far?

In retrospect, we feel that there have been some notable successes. In particular we feel the following have met or exceeded our expectations:

- The teams have accepted learning as a key aim of exhibition development.
- Visitor awareness training has dramatically improved the teams' acceptance of evaluation as a part of the exhibition development process.
- The definition of a clear target audience for each of the exhibitions has provided a clarity and focus for the teams' planning.
- The development of a structured messages document has greatly facilitated communication both within the teams and between them and the designers, sponsors and senior staff. This has also enabled us to identify where the development process is going astray.
- The communication strategy for the wing as a whole has been produced and is now driving the production of communication strategies for each exhibition.

Other aspects of the process that are proving more difficult or that have yet to be addressed include:

- The attempt to get the team to specify how different learning styles will be catered for and how different thinking skills will be encouraged has proved difficult to realise yet in practical terms.
- Getting the teams to address the problems of motivation and memorability has proved difficult. Although they accept these issues as being significant, neither they nor us can yet see how to adapt the exhibition development process to take account of them.

In conclusion, from a purely subjective point of view, we feel that we have succeeded in bringing visitors' needs, wants and expectations onto the teams' agenda and placing learning at the very heart of the exhibition development process.

References

Blud, L. (1990). 'Social interaction and learning in family groups visiting a museum', *International Journal of Museum Management and Curatorship* 9, (1).

Durbin, G. (ed.) (1996). *Developing Museum Exhibitions for Lifelong Learning*, London, The Stationery Office for Group for Education in Museums.

Gammon, B. and Graham, J. (in press). 'Putting the value back into evaluation', in Thompson, D., Benefield, A., Bitgood, S., Shettel, H. and Williams, R. (eds) *Visitor Research: Theory, Research and Practice*, Proceedings of the tenth annual conference of the Visitor Studies Association, Birmingham, Alabama, 1997.

Gardner, H. (1993). *Frames of Mind: The Theory of Multiple Intelligences*, 2nd edn, Fontana Press.

Hein, G.E. (1996). 'Constructivist learning theory', in Durbin, G. (ed.) *Developing Museum Exhibitions for Lifelong Learning*, London, The Stationery Office.

Herrman, D. and Plude, D. (1995). 'Museum memory', in Falk J. and Dierking L. (eds)

Public Institutions for Personal Learning: Establishing a Research Agenda, Washington DC, American Association of Museums Technical Information Service.

Hilke, D.D. (1993). 'Quest for the perfect methodology: a tragi-comedy in four acts', in Bicknell, S. and Farmelo G. (eds) *Museum Visitor Studies in the 90s*, London, Science Museum.

McCarthy, B.N.D. and Pitman-Gelles, B. (1989). 'The 4MAT system: teaching to learning styles with right/left mode technique' in *The Sourcebook 1989*, American Association of Museums Technical Information Service.

McLean, K. (1996). *Planning for People in Museum Exhibitions*, 2nd edn, Washington DC, Association of Science–Technology Centers.

Miles, R.S. (1988). *The Design of Educational Exhibits*, 2nd edn, Unwin Hyman.

Miles, R.S. (1993). 'Grasping the greased pig: evaluation of educational exhibits', in Bicknell, S. and Farmelo G. (eds), *Museum Visitor Studies in the 90s*, London, Science Muscum.

Perry, D.L. (1993). 'Measuring learning with the knowledge hierarchy', in Thompson, D., Benefield, A., Bitgood, S., Shettel, H. and Williams, R. (eds) *Visitor Research: Theory, Research and Practice*, Proceedings of the sixth annual conference of the Visitor Studies Association, Albuquerque, New Mexico.

Roschelle, J. (1995). 'Learning in interactive environments: prior knowledge and new experience', in Falk J. and Dierking L. (eds) *Public Institutions for Personal Learning: Establishing a Research Agenda*, American Association of Museums Technical Information Service.

Smith, P.K. and Cowie, H. (1991). *Understanding Children's Development*, 2nd edn, Oxford, Basil Blackwell.

Trevelyan, V. (1991). 'Dingy places with different kinds of bits', An attitudes survey of London museums amongst non-visitors, commissioned by the London Museums Consultative Committee, London Museums Service.

Wood, D. (1988). *How Children Think and Learn*, Oxford, Basil Blackwell.

Chapter 7

Finding evidence of learning in museum settings*

J. Griffin

Introduction

The aim of the study outlined in this paper is to develop, trial and evaluate a new approach to school–museum programmes that incorporates 'natural' learning in an informal setting. It investigates a way to optimise learning during visits to museums, so that there is a move away from the visits being isolated, one-off events totally planned and orchestrated by the teacher towards a situation where the visits are an integral part of a student-centred learning unit. An integrated approach has been developed that reflects research into the ways in which students learn science, exemplary science teaching practices, and family group learning behaviours in informal settings. This approach has been tried with upper primary grade children. One component of the evaluation of the programme is an analysis of the students' exhibited learning behaviours.

Learning in museums

The question of how to assess learning in museums is problematic. In order to investigate this question, one could look at learning outcomes and/or at the presence of learning processes or behaviours during a museum visit. A major dilemma is the difficulty in isolating and measuring cognitive learning outcomes for a one-day museum visit, and in fact to attempt to do so is in conflict with a constructivist learning paradigm, which describes learning as a developmental process involving the accommodation of new experiences with prior understandings and attitudes.

> Our constructions of life are conditioned and constrained by our experiences and this means that – since we all have different experiences – we are all likely to have different perceptions about ideas, actions, behaviours, incidents, situations, tasks, feelings and so on.
>
> (Bentley and Watts, 1994: p.8)

*Newly commissioned.

When considering pathways to answer the question of assessing learning, it is first necessary to look at the nature of learning and learning processes that take place in a museum. Learning itself is a generic process; however, the circumstances in which and the processes by which it takes place vary. Museums are informal learning settings where learning is intrinsically motivated and proceeds through curiosity, observation and activity (Ramey-Gassert *et al.*, 1994).

In museums, visitors choose their experiences, ideas may not necessarily be met in sequence, and opportunities for learning may be fragmentary and unstructured. These learning processes may be different in many respects from those normally associated with formal learning settings. The informal nature of the setting means that it is not possible to determine the specific content to which learners are exposed.

> In museums there is an increased probability that self-directed learning and generalisation beyond the specific content presented will occur, since museums tend to facilitate the learner's ability to relate content to personal experiences and backgrounds.
>
> (Falk *et al.*, 1986: p.505)

A special opportunity offered by museums is the experiential nature of learning, based on encounters with real objects. It is thus a process that involves looking, questioning, examining and comparing (Sheppard, 1993). Museum learning involves sharpening of perceptual skills and development of a sense of wonder (Voris *et al.*, 1986). In informal settings, cognitive and affective learning are fused and can enhance each other. Similarly, education and enjoyment are linked (Bitgood *et al.*, 1994). The school-oriented distinction between these aspects of learning is not apparent in a setting that involves personal action in the choice of learning.

Falk and Dierking (1992) found that museum visitors could rarely recall specific facts or concepts from a visit, and propose that the problem with measuring learning in museums by formal, school-based instruments disregards the notion that learning is incremental and museum visits form only a part of the consolidation and growth of ideas, as well as disregarding the affective aspects of learning. Visitors are often learning things in museums that are not revealed through formal tests (Birney, 1995). Falk *et al.* (1986) also discuss the difficulty of measuring museum learning due to the unstructured nature of learning opportunities, pointing out that quantitative measures of learning can only be achieved by manipulating the system, and in doing so the system now understood is not the one that was originally being investigated.

To attempt to expect many similarities between the learning of individual visitors may not be productive. The very personal nature of learning in a museum, the short time that students are involved in these distinct experiences, and the broader but individual contexts in which it occurs, make it meaningless to attempt to measure museum-based learning with the same degree of reliability as classroom learning. Further, it is recognised that learning involves making connections between experiences from all sources, hence it is not possible to determine what aspects of a visitor's understanding of a particular idea result from the museum experience alone. Learning is a continuous process; we take in information through our senses and interpret it – it grows, it rarely happens instantly. The more experiences we have had, the more information that is available to play with and develop new ideas.

In an environment where the learners are constructing their own meanings out of experience:

> the important issues involved in understanding learning are derived from analysing the actions of the learner rather than probing the nature of the subject to be learned. . . . in fact, the conditions that favour learning are such that if we maximise them, we cannot predict with certainty what will be learned . . . we cannot predict what meaning learners will make of the experiences we provide for them.
>
> (Hein, 1991, p.191)

Hein (1995) suggests consideration of the notions of 'museum as teacher' or 'museum as a place to learn'. From a constructivist perspective there is no necessary connection between opportunities to learn and learning, and maximising conditions for learning means that we cannot predict what will be learned:

> There is another whole world of learning that goes on in museums, the learning that is constructed by the visitors out of their experience and not necessarily correlated closely with our teaching efforts. In order to understand the museum visitors and find out what they have learned, we need a broad approach to museum evaluation which includes a rich infusion of qualitative, naturalistic research in the museum field.
>
> (*ibid.*: p.201)

Learning in museums involves developing understanding of concepts by looking for relationships, links, connections and patterns involving accidentally encountered ideas and previous experiences (Lucas, 1993). Learning in informal settings is non-directed, exploratory, voluntary and personal. Hence, it may be more valuable to look at *how* students are learning than at *what* they have learned. In order to investigate learning specifically during the museum visit, it may therefore be more valid to look at processes which indicate that learning is taking place.

Indicators of engagement in learning process

In a search of the literature looking for clues to indicators of learning processes, these indicators were generally found to be described as behaviours that occur in a positive learning environment. A few researchers have looked at behaviours in museums that could support learning. In their synthesis of this literature, Borun *et al.* (1996) list a number of behaviours related to learning that can be used as useful indicators of learning processes:

> asking and answering questions, talking about an exhibit, pointing to sections of an exhibit, reading label text, engaging in hands-on activities, and even 'gazing' at an exhibit.
>
> (*ibid.*: p.135)

These behaviour descriptions bear a similarity to the components of an intrinsically motivating museum experience listed by Perry (1993): curiosity, confidence, challenge, control, play and communication.

Working at the Lawrence Hall of Science, Linn and Laetsch (1976) described more task-oriented observations that indicated positive conditions for learning, including:

> observing how long students spend with materials, whether they complete the experience, in what order they carry out the activities, whether they leave and return, and whether they talk to other visitors.
>
> (p.376)

Koran *et al.* (1996) describe a study by Foster that uses a mixture of process- and task-oriented indicators:

> Time on task, task preference and verbal fluency were significant predictors of success in learning.
>
> (p.6)

Other writers, outside the museum field, have described favourable learning environments. Bentley and Watts (1994: p.16) describe seven markers of active learners:

1 initiate their own activities and take responsibility for their own learning;
2 make decisions and solve problems;
3 transfer skills from one context to another;
4 can work both as individuals and within a social grouping;
5 display their understanding and competence in a number of different ways;
6 engage in self- and peer-evaluation;
7 feel good [are confident] about themselves as learners.

Faire and Cosgrove (1988: p.28) describe students as learning successfully in science when they:

- offer their own ideas
- back up these views with evidence
- listen to and consider others' ideas
- seek clarification by probing, challenging or investigating others' viewpoints
- extend, modify or change their views when emerging evidence suggests a need
- ask questions about things that are puzzling
- ask further questions that suggest the development of important ideas and attitudes
- have ideas to assist in investigations
- devise their own investigations
- look for patterns, similarities and differences that may exist in observations
- identify ideas held before and after topics
- give reasons for a change in views or for continuing to hold a view
- explore and investigate beyond the topic and school programme
- understand important ideas about their world.

Harlen, in a chapter on indicators for teachers' self-evaluation in *The Teaching of Science* (1992: p.219), lists the following children's activities as a basis for judging learning. This is the extent to which children are:

- spending a high proportion of their time 'on task', talking to each other about their work, being busy with it;
- absorbed in their work, finding it important to them;
- understanding what they are doing, not just following others;
- working at an appropriate level so that their ideas are being used and developed;
- handling or investigating materials to answer their questions;
- using thinking and manipulative skills effectively in advancing their ideas.

Marked similarities exist between these lists of factors that can be readily melded into a useful set of indicators. Before doing so, a few other fields were briefly investigated. An understanding of family group behaviours when they are in a museum indicates the importance of social interaction, emphasised by Vygotsky's (1978) notion that what children can do with the assistance of others might be even more indicative of their learning than what they can do alone.

Two further areas that can be considered to have relevance to different members making up a family group were descriptions of adult learning, and the role of play in learning. Looking into writings on adult learning theory, there is clear congruence between descriptions of learning by adults with that described above for children. Several authors, for example Knowles (1993) and Mathew (1996), provide similar descriptions of adult learning, summarised here:

- adults have a need to know why they should be learning something;
- adults have a deep need to be self-directing;
- to an adult their experience is an integral part of them – they process new knowledge by reviewing it in the light of their experience;
- adults become ready to learn when their life experience provides a need to know;
- adults enter into a learning experience with a task-centred orientation to learning;
- adults are encouraged to learn by both extrinsic and intrinsic motivations;
- adults bring a whole agenda with them to learning situations.

Play is not always considered a significant part of the learning process – particularly beyond the junior primary school stage. Play, however, can lead to the development of skills in observation, experimentation and the testing of ideas (Semper, 1990). Duckworth *et al.* (1990) consider learning itself to be a playful process – it involves toying with ideas in an attempt to reduce complexities until simple and elegant generalisations emerge. This activity involves time to explore and become thoroughly familiar with ideas. Learning is not an efficient process that can be planned, structured, organised and streamlined.

The overwhelming impression that came from reading this literature was the similarity in views from many fields and authors on the conditions that are favourable for learning and the behaviours that reflect the presence of these conditions. Synthesis of this literature led to the development of a set of indicators of engagement in learning, which include both individual and social behaviours. These are shown in Table 7.1. By applying these descriptions to learning within a museum environment, each item can be expanded to create a set of specific indicators of engagement in learning processes within a museum; these are shown in Table 7.2.

Importantly, this tool gives no indication of what is being learned, only that a process is being used which indicates that the student may be learning. Such a tool nevertheless has potential for gauging learning, particularly when used in conjunction with measures of learning outcomes.

Table 7.1 Behaviours indicative of favourable conditions for learning

1	showing responsibility for and initiating their own learning.
2	actively involved in learning.
3	purposefully manipulating and playing with objects and ideas.
4	making links and transferring ideas and skills.
5	sharing learning with peers and experts.
6	showing confidence in personal learning abilities.
7	responding to new information or evidence.

Table 7.2 Indicators of student engagement in learning processes in a museum setting

1	showing responsibility for and initiating their own learning:
	• know what they want to look for/making choices;
	• writing/drawing/taking photos by choice;
	• talking to themselves;
	• deciding where and when to move.
2	actively involved in learning:
	• standing and looking/reading;
	• exhibiting curiosity and interest by engaging with an exhibit;
	• absorbed, close, concentrated examination;
	• persevering with a task, e.g. drawing.
3	purposefully manipulating and playing with objects and ideas:
	• handling exhibits with care and interest;
	• purposefully 'playing' with exhibit elements/using hands-on exhibits as intended.
4	making links and transferring ideas and skills:
	• comparing exhibits;
	• referring to their prepared questions;
	• comparing/referring to previous knowledge/experiences.
5	sharing learning with peers and experts:
	• talking and pointing;
	• pulling others to show them something;
	• willingness to be pulled to see others' interests;
	• group members talking and listening;
	• asking each other questions;
	• talking to adults/experts (teacher or museum staff).
6	showing confidence in personal learning abilities:
	• asking questions of displays;
	• explaining to peers;
	• reading to peers;
	• comparing information with another source.
7	responding to new information or evidence:
	• evidence of changing views;
	• evidence of discovering new ideas.

Applying the set of indicators of engagement

A school group visit to the Australian Museum in Sydney was video-recorded by a technical officer who was unaware of the specifics of the study, and therefore randomly recorded the students as they moved in the museum. About 60 minutes of video-recording was analysed. The recording was not continuous, the camera being turned off and on again as the cameraman moved from one group of students to another, or one area of the exhibit to another. The elapsed time over which the video was recorded was approximately 90 minutes.

On first viewing the videos, notes were taken of each action of individual children or groups of children doing the same thing. When the group's or an individual's behaviour changed, it was recorded as a new action. For example, a pair of students taking notes from a display was recorded as one action. If they then began talking to each other about what they were viewing, this would be recorded as a new action. An action was therefore recorded at each change in action (of the students being filmed) or each change of scene on the videotape. If individual members of a group being filmed were doing different actions, each action was recorded. One hundred student actions were noted in this way.

The noted actions were then compared with the list of indicators of student engagement in learning processes, described above. Using the indicators of engagement in learning specific to museums detailed in Table 7.2, each recorded student action was categorised into one of the seven groups of indicators or recorded as an instance of non-engagement if they did not match any indicator. The video was viewed a second time and again the actions were noted. Where the second viewing revealed different descriptions from the first, the video was viewed a third time and the list of actions finalised. The categorisation process was repeated to confirm reliability of categorisations, and then the frequency of occurrence of each category was determined.

The results of this process revealed that behaviours indicative of engagement in learning processes occurred as follows:

1 showing responsibility for and initiating their own learning: 20 actions noted.
2 actively involved in learning: 20 actions noted.
3 purposefully manipulating and playing with objects and ideas: seven actions noted.
4 making links and transferring skills: 13 actions noted.
5 sharing learning with peers and experts: 26 actions noted.
6 showing confidence in personal learning abilities: nine actions noted.
7 responding to new information or evidence: three actions noted.

On the video-recording, two instances of apparent non-engagement behaviour were noted – one of a child looking into a different gallery, and another of a child sitting, apparently 'resting'.

The significant finding from this analysis was the very high level of these students' engagement in learning processes. The variations in numbers of occurrences of each of the indicators may be affected by the difficulty in determining their occurrence; for example, some indicators rely more heavily than others on having clear audio information as well as visual information for their observance, and ambient noise made some audio recording indistinct.

This set of indicators of engagement in learning processes is neither a sophisticated nor a tested tool. However, it does provide a potential method for determining that conditions for learning are present, even if it does not directly measure learning. Unless the students' attention, described by these indicators, is directed towards something that will increase the students' understanding, learning may not occur.

References

Bentley, D. and Watts, M. (1994). *Primary Science and Technology.* Buckingham: Open University Press.

Birney, B.A. (1995). 'Children, animals, and leisure settings'. *Society and Animals,* 3(2), 171–87.

Bitgood, S., Serrell, B. and Thompson, D. (1994). 'The impact of informal education on visitors to museums'. In V. Crane, H. Nicholson, M. Chen and S. Bitgood (eds) *Informal Science Learning* (pp.61–106). Washington, DC: Research Communication Ltd.

Borun, M., Chambers, M. and Cleghorn, A. (1996). 'Families are learning in science museums'. *Curator,* 39(2), 123–38.

Duckworth, E., Easley, J., Hawkins, D. and Henriques, A. (1990). *Science Education: A Minds-On Approach for the Elementary Years.* London: Lawrence Erlbaum.

Faire, J. and Cosgrove, M. (1988). *Teaching Primary Science.* Hamilton, N.Z.: Waikato Education Centre.

Falk, J.H. and Dierking, L. (1992). *The Museum Experience.* Washington, DC: Whalesback Books.

Falk, J.H., Koran, J.J. and Dierking, L.D. (1986). 'The things of science: assessing the learning potential of science museums'. *Science Education,* 70(5), 503–8.

Harlen, W. (1992). *The Teaching of Science.* London: David Fulton Publishers.

Hein, G.E. (1991). 'Constructivist learning theory'. Paper presented at the ICOM CECA Conference: The Museum and the Needs of People, Jerusalem. 15–22 October.

Hein, G.E. (1995). 'Evaluating teaching and learning in museums'. In E. Hooper-Greenhill (ed.) *Museum, Media, Message* (pp.189–203). London: Routledge.

Knowles, M. (1993). 'Andragogy'. In Z.W. Collins (ed.) *Museums, Adults and the Humanities* (pp.49–60). Washington, DC: American Association of Museums.

Koran, J.J., Koran, M.L., Camp, B.D. and Donnelly, A.E. (1996). 'A summary of recent research and evaluation studies in the University of Florida program on learning in informal settings'. *Visitor Behaviour,* 11(3), 5–8.

Linn, M.C. and Laetsch, W.M. (1976). 'Informed decision making (evaluation you can use)'. Paper presented at the AESOP Conference, Berkeley, California.

Lucas, A.M. (1993). 'Constructing knowledge from fragments of learning?' In P.J. Black and A.M. Lucas (eds) *Children's Informal Ideas in Science* (pp.134–47). London: Routledge.

Matthew, M. (1996). 'Adult learners'. In G. Durbin (ed.) *Developing Museum Exhibitions for Lifelong Learning* (pp.70–2). London: Museums and Galleries Commission.

Perry, D. (1993). 'Designing exhibits that motivate'. In B. Serrell (ed.) *What Research Says about Learning in Science Museums.* Vol. 2 (pp.25–9). Washington, DC: Association of Science–Technology Centers.

Ramey-Gassert, L., Walberg, H.J.I. and Walberg, H.J. (1994). 'Reexamining connections: museums as science learning environments'. *Science Education,* 78(4), 345–63.

Semper, R.J. (1990). 'Science museums as environments for learning'. *Physics Today,* Nov. 1990, 50–6.

Sheppard, B. (1993). 'Aspects of a successful field trip'. In B. Sheppard (ed.) *Building Museum and School Partnerships*. Washington, DC: American Association of Museums.

Voris, H., Sedzielarz, M. and Blackmon, C. (1986). *Teach the Mind, Touch the Spirit*. Chicago: Field Museum of Natural History.

Vygotsky, L.S. (1978). *Mind in Society*. Cambridge, Mass.: Harvard University Press.

Chapter 8

The word and the world
Engaging with science in print*

J. Turney

> In the old days, we had journalists writing up and scientists writing down.
> Now educated people want the real stuff from the horse's mouth.
>
> John Brockman, quoted in Rodgers (1992: p.232)

Words on the page

How much can one understand about the world by studying words on a page? The question is as old as reading (Manguel, 1996) but has acquired a new edge in the last decade. For one thing, much of the recent emphasis in discussion of learning about science has been on discovery methods – as exemplified by developments in the school curriculum beginning in the 1960s. Then along came the science centres movement, which conveyed something of scientific principles through interaction with 'hands-on' exhibits, which have been considered in the previous three chapters.

At the same time, a succession of new schools of literary criticism have each emphasised, in their different ways, how textual worlds are constructed, and have denied authors the right to prescribe how their stories should be read. And yet, in spite of these concurrent trends, we are in the midst of a boom in popular science publishing. The writing, selling and – apparently – reading of that ostensibly old-fashioned commodity, the popular science book, has become much more prominent in the English-speaking world since the mid-1980s than it was in the previous two decades.

These books, some by professional 'science writers' but many by working scientists, lend a new edge to the question of what one can learn through text, because, of course, it is the contention of an account of science that it conveys some truth about how the world is to be understood – about 'the way things are'. Yet all the authors can use to convey their truths is their skill in story-telling, and in the arts of rhetoric. They cannot offer any *direct* experience of what they are describing, although they appear to be giving readers access to

*Newly commissioned.

aspects of reality they do not encounter in any other way, just as books always have. In some ways, text may be a poor substitute for direct experience of natural phenomena. Yet for many of us, artfully constructed texts seem a perfectly satisfactory way of finding out what we would experience if we had the opportunity of more direct contact with the phenomena.

The boom in popular writing about science has been widely remarked upon and is commonly ascribed to the spectacular success of the cosmologist Stephen Hawking's *A Brief History of Time*, published in 1988. It is true that the book was a runaway bestseller, shifting four and a half million copies in a little over three years, and is still selling today (Rodgers, 1992). But other scientists like the physicist Paul Davies and the evolutionary biologist Richard Dawkins were doing respectable business before Hawking, and many more have followed. The result goes far beyond what is frequently taken to be the previous heyday of popular writing by scientists, the 1930s, when authors like Arthur Eddington and James Jeans sold tens of thousands of copies of books about the new physics (Vincent, 1997). There are many more authors involved, and more whose books are seen as publishing 'events'. But most comment on the impact of the new wave of popular science has been from journalists. So far it has attracted little in the way of academic analysis.

This chapter, then, is one attempt to prepare the ground for such an analysis. With the profusion of science books now appearing, my comments will have to be very selective, but I want to highlight two questions in particular. First, what motivates the current crop of popular writers about science? And second, *if* their aims are straightforwardly educational, how much science can they actually convey? What limitations do they have compared, say, with formal study? Or what can professional science communication do that popular science cannot – and, maybe, vice versa?

Varieties of scientific experience

Julian Huxley, in the process of carving out a niche for himself as a popular science writer in the 1920s, offered a simple credo: that it is part of a scientist's duty 'to make available to the lay public the facts and theories of their science, and especially to try and re-create something of the mental background that is engendered by those facts and theories' (Huxley, 1926: p.v). But this is only part of the story. A moment's reflection on popular science shows that it is not a single, simple genre, or even a single type of book. This is not surprising, as it is most often defined by exclusion. It is writing about science that is not intended for an exclusively professional audience. As such, there are obviously a variety of occasions for popular science writing. The category 'popular science' stretches easily to include the following:

- *Biography* Telling the life of the scientist is likely to involve explaining something of their science, as in recent biographies of Alan Turing, Richard Feynman, Stephen Hawking and Isaac Newton.

- *Autobiography*   The necessary complement to biography, though probably more diverse. It includes 'scientific autobiographies' like Francis Crick's *What Mad Pursuit?*, which are designed mainly to show how science is done, autobiographies that are as much about the life as the science, like Francois Jacob's *The Statue Within*, and stories of 'how it was' at the time some important piece of science got done. The best-known example of the latter is, of course, James Watson's account of the solution of DNA's structure in *The Double Helix*, which Sir Peter Medawar dubbed the first example of a new genre, the scientific memoir.

- *How to/self-help/information books*   Non-fiction books with a specific pedagogic purpose, telling you how to build your own computer, how to manage your disease, or how to identify the fossil that you have just unearthed. These are closely akin to textbooks but assume a different relation with the reader.

- *Dictionaries or primers for scientific literacy*   There has been a recent rash of books like this, mostly from the United States, with titles like *The Techno/Peasant Survival Manual, 1001 Things Everyone Should Know About Science* or the *Dictionary of Scientific Literacy*. Typically, these are books that tell you what the facts of established science are, without much discussion of where they came from. They are distant descendants of an old lineage, dating back to the nineteenth century at least, but perhaps most famously exemplified by Lancelot Hogben's 1940 volume *Science for the Citizen*. Note, though, that if you actually take a look at *Science for the Citizen*, it is much more like a technical primer than such books are today, making considerable use of simple mathematics, and setting the reader problems at the end of each chapter. Hogben described his books in this vein as 'self-educators' rather than works of popularisation.

- *Intellectual entertainment*   This is probably what most people mean by 'popular science'. There is further diversity within this category, and many of the books clearly have a purpose beyond simple entertainment. Some want to argue for one side of a particular controversy, either inside science or outside. Some are concerned with what one might call problematic science – as with books that consider the ethical problems that might arise from the human genome project. Some want to debunk what the authors regard as pseudoscientific beliefs. Some have higher-level metaphysical messages to convey, or are partly or mainly concerned with 'metascientific issues' like the nature of scientific knowledge.

I am not going to list examples of all these categories – they are neither mutually exclusive nor exhaustive. It is also important to stress that there are no clear divisions between this category and professional scientific communication. Clearly, trade books published for a general readership make different demands on their authors from papers in primary scientific journals. But it makes more sense to see both as part of a continuum of science communication than as separate activities. 'Popularisations' are important for interdisciplinary and even intra-disciplinary communication, as Michele Cloitre and Terry Shinn point out in a pioneering scholarly essay on popular science.

In truth, popular texts by scientists often serve multiple ends. They may be pursuing an argument with colleagues, advertising a new research programme, or trying to persuade lay people to think about a particular set of problems in a new way. Even when the main motive is to explain complex ideas to non-professionals, the result is woven into the complex webs of science communication in ways that are often unpredictable. As one of the most successful British science writers, Richard Dawkins reflected in the second edition of *The Selfish Gene*:

> Expounding ideas that have hitherto appeared only in the technical literature is a difficult art. It requires insightful new twists of language and revealing metaphors. If you push novelty of language and metaphor far enough, you can end up with a new way of seeing. And a new way of seeing . . . can in its own right make an original contribution to science.
>
> (1989: p.ix)

A good recent example of these continuities is Antonio R. Damasio's *Descartes' Error: Emotion, Reason and the Human Brain* (1996). This is clearly a book addressed to the general reader – it is personal, recounting the author's intellectual autobiography, anecdotal, and full of allusions, asides and aphorisms. Damasio tells us that he wrote it as one side of a conversation with an imaginary friend. The impression he tries to create is that of sharing in a scientist's thoughts as he struggles with a problem.

However, the book is not only aimed at the non-scientific reader. It is also a new synthesis of Damasio's ideas about how emotion and reason interact, advancing, as he says 'a departure from current neurobiological thinking' (*ibid.*: p.xvi). So the book is a popularisation in the straightforward sense, but it is also an extended attempt to persuade his fellow neurobiologists of the virtues of his approach. It is about 'established facts, about facts in doubt, and about hypotheses, even when I could come up with nothing but hunches to support them' (*ibid.*: p.xx). It contains all the elements of his thinking, in other words, that he would be obliged to expunge from a scientific paper.

But the convenience of publishing them in this form is that citation then makes the book a vehicle for importing these ideas, at least by implication, into the professional literature. And other researchers can indicate their sympathy for his position, or use it to bolster acceptability of their own results, as suggested by the appearance of citations to the book in conventional scientific papers (Drevets *et al.*, 1997).

Damasio's 'popular' book is partly intended as a lengthy statement of the case for a particular research programme in neurobiology. And his book is not the only recent example of its type. Francis Crick's *The Astonishing Hypothesis* is in large part an attempt to convince fellow scientists that it is time to try to solve the problems of consciousness by doing experiments on the brain (Crick, 1994). As he said at the time of publication, 'I most hope it will influence the scientists in the field - especially the young scientists who will nag the older ones' (Turney, 1994: p.17). Other, more heterodox scientists, like biologist Brian Goodwin, James Lovelock, author of the Gaia hypothesis, or Roger Penrose, the physicist and mathematician, who has developed a position on consciousness and artificial intelligence that takes issue with the assumptions of many working in the field, have all advanced their ideas in popular books. None of them appears to have any great difficulty publishing in the professional literature, but they want to address a broader constituency.

So the motives of popular science authors are commonly mixed. But whatever their ambitions to influence public or scientific opinion, their work invariably involves them in explaining aspects of their science in non-technical language. How successful are they in this regard? Indeed, how successful *can* they be when they eschew the technical conventions of their disciplines and adopt unadorned English prose?

Reading is believing

Communicating about science, and persuading others that one's results are sound, has relied heavily on written accounts ever since the scientific revolution. In this light, Steven Shapin argues that the processes of professional and popular communication are essentially similar:

> The popularization of science is usually understood as the extension of experience from the few to the many. I argue . . . that one of the major resources for generating and validating items of knowledge within the scientific community under study was this same extension of experience from the few to the many: the creation of a scientific public.
>
> (1984: p.481)

Shapin is describing the style of experimental reporting developed by Robert Boyle in the late seventeenth century. The modern, specialised scientific paper, largely purged of recognisable 'literary style' by the end of the nineteenth century, is its functional descendant (Montgomery, 1996). But the difficulty that the uninitiated have in reading a scientific journal article intended for a few professionals in the same sub-field reminds us that this kind of reading is dependent on other, perhaps more direct, ways of finding out about science.

Considering these other ways of fathoming what science can tell us about the world helps to underline how much work textual accounts of science for lay readers have to do to create their understandings of the way things are. Since Boyle, we take it for granted that the most direct way to acquire knowledge of the natural world is to do experiments. Working researchers, of course, expend enormous efforts trying to devise workable experiments, and then making them go. When they read scientific papers describing experiments by others, they can be understood in terms of their own practical experience, and their own continuing conversations with other practitioners. One does not learn how to do experiments by reading papers but by working with more experienced researchers in the laboratory.

Experiments then have to be accounted for, and this is done through text. But it has also always been done through demonstration, first for scientific peers, then in popular lectures and in the classroom. In Boyle's time, demonstrations were originally a way of establishing matters of fact by multiplying witnesses. Now, they are the stuff of the Royal Institution Christmas Lectures, or of the secondary school classroom. They are carefully orchestrated exercises in 'putting meaning into matter', as one recent account of classroom science puts it (Ogborn *et al.*, 1996: p.15). Most of the 'hands-on' exhibits in contemporary science centres are also based on demonstrations of this kind.

Finally, even a classroom teacher who is not putting on a demonstration still has a range of resources to draw on – including interaction with the group, gesture and tone of voice, and the presentation of images or diagrams with a commentary tailored to the moment. Most of these resources are also available to the film-maker trying to explain science.

A popular science text has somehow to emulate the persuasive power of all these practices – experiments and the technical reporting of experiments, demonstrations and 'live' explanations – using everyday words on the page. True, many make use of images and diagrams, but the words are almost always doing most of the work. The primary relationship is between writer and reader. The writer has to *describe* observations, experiments, reports, even demonstrations, in such a way that the reader believes in them, and believes that they signify what is claimed. And he or she has to impart some understanding of the concepts in terms of which they are being interpreted. It is a testament to the flexibility of written language that even the most esoteric science is treated in so many popular books, and that texts can be composed in ways that reproduce, indirectly, some of the more direct experiences of natural science. But perhaps it is also fair to say that reproduction of these experiences through text requires, above all, success in *persuasion* – success in persuading readers that reality is as it is described and success in persuading them that they understand it.

Baudouin Jurdant has discussed the first requirement illuminatingly, focusing on the paradoxical position of popular science as a literary form that wants to make truth claims stronger than those normally granted to literature. As he puts it: 'if popularization of science is so difficult to consider as a part of literature, it is because it must deny belonging to it. Without such a denial, its truth claims would not be plausible and its reference to realities would become empty' (1993: p.370). Here, though, I want to concentrate on understanding. What might we expect to be achievable in a popular book? Some kinds of understanding are quite clearly going to be well out of reach. It is generally assumed that any kind of advanced mathematics is beyond the grasp of the general reader. Some classical theorems and results are quite often *described*, Godel's theorem being perhaps the most popular, but the majority of popular books eschew all but the simplest equations, and apologise for those. Stephen Hawking famously reports that he was advised that every equation would reduce the number of potential readers of his proposed book by half. He eradicated all the many equations from his draft, with the single exception of Einstein's iconic $E = mc^2$. So like other authors he observed a self-denying ordinance that forbids use of the formal language on which much of modern science depends for its most precise expression. I will come back to the implications of this for expository work in popular science at the end of the paper.

Nor will the reader of popular science books discover in any detail how to carry out experiments. As we have already said, no-one becomes a competent experimenter by reading, even though the biomedical sciences often rely on compendious 'recipe books' of experimental technique for laboratory reference. And it is not the intent of any of these authors to describe the real detail of experiments. So the reader will not find in these texts either the details of scientific practice or of its results as they would be discussed by professionals. What, then is being popularised? Or, as Shapin put it, what kind of experience is being extended from the few to the many?

One way of getting a sense of the kind of experience on offer is by examining perhaps the most widely read (certainly the most widely bought) popular science book of recent times, *A Brief History of Time*. As Michael White and John Gribbin tell the story in their biography of Hawking, the main motive behind the book was financial. Hawking wanted security for his family and support for his own medical expenses and nursing care, and hoped that a successful book would do the trick. He was quickly told that his rough drafts were far too technical, and not just because of their use of what he regarded as simple mathematics. A colleague at Cambridge University Press who examined them told the prospective author: 'It's like baked beans. The blander the flavour the broader the market. There simply isn't a commercial niche for specialist books like this' (White and Gribbin, 1992: p.222).

Later, when he had secured a suitably large advance from the American publisher Bantam, he had an enormously detailed editorial advice on further drafts – this after turning down his agent's earlier suggestion that he bring in a professional writer as co-author. The same agent later suggested that 'I would guess that, for every page of text [the editor] wrote two or three pages of editorial letters, all in an attempt to get Hawking to elaborate on ideas that his mind jumps over, but that other people wouldn't understand' (*ibid*.: p.229).

The book that resulted, as is well-known, was an attempt to address the questions that Hawking said had led him to cosmology in the first place: Where did the universe come from? How and why did it begin? Will it come to an end, and if so, how? Having eschewed mathematics, the author described his explanatory goals as follows: 'I think in pictorial terms and my main aim in the book was to describe these mental images in words with the help of familiar images and a few diagrams' (Hawking, 1993: p.31).

Hawking's explanatory techniques are similar to those of other popular science writers. Katherine Rowan (1992) suggests that there are three basic ways in which a reader may misunderstand a piece of technical exposition, and three corresponding kinds of explanation to help them get over such misunderstandings. If the problem is failure to grasp the meaning or use of a particular word, the relatively straightforward answer is an elucidating explanation that gives the critical features of a concept, with examples. A more demanding case is where lack of understanding stems from a failure to make a useful mental model of some phenomenon, to register what it is *like* in a way that makes sense to the reader. This calls for what Rowan terms a quasi-scientific explanation, which is intended to help one to model some unfamilar aspect of reality. The third difficulty is a complication of the second, when the reader fails to replace an existing mental model or structure of images with a new one that is more appropriate for the subject matter. This requires what she calls a transformative explanation – explaining, perhaps, why the 'hole' in the ozone layer is not really a hole.

Of the three, transformative explanations tend to be the most demanding. And as the science Hawking wishes to introduce is many stages beyond our common understanding, this is the kind he has most need of. Take his treatment of gravity in *A Brief History of Time*, for example. He begins with the familiar Newtonian view of gravity, that 'each body in the universe was attracted to every other body' (p.4) and states the relation between force, mass and distance in two stages. First, he tells us that 'the force between two bodies would be twice as strong if one of the bodies (say, body A) had its mass doubled' (p.16), then that 'gravitational attraction of a star is exactly one quarter that of a star at half the distance' (p.17).

He goes on to say that Newton's gravity predicts the orbit of the Earth around the Sun. However, this view is transformed during the subsequent exposition of Einstein's relativistic account of gravity. Now we discover that 'Einstein made the revolutionary suggestion that gravity is not a force like other forces, but is a consequence of the fact that space–time is not flat . . . it is curved or "warped" by the distribution of mass and energy in it' (p.29). A consequence of this view is that 'the mass of the Sun curves space–time in such a way that although the Earth follows a straight path in four-dimensional space–time, it appears to move along a circular orbit in three-dimensional space' (p.30).

Here, Hawking is following many other popular writers in offering a transforming explanation that follows the historical course of physical theory, but without benefit of any of the mathematical tools that allowed the theorists involved to rethink their own frameworks. He follows the same, essentially descriptive, path in offering the further transformation incorporated in the quantum theory of gravity. Seventy pages after being introduced to Newtonian gravity, we are told that:

> In the quantum mechanical way of looking at the gravitational field, the force between two matter particles is pictured as being carried by a particle of spin 2 called the graviton. This has no mass of its own, so the force that it carries is long range. The gravitational force between the Sun and the Earth is ascribed to the exchange of gravitons between the particles which make up these two bodies. Although the exchanged particles are virtual, they certainly do produce a measurable effect – they make the Earth orbit the Sun!
>
> (p.70)

This passage occurs in a 16-page chapter on 'Elementary particles and the forces of nature' and is the first of four short specifications of the four 'categories' of fundamental forces – gravity, electromagnetism, and the strong and weak nuclear forces. The chapter begins with an extremely brief historical recapitulation of transformations in ideas about atoms, then describes how quantum mechanics indicates that forces are carried between matter particles by virtual particles, of which the graviton is the first example discussed. We have also been reminded of wave–particle duality, discussed in an earlier chapter, and the gravitational passage concludes with the observation that 'real gravitons make up what classical physicists would call gravitational waves, which are very weak – and so difficult to detect that they have never yet been observed' (p.70).

Almost the whole chapter, highly compressed to match the rest of the book, is written in this very spare descriptive style, with virtually no analogies, or even adjectives. The only exception is a short passage explaining that what physicists mean by particle 'spin' is not the everyday meaning of the term, which includes a diagram picturing two playing cards.

The scheme for the four fundamental forces, and their partial unification, which Hawking outlines in these few pages, summarises most of the new physics of the middle part of the twentieth century. What the naive reader might make of it is hard to tell. It deals with concepts far outside everyday experience, describing entities whose behaviour does not conform to our normal intuitions. There is very little attempt here, it seems to me, to refer back to the frameworks that we probably try to apply to such a description to help us to visualise what might be going on, or to encourage us to adapt our world view to incorporate the existence of the strange phenomena being described. Even the discussion of spin asserts bluntly that one must not think of it as describing particles spinning like little tops around an axis, 'because quantum mechanics tells us that the particles do not have any well-defined axis' (p.66). Generally speaking, we are simply given the new framework, put in as few words as possible rather than in a system of equations, and the mind is left to scrabble away at imagining what kind of stuff the particles are, not to mention the virtual particles. If good expository writing tries to anticipate questions arising in the reader's mind, and answer them before they create unease or incomprehension, there are surely many questions here left unanswered.

But perhaps looking for an adequate transformative explanation of particle physics in a popular book is applying a test that is impossible to pass. Like Hawking, other popular science authors often describe their aims as to offer an exposition of the way scientists think. By this I mean both the kinds of entities that they think about and how they understand their relation to everyday experience. The overall intention may be to enlarge or alter the world view of the reader so that it accommodates some of the notions that are important to the scientists working in the area under discussion, rather than to impart a detailed understanding. There is, after all, no examination at the end.

Lawrence Krauss has worked towards such a goal in *Fear of Physics*. 'My intent', he writes, 'is more to present the flavor of physics than it is to master its substance. I think it is insight, rather than a working knowledge, that is most useful and is needed by nonscientists in today's world, and so it is insight that I am aiming at' (1996: p.xi). This, it appears, is a kind of inversion of Julian Huxley's credo quoted above – not re-creating the mental background *engendered by* facts and theories, but trying to convey the mental background that *engenders* those facts and theories.

This approach stems in part from an honest recognition of the limitations of what can be achieved in a popular book. They are, inevitably, impressionistic, and it is easy to find well-founded expressions of scepticism about claims to offer more than an impression of some crucial areas of science. Carl Sagan, no mean popular writer himself, wrote a laudatory forword for *A Brief History of Time*. But elsewhere he is more sceptical about the results of such efforts:

> Imagine you seriously want to understand what quantum mechanics is about. There is a mathematical underpinning that you must first acquire, mastery of each mathematical subdiscipline leading you to the threshold of the next. In turn you must learn arithmetic, Euclidean geometry, high school algebra, differential and integral calculus, ordinary and partial differential equations, vector calculus, certain special functions of mathematical physics, matrix algebra, and group theory. For most physics students, this might occupy them from, say, third grade to early graduate school – roughly fifteen years. Such a course of study does not actually involve learning any quantum mechanics, but merely establishing the mathematical framework required to approach it deeply. . . .
>
>   The job of the popularizer of science, trying to get across some idea of quantum mechanics to a general audience that has not undergone these initiation rites, is daunting. Indeed, there are no successful popularizations of quantum mechanics in my opinion, partly for this reason.
>
>   (1997: p.237)

So is quantum mechanics a special case, or does it point towards a more general limitation in popular writing? Taking a view on this involves considering the role and utility of metaphors and analogies for explaining and understanding science. In many fields, the indispensability of metaphor for communicating scientific ideas to non-professionals is not a barrier to popular writing. Rather, the writing blends seamlessly with the use of metaphor in technical or theoretical discourse. This is not the place to review the literature on metaphor and science, but I sympathise with Boyd's conclusion that 'the use of metaphor is one of many devices available to the scientific community to accomplish the task of accommodating language to the causal structure of the world' (1993: p.483).

The would-be populariser then has a choice: to elaborate the metaphors already built into the conceptual structure of the field, perhaps in ways that would not be legitimate in the technical discourse, or to coin new ones. Again, the effect may well be to influence the technical understanding of the field in question, as my earlier quotation from Richard Dawkins suggests.

Dawkins' popular books provide an excellent example of the different roles that metaphors can play here. His technique in each book is similar, in that each is structured around a single guiding metaphor, always signalled in the title. But the metaphors he uses are, it seems to me, different in kind. His first and most controversial book, *The Selfish Gene*, reformulates ideas from neo-Darwinian theory about inclusive fitness in such a compelling manner that many Darwinian theorists still work under its influence. *The Blind Watchmaker* (1986) builds from a very old analogy in discussion of evolution and objections to the argument from design. *River out of Eden* (1995) is an extended meditation on a new analogy, coined for the occasion, that likens the flow of genes through time to an ever-branching stream, and speciation to separation of the branches. *Climbing Mount Improbable* (1996), by contrast, is based on a relatively straightforward reworking of a standard idea in the field – that of so-called fitness landscapes, with peaks and troughs that represent particular possible states of an evolving organism in its environment.

Dawkins also makes regular use of other metaphors, which often turn into subsidiary motifs as he gets into his expository stride. In *The Blind Watchmaker*, for example, he offers the notion that genes are a recipe as a better metaphor for what genetic instructions are than the often-used blueprint metaphor. 'A recipe in a cookbook', he writes late in the book in a discussion of embryology, 'is not in any sense a blueprint for the cake that will finally emerge from the oven' (p.295). He then devotes a long paragraph to explaining in detail exactly why a recipe is different from a blueprint, and asserts after this that 'the indications are very strong that the genes are much more like a recipe than like a blueprint' (p.296).

Having established the grounds of the metaphor in such detail, he then has a new framework established in the reader's mind that can easily accommodate the further additions he wants to make, such as that:

embryonic development is a process. It is an orderly sequence of events, like the procedure for making a cake, except that there are millions more steps in the process and different steps are going on simultaneously in many different parts of the 'dish'.

(p. 296)

This is a more elaborate use of metaphor than almost anything in Hawking's book, and a very effective one. But it is something that the concepts of information in the life sciences seem to lend themselves to particularly well. Even critics of Dawkins' brand of Darwinism, like biologists Steven Rose and Brian Goodwin, argue their case in terms of better, or more insightful, metaphors, rather than suggesting that the use of metaphor itself is impermissible, or unhelpful.

But what about the phenomena studied by other sciences, especially the physics that Sagan highlights? Here, just as there is a strong argument that it is misleading to pretend to explain quantum mechanics to someone who has not studied the mathematics required, there are also arguments that the traditional advice to popular writers to use metaphors and analogies runs into the buffers.

These have been put most clearly by John Barrow in an article in which he develops points that he touches on more briefly in his popular book about the nature of mathematics, *Pi in the Sky* (Barrow, 1993). Analogies as a pedagogic device are fine, says Barrow, but only up to a point. He demonstrates where that point might be through a discussion of *A Brief History of Time*, and in particular its rendition of Hawking's ideas about the initial quantum state of the universe.

Many readers have difficulty with this notion, Barrow suggests, because it involves time becoming 'another dimension of space' in the gravitational environment of the Big Bang. But what use is this assertion that time becomes another dimension of space, asks Barrow? 'We know what every word in this statement means. It makes sense in ordinary English in some vague way that makes us think we understand its content. But is any meaningful information conveyed to the lay reader? The answer is probably "no"' (p.15–16). The reason, he argues, is that this is a scientific idea which does not fit any analogy we can think of. 'One cannot say time becomes space is like a chrysalis becoming a butterfly or a water droplet evaporating or whatever. It is more like "the sound of one hand clapping". It is just a bare statement of mathematical reality' (p.15–16).

The question then is whether this and similarly intractable concepts in theoretical physics and cosmology – superstrings come to mind – are simply waiting for a sufficiently ingenious writer to come along, or do they signal something more profound? Barrow thinks that they do. When no analogy exists for some new idea that is described mathematically, he suggests, that is a sign that it really is a *new* idea, that we are really getting somewhere in the effort to gain a fundamental understanding of the world. 'When analogies from everyday experience are not readily available to illustrate new ideas in fundamental science it may be a good sign that we are touching some brute fact of reality that cares not one whit whether there exist analogues elsewhere in the world' (p.15–16).

Maintaining this position, as Barrow is well aware, raises further, philosophical, questions about whether the true language of realism is the language of mathematics. Either way, it suggests one limit on the kind of understanding that can be conveyed through popular writing which will be extremely difficult to overcome. But that does not diminish the importance of the fact that many people's informal learning of science is largely through reading selections from the current profusion of popular books. Nor does it seem likely to deter eager authors from trying to outdo Hawking in their efforts to explain science to such readers.

Acknowledgement

I would like to thank the students on my undergraduate course in Rhetorics of Popular Science at University College London for discussion which helped to develop and refine the ideas in this chapter.

References

Barrow, J. (1993). 'In the world's image', *Times Higher Education Supplement*, April 16, pp. 15–16.

Boyd, R. (1993). 'Metaphor and theory change: What is "metaphor" a metaphor for?' in Ortony A. (ed.), *Metaphor and Thought*, 2nd edition. Cambridge University Press.

Brockman, J. and Matson, K. (eds) (1995). *How Things Are – A Science Tool-Kit for the Mind*, Weidenfeld & Nicolson.

Crick, F. (1994). *The Astonishing Hypothesis*, Touchstone Books.

Damasio, A. (1996). *Descartes' Error – Emotion, Reason and the Human Brain*, Papermac.

Dawkins, R. (1986). *The Blind Watchmaker*, Longman.

Dawkins, R. (1989). *The Selfish Gene*, 2nd edition. Oxford University Press.

Dawkins, R. (1995). *River out of Eden*, Weidenfeld & Nicolson.

Dawkins, R. (1996). *Climbing Mount Improbable*, Viking.

Drevets, W. *et al.* (1997) 'Subgenual prefrontal cortex abnormalities in mood disorders'. *Nature*, 386, 24 April, 824–7.

Hawking, S. (1988). *A Brief History of Time*, Bantam.

Hawking, S. (1993). *Black Holes and Baby Universes*, Bantam.

Hogben, L. (1940). *Science for the Citizen: A Self-Educator Based on the Social Background of Scientific Discovery*, Allen & Unwin.

Huxley, J. (1926). *Essays in Popular Science*, Pelican (1937), p.v. (First published 1926.)

Jurdant, B. (1993). 'Popularization of science as the autobiography of science', *Public Understanding of Science*, 2, 365–73.

Krauss, L. (1996). *Fear of Physics – A Guide for the Perplexed*, Vintage.

Manguel, A. (1996). *A History of Reading*, HarperCollins.

Montgomery, S. (1996). *The Scientific Voice*, 'In Equal Number of Words: Notes for a History of Scientific Discourse', New York, Guilford Press.

Ogborn, J., Kress, G., Martins, I. and McGillicuddy, K. (1996). *Explaining Science in the Classroom*, Buckingham, Open University Press.

Rodgers, M. (1992). 'The Hawking phenomenon', *Public Understanding of Science*, 1, 231–5.

Rowan, K. (1992). 'Strategies for enhancing comprehension of science', in Lewenstein, B. (ed.) *When Science Meets the Public*, AAAS.

Sagan, C. (1997). *The Demon-Haunted World – Science as a Candle in the Dark*, Hodder Headline.

Shapin, S. (1984). 'Pump and Circumstance: Robert Boyle's Literary Technology', *Social Studies of Science*, vol. 4, 481–520.

Shinn, T. and Whitley, R. (1985). 'Expository Science: Forms and Functions of Popularization', in *Sociology of the Sciences Yearbook*. Dordrecht, Reidel.

Turney, J. (1994). 'Mind over matter', *Times Higher Education Supplement*, May 17.

Vincent, B. (1997). 'In the name of science', in Krige, J. and Pestre, D. (eds) *Science in the Twentieth Century*. Harwood Academic.

White, M. and Gribbin, J. (1992). *Stephen Hawking – A Life in Science*, Viking.

Chapter 9

Einstein for young people*

R. Stannard

Introduction

At first sight, the *Uncle Albert* trilogy[1] seems to consist of science fiction adventure stories much like any others. They can be read purely for enjoyment and relaxation. Indeed, when it appeared in 1989, the first tale in the series, *The Time and Space of Uncle Albert*, was shortlisted for the Whitbread Children's Novel of the Year.

But these are no ordinary stories of journeys into space. The girl character piloting the spacecraft is named Gedanken. Her mission? To experience the 'thought (or *gedanken*) experiments' of Einstein. The properties of space and time, and the behaviour of matter at the subatomic level, are as bizarre as any that can be found in science fiction – only these are science *facts*. Behind the fun and excitement of the storyline, there lies a serious educational intention: to introduce young people of 11–12 years to Einstein's theory of relativity, and to quantum theory.

How successful are the books? They are certainly popular. Currently they are in 15 translations. The third book in the series, *Uncle Albert and the Quantum Quest*, became the Number 1 children's best-selling book for a month, even reaching Number 5 in the overall (adult) paperback bestseller list for a week! Furthermore, developmental testing of the books prior to their publication reveals that many children learn a considerable amount of physics from them – sufficient to encourage the Institute of Physics to distribute free copies of the first book to all its 1,000 affiliated schools. The books have been shortlisted for the Rhone-Poulenc Children's Non-fictional Science Book Prize.

Motivation

But why attempt such a task in the first place? There are several reasons. For a start it is surely a scandal that almost a hundred years since its formulation, the ideas of relativity theory have yet to be absorbed into the common culture.

*Newly commissioned.

Unlike, for example, the theory of evolution by natural selection, it plays no part in the thinking of most people, even those highly educated in other fields. Relativity, to say nothing of quantum theory, has gained such a reputation for being 'difficult' that most people automatically assume themselves to be incapable of understanding it. It is important therefore to get in quick before children have a chance to learn that they are not supposed to be able to understand such matters. In addition, a book ostensibly aimed at young children might encourage adults to give it a try.

The findings of relativity are strange. For example, no matter how hard you push, you cannot make anything exceed the ultimate speed barrier – the speed of light (300,000 kilometres per second). As that limit is approached, space squashes up and time slows down (you could live for ever!). Whether two events occurring at different locations are to be regarded as taking place simultaneously, or one after the other, depends on your state of motion relative to them. Relativity theory further reveals that inert matter, such as the chair you are sitting on, is an enormous stockpile of locked-up energy – an idea summed up in the equation linking mass (m) to energy (E) through the speed of light (c): $E = mc^2$.

Such consequences appear to defy common sense. But it was Einstein himself who once dismissed common sense as 'that layer of prejudice laid down in the mind before the age of 18'. If this is so, it can again be argued that one's first acquaintance with modern physics should occur as early as possible – before one's thinking has become too set in its ways.

Besides enriching the culture generally, a greater awareness of relativity could lead to more people being encouraged to study physics seriously. A survey has shown that it is the prospect of studying *modern* physics (special and general relativity, elementary particles, quantum theory, and astrophysics) that has the most influence in persuading students to study physics at university level.[2] Yet little is done systematically to introduce young people to these 'shop window' topics at school. It is largely left to chance whether children casually pick them up through the press or television. Not that one wishes to denigrate the importance of laying a good school grounding in traditional classical physics. What is advocated is a balance – one struck between what physics teachers know students *ought* to learn and what the students themselves *want* to learn. Rather than taking students' interest for granted, we must capture and stimulate it by consciously and deliberately seeking ways of making physics more attractive.

A further reason for trying to approach the frontiers of physics as quickly and economically as possible has to do with the needs of the exceptionally gifted child – the Einsteins of the future. So often one finds radically new physical ideas springing from the flexible minds of theoretical physicists at the commencement of their professional careers – in their twenties. Though the work of their later years might rank as good solid achievement, it is unlikely to have the audacity of their first forays into the unknown. So how can we encourage this flexible thinking?

To push back the frontiers of knowledge, the researcher has to know enough physics to appreciate what the outstanding problems are. But in gaining that essential background, it is difficult not to succumb to the particular mind set in which that information has been couched – a mind set that has so far failed to lead to a solution of the problem in hand. The researcher, having absorbed the information, has then to break the mould of that conventional thinking and see the problem from a different angle. Openness to lateral thinking of this type seems to be the hallmark of the younger mind. Later in life, it becomes increasingly difficult to resist being made to conform to whatever is the prevailing world view. By not imposing the strait-jacket of classical thinking on young children, allowing them from their earliest days to know that Newtonian mechanics, despite its indispensable usefulness, is but an approximation to the truth – moreover, one based on a totally erroneous view of the nature of space and time – we might hope to induce a greater flexibility of thinking, especially in the mind of the budding theoretical physicist.

Such then are the reasons for trying to introduce Einstein's ideas to children.

Readiness for modern physics

> Any subject can be taught effectively in some intellectually honest form to any child at any stage of development.

This well-known statement by US child psychologist Jerome Bruner[3] was the trigger for the project. Without the encouragement of that positive, optimistic pronouncement, a start would never have been made. However, it still left unresolved the question: at which age precisely should the project be aimed? Though it is desirable to reach the youngest possible age group, it is also required that the children should have reached a stage in their cognitive development where their ability to benefit is at a sufficiently useful level of understanding to make the project worth while.

There are various preconditions for appreciating relativity: the child first needs a basic understanding of what is meant by the terms 'space', 'time' and 'speed' (the latter being distinguished from 'acceleration'). Then, in order to appreciate the significance of the idea that objects behave as though they are heavier at high speed, there needs to be an awareness of what it is for certain physical properties to be constant. Matter–energy interchange requires an intuitive knowledge of energy and an acquaintance with the idea of conservation. It is further necessary to be able to imagine hypothetical situations that are simple extensions of everyday experience – for example, what it would be like to go faster and faster.

According to Piaget and his co-workers,[4] these various requirements are met when a child reaches a stage in its development known as the late concrete operations period (COP). Equipped with such abilities, a child might at least be able to accept an account of relativistic effects as a *description* of what happens. Appreciation of the *reason* for these effects, however, might be another matter. Further demands are made in order to be able to accept that all the effects stem from (1) the fact that all observers, regardless of their motion relative to each other, find the same value for the speed of light; and (2) the Principle of Relativity, which states that the laws of physics are the same for everyone in uniform relative motion (hence there is no way of choosing a privileged observer who is stationary in any absolute sense – crudely speaking, 'all motion is relative').

In order to grasp this, the child must in the first place have developed a facility for being able to think of situations from different points of view – those representing observers in relative motion. This entails a rather sophisticated measure of 'freedom from egocentricity' – as cognitive psychologists put it. Second, the child must be able to follow through the logic of an argument, even though its content appears at first sight to be 'wrong'. (For instance, having established that someone on Earth sees the clock on a high-speed spacecraft going more slowly that the one on the ground, the Principle of Relativity requires that the astronaut see the clock on the Earth going slower – not faster – than the one in the spacecraft.) Third, one must be able to compare reality with a set of formal assumptions and look for correspondences and consequences.

According to the Piagetian scheme, these skills mature only in the formal operations period (FOP) – the period that follows COP. Thus, we conclude that while one needs to have reached only the late COP stage to begin to appreciate relativity as a relationship between pairs of observables (speed and inertial mass, speed and length, speed and time), it is necessary to have made the transition to FOP in order to understand the reasons for these relationships as they are contained in the axiomatic statements of the underlying theory.

At what ages are these cognitive stages of development reached? Piagetian theory originally placed the transition from COP to FOP at around 11–12 years. However, later work by Shayer and Wylam[5], using large samples of children, demonstrated that the average age of the transition is far higher. By 12 years, less than 15 percent of children have reached FOP. Even as late as 16 years, only 30 percent of girls and 35 percent of boys have accomplished the transition to FOP. Indeed, the achievement curves tend to flatten off at around 15–16 years, giving rise to the suggestion that possibly more than half the adult population *never* reaches FOP.

In the light of these findings, we must conclude that there can be no easy answer to the question: what is the best age at which to encounter relativity for the first time? Whatever age is chosen, only a minority will have made it to FOP and thus be capable of appreciating a full formal treatment of the subject. In the event, it was decided to aim the work at the 11–12-year-old age group, that being the age by which most have at least reached late COP.

Design strategy of the material

The rough age group having been decided, the next problem was to find a way of structuring the ideas of relativity in such a manner as would correspond to the way of thinking characteristic of children at this stage in their development. As Bruner puts it, the need is to find 'a courteous translation'.

Because it is necessary to deal in concrete operations, it would clearly be inappropriate to begin with bald statements of the Principle of Relativity and of the constancy of the speed of light, and expect the child to follow an argument from these axioms to their practical consequences. This approach, common to the teaching of adults, will not do.

> What is most important for teaching basic concepts is that the child be helped to pass progressively from concrete thinking to utilization of more conceptually adequate modes of thought. But it is futile to attempt this by presenting formal explanations based on a logic that is distant from the child's manner of thinking and sterile in its implications for him.
>
> (Bruner[6])

The material has accordingly been designed to follow a scheme of developing thought that runs largely *counter* to the more normal axiomatic approach. We begin with the practical effects – those you would experience on going faster and faster. Only later do we arrive at the formal statement of the Principle of Relativity. In this way, those children who can order their understanding only in concrete terms – working outwards from their experiences (actual or imagined) rather than from within some chosen theoretical framework – will at least have gained something from their study before the increasing formality of the material towards the end goes beyond their present capabilities. This general approach to science education is in line with that advocated by Shayer and Adey.[7] They point out that such a strategy is essential for most *adults*, let alone children. They further suggest that an approach through concrete operations might be preferable even for those who have made the transition to FOP (including future science specialists) when first encountering a new topic.

Having decided on the underlying strategy, the next aspect of a 'courteous translation' to be addressed is the selection of a suitable mode of presentation. If young children are not naturally drawn to reading textbooks, it is no use writing the book in that form. To establish what kinds of books children currently read, an examination was made of the frequency with which various types were borrowed from the local library (this being deduced from the number of date stamps appearing on the inside cover). Commonly recurring features of popular books were identified. These included:

- a strong storyline incorporating a sense of adventure;
- an element of fantasy so as to allow the child to exercise his/her imagination;

- lots of conversation in order to break up the page and give it a dynamic look;
- short chapters, so enhancing the child's sense of achievement at having read another one;
- illustrations;
- humour;
- a main character with whom the reader can identify;
- finally, the book should be written from the child's point of view looking up at the adult world (not always understanding what is going on up there), rather than a condescending adult view looking down on the child's world.

With these characteristics in mind, I wrote *The Time and Space of Uncle Albert*. It consists of an adventure story, involving two main characters. Uncle Albert is based closely on Albert Einstein and is a rather loveable uncle figure. This is deliberate, the intention being to allay any feelings the reader might have that Einstein, because he was a genius, must have been remote and aloof (and consequently his theories be likewise distant and unapproachable). The second protagonist is his niece Gedanken. The choice of a girl rather than a boy was deliberate, given the acknowledged need to make a special point of trying to attract girls to take an interest in physics.

The general format of the story is that Uncle Albert thinks so hard he is able to create a 'thought bubble'. His niece Gedanken is then beamed up into the world of the bubble, where she goes on imaginary space journeys. She makes 'discoveries' about the peculiar properties of space and time as speeds close to that of light are approached. The significance of these various discoveries is then discussed with Uncle Albert.

In the first journey, for example, she discovers that no matter how powerful the space rocket, she cannot catch up with a light beam. This closely parallels Einstein's original *gedanken* experiment in which he tried to imagine what it would be like to catch up with, and subsequently coast along with, a light beam. His inability to account for that situation (because movement is such an integral part of what light is that it was inconceivable for it *not* to be moving relative to oneself), was, in fact, the historical trigger for the development of his theory. The connection between Gedanken's adventures and the real science of Einstein is spelt out in a postscript to the book.

It is important to note that Gedanken at all times plays a crucial role, first providing the basic observational data and later helping to develop the ideas springing from them. It has to be remembered that the reader will be identifying in the main with her rather than with Uncle Albert, so she must not be cast in the role of a mere passive foil to the brilliance of her uncle.

Gedanken, on handing in her school project based on her adventures, rather cheekily sets her teacher a test to see whether he has understood her discoveries. This brings into the storyline itself a self-assessment test that readers can – and in practice usually do – try out on themselves. (In fact, each of the three *Uncle Albert* books finds some pretext for including a test within the storyline itself.)

A readability test[8] on the text was to show that the language level is that suitable for the average 12-year-old.

Developmental testing

Because of the novelty of the approach, it was decided to test the draft of the book developmentally before submission for publication. A sample of 63 schoolchildren aged 11–12 years took part. In choosing the children to be tested, the decision was made not to call for volunteers to read the book. Such a move would have led to the self-selection of the more able and scientifically inclined children. Instead, the teachers selected a random sample of all interests and abilities, including some children classed as remedial. They were chosen from two schools situated in small provincial towns. They were supplied with typed copies of the book, and were told to read it in their own free time. After a period of about one month, they were tested. Two-thirds of the tests were carried out at one of the schools under examination conditions. The remaining children filled in the questionnaires in their own time at home. There was no detectable difference in performance in the two sub-samples.

The questionnaire was based on 18 multiple-choice questions designed to test how much of the physics they had absorbed. Such questions, by their very nature, do not readily lend themselves to the more open-ended, problem-solving type of exercise. Nevertheless, each question did require the respondent to demonstrate comprehension, either by drawing out some simple inference not specifically stated in the text, or by applying the ideas to novel situations. Each question was supplied with a 'Don't know' option among its list of possible responses. The rubric stated that the respondent should *not* guess. The intention behind this instruction was to minimise the number of cases where the correct option was chosen by pure guesswork. Among the distractors there was always one that corresponded to 'common sense', i.e. one that implied no relativistic effect. In cases where less likely incorrect options were chosen, the initial suspicion was that guessing had been at work – despite the instruction in the rubric. However, spot checks revealed that in each case the child had some reasoned (though wrong) explanation for their choice; they had genuinely misunderstood the physics and had not simply guessed. This encourages the view that correct answers to the questions can be taken as a fairly reliable indication of the level of comprehension.

Results of the evaluation

Not surprisingly, the tests revealed a wide range of performance. Some of the children did badly; either they were intellectually not ready for the material, or they regarded the exercise as an imposition and hence reacted against being compelled to read the book as an extra-curricular activity. On the other hand, there were those who took the task seriously, did consistently well, and displayed a good grasp of the subject matter. The overall average score on the test was a commendable 53 percent. Within the limited statistics available, it was not possible to discern any difference in performance between 11- and 12-year-olds, or between boys and girls.

Looking at the results in more detail, we can examine how the children responded to the various teaching points made in the book. For each specified teaching point listed in Table 9.1, the percentage of correct replies to questions related to that objective is quoted.

In addition to testing for comprehension, the evaluation examined general affective attitudes towards the book. In this respect, it should be noted that the reply sheets did not carry the name of the respondent, thus encouraging, under the cover of anonymity, a frank response. Also, it was felt important that, at this stage of the evaluation, there should have been no direct contact between myself as author and the children; I did not want the children to form a personal relationship with me, which might subsequently have inhibited their frank response in the event that they did not like the book. For this reason, I worked initially through the children's teachers. Only after all the completed questionnaires had been gathered in and studied did I meet the children directly in order to discuss with them in depth some of their replies. The questions and percentage replies are shown in Table 9.2.

Table 9.1 Results of developmental testing of *The Time and Space of Uncle Albert* (cognitive domain)

	Teaching objective	Correct replies
1	It is impossible to go faster than the speed of light	83%
2	The faster an object's speed, the heavier it appears to become	91%
3	At high speed, time slows down	45%
4	This does not mean one can go *backwards* in time	62%
5	At high speed, lengths contract	64%
6	At high speed, agreement over simultaneity is lost	65%
7	Relativistic effects are always present but are negligible at low speeds	72%
8	Matter and energy are equivalent	47%
9	The same relativistic effects are found by *all* observers	23%
10	The laws of physics are the same for all uniformly moving observers	22%

Table 9.2 Results of developmental testing of *The Time and Space of Uncle Albert* (affective domain)

	Question	Replies
1	How interesting did you find the book?	
	• very interesting	32%
	• interesting	46%
	• not very interesting	15%
	• boring	7%
2	How enjoyable did you find the book?	
	• very enjoyable	28%
	• enjoyable	49%
	• not very enjoyable	23%
	• not at all enjoyable	0%
3	What do you think is the right age for someone to read this book?	
	• someone a lot older than me	7%
	• someone a bit older than me	30%
	• someone of my age	49%
	• someone a bit younger than me	12%
	• someone a lot younger than me	2%
4	Suppose you saw in the local library a second book in the series in which Uncle Albert and Gedanken make further discoveries about space and time. What would be your reaction?	
	• I would definitely borrow it	37%
	• I would probably borrow it	22%
	• I might borrow it	25%
	• I probably would not borrow it	13%
	• I definitely would not borrow it	3%

On the basis of these results, there can be no doubt that some of the thinking behind special relativity is accessible to 11- and 12-year-olds, and that *The Time and Space of Uncle Albert* goes some way towards providing a 'courteous translation' of the subject matter for this age group.

The main problem concerned the teaching of objectives (9) and (10) in Table 9.1. These arise out of the material contained in the final chapter – the one dealing with the Principle of Relativity. Up to this point in the book, the relativistic effects have been handled in very concrete terms. These effects have been presented from a particular point of view – that of the Earth-bound 'stationary' observer. All the peculiar effects are associated with the moving spacecraft; it is the craft that undergoes mass increase and length contraction, and in which the time processes are slowed down. In the last chapter, however, readers have to switch viewpoints and accept that for someone in the spacecraft, it is the craft that is to be thought of as 'stationary'. As far as this second observer is concerned, the immediate environment within the craft behaves normally, and all the peculiar effects are to be attributed to conditions prevailing on the Earth – a consequence of the Principle of Relativity.

So, for example, there was a question that asked: 'When Gedanken is up to high speed, as far as she is concerned, because of their relative motion, the Earth is heavier than normal, lighter than normal, or has the same mass as normal?' The correct option is that the Earth appears to Gedanken to be heavier (in the same way as her rocket appears to someone on Earth to be heavier).

Likewise, a second question asked whether a measured distance along a road would be that same distance to someone riding a bike. The correct answer is that it would not; it would be very slightly shorter (in the same way as Gedanken's rocket appeared shortened to someone 'stationary' on Earth).

These ideas are very difficult to grasp. It is only natural to think that if an object appears shortened relative to a second object, then the second must appear lengthened relative to the first. But this is *not* the conclusion of the Principle of Relativity. To appreciate the import of this principle, readers must be capable of performing a change of viewpoint – moreover one that is hard to reconcile with the first – which requires an exceptionally high degree of emancipation from egocentricity. They must allow themselves to be carried along solely *by a line of argument from a set of theoretical propositions* – a very formal operation. As we see from Table 9.1, only about a quarter of the children were able to do this. This is not surprising, however, when one recalls that only 15 percent of this age group are expected to have made the transition to FOP.

With regard to the affective domain, one can but express satisfaction at the results of the survey. One of the main purposes was to stimulate interest in the subject and encourage readers to pursue their studies of physics further. The aim appears to have been achieved inasmuch as well over half the children not only expressed their enjoyment and interest but also went on to assert that, given the opportunity, they would definitely or would probably borrow further literature on the subject. This is perhaps the single most encouraging feature of the evaluation. Whereas one might debate the value or otherwise of the level of understanding capable by the concrete thinker, there can be no argument about the desirability of encouraging people to be aware of relativity and to want to learn more about it.

General conclusions from the evaluation

The first important conclusion to be drawn from the developmental testing is that children can indeed appreciate and enjoy certain aspects of modern physics – subject matter customarily regarded as too difficult for most adults, let alone children.

The second is that this can be done only through approaching the subject in a concrete, rather than formal, manner. This means presenting the material as though one were experiencing the effects at first hand. The approach must be of the form: 'If I do this, what will happen next?' It is pointless setting up theoretical models, based on some set of axioms and then working out the consequences of those axioms, and comparing them with experiment. No matter how carefully and logically this might be explained, most readers simply will not 'get it'. That is not how concrete thinkers structure their understanding of *anything*.

And this conclusion applies not just to child readers but to the majority of adult readers as well. I personally have lost count of the number of adults who, having read *The Time and Space of Uncle Albert*, have remarked to me 'At last I understand relativity'. Generally these are people who have tried other popular-isations of the subject but failed to progress. This is almost certainly because they are concrete thinkers. Perhaps the single most profound condition to be observed when it comes to the popularisation of science – for adult as well as child readerships – is to make prolific use of concrete models and analogies drawn from normal everyday experience.

Further developments

The popularity enjoyed by the first *Uncle Albert* book encouraged the view that one should perhaps try something even more adventurous: Einstein's *general* theory of relativity. This encapsulates our modern understanding of gravity and is the basis of cosmology. But would children of the target age group be capable of coping with what at first sight appear even heavier demands?

To answer this, a survey was organised to find out, in advance, what children knew (or *thought* they knew) about the topics on which I would have to draw. Two hundred and fifty twelve-year-olds were involved.

In answer to a question probing whether they knew what it would be like to accelerate fast in a high-speed lift, they spoke of being 'pressed to the floor', 'feeling heavier' and 'your tummy gets pulled down into your shoes'. This was encouraging because it revealed that the children were making a connection between acceleration on the one hand and an effect normally associated with gravity on the other. This was important because it is this connection, through what is called the equivalence principle, that is the crucial idea lying at the heart of the general theory of relativity.

On the other hand, the survey went on to highlight some surprising mis-understandings on the part of the children. For instance, 65 percent had no idea what a star was (i.e. a large sun). How is that possible for devotees of *Star Wars* and *Star Trek*? The answer appears to be that astronauts never, of course, travel to stars – only between planets; stars remain insignificant points of light in the background.

Another surprise was that on being asked what would happen if an astronaut holding a hammer and a feather in each hand were to release them, 46 percent replied that the two objects would simply stay where they were, floating in space. On being asked to explain this behaviour, the reply was that the astronauts were out in space and there is no gravity out there (this despite the fact that the astronauts themselves were clearly being pulled down to the surface of the Moon when they jumped). This was a particularly important misunderstanding to uncover, because the route into general relativity is the recognition that in the absence of air resistance (as is the case on the Moon) objects of different mass accelerate under gravity at the same rate. Clearly if the reader is wondering why they are falling at all, let alone at the same rate, one is in trouble! The survey graphically illustrated the pitfalls that can lie in wait for the unsuspecting would-be populariser of science.

Bearing these matters in mind, *Black Holes and Uncle Albert* was written and, like the first book, tested developmentally. This in its turn was to be followed by *Uncle Albert and the Quantum Quest*, thus completing the trilogy that taken together covers the work of Einstein.

Further books were to follow.[9] For example, *World of 1001 Mysteries* presents a whole kaleidoscope of interesting physics through an updated version of *The Arabian Nights*. Again the physics is woven into a storyline that can be read and enjoyed for its own sake. As one young reader put it: 'What I like about your books is that they teach you things without you knowing it'.

References

1 *The Time and Space of Uncle Albert*, *Black Holes and Uncle Albert* and *Uncle Albert and the Quantum Quest*, by Russell Stannard (Faber & Faber, 1989, 1992, and 1994, respectively).
2 P.I.P. Kalmus, *Physics Bulletin*, 36, 168 (1985).
3 J.S. Bruner, *The Process of Education*, p.33 (Harvard University Press, 1977).
4 See, for example, J. Piaget and B. Inhelder, *The Psychology of the Child* (Routledge and Kegan Paul, 1969).
5 M. Shayer and H. Wylam, *Br. J. Educ. Psychol.*, 48, 62 (1978).
6 J.S. Bruner, *op cit.*, p.38.
7 M. Shayer and P. Adey, *Towards a Science of Science Teaching* (Heinemann, 1981).
8 Using the test devised by R.F. Flesch, *How to Test Readability* (Harper, 1951).
9 *World of 1001 Mysteries* (Faber & Faber, 1993). *Our Universe* (Kingfisher, 1995). *Letters to Uncle Albert* (Faber & Faber, 1996). *More Letters to Uncle Albert* (Faber & Faber, 1997). *Ask Uncle Albert; $100\frac{1}{2}$ Tricky Science Questions Answered* (Faber & Faber, 1998).

Chapter 10

Science fiction and the communication of science*

R. Lambourne

Introduction

Science fiction in all its forms – books, comics, films, TV, computer games, etc. – occupies a substantial fraction of the contemporary global entertainment market. Much that is sold under the banner of science fiction has little or nothing to do with science and is irrelevant to the study of science communication. However, given the industry's titular link with science, its size and diversity, and its particular appeal to the young and to those with technical interests, it is not surprising that there is also a good deal of science fiction that does communicate science, and does so on a variety of levels. This part of science fiction is relevant to any comprehensive study of science communication and merits serious attention.

The purpose of this short article is to determine which aspects of science are most commonly communicated by science fiction, to identify those areas of science fiction where authors aim to communicate science, and to describe how the science is most commonly communicated. In short, the aim is to answer the what, where and how questions regarding the communication of science in science fiction.

Which aspects of science can be found in science fiction?

When looking for signs of science in science fiction it is important to be clear about what is meant by 'science'. When an author or film maker interrupts an unfolding plot to explain the nature of dinosaur DNA, or to outline the basic properties of an Einstein–Rosen bridge, then it is clear that an act of communication concerning the 'facts and theories' of science is taking place (or at least being attempted). Such acts are easy to identify – many critics would say they stick out like sore thumbs – but they are certainly not the only acts of science communication that occur within science fiction. More subtle examples of science communication in a fictional setting may concern the nature and

*Newly commissioned.

purpose of science, the process of science, the character and experience of scientists, or the historical, political and sociological aspects of science, including its impact on society. It is science in this general sense that will be of interest to us in this study.

The relatively simple task of gauging the coverage of scientific 'facts and theories' within science fiction has already been undertaken by a number of authors (Nicholls, 1982; Lambourne, 1990). Their general conclusion is unsurprising: the coverage is wide but patchy, with a strong concentration on physics and astronomy (including planetary science), the science that underpins space exploration and some parts of biology (notably molecular biology, genetics and ecology). Stories concerning chemistry and earth science are scarce, those concerning cosmology and the beginning or end of the universe relatively common. More recent studies would probably reveal a substantial growth in the coverage of information technology and computer science, though the preface to one collection of mathematics-based stories points out that new stories relevant to that theme are rare, appearing at the rate of only one or two per year (Rucker, 1989). Nonetheless, there are a number of topics, including black holes, comets, the solar system and even the individual planets that it contains, that have been revisited so many times and by so many authors that they have become the subjects of specialised 'themed' anthologies containing stories by various hands. Such works often contain factual essays that compare the assertions made in the stories with the currently perceived reality, indicating the feeling of many authors and editors that science fiction should, somehow, reflect scientific fact.

The presence of factual scientific information, often presented in a crassly instructive style, has always been a striking feature of science fiction. The founding fathers of the field, Jules Verne and H.G. Wells, both had a propensity towards pedagogy. Verne was essentially an autodidact in scientific matters, showing the common enthusiasm of the self-taught for passing on newly acquired knowledge, especially in the many books he wrote for the publisher Hetzel, with a juvenile audience in mind. Wells was less inclined to discuss technical details in his scientific romances, yet, ironically, it was he who trained to be a science teacher and it was he who worked for a time at the University Correspondence College, a sort of nineteenth-century precursor of the Open University.

The same tendency towards didacticism can be seen in the American 'pulp' magazines published by Hugo Gernsback and others in the mid and late 1920s. It was Gernsback's magazines that brought the term 'science fiction' into widespread use and did much to create a market and a loyal readership for the genre. Some of those early magazines even included science quizzes based on the factual content of the stories, and, in the case of *Science Wonder Stories*, boasted a panel of associate editors composed of distinguished scientists who 'pass upon the scientific principles of all stories'. The era of such devices is now long gone, but the factual content of some modern stories remains high, despite the view of many authors that they should 'never let the facts stand in the way of a good story'. (See Forward, 1992, for example.)

The task of assessing the scale and focus of the less overt acts of science communication in science fiction is much harder than that of spotting insertions of 'science fact'. Occasional insights into science and its role in society may be gained from a wide variety of science fiction works, many of them, superficially at least, highly unlikely repositories for such wisdom. Most of these glimpses of scientific tigers amidst the fictional undergrowth are little more than accidents, but there is a body of material, mainly in the form of novels and printed short stories, that provides a good deal of deliberate insight into the way that science is really done.

Not surprisingly, many of the works that communicate recognizable views of how science is really done are produced by trained scientists. The nature of their fictionalized accounts can be seen in bulk in those anthologies that deliberately draw together such stories. 'To Explain Mrs Thompson' by the American astronomer R.S. Richardson, in the collection *The Expert Dreamers* (Pohl, 1963), is a good case in point. The story itself is of little literary merit and has not been widely anthologized, but it does portray credible scientists confronted by a newly observed phenomenon formulating and pursuing research programs that might clarify the phenomenon and/or refute hypotheses about its nature. Similar portrayals of the process of scientific investigation can be seen in *Great Science Fiction by Scientists* (Conklin, 1962). It is interesting to note that science fiction authors who are also practising scientists (as opposed to authors who have simply had a scientific training) are relatively rare and are often not rated particularly highly by the readers of science fiction. The impact of such authors therefore tends to be relatively slight, though there are some notable exceptions to this generalization. It is also interesting to note that when scientists do write science fiction it is often with humorous or satirical intent. This is demonstrated in Pohl's collection by Otto Frisch's mock technical report, written from the perspective of a nuclear scientist in the year 4995, 'On the Feasibility of Coal Driven Power Stations', and, in Conklin's collection by Ralph S. Cooper's story 'The Neutrino Bomb'.

Amongst the longer works providing insights into science is *Timescape* (Benford, 1980), an award-winning novel by Gregory Benford – a professor of physics at the Irvine campus of the University of California. At the start of the book Benford says that his aim is 'to illuminate some outstanding philosophical difficulties in physics' but, as his story develops and his philosophical concerns are exposed, he also manages to convey a strong sense of what being a physicist entails. Mainly set in Cambridge, England, where Benford spent time as a visiting fellow, and located in a fictional 1998 (the book was published in 1980), *Timescape* provides a vision of a decaying, underfunded university system in a world that is descending into anarchy and ruin. This vision, which despite its exaggerations some would be tempted to describe as 'prophetic', illustrates the sort of financial pressures that confront many real scientists and would certainly communicate to its readers some important aspects of science, though those aspects would be inextricably intertwined with other elements that are still, thankfully, entirely fictional.

Another informative view of life in a modern physics department may be obtained from *Twistor* (Cramer, 1991) by University of Washington physicist John Cramer. This has an interesting emphasis on the lot of the graduate student and the post-doctoral researcher; the tenured staff play a more distant, if not downright disreputable, role that will amuse many readers. Similar, but somewhat more dated, is *The Black Cloud* (Hoyle, 1957), by the British astrophysicist and cosmologist Fred (now Sir Fred) Hoyle. This book also provides many insights into the way that scientific communities really work, though it is best known for its conception of a vast, coldly intelligent, cloud-like life-form that approaches the Earth from deep space.

It is not only in written science fiction that realistic portrayals of science can be found. A large element of what might be termed the 'science procedural' (by analogy with the use of 'police procedural' to describe certain kinds of detective fiction) can be seen in at least two major science fiction films, *The Andromeda Strain* (1970), and *Contact* (1997). The procedural elements are more important, though less realistic, in the former than the latter, but the scientific method has a prominent role in both. Interestingly, both films were based on published novels. *The Andromeda Strain* (Crichton, 1969) by Michael Crichton, a graduate of the Harvard Medical School who became a successful writer and film director, tells of the intensive five-day laboratory investigation of a virulent infection returned to Earth by an unmanned satellite. *Contact* (Sagan, 1986), by the distinguished Canadian/American astronomer and science popularizer Carl Sagan, describes the reception and decoding of the radio signals from intelligent extra-terrestrials, and the events that ensue. In both cases, the books give a more credible portrayal of science than the corresponding films, but in neither case does the film resort to the crude scientist-as-unworldly-egghead or scientist-as-man-of action caricatures that were such a strong feature of the science fiction films of the 1950s. As Crichton warns his readers at the start of *The Andromeda Strain*:

> This is a rather technical narrative, centring on complex issues of science. Whenever possible, I have explained the scientific questions, problems and techniques. I have avoided the temptation to simplify both the issues and the answers, and if the reader must occasionally struggle through an arid passage of technical detail, I apologize.
>
> (p.12)

Although it would be wrong to think that only scientists are capable of writing fiction that communicates the non-factual aspects of science with any hope of getting the issues straight, it is worth noting that many of the less thoughtful efforts by non-scientists are hopelessly flawed and misleading. Anyone hoping to find that their scientific career will be anything like that of Dr Indiana Jones or Star Trek's Science Officer Spock is likely to be sadly disappointed. Of course, that failing does not in any way diminish the stories that introduced those characters, but it should remind us that most fictional scientists operate in a way that is very far from reality. Not every account of a cash-strapped scientist resorting to desperate measures to push forward the boundaries of knowledge is necessarily a penetrating insight into modern science; it may be no more than a simple plot device intended to allow an author to move a story forward as quickly as possible.

The problem of identifying 'true' science communication in science fiction is further complicated by the presence of what is usually termed *imaginary science*. Imaginary science is basically deliberate hokum – the use of jargon and a recognizably 'scientific' style to convince the reader that the unlikely, or even the downright impossible, has been achieved, thanks to an advance in science or technology. In most cases, imaginary science is useful nonsense that communicates nothing about science but keeps a story moving along. However, there are examples of imaginary science that do convey important messages about real science and these too deserve inclusion in our study. The mere fact that imaginary science exists at all is a clear indication of the gulf between science and other cultural pursuits. Were it not for this divide science would be beyond the sort of mimicry that imaginary science represents. Imaginary science is an ironic form of science that uses the trappings and outward forms of science without ever treading on the heartland of real science – empirical contact with the real world.

As an example of the kind of imaginary science that reveals little or nothing about real science, witness Rundle Detteras' description of symbology, taken from Jack Vance's novel *The Star King* (1966: p.85):

It is a skill or habit of observation born of long years of study. I formerly specialised in Symbology, until I decided that I'd cropped that particular pasture as short as my teeth were long, and as far as my tether would reach. So here I am in Galactic Morphology. A less complicated field, descriptive rather than analytic, objective rather than humanistic. Still, I occasionally find application for my previous field. Now is a case in point. You come into my office, an utter stranger. I assess your overt symbolic presentation; skin colour; shape, condition, colour of your hair; features, clothes, your general style. You will say, this is a common practice. I reply true. Everyone eats, but a skilled taster is rare. I read these symbols with minute exactitude, and they provide me with information about you personally. I, on the other hand, deny similar knowledge to you. How? I bedizen myself with random and contradictory symbols. I am in constant camouflage, behind which the real Rundle Detteras watches as calm and cool as an impresario at the hundredth performance of a glittering carnival extravaganza.

Now contrast this with the late Isaac Asimov's famous explanation of the imaginary science of psychohistory, as given in the (equally imaginary) 116th Edition of the Encyclopaedia Galactica (1953: p.16):

> PSYCHOHISTORY . . . *Gaal Dornick, using non-mathematical concepts, has defined psychohistory to be that branch of mathematics which deals with the reaction of human conglomerates to fixed social and economic stimuli. . . . Implicit in all these definitions is the assumption that the human conglomerate is sufficiently large for valid statistical treatment. The necessary size of such a conglomerate may be determined by Seldon's First Theorem which. . . .*
>
> *A further necessary assumption is that the human conglomerate be itself unaware of psychohistoric analysis in order that its reactions be truly random. . . . The basis of all valid psychohistory lies in the development of the Seldon Functions which exhibit properties congruent to those of such social and economic forces as . . .*

Psychohistory is every bit as bogus as symbology, yet it is hard to avoid the feeling that a reader who had absorbed Asimov's definition would be better equipped to recognize definitions of real sciences than one who knew only Vance's. Psychohistory may not be 'real', but it does capture and convey some part of the spirit of real science. Most significantly, it sounds like a scientific advance that *might* be real. It is of course no accident that Asimov has such a ready familiarity with the outward forms of science; he was the holder of a PhD in chemistry, and was at one time an associate professor of biochemistry at the University of Boston. Of course, it must be accepted that the ironic aspects of Asimov's definition can only be fully effective if the reader is already familiar with such dictionary-style definitions of sciences. But it is unlikely, even given the relative youth of many of science fiction's most avid readers, that many would encounter psychohistory before they had already met a science such as chemistry or biology.

Where is the science in science fiction?

Although pockets of science communication can be found in each of the science fiction media, there can be no doubt that the widest and deepest representation of science is in the printed literature of the field. The coverage provided in films and on TV is shallower, though, owing to the nature and popularity of those media, it may have much greater impact. (Similarly, although it is possible to identify thousands of carefully imagined scientists in the literature of science fiction, the stereotypical scientist that most people recall from their encounters with science fiction is mainly a blend of the wide-eyed obsessive who features in old Frankenstein movies and the coldly logical Mr Spock of television's *Star Trek*.) In view of the relative weight of science communication carried by the different media, this article will mainly concentrate on printed stories and novels, but some acknowledgement of other media will be made, especially by comparing written and filmed versions of stories that have made the transition from one medium to the other.

Within the printed literature of science fiction there is a recognized tradition of so-called 'hard' science fiction, which strives to be serious and authentic in its dealings with science. This is the sub-genre in which the communication of the facts, theories and methods of science is most densely concentrated; only a detailed consideration of the impact of science would require us to spend much time looking elsewhere for science in science fiction.

Hard science fiction has already been the subject of a number of serious studies (see Bainbridge, 1986, for example) and has attracted a correspondingly large number of definitions. The style is easy to identify and to caricature, so the proliferation of definitions, many of them tongue in cheek, is not surprising. Three representative definitions can be found in the short introduction to *The McAndrew Chronicles* (Sheffield, 1983), a collection of indubitably hard science fiction stories about the potential uses of low mass, electrically charged, rapidly rotating mini black holes (Kerr–Newman solutions to the Einstein field equations, in the language of general relativity). According to the collection's author, Charles Sheffield – a British-trained physicist who has spent much of his career working in the US satellite industry – one popular definition holds that in a hard science fiction story, 'the scientific techniques of observation, analysis, logical theory and experimental test must be applied, no matter where or when the story takes place' (*ibid.*: p.2) However, Sheffield readily admits that his own preferred definition is the operational one, which asserts that 'if you can take the science and speculation away from a story and not do it serious harm then it was not hard science fiction anyway' (p.2). An altogether simpler and less contrived indication of what makes science fiction 'hard' can be glimpsed in the closing lines of Sheffield's introduction, where he says of the scientific content of his stories that 'even the invented material is designed to be consistent with and derived from what is known today' (p.4). Here then is fiction with a significant (overt) scientific content that is intended to be extrapolative and credible though not necessarily predictive or correct.

Although it may be argued that hard science fiction originated with Verne and Wells, it really makes more sense to see it as a tradition that has always been present in science fiction, but which only needed to define itself in opposition to other traditions that did not treat science with the same respect (James, 1994). These other traditions were conventionally lumped together under the title of 'fantasy' or even 'science fantasy', at least until the early 1960s, but since that time a number of other movements have arisen, and two in particular have achieved such wide recognition that they deserve explicit mention. First came the 'New Wave' of the mid to late 1960s, a movement spearheaded by authors such as J.G. Ballard, Brian Aldiss, Michael Moorcock and Samuel R. Delaney and characterised by literary experimentation, a concentration on non-technical themes, and a greater concern for the 'inner space' of the human mind than the outer space that had played such a important part in earlier forms of science fiction. More recent times have seen the emergence of an even more prominent movement known as 'Cyberpunk'. Essentially the creation of the American writer William Gibson and his 1984 debut novel *Neuromancer*, Cyberpunk attitudes were quickly taken up and developed by others, most notably Bruce Sterling, who did much to codify the movement in his 1986 anthology *Mirrorshades*. Cyberpunk stories are characterized by an obsession with high technology, particularly computer technology (hence the 'cyber') and a rejection of conventional cultural standards (hence the 'punk'). Cyberpunk is hard-edged, fast-moving, violent and kaleidoscopic. Its fusion of counter-cultural and highly technological elements in a single movement has caused some to refer to Cyberpunk as 'radical hard science fiction', but it should be recognized that Gibson and most of his followers have little technical knowledge and none of the regard for science that typifies truly 'hard' science fiction. Their interest in technology is that of the consumer rather than that of the producer.

Of course, the recognition that a group of thirty or so authors such as Charles Sheffield and Gregory Benford, together with Larry Niven and the British author Stephen Baxter, are currently writing in a 'hard science' tradition necessarily implies that they had their precursors in the earlier decades of this century. In the case of these particular authors it is easy to identify their co-traditionalists and the soil from which they sprang. The pivotal event in the founding of the hard tradition, as in so many other features of American science fiction, was the appointment of John W. Campbell as the editor of the US magazine *Astounding Science Fiction* in 1937. (At the time of his appointment the magazine was actually called *Astounding Stories*; the change of title was a typical Campbell action.) Campbell, a physics graduate from Duke University, whose first published story appeared while he was still an undergraduate, used his editorial position to bring a new seriousness to the writing of science fiction and to its treatment of science. Despite the pretensions of Gernsback's publications, with their quizzes and panels of experts, some might argue that many of the authors who wrote for them were professional hacks to whom science fiction was just one more money-making sales category. Campbell achieved his revolution by sidelining many of these established authors and developing his own stable of young malleable writers, several of whom had received, or were in the process of receiving, a technical education. Prominent amongst this group were Isaac Asimov and Robert Heinlein, the authors who, along with the British writer Arthur C. Clarke, were to dominate science fiction throughout much of the 1950s and 1960s, and beyond.

Campbell's success in making *Astounding* the natural home of good quality science fiction – a category that hardly existed *until* Campbell provided a home for it – ushered in the six- or seven-year period that is generally referred to as the 'golden age' of science fiction and provided a fertile meeting ground for serious and informed depictions of science. *Astounding* changed its title to *Analog: Science Fiction/Science Fact* in the1960s, but under Campbell's editorship, which continued up to his death in 1971, it remained a major focus for hard science fiction, and one of the few fiction magazines in which readers were quite likely to be expected to take equations in their stride. Other US monthlies, notably *Galaxy* and *If*, provided a home for stories that concerned the impact of science, those that, in the phrase of *If*'s sometime editor Fred Pohl, predicted the traffic jam rather than the motor car, but *Astounding/Analog* remained the market of choice for the most talented of 'hard' writers.

Another author who deserves to be included in any discussion of hard science fiction is Hal Clement. Clement – in reality American high-school chemistry teacher Harry Clement Stubbs – has never attained the wide popular readership of Clarke or Asimov, but he did produce some of the most strongly 'science-based' of all science fiction prior to the emergence of Robert L. Forward in the early 1980s. Clement's first published story was 'Proof', written while he was still a college junior, studying science at Harvard. 'Proof' appeared in *Astounding* in June 1942 but was such a science-laden debut that it was republished in *Where Do We Go From Here?* (Asimov, 1973), an anthology produced with the intention of showing how science fiction might be used in the teaching of science. (The collection includes questions and suggestions written by Asimov as well as comments on the extent to which the progress of science has made some of the older story elements obsolete.) Notable as many of Clement's short stories are, there can be little doubt that his enduring popularity is mainly the result of a single work, his 1954 novel *Mission of Gravity*, the tale of an epic journey from the equator to the pole of an ultra-dense, rapidly spinning planet where the effective surface gravity varies from 3 to 700 g. The gradual un-packing of the ramifications of such a substantial variation in surface gravity provides the scientific spine of the book, linking together a number of quite separate technical puzzles that the reader is invited to solve along with the alien protagonists who can survive such extreme conditions.

As indicated earlier, the author who has emerged to take on the mantle of Hal Clement is Robert L. Forward, who was working as a senior scientist at the Hughes Research Labs in California when he shot to prominence in science fiction circles with his novel *Dragon's Egg* (1981). Not altogether coincidentally, Forward, who holds a PhD, is in the field of gravitational astronomy, set *Dragon's Egg* in a somewhat Clement-like high-gravity envir-onment – on the surface of an ultra-dense neutron star. Both Clement and Forward have written interestingly about the way in which the dictates of science determine, or at least constrain, the flow of their respective narratives, in Clement's case in a non-fiction article for *Astounding* (Clement, 1953) and in the afterword to a collection of his short stories (Del Rey, 1979), and in Forward's case in the illuminatingly entitled 'When the Science Writes the Fiction' (Forward, 1986).

As mentioned earlier, the cadre of 'hard' authors is currently only about thirty strong. Nonetheless, they and their predecessors in the hard tradition have had and will continue to have an influence on the perception and form of science fiction that is out of all proportion to their number.

How is the science communicated?

The need to communicate scientific information in an interesting and engaging way creates as many problems for the author of fiction as it does for the teacher. These problems can be particularly acute when the author feels it necessary to communicate a large volume of technical information, and to do so with a fair degree of accuracy.

The standard problem of communicating science in the course of a story has a number of standard solutions. In the case of longer works, such as novels, one approach is to introduce the science via quotes from (usually fictional) reference works. This is an especially common technique for introducing pieces of imaginary science, perhaps because it lends them a quite spurious authority; but it can also be used for real science. In the context of imaginary science the technique is well illustrated in the BBC radio series *The Hitch-hiker's Guide to the Galaxy* (first broadcast 1978), where Douglas Adams' humorous narrative includes frequent interruptions by 'the voice of the book' explaining vital pieces of background information such as the operating principles of the Babel fish or the recipe for a Pangalactic Gargleblaster. More serious examples can be found in David Brin's monumental *Earth* (1990), where in addition to quotes from non-existent books, the reader is also treated to screen dumps on plate tectonics and the space–time geometry of general relativistic singularities. A similar, though somewhat more traditional approach is to introduce into the text a letter or e-mail from a scientist (in films this often takes the abbreviated form of a newspaper headline). James Blish's *They Shall Have Stars* (1956) contains just such an epistolary discussion of the Blackett–Dirac equation, including comments on its dimensional consistency.

If authoritative messages or quotes are inappropriate or simply not able to deal with the quantity of technical information, a more flexible technique is to introduce a real live scientist (usually fictional, of course, though a number of stories involve resurrecting Newton or Einstein, or some other historical expert.) Once a scientist has made an appearance the author can start communicating science on a variety of levels. Carl Sagan's novel *Contact* (and the 1997 film of the same title) illustrates most of the tricks of this particular trade. Apart from the almost inevitable 'Tell me professor . . .' passages where a scientist speaks to one or more non-scientists, there are also passages in which one scientist talks to another, a scientist provides information to a junior or requests/demands information from a junior, and even a passage where a scientist asks of herself 'what did I learn in that lecture about . . .' and then proceeds to present herself with a three-paragraph summary.

If scientists are not deemed to be adequate communicators, science fiction authors may find themselves in the fortunate position of being able to call on aliens or intelligent computers to perform the deed. Robby the Robot in the 1957 movie *Forbidden Planet* was a master of this technique, never tiring of providing the crew of United Planets Cruiser C-57-D with useful information. In the *Star Trek* universe, Vulcans such as Mr Spock and his various successors play a similar role.

Of course, if all these techniques for making scientific explanations a 'natural' part of the plot fail, the author can still adopt a head-on approach to the communication of science and simply come straight out with the requisite information. This approach is used to good effect in Stephen Baxter's *Timelike Infinity* (1992). Baxter, who possesses a first degree in mathematics and a PhD in physics, clearly has a broad familiarity with modern physics and uses this repeatedly in his books.

One of the most interesting ways in which science is communicated in literature, as in life, is via the process of discovery. Some of the most gripping of hard science fiction is that in which the reader shares with the protagonists a gradual process of discovery. The authors who manage to carry this off with the greatest success are often scientists themselves who, even if they have not personally made scientific discoveries, have observed those who have. Examples include some of the books mentioned earlier: Fred Hoyle's *The Black Cloud*, Carl Sagan's *Contact* and John Cramer's *Twistor*, together with Paul Preuss's particle physics adventure *Broken Symmetries* (1983). The Charles Sheffield short story collections *Vectors* and *Hidden Variables* (1979 and 1981) both contain many examples of this kind of communication.

One final form of science communication that deserves mention is what may be loosely termed the 'technical appendix'. Just as the authors of historical novels often feel the need to conclude their works with an historical note indicating the exact dividing line between fact and fiction, so the authors of science fiction sometimes feel a similar need to distinguish rational speculation from wild invention. In a few cases this is achieved by simply adding a set of factual notes to the end of the book; John Cramer's *Twistor*, mentioned above, provides an example of this. However, a more interesting variant of the same approach occurs when the note itself is somehow woven into the fabric of the narrative. Robert L. Forward is particularly fond of this approach and has used it in many of his books (see Forward, 1981; 1992; 1993, for example).

Conclusion

Despite the claims of some of its younger fans, the enjoyment of science fiction is not an effective substitute for the study of science. Communicating science is rarely a primary goal of a science fiction author and is often not a concern at all. Nonetheless, there is a small cadre of 'hard' science fiction authors who follow a tradition that attempts to treat science seriously while not being completely bound by its strictures. The work of this group, and of many of their pre-decessors in the tradition, certainly makes use of imaginary science, but it may be characterized as extrapolative rather than predictive and can therefore convey an element of science even in its fictive elements. Quite apart from the work of this small group, there is a much wider body of science fiction storytellers who pass on some element of science (including its impact on society) in their narratives. For all of these authors, the communication of scientific information of all kinds is a substantial challenge that has been overcome in a variety of ways. The main use of science in science fiction has always been to enable audience members to attain the willing suspension of disbelief that is, for many, an essential precursor to igniting the sense of wonder; in achieving this the effective communication of science often plays a vital role.

References

Asimov, I., 1953; *Foundation*, Weidenfeld & Nicolson.

Asimov, I. (ed.) 1973; *Where Do We Go From Here?*, Michael Joseph.

Bainbridge, W., 1986; *Dimensions of Science Fiction*, Harvard University Press.

Baxter, S., 1992; *Timelike Infinity*, HarperCollins.

Benford, G., 1980; *Timescape*, Gollancz.

Blish, J., 1956; *They Shall Have Stars*, Faber & Faber.

Brin, D., 1990; *Earth*, Macdonald and Co.

Clement, H., 1953; 'Whirlygig World', *Astounding Science Fiction*, June 1953.

Clement, H., 1954; *Mission of Gravity*, Doubleday.

Conklin, G. (ed.) 1962; *Great Science Fiction by Scientists*, Collier.

Cramer, J., 1991; *Twistor*, New English Library.

Crichton, M., 1969; *The Andromeda Strain*, Cape.

Del Rey, L. (ed.) 1979; *The Best of Hal Clement*, Del Rey Books.

Forward, R.L., 1981; *Dragon's Egg*, New English Library.

Forward, R.L., 1986; see *Hard Science Fiction*, edited by George Slusser and Eric S Rabin, Southern Illinois University Press.

Forward, R.L., 1992; *Timemaster*, Tor Books.

Forward, R.L., 1993; *Camelot 30K*, Tor Books.

Gibson, W., 1984; *Neuromancer*, Gollancz.

Hoyle, F., 1957; *The Black Cloud*, Heinemann.

James, E., 1994; *Science Fiction in the 20th Century*, Oxford University Press.

Lambourne, R. *et al.*, 1990; *Close Encounters? Science and Science Fiction*, Adam Hilger.

Nicholls, P. (ed.) 1982; *The Science in Science Fiction*, Mermaid Books.

Pohl, F. (ed.) 1963; *The Expert Dreamers*, Gollancz.

Preuss, P., 1983; *Broken Symmetries*, Pocket Books.

Rucker, R. (ed.) 1989; *Mathenauts*, New English Library.

Sagan, C., 1986; *Contact*, Century Hutchinson.

Sheffield, C., 1979; *Vectors*, Ace Books.

Sheffield, C., 1981; *Hidden Variables*, Ace Books.

Sheffield, C., 1983; *The McAndrew Chronicles*, Tor Books.

Sterling, B. (ed.) 1986; *Mirrorshades*, Collins.

Vance, J., 1966; *The Star King*, Dobson Books.

Chapter 11

Science on television

A coming of age?*

J. Bennett

What view of contemporary science and technology do the mass media present to the public? This paper is confined to the medium of television, not only because this is the main medium in which I have worked, but because television is probably the largest source of information on contemporary science used by the general public outside formal education. I would not claim that television can offer science museums and science centres a way forward as they seek to increase their coverage of topical science stories and new developments. But, as a programme maker, I would argue that museum professionals will draw some interesting parallels with the changing nature of contemporary science programming over the past 30 years. Exhibition developers may find some useful information in the research we have used to shape our current approach. If museums and science centres are to begin to tackle subjects and issues which up to now have only been covered in other media, then I suspect we may face some similar challenges.

However, a warning about evidence: the television industry is not very sophisticated in terms of its qualitative research methods, and available data on the contents of science programming and audience responses to it are not conclusive. However, the data that exist and the quantitative research that measures viewer numbers, demographics and viewing habits are both revealing and robust.

One common challenge which is increasingly facing both the museum world and that of television is the search for audiences – for 'visitors'. In both museums and increasingly television there is a need to recruit our audiences in competition with the plethora of other possible activities, from video games, theme parks, the World Wide Web and, in the BBC's case, from cable, satellite and shortly from hundreds of competing stations transmitting via digital technology. We are in a world of fewer and fewer captive audiences. Audiences are also seeing their time as a form of leisure expenditure which they will decide how to broker for themselves. They will make the choice between theme park

*Previously published in 'Here and Now: contemporary science and technology in museums and science centres' (1997). The Science Museum, pp. 51–64.

and museum, between a BBC programme and a computer games console. The media will have to focus clearly on what it can and cannot do in order to provide something attractive to them. By identifying some of these trends, the BBC has become more audience-focused and less paternalistic in its science programme provision. Given that, as programme makers, we have less and less influence over what people watch, this seems to be the right focus.

There is another common force operating for both museums and television: the interest that people have in knowing more about science and technology. The link between science, technology and industrial expansion is encouraging many populations to become more technologically literate. People in other countries may be more aware than those in Britain of the importance of understanding the impact of scientific development.[1] Thus it is no accident that the BBC is continuing to expand the coverage of science on World Service Radio through its news and features coverage. This expansion is continuing on television channels, not just in the USA and the UK but also elsewhere in the world.

I have painted a rather optimistic picture of infinite thirst for scientific and technological information. A subsequent question is: demand for what? It is important to ask what approach to science and technology is needed or indeed wanted. Is the depiction of science by the media utopian or does it adopt a critical approach?

A short history of British television's science coverage

Science on television grew out of the fact that television itself is a technological wonder. Sixty years ago the first BBC television broadcasts merely screened what they found in the real world, or, more often than not, what they found in the Alexandra Palace studios. Even 33 years ago the original mission of the flagship *Horizon* programme, 'The World of Buckminster Fuller', transmitted on BBC2 on 2 May 1964, was to translate the ideas of contemporary science on to the screen for a lay audience and to act as an interpreter for the scientists:

> The aim of *Horizon* is to provide a platform from which some of the world's greatest scientists and philosophers can communicate their curiosity, observations and reflections, and infuse into our common knowledge their changing views of the universe. We shall do this by presenting science not as a series of isolated discoveries but as a continuing growth of thought, a philosophy which is an essential part of our twentieth-century culture.[2]

That was, of course, only for those scientists who were vulgar enough to use the medium at all. There have been many stories of how scientists were spurned by their colleagues for having 'supped with the television devil'. Even now it is sometimes considered harmful for a scientist to have appeared 'on the box'.

From Professor Jacob Bronowski onwards, 'telly boffins' have sometimes had a bad time back at the lab. Bronowski, presenter of the renowned *The Ascent of Man*, felt he was held in less high regard as an academic because of his role in popularising (vulgarising) science. However, this mode of passive translation coupled with the broadcaster's initial deference to science ensured that the first television science broadcasts presented an optimistic view of the future which could justifiably be called utopian. An episode of *Horizon* from 1964 illustrates this attitude of awe and belief in the future being built by science and technology (excerpt 1).

EXCERPT 1   Programme *Horizon*: 'The Knowledge Explosion', transmission 21 September 1964 on BBC 2, producer Michael Lathamboth

Narrator:

What remains for science to do? How will it affect our lives? This is a city of the near future, planned by scientists and designers for the General Motors exhibit at the World's Fair in New York. They see a future where man will be making fuller use of the world's at present untapped resources. Improved technology will make it possible to penetrate jungles and build roads with tools so efficient that from tree cutting with a laser beam to laying road foundations will be a matter of only a few short hours with equipment like this. In this world of tomorrow overland communications will be vital, say the experts at the World's Fair. So super highways will cross areas which are now served only by cart tracks.

Arthur C. Clarke:

The only thing we can be sure of about the future is that it will be absolutely fantastic.

This typifies how modern science on television started out with a utopian but also a genuflecting outlook. The programme makers were granting the viewers the privilege of an audience with the scientist on the screen. This left little room for debate, critique or comment. However, it is important to stress that the treatment of politics was much the same on television at this time.[3]

Science on television has been very much a product of the age. Consequently, television was swept along by the social upheavals in the 1960s, and so the critical social documentary was born. English science programmes were no different from the rest of the media, or indeed the rest of society. Producers were not doing their job if they were simply passive translators. Society at large was taking on big issues and by the late 1960s science television was following suit. It wanted to have a point of view. Anthony Wedgwood Benn, the incoming Labour government's Minister of Technology, was invited to present a whole programme discussing the impact of technology on society.[4] Campaigning journalism extended to television, where the latest science became a provider of evidence, used to attack or expose targets that ranged from the dangers of blue asbestos and tobacco to people's tendency to obey authority. This shift in attitude represents neither a negative nor a utopian view, but is a recognition of the power of science to do good or evil. Television producers also utilised science information themselves to pursue an issue. In a famous *Horizon* 'You Do as You Are Told' programme,[5] audiences watched stunned as ordinary volunteers administered ever more intense electric shocks to a recalcitrant subject who was being told that they must obey. When they did not obey they had to be punished. Only later did viewers, and indeed the punishers, discover that the near-lethal voltages were merely buzzers making a noise and that the person on the other side of the screen was an actor. The programme demonstrated how far psychological techniques could be used to make somebody into someone who would just take orders. This was at a time of great concern about brainwashing, about the Vietnam War, about the military-industrial complex – all with a fair degree of paranoia thrown in. 'You Do as You Are Told' and other programmes marked an increased suspicion about contemporary science in the late 1960s and through much of the 1970s: what was science being used for?

By the 1980s, media attention had moved to the politics of science itself: how the scientific community functioned as an industry in its own right. 'Star Wars' was the subject of a half-hour special devoted to the politics and technology of the space-based strategic defence initiative on the prime-time magazine show *Tomorrow's World*.[6] HIV and AIDS received a similar treatment,[7] as did Chernobyl on BBC 1.[8] The Chernobyl programme was presented from the studio and, rather dangerously it seemed at the time, live from the lid of a nuclear reactor.

A comparison of three programmes on genetic screening and its potential uses outlines three different approaches and indicates where science broadcasting is heading. 'Brave New Babies' (excerpt 2) was produced by *Horizon* in the 1980s. This dramatisation shows two parents selecting their future child's physical make-up and character with a medical technician, who enters their requirements into a computer. The next transcript is from the *Antenna* magazine programme in the early 1990s (excerpt 3). It dramatised a situation in which the health insurance salesman of the future is doing a genetic profile of his client, a rather anxious young man. The third is from a 1996 broadcast, the BBC 2 series *In the Blood* (excerpt 4). The series about genetics had a more down-to-earth approach to genetic screening – in this case showing how a family deals with a rare and inherited cancer. The 1996 television treatment of genetic issues is no longer tinged with suspicion, but is practical. In this extract, a mother of two young children talks to Professor Steve Jones, a geneticist, about genetic testing of her daughters for an inheritable bowel cancer. These programmes show a progression from a fearful attitude towards genetic engineering, using dramatic futuristic scenarios in the two earlier examples, to a more immediate and information-rich perspective as the science comes closer to home, as portrayed by *In the Blood*. Although part of this change may be because genetic screening is a reality today and not just some prophecy belonging to a future world, I would suggest that the media's attitude has also shifted from one of fear to one of 'let us assess and debate'. *In the Blood* aimed to cover the public debate about the possible dangers of genetic screening, yet avoided scare tactics. The *Horizon* 'Brave New Babies' approach of using drama or satire to make a futuristic point is less likely to be used today by science programme makers. Perhaps this is because a more mature relationship is developing between the media and science. Whether television and society are well prepared to deal with some of the stranger effects of medical technology such as selective termination of pregnancy and cloning is, however, still questionable.

EXCERPT 2   Programme *Horizon*: 'Brave New Babies', transmission 15 November 1982 on BBC 2, producers David Dugan and Oliver Morse

Medical technician:	You've had a chance to view the data at home?
Mother:	Yes. We've narrowed it down to zygotes three and six. We're not really sure which one to choose.
Medical technician:	What sort of characteristics were you thinking of?
Father:	Well we definitely don't want to tamper with the physical side of things in any way.
Mother:	No, except that we would like her to have my father's red hair.
Medical technician:	Ah! Oh well that's easy. We can make her homozygous on the three hair-colour genes. What about her character and emotions?
Mother:	Ah, well yes there are a few things we'd like to have modified if possible. We'd like to reduce shyness, and susceptibility to depression, without necessarily damaging any artistic potential. Also we'd like her to be musical and if possible, also we want her to be ambitious.
Father:	Of course we want her to be as healthy as possible.

EXCERPT 3   Programme *Antenna*: 'Nobody's Perfect', transmission 16 January 1991 on BBC 2, producer Tim Haines

Insurance salesman:	OK Jose! Let's see what the men in white coats made of you.
Client:	What are you looking for these days? I mean, there seems to be more and more added each year.
Insurance salesman:	Only the main 'baddies'. Oh yeah we have a very strict code

on that one. Only those approved by the committee. Heart, mind, lungs, stomach. Yeah. Pretty much everything, but the more we have the more we can tailor the policy to your needs. And of course, all these juicy facts about you John are for my eyes only.

Client: Yeah, I bet.

Insurance salesman: Good, good. Well . . . .

EXCERPT 4   Programme *In the Blood*: 'The End of Evolution', transmission 24 June 1996 on BBC 2, producers Robin Brightwell and Dana Purvis

Mother: I don't have worries or concerns about myself because I go for regular tests, but I do worry about the girls obviously because I'm a parent and they're my children. I worry if I have passed something on.

Father: This is one of the things that we discussed when we tried to have children: it could be anything. It's not as if we think it's a special case, it's just part of life, and a lot of people will be affected by various genetic diseases.

Mother: Hopefully, by the time they're due to be tested – round about 13 or 14, you know when they reach adolescence, they'll be able to find out from blood tests so that they don't have to go through the examinations that I did.

Steve Jones: What would your advice be to other people who might be dubious about having genetic tests?

Mother: I would have them.

Father: If Deborah hadn't had any of the tests she wouldn't have been here now. So obviously if there is a risk of something, then you have got to be tested and if things are caught early enough, then modern medicine can get it sorted out.

Professor John Burn: People come along and say 'Have I got the gene for this because my dad died of it?' and the answer is I need your dad's blood sample to answer the question because I need to know which of the thousands of possible spelling mistakes actually caused the disease in your father. You can get round it to some extent, but if we've stored samples from affected family members it makes an enormous difference and that's what we are doing now. We've got something like 16,000 people's DNA stored away for a rainy day.

Steve Jones: And how many will you have in 20 years?

Professor John Burn: I hate to think, but the power bill could be enormous.

Science television grows up

I have suggested that there may be a new, more mature relationship between the science community and the media. There is, however, another factor: the increased need for the media to understand and respond to audiences' interests and likes.

In an analysis of news bulletins from February 1994 conducted by the BBC,[9] researchers were interested in what provides a news item's appeal, and what prevents it being effective as far as viewers are concerned. The survey established that there is potentially more interest in science stories in the news than in coverage of the arts, sports, finance or party politics. Genetics, medicine, environmental issues and other science stories that have relevance to people's lives aroused particular interest. Importantly, for a science story to qualify as newsworthy, the ordinary viewer has to be able to understand it. This creates problems for coverage of modern science.

Likely to fail vs likely to succeed

Table 11.1 highlights the difficulties caused by the very nature of science as a discipline. Much of science is based on claims and hypotheses, and real milestones and achievements are sparse. Much of what science is about is painstaking testing and uncertainty, yet this is something which, if concentrated on, is likely to make a 'story' fail. The complex, the difficult, the technical and the concentration on the 'how' are essential to actually understanding what a scientific development really means. Science for science's sake is very important within science, and many scientists rightly feel passionately about this, but it often leaves television viewers cold. In contrast, what is likely to succeed is media-hyped science, claiming a real milestone, real certainty and achievement. Take the case of the 1996 Nobel prize winner Sir Harry Kroto's discovery of buckminster-fullerenes or 'bucky balls'. To say this new form of carbon is directly relevant to our lives would be an exaggeration, and yet this was an exciting science story. There are, therefore, some aspects of science itself which do not lend themselves to successful science communication.

Newsworthiness of science items

Table 11.2 shows 23 science stories rated by focus groups according to newsworthiness. What comes across is that the clear key to the more newsworthy stories is relevance. One respondent said about 'Missing Matter', a clear 'loser': 'Why should I care? I didn't even know it was missing'. An item entitled 'British Scientists Race towards Absolute Zero' fell to the bottom of the league table because the story appeard to rely upon science for science's sake. The analysis of why stories fail reveals that the viewing public has a sophisticated screening system for relevance.

Table 11.1 Characteristics associated with science items in the news that indicate whether a programme is likely to succeed or fail

Likely to fail
- 'Science for science's sake'
- No relevance to everyday life
- Does not indicate *why* we should be interested
- 'Claim'/hypothesis
- Viewer knows nothing about area
- Complex/difficult/technical/concentrates on *how* research is done
- Footage of boffins/machinery
- Scientific/technical jargon
- Long/rambling
- Covers many areas
- Gives publicity to vested interests/shows bias
- Ignores viewers' worries

Likely to succeed
- 'Science for the human race'
- Could affect us all
- Indicates *why* we should be interested/why we are being told *now*
- Fact/real achievement/milestone
- Viewer already knows enough to be able to integrate new information
- Presented simply, without too much explanation of technical/theoretical background
- Clear, explanatory graphics
- Layman's language
- Short
- Focuses on one clear issue
- Performs public service (warns of danger/flags where help available)
- Shows awareness of viewers' concerns

Programme makers have to take account of this negative response to pure science when thinking of how to cover scientific news: rare diseases, foreign achievements, continuing projects without new milestones or with no solution in sight, government shake-ups, a lead in technology that is likely to be lost, or raising false hopes such as whether cancer treatment is promising too much – this is a long list of 'loser stories'. I believe that programme makers should be covering these issues – although with care – even if they are not considered to be immediately high up in the news agenda or even on the news agenda.

What is needed is a filter of relevance, or a mechanism for constructing that relevance if necessary through the way the story or subject is presented. For instance, *Horizon*: 'Assault on the Male' made specialist science relevant for the non-news-programme audience, yet was presented in the form of an extremely newsworthy 'scoop' documentary, as is illustrated in excerpt 5. This was the first time any broadcaster had gathered together the news about new oestrogens in the environment.

Table 11.2 Number of focus groups rating a science item as 'newsworthy'

Science items	Yes	Don't know	No
1 Government go-ahead for genetically altered food	8		
2 Scientific advances in genetic screening raise serious moral concerns	8		
3 Nuclear reprocessing: government gives go-ahead for Sellafield tests	8		
4 Trials begin of a new treatment for breast cancer	8		
5 Americans clone identical twins	8		
6 British scientist receives Nobel prize for medicine	8		
7 Gene therapy gets the official go-ahead	7		1
8 A thousand women in the West Midlands recalled after examinations for cervical smear tests	7	1	
9 Nuclear fusion: American scientists claim major advance	6	2	
10 Ice-core research throws doubt on global warming	6	2	
11 Hubble telescope: astronauts replace faulty parts	6		2
12 Experts say there is no evidence to link children's skull deformities with polluting chemicals – but North Yorkshire parents demand full investigation	6		2
13 AIDS: Department of Health report predicts sharp rise in number of British heterosexuals contracting HIV virus	5	3	
14 US researchers think they have located 'gay gene' – but worry that it may lead to sex orientation checks on the unborn	5	2	1
15 A new British clinic offers sex selection of your baby	5	1	2
16 Trials of anti-AIDS drug AZT show that it does not delay the onset of the disease	4	4	
17 President Clinton announces plans for new US Space Station	4	2	2
18 Government reveals plans for shake-up of science and technology	3	4	1
19 Video games are turning many young people into addicts and making them aggressive	3	3	2
20 New telephone technology paves the way for home banking	3	3	2
21 Computer scientists warn that British lead in technology could be lost	2	2	4
22 Australian scientists find universe's missing matter	1	4	3
23 British scientists race towards absolute zero	1	1	6

EXCERPT 5   Programme *Horizon*: 'Assault on the Male', transmission 31 October 1993 on BBC 2, producer Deborah Cadbury

Narrator: Lake Apopca, Central Florida. A scientific team was called in to investigate the declining number of alligators. They found more than they bargained for.

Professor Louis Guillette: We were astonished at what we found. Things that we were seeing were so dramatic. We were actually seeing sex reversal. I mean things were changing sex. At least 25 percent if not 30 percent of the male alligators on this lake have some kind of abnormal phallus or abnormal penis. Mostly it appears that the abnormality is small size, as much as a half or two thirds reduced. For this size animal, it's normally about twice this wide at least. But it doesn't ever have this hook to it like this.

Narrator: Similar changes to males of other species have been found in Europe and America and now there are signs that human reproduction could be in trouble.

Professor Louis Guillette: Everything that we are seeing in wildlife has an implication for humans. I believe that we have the potential to have major human reproduction failures.

Narrator: These are human sperm. They show a high level of abnormality. These have grossly deformed heads. Whereas these have no tail, this one is all tail. And this sperm has two tails. Here the neck is enlarged with cytoplasm, which should have been shed earlier. And while some are hyperactive, others don't move at all. It was these sorts of abnormalities which scientists from Copenhagen began to study two years ago. At the University Hospital, Professor Skakkebaek was surprised to find some healthy normal men had more than 50 percent abnormal sperm.

Even though there is quite a lot of science and chemistry in this programme, the point of relevance, the abnormal alligator genitalia, was never exaggerated but always driven home. This made a very successful programme and one which has exposed the subject to a lot of public debate.

A second lesson is that of following a process. Involving audiences in the conduct of contemporary science enables difficult and abstract science topics to work for audiences – especially for longer reports such as documentaries of more than 30 minutes in length. Seeing science as a process, as method in action, also links science as an activity to other areas of human endeavour. *Horizon*: 'Ulcer Wars' is an example which combines process with relevance and hence subsequently involves the audience. This extract illustrates an unusually direct way of testing an unusual hypothesis: that ulcers could be caused by a bacterium, *Helicobacter pylori*, which, if true, could theoretically be cured with antibiotics. The test was unusual because it was first tried out by the friends of the scientist involved, Barry Marshall (excerpt 6).

EXCERPT 6   Programme *Horizon*: 'Ulcer Wars', transmission 16 May 1994 on BBC 2, producer Michael Mosley

Narrator: One of the first to try his antibiotic cocktail was Win Warren, his colleague Robin Warren's wife.

Win Warren: Once it was clear that I was one of the folk who had these bugs growing in my stomach, it was arranged that I should go to Freemantle Hospital for gastroscopy, which I didn't find an entirely delightful procedure. There was lots of grizzling, from Barry in particular, about the fact that I kept chewing on his gastroscope, which I was informed cost several thousand dollars and had to be treated with respect. I'd have liked a little respect myself at the time. So that bit of a treat, swallowing the gastroscope, was followed by great excitement on Barry's part because lo and behold there was the ulcer. I could have lived without sharing his enthusiasm because he insisted that I looked down the eyepiece. There's something disgusting and obscene about looking at the inside of one's own stomach but he seemed to think it was the most exciting thing he'd seen for a long time. After that it was very clear that I was part of the trials as far as taking medication was concerned, and that was a relatively simple thing to do. There were no major side effects of the pills, and before very long I was nicely cured and eating well again. That was nearly ten years ago and I've had no recurrence whatsoever. Sometimes when my weight goes up too much, I think maybe a recurrence wouldn't be such a bad thing but I think the likelihood is nil.

This was an example of a patient with *Heliobacter pylori* bacterium, the discovery of which was overturning the prevailing stomach ulcer hypothesis. It proved to be a contentious issue, as the drugs industry had not really moved with theory. The point emphasised in the programme was that a scientist, Barry Marshall, was ahead of the pharmaceutical industry's ideas and was ignored because he had an unconventional idea which also challenged a hugely lucrative industry. Such approaches to science in television are basically journalistic, although not in the traditional way of news. This does not represent a utopian or critical vision, but a practical view of science which assesses the current standing of scientific ideas.

Horizon concentrates on process, on relevance, on stories from the world of science with occasional uncertainty and human failings thrown in. Yet, while wanting to be contemporary and timely, it does not always strive to be topical. The science comes across as an area of rolling human activity with few points of absolute discovery, while the highlighted moments may or may not stand for 'good' progress.

'Good' vs 'bad' science

What effects do the good news or bad news messages within programmes have upon viewers? Assessing *Horizon* by topic using audience appreciation scores[10] provides an interesting perspective on its 33-year history. In the audience appreciation index, a high score is in the high 70s to the mid-80s and a lower score is the mid-70s. Contemporary topics with worrying secondary issues (AIDS or the non-ethical introduction of Norplant, the implantable female contraceptive, into developing countries, for example) received lower scores in the audience appreciation indices than 'discovery' programmes. The *Horizon* programme 'AIDS: Behind Closed Doors',[11] for example, received a score of 75, and 'The Human Laboratory'[12] (the Norplant story) scored 76. A more popular story called 'The Planet Hunters',[13] about discovering a new planet, recently scored 80.

On the same scale, a programme on the ethics of non-lethal weapons and the politics of land mines, *Horizon*: 'Small Arms, Soft Targets'[14] received a score of only 74. Socio-political issues and campaigning films seem to be given relatively low scores by the audience, unless they have empowering and optimistic endings. My interpretation of the audience appreciation scores suggests that the audience is searching for hopeful messages: for stories from the world of science which are enriching and perhaps complicated, yet which do not give prominence to worrying issues.

An important exception to this rough-and-ready rule was coverage of bovine spongiform encephalopathy (BSE), a serious subject which was ranked highly in the audience appreciation index. This is a particularly British contemporary issue about which viewers are worried and personally interested. Seventy-four percent versus 21 percent of viewers in our focus group research stated clear preferences for narrative rather than 'fact-file' approaches. This supported the approach taken by the producer of the recent *Horizon* programmes examining BSE, illustrated in excerpt 7, which focused on a strong personal story within the wider scientific framework. The programme covered prions, public policy and scientific uncertainty. The point about uncertainty was that in the case of CJD we do not know where we are on any possible epidemic curve. Are we at the beginning of a large curve, or will there be only a few cases? The programme discussed epidemiology and how epidemics can or cannot be identified, a debate which will obviously be important in terms of future health policy. What stance does such a narrative approach take to science? In the case of BSE, the most important question is how the developments in a particular field may affect public policy. Science is not exactly value-free but is reported as an activity, much as we report on politics, the arts or industry.

EXCERPT 7   Programme *Horizon*: 'The Human Experiment', transmission 18 November 1996, producer Bettina Lerner

A surgeon changes into clothes preparing to begin a Creutzfeldt–Jakob disease (CJD) autopsy.

Narrator:	In 1990 the government set up a small research unit with one sole purpose – to detect the earliest signs of a human epidemic of mad cow disease. They were to study every case of CJD in Britain, to look for any change in the normal pattern of disease, a new variant that would reveal that BSE had crossed into humans. One member of the team had the job of examining the brains of everyone in Britain who died of CJD, looking for anything unusual. But a CJD autopsy is unlike any other a neuropathologist ever has to perform.
Dr James Ironside:	I've now changed into the clothes I'll wear to do an autopsy in a case of suspected CJD, and these garments are disposable because they will be incinerated after the autopsy. These are the gloves. On the top is a chain-mail hand piece. And this is flexible and allows my hand to be protected from any cuts while the autopsy is being performed, and I wear another pair of rubber gloves on top of this just to make the whole thing as waterproof as possible. And this is the helmet. I'll just put it on. The instruments that I use in the post-mortem room and the instruments that technicians use in our dedicated laboratory – really we regard these as being permanently contaminated, so we use those for CJD cases alone because there is no effective way of guaranteeing decontamination in this disease. Unlike other viruses and bacteria, it can resist extremes of heat, cold, chemicals, enzymes – everything practically, and I don't think any of us believe that we can fully decontaminate anything with this agent.

The future

This mix of narrative and reporting was reflected in a recent science fiction series that the BBC made, *Future Fantastic* (excerpt 8).[15] This incorporated wonder, yet portrayed visions of the future that had the potential to be good, bad or just plain disturbing.

EXCERPT 8   Programme *Future Fantastic Promo*, series transmission 21 July to 30 August 1996 on BBC1, series producer David McNab

Narrator:	'Future Fantastic' reveals over a century of dreams. And how scientists past and present have turned those dreams into reality.
Professor Charles Vacanti:	Any organ that you can think of that fails in the human body has a potential to become a tissue-engineered organ. I believe we're ready to start doing it in humans now.
Narrator:	This major new series unveils the startling truths about our future. Can tomorrow's scientists deliver today's science fiction? Are we ever going to conquer space or make contact with aliens? Will our children live on Mars? Will we achieve eternal health and beauty? Will we see advanced bionic people or regrow lost limbs? Teleport around the world or even travel in time? Could today's science-fiction visionaries actually have got our future right? 'Future Fantastic' – it's nearer than you think.

The programme asked whether 'change' would be equivalent to progress. This was left very much as an open question and was an attitude which the producers believe worked very well for a young audience. *Future Fantastic* attracted more younger people in the 16- to 24-year-old age groups than is usual for a BBC 1 prime-time factual programme.

The contract of *Future Fantastic* with the first extract on the future is interesting in that it suggests that today's visions belong both to science fiction and to science. The programme is saying that these visions are not necessarily utopian, but they are subject to reporting based on what is happening today.

Conclusion

There are challenges ahead for science communication, both in television and in other media such as exhibitions. The audience is curious and has a sense of wonder, and this needs to be tapped. As Professor Richard Dawkins said in the BBC's 1996 *Richard Dimbleby Lecture*:

> The popularity of the paranormal, oddly enough, might even be grounds for encouragement. I think that the appetite for mystery, the enthusiasm for that which we do not understand, is healthy and to be fostered. It is the same appetite which drives the best of true science, and it is an appetite

which true science is best qualified to satisfy. Perhaps it is this appetite that underlies the ratings success of the paranormalists.[16]

At the same time, there is a huge interest in the paranormal and it is an immense challenge to establish where science communicators should be placing themselves in terms of either tapping into or ignoring that interest.

There is also a great need to continue to look at how programmes can be relevant and how broadcasters can drive that relevance home. The audience should be compelled to participate, whether by evoking the notion of process in a film, the narrative of a story or, increasingly, by interactivity in the form of Web sites.

Exemplifying this is the *Horizon* Web site,[17] which allowed viewers to follow an expedition to find a Peruvian mummy. Despatches from television cameras were sent to the Web site and on to our international site shared with the Public Broadcasting Service network in America. Viewers were able to participate in the actual expedition they would see on the *Horizon* programme 'Ice Mummies: Frozen in Heaven'[18] some weeks later. The site gave an opportunity to the public to write to the members of the expedition and to the scientists in Peru, an interactivity which created a new interface for the audience.

As I have shown, the presentation of contemporary science on British television has changed during the past 30 years. While it was once possible to criticise science programming as deferential and portraying a universally positive view of science, this is no longer the case. In the 1990s, some of the key features of science coverage on television are the search for relevance, a focus on the impact of breakthroughs and discoveries, and a concentration on process and the narrative when covering science in documentary format. Today, in general, science and technology is treated both as a part of people's daily lives and as part of industry. If science museums and science centres are to follow television in communicating the science that is in the news, then these features should be assessed for their potential to translate into successful exhibitions.

Finally, it is worth considering whether science is now taken for granted by television – have we as programme makers lost our sense of wonder, and could we be in danger of underrating the power of science by taking a rather cooler look than perhaps in the past? The answer is 'not necessarily'. Broadcasters need to preserve their ability to give a sense of excitement and to reflect on the major developments and genuine discoveries that science offers up. In so doing, we will be able to help to distinguish the enormous force for change – for progress – contained within the world of modern science.

Notes and references

1 *European Report on Science and Technology Indicators* (Luxembourg: European Community Publications, 1994) quoted by Robert May, UK Government Chief Scientific Adviser, Office of Science and Technology, London.

2 Daly, P., 'Horizon', *Radio Times* (30 April 1964).

3 For example, Robin Day was acknowledged to be the first severe questioner of politicians in the late 1950s.

4 *Horizon*: 'Machines and People', transmitted on BBC2 on 5 June 1969, producer Robert Vas.

5 *Horizon*: 'You Do as You Are Told', transmitted on BBC 2 on 28 October 1974, producer Christopher La Fontaine.

6 *Tomorrow's World Special*: 'Star Wars', transmitted on BBC1 on 14 November 1985, producers Martin Freeth and Martin Hughes Games.

7 *Tomorrow's World*, transmitted on BBC1 on 1 December 1988, producer Martin Mortimore.

8 *After Chernobyl – Our Nuclear Future?* transmitted on BBC1 on 27 May 1986, producer Philip Harding.

9 BBC Broadcasting Research, *Science in the News – Qualitative Research SP93/98/3125*.

10 BBC Broadcasting Research, *Horizon: Winter 1996 Series Broadcasters' Audience Research Board (BARB) Analysis 6144TV*. Audience appreciation indices (AI) measure how much a sample of viewers have enjoyed or appreciated a programme. Their response is measured immediately after a programme has been transmitted. Respondents' opinions are used to calculate an AI for every BBC, ITV and Channel 4 television programme. The AI ranges from 0 to 100, a high AI indicating a high level of appreciation. AIs are calculated as simple averages of the scores given by respondents. The AI is based on the number of panel members who rated the programme each week. In this respect, a panel member who returns a diary is included in the analysis even if he/she has not watched any programmes during the week. For every programme, the number of viewers who marked each position on the 11-point scale is determined. The scale positions 10, 9, 8, 7, 6, 5, 4, 3, 2, 1, 0 are then treated as, respectively, 'scores' of 100, 90, 80, 70, 60, 50, 40, 30, 20, 10, 0, and an average is taken.

11 *Horizon*: 'AIDS – Behind Closed Doors', transmitted on BBC 2 on 4 December 1995, producer Andrew Chitty.

12 *Horizon*: 'The Human Laboratory', transmitted on BBC2 on 5 November 1995, producer Deborah Cadbury.

13 *Horizon*: 'Planet Hunters', transmitted on BBC2 on 11 March 1996, producer Danielle Peck.

14 *Horizon*: 'Small Arms, Soft Targets', transmitted on BBC2 on 10 January 1994, producer Martin Freeth.

15 *Future Fantastic* was a nine-part series transmitted weekly on BBC1 from 21 June to 19 July 1996 and from 9 August to 30 August 1996, series producer David McNab.

16 *Richard Dimbleby Lecture: Science, Delusion and the Appetite for Wonder*, by Richard Dawkins, transmitted on BBC1 on 12 November 1996, producer Charles Miller.

17 http://www/pbs.org/wgbh/pages/nova/peru/index.html

18 *Horizon*: 'Ice Mummies – A Three-Part Special', transmitted on BBC2, producer Tim Haines. **1**: 'The Ice Maiden', transmitted on 30 January 1997; **2**: 'A Life in Ice', transmitted on 6 February 1997; **3**: 'Frozen in Heaven', transmitted on 13 February 1997.

Part III

Science and the media

Introduction

Simeon Yates

One of the most important areas of science communication is that which takes place through the mass media. Today the term 'mass media' covers everything from newspapers and television, through magazines and films/videos to digital broadcasting of various forms. The communication of science in all these media takes place through various genres. These include such things as science fiction, specialist TV programmes and magazines for lay and specialist audiences, and general news coverage. It is this presentation of science in news media that forms the theme within the six chapters presented in this part of the book. In one way or another each of these pieces is concerned with what Holliman in Chapter 17 calls 'public affairs media'. This category covers all the print and TV broadcast output that is oriented to news and current affairs coverage.

The first chapter addresses the reasons why a range of people have come to study 'science in the media'. The chapter notes that one of the main forces behind such research is a perceived need to 'improve' science communication in general and science journalism in particular. Dornan takes a critical eye to such arguments and asks if this is not too narrow a focus. He concludes by asking what studies of science in the media can tell us about the 'public sphere' in modern societies.

The second chapter is a newly commissioned piece and takes up this issue of science communication and the 'public sphere' and explores how four key social groups, social institutions, the press, the public and decision makers, interact in the production of science news. Miller uses a model of the 'circuit of mass communication' in exploring these ideas. This chapter emphasises the manners in which science is always 'mediated' during the process of communication. The form in which the science is mediated depends upon the interaction of Miller's four key groups of actors.

The third chapter examines the various ways in which scientists and science have been represented in the mass media. Nelkin highlights four different types of representation: scientist as star, science as a public resource, science as pure and science as authority. This chapter highlights the fact that science and scientists are never presented in a neutral way within the media. As science and scientists are part of public cultural life, they are part of the set of representations of science, and scientists have tended to emphasise such things as the 'brilliance' of a scientist or a specific story and the authoritative usefulness of science.

The fourth chapter continues the theme of exploring the representation of science in the media by looking at a specific case. The chapter presents a study that attempted to explore how the manner in which a scientific debate around biotechnology had been presented in the media – how it was framed – actually impacted on the public understanding of the debate. The chapter argues that within the US media the biotechnology debate had been framed by the commercial needs of major companies. This commercial framing was also found in the public's interpretation of the debate.

The fifth chapter presents a study of the relationship between science journalists and scientists. Peters points out the ways in which the professional cultures in which both journalists and scientists work lead them to differing views on what makes good science communication.

The final chapter is a newly commissioned piece that explores the life of one science story – the claim by NASA to have found evidence for the previous existence of life on the planet Mars. Holliman makes use of a number of the research methods employed by authors of the previous chapters in order to explore the content and presentation of the story over time, the public understanding of the story, and roles of scientists and journalists in the production of the story.

Chapter 12

Some problems in conceptualizing the issue of 'science in the media'*

C. Dornan

The recognition that science is an enterprise crucial to the welfare of Western societies has become commonplace, along with the recognition that public acquaintance with science is equally essential. As a result, especially in recent years, considerable attention has been paid to the role of the media in the public communication of science.

However, the manner in which questions of 'science and the media' have been posed, and the nature of the answers that have been forthcoming, are themselves deserving of scrutiny. This article presents a critical examination of the dominant approach that has been taken *vis-à-vis* popular coverage of science. In making this examination, there has been an attempt to survey the extant literature from 1967 to 1987 as exhaustively as possible. Hence the bibliography at the end of this article should represent fairly comprehensive coverage of the subject matter.

The remainder of this article will approach, in turn, each issue that is epistemologically and/or methodologically salient or that can be critically interrogated based on an examination of the literature. The conclusion attempts to show certain relationships between the various issues and point to future approaches to the science/media question.

Reiteration

Although concern over media coverage of science began to be voiced almost immediately after the Second World War (see Dornan, 1988), it was not until 1967 that the first book devoted to the subject, Krieghbaum's *Science and the Mass Media*, was published. In brief, Krieghbaum argued that the media generally ignored science and, even when they did not, they all too often sensationalized it, exploiting scientific inquiry as a source of startling narratives. In a context in which science was seen to play an increasingly prominent role on the political stage, this exploitation was taken to be deleterious to the workings of democracy: a 'scientifically illiterate' polity could not possibly come to sound

*Previously published in *Cultural Studies in Mass Communication* Vol. 7 (1990), pp. 48–71.

or rational decisions. What was required, in Krieghbaum's view, was a press diligent and responsible in its attentions to science, one that would apprise its readership of the latest in scientific findings, instill public confidence in the enterprise, and cultivate a popular excitement for the advances in knowledge it made possible.

Since 1967, at least a dozen other such works have come into print. All of these have been slim volumes, commonly less than 200 pages, even those that include a number of articles and essays. The sole exception is *Scientists and Journalists* (Friedman, Dunwoody and Rogers, 1986), an anthology that boasts three editors and 33 other contributors.

This observation points to an important feature of commentary on science and the media. Books on the subject are brief because each reiterates an argument that is straightforward, widely accepted, and therefore all but free from challenge. While other areas in media studies have developed via contest or comment, academic discourse on science popularization has been marked by an enduring consensus, in which individual contributions work to entrench the positions first articulated by Krieghbaum. The need to 'better' public under-standing of science has seemingly motivated and informed academic attention to media coverage.

A search of the literature reveals only a single instance in which this argument is directly contested and one other in which reservations are raised. Alone among those who have addressed the topic, Trachtman (1981) describes the efforts to enhance science communication as 'missionary activity' and questions

> the glib assumption that a *scientifically informed public* is a prerequisite for effective functioning of a democratic society in an age dominated by science and technology and the corollary of this assumption that a major policy commitment should be made to further public understanding of science.
>
> (p.14, emphasis in original)

Trachtman's survey of the literature reveals that this central assumption is based on three major premises. First, knowledge is simply good in and of itself. Second, people will be able to make more intelligent consumer choices if they are more knowledgeable about science and technology. Third, the very structure of a democratic society depends upon the existence of an enlightened citizenry (*ibid.*: p.10).

Trachtman has no quarrel with the first premise, although he maintains that it alone can hardly justify the considerable expense involved in mounting a media campaign of forced public education. As for the second, he argues that there is little evidence to suggest that individuals' habits of consumption are much influenced by their levels of technical sophistication; in any case, it is unlikely that consumption is an activity in which there are 'right' or 'best' choices as that can be determined on scientific grounds. Even in those areas where scientific expertise conceivably might be relevant – choices as to medication, for example, or diet – the available 'scientific' evidence is ambiguous, unclear, and continually subject to revision.

The third rationale – that a scientifically literate public is essential to democracy – Trachtman finds equally specious, first on the grounds that scientific work is often of little relevance to the ethical, moral or political problems posed by social organizations. Thus, he points out that

> people who are consistently willing to make economic sacrifices in the interests of environmental preservation – or their opposite numbers – are unlikely to have their convictions and political activities modified by learning more about the life cycle of the Chesapeake Bay oyster.
>
> (p.12)

Second, he notes that if crucial social questions actually did depend on scientific pronouncements, the public's ability to come to decisions would be seriously impaired, if only because on any given issue there is a wealth of contradictory, tentative, qualified information and supposition. In areas of political controversy (nuclear power, pesticide use, population control, and so on) the scientific community is itself divided. To rely on the pronouncements of science in such instances would paralyse, not aid, decision making.

The champions of an enhanced science writing might respond that Trachtman proposes a surrender to ignorance, or that he has insufficiently explored how a sound acquaintance with science might influence political choice. However, the proponents of greater public understanding of science themselves neglect to say how widespread scientific literacy would in practice better the operations of democracy.[1] It is assumed, not established, that lay knowledge of science is less than sufficient. No examples are given of how this inadequate understanding has harmed the performance of democratic governance. No mention is made of what would constitute 'adequate' public understanding. The suggestion is simply that a laity enthusiastic about science is preferable to one that is wary, indifferent or ignorant.

Nevertheless, even if Trachtman were correct in his contentions, his opponents might still fall back on the assertion that a public alienated from science might lose the resolve to support its inquiries. A campaign of public education would still be justified, therefore, as a means of instilling in the laity the requisite respect for the scientific venture.

However, Mazur (1981b) notes that the widely held assumption that the American public harbors a growing distrust of science is not confirmed by a series of ten national opinion surveys conducted from 1966 to 1980. He finds that confidence in *all* US institutions dropped sharply from 1966 to 1971, rose to a minor peak in 1974, and then remained relatively stable from 1975 to 1980. Indeed, science fared better in public esteem than most institutions, enjoying more confidence throughout the 1970s than any save medicine. He concludes that these data not only challenge the frequent assertion of a rising public distrust of science but also throw into doubt the need to raise public confidence in science.

Nonetheless, in the wealth of material on science and the media published since 1981, neither Trachtman's nor Mazur's objections are anywhere mentioned or noted.[2] The near-uniform call for a redoubled science journalism has nowhere questioned or elaborated its own basic assumptions. It has been preoccupied, rather, with ascertaining the deficiencies of press coverage of science and with formulating strategies and tactics whereby science communication might be 'improved'.

In that regard, the dominant concern has served to advance an essentially positivist portrayal of science as a heroic, apolitical and inherently rational endeavor; it has indeed insisted that 'good' science writing should promulgate just this portrayal for popular consumption. In the end, it has served those interests that have found in science a vehicle for the legitimation of the prevailing social order.

Transmission

Notwithstanding that science and scientists feature regularly in television, films, and advertising of all descriptions – and despite the fact that commentators refer frequently to the problem of science and the *media* – the dominant concern has in fact been *journalistic* coverage.[3] Most studies of the representation of science have limited their attentions primarily to the press and secondarily to documentary accounts in broadcasting. This limitation is probably based on two assumptions. First, the goal of fictional representation supposedly is not to impart a substantive knowledge of science or its findings. Second, therefore, fictional representation of science is neither guided nor constrained by canons of objective representation and thus does not figure largely in the 'problem' of science and media.

In focusing near-exclusively on nonfictional accounts of science, research has been dominated by a discrete, mechanical sender–receiver model of communication (see Friedman *et al.*, 1986, part I). Science is seen as an avenue of access to assured findings, and scientists – in the dissemination of these findings – as the initial sources. The members of the laity are understood purely as recipients of this information. Journalists and public relations personnel are viewed as intermediaries through which scientific findings filter. The task of science communication is to transmit as much information as possible with maximum fidelity.

Such a formulation of the problem has two pre-eminent consequences. First, it drives inquiry toward examining the operation and interaction of the various elements in the process (as they have been specified by the basic model). Second, from the very outset it establishes the scientist as hierarchically dominant over all other actors. Since the goal is undistorted communication, success must be measured against how well the final product matches the intentions of the scientist-source. Although the limitations of the audience and the organizational constraints of the media must be taken into account (so that 'successful' popularization is rarely a matter of reproducing the content of scientific texts or mimicking the exposition of scientists), it is the scientific community that is privileged as the ultimate arbiter of the adequacy of science coverage. Indeed, the interrogation of the communication process is most commonly conducted in light of the hierarchical dominance of the scientific camp.

Accuracy

Given that attention to popular science has been marshalled as a lobby for its improvement, the deficiencies of the press recur throughout the literature as a leitmotif. The corpus is rife with anecdotes illustrating how the fourth estate has ignored, misunderstood or otherwise misrepresented scientific work.

Occasionally these anecdotes, whatever their rhetorical utility, are apocryphal. For example, in two contributions Franklin recounts the same tale: 'back in the 1950s' (Franklin, 1981: p.100) or 'in the late 1960s' (Franklin, 1986: p.131), the first pulsar was discovered through the use of Cornell University's radio telescope at Arecibo, Puerto Rico. It is now accepted that pulsars are rapidly spinning magnetized neutron stars, but, at the time, all that was known was that something in the galaxy was emitting seemingly regular bursts of electro-magnetic radiation.

The astronomers, Franklin continues, judged that their discovery was of sufficient significance that the public should be informed. Initially unsure as to how to publicize their find, they contacted the largest circulation newspaper in the country, which duly dispatched a correspondent who toured the facility. Intrigued that the astronomers were at a loss to account for the regularity of the radio signals, the reporter asked whether they might not be artificial in origin – the product of an extraterrestrial intelligence.

> The astronomers laughed, sort of pleased that the fellow was beginning to grasp the basic vagueness of science. Sure, I suppose, sure. It could be anything. . . . And so it was that the most important astronomical discovery of the decade was announced on the front page of *The National Enquirer*. The banner headline, in 72-point type, said something like: ALIENS CONTACT EARTH.
>
> (Franklin, 1986: pp.1132–3)

Franklin tells (and retells) the story ostensibly to illustrate the pitfalls of science popularization. The scientists are chided for their naivete; *The National Enquirer* is derided for its flagrant misrepresentation of an important scientific discovery; and its vast readership is deplored for its gullibility and taste for sensation.

However, the anecdote itself cannot be true, and not simply because certain of its elements ring false. (Why were the astronomers so blissfully ignorant of the character of *The National Enquirer*? Do Cornell scientists not frequent supermarkets? And why, in any case, would they announce their find first in the popular press, bypassing their peer review journals, when they themselves were unsure what they had discovered?) The first pulsar was not discovered by the Arecibo dish; it was detected in late 1967 by graduate student Jocelyn Bell, working under the direction of Anthony Hewish and using an array at the University of Cambridge.

Neither would the supposed *Enquirer* treatment have been altogether a misrepresentation. The first pulsar is now designated as CP 1919 (Cambridge pulsar at 19 hr 19 min right ascension), but the signals detected in 1967 were so regular – flashing once every 1.33730 seconds – and therefore so anomalous that Bell and Hewish named the source LGM-1, an abbreviation for Little Green Men. Cornell University astronomer Carl Sagan recounts that when he heard of the discovery he was moved to speculate that the source might be an interstellar navigation beacon of a spacefaring extraterrestrial civilization (Sagan, 1973: p.260). Indeed, the announcement of the find was delayed until February 1968, in part because Hewish and his colleagues wondered whether the signals might not be artificial in origin.

Franklin is a Pulitzer Prize-winning journalist, and in committing such an anecdote to print without first verifying its contents he seems to have breached routine journalistic conduct. Ironically, he demonstrates by example precisely the complaints raised by the critics of popular science coverage: that the press might sacrifice accuracy in its zeal to tell an engaging story.

Accuracy of science coverage is an important element in the literature, and there have been attempts to assess the correspondence between journalistic accounts and the science being described. Broadly, these studies have taken two forms. First, some seek to quantify reporting accuracy by placing a numerical value on journalistic success in disseminating scientific information. Most of these studies have been published in *Journalism Quarterly*, although the error rates revealed are quoted widely elsewhere in the literature. Second, a number of case studies examine ongoing coverage of established scientific issues (stories followed by a number of different news outlets).

Typical of the former is the study by Tankard and Ryan (1974) in which 242 researchers who had served as sources for science articles were sent clippings of these reports, along with a four-page questionnaire in which they were asked to check for inaccuracies. The scientists could select from 42 different types of error, ranging from errors of fact to spelling mistakes and including such categories as misleading headlines, misquotations, omission of relevant information, science reported in a humorous vein, and so on. In the second part of the study, the authors attempted to measure scientists' attitudes to science writing in general.

The results showed a markedly higher incidence of error in science stories (a mean of 6.22 per article) than had been detected in previous studies of 'straight' news (which had been found to contain on average 1 error per story). Only 8.8 percent of the science stories were judged to be error-free, as opposed to about 50 percent of 'straight' news accounts. In general, the scientists reported considerable dissatisfaction with the accuracy of science stories, 82.4 percent of respondents agreeing that headlines were misleading and 76.3 percent agreeing that information crucial to the understanding of research results is often omitted from news stories.

Complementing such analyses have been the more general case studies of press performance, of which the Freimuth *et al.* (1984) examination of media coverage of cancer is typical. Newspaper reports were analysed to determine how closely they corresponded to the actual nature, incidence and body sites of the disease. Data from a content analysis of press reports dealing with cancer were compared with data supplied by the National Cancer Institute (NCI).

The authors enumerate a number of discrepancies between overall press coverage and the NCI data. Statistics on the incidence of cancer in general were lacking in the newspapers examined; colon–rectum cancer was under-reported relative to its actual incidence; coverage tended to emphasize dying rather than coping; approximately half of news stories mentioning the causes or risks of cancer carried headlines that were coded as 'fear arousing'. It is suggested that many cancer victims could be saved if journalists would publicize the proctosigmoidoscopy, a means of early detection for colon–rectum cancer.

These studies may be taken as representative. Both are attempts to pronounce on the accuracy of the press. Both render their judgment on the basis of a view of what press coverage *should* contain, and both reserve such judgment for the scientific community. Importantly, the Freimuth *et al.* study selects as its object of analysis an issue of manifestly political dimension – the correct attitude to adopt to caner and its treatment – and presumes to rule on press representation by appealing solely to the testimony of a scientific agency.

In that regard, the prominence of *accuracy* as a guiding concern assumes a further significance. It is difficult to contest that press reports on scientific work should be answerable to the scientist-authors for the accuracy with which their work has been represented. It makes little sense to argue that the journalist might 'understand' the scientist's findings better than the scientist himself or herself, or that the journalist's assessment of a work's scientific import is some-how superior to that of the scientist's peers. However, on the basis that the purely technical content of science journalism should be 'accurate' (in the eyes of the scientific community), the further claim is made that science is the rightfully dominant authority over the adequacy of press coverage of any issue to which science contributes. There is a slide from the premise that journalism should be required to get the scientific details right to the assertion that these details themselves dictate the form and tone that coverage should adopt.

Thus, Freimuth *et al.* implicitly blame the press for public 'misapprehension' of cancer, characterized presumably by inordinate fear and pessimism. That is, they assume not only that the NCI findings speak the 'reality' of cancer, but that there is a correct attitude toward the disease which derives from these data, and that in its misrepresentation of the available figures the press also promulgates a flawed and damaging public sentiment.

Translation and sensation

Although the dominant position accepts that there are consistent, systematic distortions in science coverage, the notion of 'bias', interestingly, does not figure largely. In other contexts, when the press is accused of 'bias', the charge implies that the inaccuracies work to the benefit of select parties. However, in the case of science reporting, there is no suggestion that any interest is served by the distortions characteristic of popular science. Rather, the deficiencies of the fourth estate in this regard are seen as issuing from the structural difficulties involved in reconciling the demands of science with the exigencies of newswork. Constraints of space and air time, the pressures of deadlines, the education of reporters, and so on, are seen to frustrate the goal of responsible and detailed coverage (see Friedman, 1986b; Goodfield, 1981: Chapter 1). This gives rise to what are identified as the two major sources of distortion in science coverage: the problem of translation and the danger of sensationalism.

The former derives from the fact that, while scientific theories or research findings emerge from the context of a specialized knowledge and are couched in terms of an equally specialized vocabulary, successful popularization demands that they be recast in the vernacular and that their comprehension require minimal reference to other knowledge. The issue, therefore, is whether and under what circumstances it is possible to 'translate' scientific work into a lay idiom without also corrupting it.

The danger of sensationalism is related to this problem. Many commentators apply the label 'sensational' to any science writing they deem so simplified that it can hardly do justice to the work it describes. Others use the term to designate reports that abandon the goal of undistorted communication to tell a flamboyant, exciting story.

However, as central to the dominant concern as the problem of translation and the danger of sensationalism may be, they have proven obstinately difficult to engage in a rigorous fashion. The problem of translation, for example, strikes to the heart of broad questions of pedagogy. How is it that individuals come to be conversant with previously unfamiliar concepts? What is the nature of explanation? In what does understanding consist?

The difficulties associated with sensationalism are similar. At what point does the journalistic labor of the science writer cease to be beneficial (by cultivating lay interest) and begin to detract from the overall goal (by obscuring scientific fact)? On what grounds can the charge of 'sensationalism' be proved?

Consequently, most commentators are content merely to point to the difficulties of adequate translation and to the lurking danger of sensationalism, without exploring their details. Studies that do directly engage the topics have been few and of limited worth.

In the case of the problem of translation, Hunsaker (1979) found that less 'difficult' science journalism elicited more reader enjoyment than complex accounts using unfamiliar terminology. In more detailed studies, Funkhouser and Maccoby (1971; 1973) concluded that it is possible to present the same scientific information in a range of styles, from that available in popular science magazines to that available in professional journals; that differences in style result in measurable differences in the effects on educated lay readers; and that 'simplified' science writing is enjoyed at all levels of readership, not merely at the lowest. On that basis, the 1973 study generated ten 'rules' of effective composition, urging science journalists to be explicit, use analogies, employ short sentences with short words, mention practical applications, and so on.

Although it is difficult to imagine any science writer deliberately favoring a specialized vocabulary and opting for convoluted exposition, these guidelines represent the most direct attempt to address the problem of translation. Despite the frequent citing of the problem as an inherent obstacle to science communication, its features are explored in only the most cursory manner.

The danger of sensationalism, too, is commonly mentioned but only sparingly examined. Attempts to document the presence of sensationalism in press coverage are limited to Glynn (1985) and Glynn and Tims (1980; 1982).

The latter two papers are near-identical reports on news coverage of an environmental debate. The authors conducted a content analysis of coverage in *The Knoxville News-Sentinel* and *The New York Times* over the space of six years. In brief, the study found that 'sensationalism' was rife in both papers and concluded that organizational constraints specific to the press – in particular, the need to concentrate on 'newsy' aspects that pander to reader interest – work to skew coverage to the detriment of adequate and fair attention to substantive issues.

However, despite the authors' insistence that their content analysis is a 'quantitative procedure which provides an objective measure of the importance and emphasis of explicitly defined content' (Glynn and Tims, 1980: p.102), the criteria according to which 'sensationalism' was measured are shot through with subjective assessments and value judgments. Stories were judged to be sensational if they contained what '*seemed* to be an *obvious overstatement* of fact' (although it is not specified what would constitute an overstatement of fact); if they 'placed *exceptional* emphasis on *unique* aspects of the situation' (neither 'exceptional' nor 'unique' being defined); if they 'introduced *apparent* bias'; if they 'associated the subject of the story with an *irrelevant* issue'; or if they 'treated the story in a *frivolous* manner' (*ibid.*: p.102, emphases added).

Once again, the charge of sensationalism stems simply from a view of what coverage *should* have contained and what emphasis it *should* have adopted. It is only in light of such an alternative that coverage can be characterized as irrelevant, frivolous, or carrying undue emphasis on certain aspects. However, in this instance, there has been a shift from scientist-sources as the arbiters of press accuracy to the media researchers themselves. It is Glynn and Tims who seemingly reserve the right to determine adequacy of coverage.

Strategies and tactics

Because 'noise' in science writing seems to derive predominantly from the press, the practical efforts at reformation have been directed to softening or limiting the mediating influence of the press – to reassert that the norms of science are hierarchically dominant over those of news production and that the latter, when necessary, should be suspended (or circumvented) to ensure accuracy.

The lobby for reform has advocated three distinct but complementary strategies for the pursuit of this end. First, journalists are to be better schooled in the procedures of science, so as to respect their sanctity. Second, scientists are to be made aware of the constraints of the media, so that in their dealings with the press they might be better able to compensate. Third, scientists are to be encouraged to bypass the journalistic community altogether and to advance the science communication project by addressing the public directly.

The first strategy calls for the expansion of science and technology as a specialized beat within journalism. The notion is that the general reporter cannot do justice to the complexities of science. At its most basic, the aim is to minimize the errors in science news caused purely by the ignorance of journalists. However, the expansion of science as a special topic of coverage offers other advantages.

To begin with, the position of science writer should require a background in science, or at least exposure to it at the university level. It is widely agreed that this would not only provide a grounding in the content of the sciences but would equip the reporter with a fundamental commitment to the values of the scientific enterprise (see Ryan and Dunwoody, 1975).

As well, the lobby for reform advocates university-level training in science communication for science and engineering as well as journalism students. Nelkin (1987) notes that there are already 43 programs in science journalism in 67 US colleges and universities, 14 of which offer graduate degrees (p.181). Seminars and university science instruction for practising science journalists are similarly encouraged (Goldstein, 1986: p.8).

In addition, the creation of a full-time science beat within a news organization means that science is no longer a topic to be covered sporadically but a subject on which coverage must be made available consistently. This makes the science writer dependent on the cooperation of the scientific community, particularly since, unlike the court reporter or the city hall correspondent, the science journalist has no set forum whose affairs can be covered on a daily basis. If science is to be a ready source of material, then the journalist must cultivate the trust of scientists. This can be accomplished only by producing coverage of which scientists themselves approve. Thus the literature is dotted with the reminder that, in the words of Nathan S. Heseltine of *The Washington Post*, 'the successful science writer builds his success on the esteem of the scientists' (quoted in Krieghbaum, 1967: p.120).

Furthermore, the position of science writer – the nature of the work it involves and its place in the hierarchy of the newsroom – encourages little mobility. As Dunwoody *et al.* (1981) confirm, whereas other journalists often shift beats or careers, science writers tend to stay with what they do. This, too, is seen as an advantage, in that numerous years of service bespeak not only a continuing on-the-job education in science, but also an individual who shares the excitement of science and who believes that its popularization is an important endeavor. As well, a science writer of long standing must presumably have won the respect of the community on which he or she reports.

The overall result is that the role of the science writer differs markedly from the traditional role of the journalist. The able science reporter is constructed as considerably more deferential to his or her subject matter, more answerable to the constituency being covered, than would be appropriate in other departments of the newsroom. There is no allowance for performance as gadfly, watchdog or adversary, as there is in the political bureaus, on the city desk, or even in the financial section. Rather, the role advocated is that of a skilled and sympathetic translator.

There is no overt suggestion that the journalist should serve as merely a spokesperson for science. On the contrary, the science writer is extolled not to 'try to hide the human, institutional, and theoretical difficulties of science and the misdemeanours of scientists' (Farago, 1976: p.13). Nonetheless, this criticism must always be conducted in the service of the larger enterprise, since the science writer 'must believe that in their totality the aims, ideas, thought-processes, and motivations incorporated in science are on balance beneficial to the world at large' (p.13). The consequences, otherwise, will be dire:

> If he does not believe all this, although the belief may be only half-conscious, his work is pre-judged to be sterile, and his efforts will be in vain, not only for the two publics he serves but for himself. He will be destroyed not only as an expert and a craftsman, but also as a human being.
> (p.13)

In addition to calling for more specialized science writers the lobby for reform advocates greater awareness on the part of scientists of the constraints of media work. Hence many of the texts on science and the media address themselves as much to interested scientists as to journalists or public information personnel. A few, such as Gastel (1983), Goldstein (1986) and N.E. Miller (1986b), presume a readership composed predominantly of scientists.

It is the Goldstein anthology, however (*Reporting Science: The Case of Aggression*), that is the most militant in its advocacy of scientist control of the communication process and therefore makes most evident certain of the motives that underlie such a demand. The volume presents itself at the outset as an analysis of news coverage of research on the causes of, and remedies for, 'aggression' in humans. However, it largely develops into an angry complaint on the part of aggrieved scientists that their research has been harmed by consistently unkind press portrayals. As well, it agitates in favor of the continued use of animals in experimentation, on the grounds that this work may eventually lead to solutions for problems of urban violence and national militarism. Central to its complaint is the charge that undue attention to animal experimentation has distorted public understanding of aggression research.

The anthology is therefore a primer for scientists on relations with the press, its aim being to educate those who conduct research using animals in the rigors of dispensing 'sound information' to the public. The tactic in doing so is fairly straightforward. Scientists are to cultivate the ability to present their work calmly and lucidly, playing on the image of science as supremely rational and pristinely objective:

> If you are invited to appear with an animal activist on a talk show or other program, you should accept . . . You should have prepared a few key points that you will try to make clearly and briefly if given even the remotest chance. You should try to avoid being distracted into spending your time answering your opponent's horrible examples. You should resist being interrupted just as you are about to make a telling point and, if your opponent succeeds, you should resume with 'I would like to complete what I was saying when you interrupted me'.
>
> (N.E. Miller, 1986a: p.viii)

The same theme is reiterated throughout the volume. Groebel (1986), for example, complains that in a *Der Speigel* cover story his findings on the effects of TV violence were presented alongside the dissenting opinions of the less well informed:

> I am not suggesting that the scientist's opinion should be above the others, but it is my belief that empirical work has a different analytical value compared to the essayistic opinions of ad-hoc experts. Consider the situation of a TV discussion where you have presented your results and are then told '. . . but I *think* the contrary'.
>
> (p.47)

Nevertheless, it is difficult to construe this as anything other than a suggestion that the scientist's voice should be dominant. Groebel's view seems to be that scientists' findings are objective, uncontestable, and enter into public discourse only so as to be recognized as true. Dissent is fruitless (in the long run), an annoyance (in the short run), and ultimately counter to the public interest.

Finally, the lobby for reform advocates purging the communication process of tainting influence by having scientists and scientific institutions publicize their work themselves. In part, what is meant here is that more scientists should participate in popularization via books, op-ed or feature articles in local newspapers, documentary production for local television, and so on. The most likely form such participation might assume, however, is collaboration with the public information office of the scientist's own institution.

In the United States, most large research universities maintain news offices or media centers that publicize the institution's achievements. Because media office personnel are not employed by the press but by the university (or hospital, or scientific organization), they are considered to be insulated from many journalistic pressures. In particular, they are directly accountable to the researcher for the accuracy and tone of the coverage produced, and therefore scientist involvement with a public information department is commonly seen as direct public address, or as near as is possible.

Thus, for example, Walum's (1975) 'modest proposals' to the American Sociological Association for the solution of 'major problems' in public communication include having the association's Committee for Public Information prepare a manual briefing members on relations with the press; developing a public relations office; employing a clipping service to monitor press attention to sociology and, where necessary, to correct 'misstatements'; and making efforts to secure the employment of sociologists as technical advisers for television programs (p.31).[4]

These, then, are the basic strategies advocated to rectify the problem of science and the media. Journalists are to respect the demands of science in their coverage and to be held accountable to scientists for their errors. Scientists are encouraged to participate in the communication process and are to be drilled in how to handle the press. Scientists are to forgo the press entirely and establish their own agencies of communication. The tactics in each case are left vague, but the goal is clear: to minimize journalistic interference.

There are only two issues in the literature left outstanding. The first is the reservation, only recently raised, that the campaign for reform has had the effect of rendering the press overly compliant to the scientific estate, thus contributing to a glorified (and therefore skewed) portrayal of science. The second is the more longstanding worry that, if the press *were* wholly responsible in its science coverage, eliminating all tendencies to sensation, there would be nothing to ensure reader interest. The first is the problem of deference; the second is the problem of disinterest. They are the only instances of disagreement within the dominant concern.

Deference

Although the subtitle of Nelkin's (1987) volume is *How the Press Covers Science and Technology*, the title itself is *Selling Science*. The book, like its predecessors, argues that science is unfortunately ill-understood by the majority and that media performance in its coverage has been less than exemplary. Nelkin, however, contends that the US press has been unduly subordinate to the scientific community and that the science communication effort overall has assumed the form of an institutional advertisement.

She charges that the interests of both scientists and journalists conspire to skew coverage so that science is typically represented as progressive, problem-solving and beneficial. The result, she argues, is a superficial and ultimately erroneous portrayal that neglects both the tentative nature of scientific inquiry and its political context.

Within the dominant concern, this is a relatively subversive contention; certainly it would seem to call for a reversal of the hierarchical scientist–journalist relationship championed by the mainstream lobby for reform. Nonetheless, the form in which the complaint is rendered – that press attention to science is shallow and unrealistic – is not only one with which scientists themselves presumably would have little quarrel, but is also merely a variation on the charge, first voiced in the 1950s, that popular science is too 'gee whiz', too preoccupied by the power and success of science to probe the complex processes by which it works.

The recent divergence on the question of press deference is best illustrated in the different assessments of the management of the press during the debate over recombinant DNA in the mid-1970s, and in particular during the conference on international safety held at Asilomar, California, in February 1975.

It was thought, in the mid-1970s, that recombinant techniques harbored the potential for industrial application. Cultures of the host bacteria might in effect function as cheap and efficient factories for the production of marketable biological products, such as human insulin or growth hormone. However, there were perceived risks attached to recombinant DNA research. Goodfield (1981) calls these 'hazards' and avoids specifying their nature. It is a curious omission, since the Asilomar conference she goes on to describe concerned itself precisely with the question of safety guidelines to minimize any risks.

The concerns about risk sprang from the recognition that one could not be certain that genetically altered micro-organisms, if released from the laboratory to the larger environment, would not be harmful. The popular press played up a number of worst-case scenarios. One involved the fear that a hardy carcinogenic microbe, originally designed for the study of cancer, might escape its containment and cause pandemics of incurable disease. Another concerned the worry that a bacterium designed initially to digest oil spills would spread throughout the environment, feeding on the world's oil supplies.

At the Asilomar conference, called to draw up guidelines for recombinant DNA experiments, nonscientist involvement was limited to a panel composed (apparently by accident) exclusively of lawyers and to the presence of 16 invited journalists, who acted only as observers, were enjoined to stay for the entire three-and-a-half day conference, were permitted to file stories only when the proceedings had concluded, and were denied the use of any but still cameras (thus eliminating television coverage). Goodfield lauds such organization, noting that the conference produced not only three award-winning articles but also a marriage between two of the attending journalists. Coverage was further enhanced by the fact that 'the most vivid publications stayed away', and the eventual result, she concludes, quoting Richard Hutton, was that 'informed public scrutiny of science had become a real possibility' (Goodfield, 1981: p.49).

In Goodfield's view, therefore, the most appropriate and advantageous relationship is one in which the scientific community takes a small number of carefully selected journalists into its confidence, isolates them from outside sources, and stands in judgment of their ability to reproduce scientists' own understanding of the proceedings. It is a view shared by others (Russell, 1986: p.93).

It is also a view that lately has been contested, notably by Altimore (1982) and Goodell (1986). Goodell's study is the more detailed, seeking to show that American science writers are both dependent upon and subordinate to the priorities of science as an institution and that this relationship involves the complicity of the press. Her reconstruction of the debate over recombinant DNA from 1974 is one that emphasizes the gradual increase of the influence of the scientific community on press coverage.

She notes that reporting of the debate prior to the Asilomar conference was precisely of the sort deplored by scientists, emphasizing as it did the hypothetical, the dramatic and the threatening. As the *The Philadelphia Bulletin* announced in a 19 July 1974 headline: 'Genetic scientists seek ban – world health peril feared'.

As a result, the scientists resolved to exercise greater control over the press at the Asilomar conference. It was not, as Goodfield contends, that 'the most vivid publications stayed away'. It was that they – along with organizations such as the Canadian Broadcasting Corporation – were denied press credentials.

At the time, the coverage of Asilomar was widely praised for its quality and clarity. As Goodell observes, however, the embargo had the consequence of encouraging reportage that adopted the terms favored by the scientists present.

In the wake of the conference, Goodell observes first the curtailment of debate in the press over safety concerns and subsequently a shift in reporting to the bold promise of the genetic engineering industry, spurred by a public relations campaign that promoted the potential for benefits and profits. Once again, she argues, coverage followed the views of scientist-spokespersons and neglected the cautions of health specialists, financial analysts, or critics of any hue.

Goodell accepts that some variant of the relationship between scientists and the press obtains in all avenues of journalism, but she suggests a number of reasons that its features should be so pronounced in the case of science writing and therefore so 'unhealthy' (1986: p.177). First, journalists are just as intimidated by science as other lay folk. As a result, editors are inclined toward stories that feature sources with obvious credentials and pre-established credibility – a policy that tends to focus press attention on the mainstream of scientific work and opinion.

Second, inexperienced journalists are unlikely to embark on investigative ventures that involve acquiring and evaluating information that has not been volunteered by the scientific community. Even experienced journalists are wary of such reporting, since it might well jeopardize the relationship they have developed over time with a distrustful scientific estate. As well, veteran writers all too often share scientists' enthusiasm for science and worry that reporting on its political aspects will merely tarnish its image. The end result is that

> scientists and science reporters have frequently assumed that the views of scientists on scientific issues are definitive, the product of expertise and collective wisdom, and that the views of lay participants, such as environmentalists, labor leaders, or religious leaders, are somehow inferior or extraneous.
>
> (*ibid.*: p.177)

As a consequence, it would appear that within the dominant concern a relatively new criticism has begun to emerge: far from ignoring or distorting science, the press is in fact complicit in the advancement and protection of the interests of the scientific estate. The significance of such a charge lies in the implication that the agitations for 'improved' science communication have been successful and in the suggestion that the end result is not necessarily in the public interest.

However, this is not a radical departure from the strictures of the dominant concern, principally because it has not yet embraced the perspective of the critical tendency in communication studies. That is, Nelkin and Goodell fault current science writing for its acritical stance *only relative to standard journalistic practice*. While the journalist in general is taken to be autonomous, skeptical and adversarial, the science writer, by comparison, is chided for being a shill for scientific interests. The charge is that the 'proper' relationship between the press and its objects of coverage in this instance has been abrogated, not that the fourth estate invariably and inevitably services the interests of the prevailing order – and that the compliant portrayal of a heroic scientific rationality is only one means among a myriad whereby this is accomplished. In that regard, the complaints of Nelkin and Goodell amount merely to a call for the 'toughening' of journalistic standards, not for a wholesale revision of the very foundations of academic discourse on science and the media.

Disinterest

There remains one final problem for those who would 'improve' science reporting. Given the finding by Miller and Barrington (1981) that the public 'attentive' to science is at most one-fifth of the total population, and given the drive to purge science coverage of 'sensational' elements that appeal to reader interest, the issue becomes how, in practice, to produce a science writing that, while true to science, is nonetheless sufficiently arresting to capture widespread public attention. That is, even if the press dramatically increased the quantity and quality of its science coverage, what would guarantee that the laity would respond? Would the simple presence of more and 'better' science news result eventually in a scientifically literate population?

In essence, after all the studies, the content analyses, the ruminations and recommendations, what remains is the rarely spoken fear that *without* the narrative artifice that comes with press handling, science makes for unfortunately dreary subject matter. Thus, a report commissioned by the Canadian Ministry of State, Science and Technology emphasized that 'science news and science features need not be dull; science need not be irrelevant and it need not be technical' (Dubas, 1976: p.13). Nonetheless, such statements suggest that at present science coverage is indeed dull and that this is in part responsible for lay ignorance (see also Farago, 1976: pp.33–4, 42).

Nevertheless, if science writing is to be successful, it must entice readers; to attract a readership, it must promise a pleasure in return. Barring startling tabloid-style treatment or coverage stressing imminent technical benefits, science has in fact only one pleasure to offer: the pleasure scientists themselves derive from their work. The duty of the science writer therefore comes to include not only the transmission of scientific content, but also the communication of the sense of wonder and adventure that drives science. However, the problem of how to capture and reproduce the pleasure of inquiry remains. The only solution proposed is to emphasize *investigation*. As a tactic, this has a number of advantages.

First, it serves to divert attention from the 'sensational' preoccupation with technical application and instead focuses on the processes of inquiry – a factor consistent with the agitations of the dominant concern.

Second, in detailing the researcher's own procedures of inquiry, the journalist presumably comes closest to capturing the joy of scientists themselves: the achievements rooted in the mundane.

Third, the journalist acquires the narrative element necessary to attract reader interest: a readily available mechanism whereby the contents of scientific *reports* might be transformed into science *stories*. Clearly, the pleasure offered the reader is that of the detective story, in which a mystery is solved, a puzzle is pieced together and a solution is eventually revealed by dint of effort, expertise and a flash of either genius or luck.

This basic format allows the science writer a good deal of latitude, just as it does the mystery writer, and the experienced journalist will likely have written a number of variations on the central theme. Drama is invariably heightened, however, when the stakes are high and time is of the essence. Hence two common variants are the 'race against the clock' and the 'race against a competing research institution'. (Witness coverage of everything from the Apollo program to AIDS to cold fusion.)

As a consequence, it is the process of investigation that is stressed in the literature, both as more true to the nature of science itself and as more likely to cultivate lay interest (Farago, 1976: p.11). Nonetheless, while the tactic is common, it also admits of the complaint that it portrays science in altogether too heroic a fashion. Although this complaint is similar to that made by Nelkin and Goodell, in this instance it is raised by scientists, and on quite different grounds.

In particular, the narrativized portrayal works to feed the sentiment that the scientist who makes extensive contact with the media does so out of motives of self-promotion. Individual scientists may register no complaint in being cast as the heroes of grand procedures of investigation, but their colleagues may well resent and deprecate such a representation.

As well, if widely and repeatedly applied, science-as-investigation stories may work to portray science in far too successful and reliable a light for the comfort of many scientists. Unless they are exceptional variations on the theme, such stories require that the investigation actually result in findings of merit. The mystery must be unravelled if the reader is not to feel cheated. As a result,

> the public image of science tends to be one of a methodical force, ruthless and unstoppable in its logical and rational assault on the problems that face mankind. To use C.D. Darlington's analogy, what comes across is a picture of science as a giant steamroller, 'cracking its problems one by one with even and inexorable force'.
>
> (Trachtman, 1981: p.14).

Such an image, flattering though it may be, is judged naive by scientists themselves, who are all too aware that though their work *can* be personally and socially rewarding, it is not perpetually so. Moreover, the portrayal may inflate expectations about what science can accomplish. These sentiments are most commonly expressed in the complaint that the press, in focusing on the successful outcome of investigations, cheapens science by representing it as a series of 'breakthroughs'. Krieghbaum (1967) made the point by quoting Edward L. Tatum, a 1958 Nobel Prize winner in medicine and physiology, who objected not only to the overuse of such words as 'breakthrough' and 'major advance' but also to 'those stories written as if the most recent findings were completely new, instead of based simply on, and continuing from, earlier work' (p.165). Almost 20 years later, Jerome (1986a) lamented that still:

> All too often, the 'Eureka!' approach to reporting science prevails. A review of cover headlines in *Discover*, *Science 82*, and *Science Digest* for the first half of 1982 shows that 'New!' was still the headline-writer's favorite word: 'New Science and Fireworks,' 'New Facts Stun Paleontologists,' 'New

Physiology,' 'A New Science That Can Predict Winners and Losers at Sex,' 'A New Geometry of Nature,' 'New Windows on the Body'.

(p.150)

Like Nelkin and Goodell, Jerome advocates coverage that would concentrate on 'science policy' matters. However, beyond the vague call for a science writing that would scrutinize the institutional aspects of science – its politics and economics, presumably – there is no attempt to specify what form such coverage might take, whether the scientific constituency would welcome such a development, whether editors would agree to it, and whether readers would find it an attractive innovation. That is, the call for the 'politicization' of the science beat has thus far failed to set out what this entails and how it might be effected. It rests for the present purely on a dissatisfaction with the science coverage currently available – which is, after all, how concern over the 'problem' of science and the media was initially broached.

The dominant concern, reconsidered

There is an irony to the dominant concern that is revealed only following a review of the literature. In 1977, Goodell pointed out that public contact with scientists via the media was largely limited to a relatively small group of 'visible scientists', whose members displayed similar traits and outlooks. Dunwoody (1978; 1980; Dunwoody et al., 1981) documented the existence of an 'inner club' within the ranks of American science writers: a relatively small, collaborative group of journalists who dominated the science coverage made available.

The irony is this: the discourse on science and the media seems itself to have been dominated by a comparatively small group of academics who made the subject their speciality, whose work established a mutually held agenda, who collaborated often, and who together largely fixed the terms in which the problem was to be understood. Often these individuals have been attached to a department in which science communication is an emphasis, and hence they have educated their students in light of the dominant concern. They have organized and attended the meetings and conference sessions devoted to science communication and appear as a group sufficiently closed so that writers working counter to the dominant concern (e.g., Trachtman) have been ignored. In addition, they have enjoyed extensive links with organizations devoted to the advancement of science's interests and the improvement of its public image.[5]

The result has been that the science communication project, in the United States at least, has been inextricably allied with the efforts of scientific organizations to engineer dutiful coverage and to create a public that will accede to science's claim on rational authority. Although the champions of improved science writing admit forthrightly that they are devoted to the cause of advancing science, they nonetheless deny that their work has been in the service of political interests, since science itself is taken to be a politically disinterested endeavor. Because the dominant view has remained isolated from developments in other academic disciplines (in particular those that point to the role of science and scientific rationality in the preservation and management of social order), it has promulgated a view of science that sees the enterprise purely in its guise as objective inquiry – and, indeed, the overall effort has been to entrench this view in press coverage and in the popular imagination.

Nevertheless, even within its own terms the dominant concern comes to an untidy conclusion. It has been enormously successful in fixing the terms in which popular science is to be addressed; it has been fully participant in the expansion of science communication as a field of employment; and it has established itself as the prevailing context for the actual practice of science journalism. But in the final analysis, the premises on which it has been founded have been assumed, rather than demonstrated; certain elements of the corpus are questionable in their method; and despite the fact that it is at root a prescriptive discourse, no definitive program to implement a sound science journalism that will also ignite popular interest has been forthcoming.

Indeed, as staunch as the consensus has been, it unravels when called upon to elaborate techniques or content of optimal science journalism. What remains, therefore, is a powerful discourse, firmly entrenched in the universities, promoted by scientific organizations and supported by constituencies of journalists and science information personnel, the major thrust of which has been the incessant, insistent reminder that lay acquaintance with science is insufficient and that press coverage is inadequate.

However, the point is not simply that the dominant concern is limited and repetitive, but rather that it performs an ideological labor. It works continually to shore up the traditional, heroic, positivist understanding of science as an assured avenue of access to the real – an understanding that has not only been seriously questioned in the philosophy of science but has also been identified within social theory as an ideology crucial to the workings of late capitalist society. Thus the dominant concern, in largely ignoring the ideological aspects of science, actively closes off the type of critical perspective offered by writers such as Feyerabend (1978), Foucault (1970; 1972), Habermas (1970), Lewontin, Rose and Kamin (1984), Marcuse (1964) and Reiss (1982). While other areas in media studies have come to be informed by a broad critical perspective, the representation of science has been examined in light of a stolidly mainstream and increasingly antiquated heuristic.

It is true that there have been some attempts to address media coverage of science in terms wholly opposed to the dominant concern,[6] but these have been relatively recent and as yet comprise no uniform critical corpus. It may be that no critical project will be able to gather momentum until the dominant concern has been unseated *as* the dominant concern. That will occur only when the traditional 'problem' is itself made the object of critical scrutiny – a task to which this article has attempted to make an initial contribution.

Notes

1 Indeed, on those few occasions when the notion of democratic involvement in science is considered, it is rebuffed as a perversion of the scientific process. Farago (1976), for instance, holds that 'the lack of public concern [for science] is genuine, and may it long remain so, for if a camel is a horse designed by a committee, a new chemistry developed by public request would be a horrendous monster indeed' (p.49). It would appear that the democracy envisioned by the champions of greater scientific literacy would not extend to lay supervision of science.

2 Nelkin (1987) does cite Trachtman's paper in an endnote (chapter 10, note 7), but only to support the assertion that science writers, required to entertain as well as inform, 'are attracted to nonroutine, nonconventional, and even aberrant events' (p.175). She ignores the substantive contents of his paper. Friedman *et al.* (1986) include in their anthology a bibliography of research on mass media science communication that lists 95 books, articles and conference papers. Two of these articles are by Mazur (although not the article at issue here).

3 The sole prominent exception has been the content analysis of US network television (Gerbner *et al.*, 1981).

4 In fact, many large American scientific organizations maintain precisely this sort of public information arm. The American Psychological Association, for example, published a *Media Guide* by K. Holmay in 1980 and a handbook on *Communicating with the Public via the Media about Psychology* by M.M. Olean in 1977. The American Institute of Physics has published *Physics Goes Public* (1981) and the American Chemical Society makes available a similar publication. The American Institute of Physics, with money from the National Science Foundation, produces two-minute video clips about physics that are sent to television stations across the country. Indeed, since the debut of the 'problem' of science and the media, the growth in science communication personnel has not been concentrated in the press so much as in public information offices attached to hospitals, universities, museums, research institutions, the research and development laboratories of large corporations, and so on. At present, a student specializing in science communication is far likelier to find employment as an information officer than as a science journalist proper.

5 Indeed, much of the work on science and the media has been produced with the financial assistance of scientific agencies. The volume *Communicating University Research* (Alberger and Carter, 1981) is based on the proceedings of an October 1980 conference financed by the Public Understanding of Science program of the National Science Foundation. Gastel's (1983) primer was published by the Institute for Scientific Information. Goodfield's (1981) volume was published by the American Association for the Advancement of Science (AAAS). Friedman *et al.*'s (1986) anthology emerged from a workshop and symposium organized by the editors at the 1982 AAAS meeting, and although published by a division of Macmillan, the book was prepared under the aegis of the AAAS.

6 For a discussion of such critical appraisals of popular science and the challenges that lie ahead for future work, see Dornan (in press).

References and related readings

Alberger, P.E. and Carter, V.L. (eds) (1981). *Communicating University Research.* Washington, DC: Council for Advancement and Support of Education.

Altimore, M. (1982). The social construction of a scientific controversy: Comments on press coverage of the recombinant DNA debate. *Science, Technology & Human Values*, 7, Fall.

American Institute of Physics. (1981). *Physics Goes Public*. New York.

Amor, A.J. (1986). Science journalism in Asia. In J.H. Goldstein (ed.), *Reporting Science: The Case of Aggression*. Hillsdale, NJ: Lawrence Erlbaum.

Bander, M. (1983). The scientist and the mass media. *The New England Journal of Medicine*, 308, May.

Bennett, W. (1979). Science goes glossy. *The Sciences*, 19 (7).

Bennett, W. (1981, January–February). Science hits the newsstand. *Columbia Journalism Review*.

Berry, D. (1984, July). Science and technology on TV: Why so little research? Paper presented at the first International Television Studies Conference, British Film Institute, London.

Bevan, W. (1976). The sound of the wind that's blowing. *The American Psychologist*, 31 (7).

Branscomb, A.W. (1981). Knowing how to know. *Science, Technology & Human Values*, 36, Summer.

Broad, W.J. (1982). Science magazines: the second wave rolls in. *Science*, 215 (4530).

Bromley, D.A. (1982). The other frontiers of science. *Science*, 215 (4536).

Burkett, D.W. (1973). *Writing Science News for the Mass Media*. Houston: Gulf Publishing.

Carter, V.L. (1981). Introduction. In P.L. Alberger and V.L. Carter (eds), *Communicating University Research*. Washington, DC: Council for Advancement and Support of Education.

Cohen, I.B. (1981). Fear and distrust of science in historical perspective. *Science, Technology & Human Values*, 36, Summer.

Crisp, D.W. (1986). Scientists and the local press. In S.M. Friedman, S. Dunwoody and C.L. Rogers (eds), *Scientists and Journalists: Reporting Science as News*. New York: Free Press.

Cronholm, M. and Sandell, R. (1981). Scientific information: A review of research. *Journal of Communication*, 31 (2).

Cunningham, A.M. (1986). Not just another day in the newsroom: The accident at TMI. In S.M. Friedman, S. Dunwoody and C.L. Rogers (eds), *Scientists and Journalists: Reporting Science as News*. New York: Free Press.

Doemel, W. (1986). Newspaper columns for fun and profit. In S.M. Friedman, S. Dunwoody and C.L. Rogers (eds), *Scientists and Journalists: Reporting Science as News*. New York: Free Press.

Dornan, C. (1977). The science writers: like it or not, most people look to them to demystify science. *Science Forum*, 10 (4).

Dornan, C. (1988). The 'problem' of science and the media: a few seminal texts in their context, 1956–1965. *Journal of Communication Inquiry*, 12 (2).

Dornan, C. (in press). Science and scientism in the media. *Science as Culture*.

Drake, D. (1972, April). A science writer looks at the American newspaper. *American Association for the Advancement of Science Bulletin*, 17.

Dubas, O. (1976). *Media Impact: Vol. 3. The Scientific Community and the Mass Media*. Ottawa: Ministry of State, Science and Technology.

Dunwoody, S. (1978). *Science writers at work*. Research Report No. 7, School of Journalism and Center for New Communications, Indiana University, Bloomington.

Dunwoody, S. (1980). The science writing inner club: A communication link between science and the lay public. *Science, Technology & Human Values*, 5, Winter.

Dunwoody, S. (1986a). The scientist as source. In S.M. Friedman, S. Dunwoody and C.L. Rogers (eds), *Scientists and Journalists: Reporting Science as News*. New York: Free Press.

Dunwoody, S. (1986b). When science writers cover the social sciences. In J.H. Goldstein (ed.), *Reporting Science: The Case of Aggression*. Hillsdale, NJ: Lawrence Erlbaum.

Dunwoody, S., Petrusky, B. and Rogers, C. (1981). The gatekeepers: The inner circle in science writing. In P.L. Alberger and V.L. Carter (eds), *Communicating University Research*. Washington, DC: Council for Advancement and Support of Education.

Dunwoody, S. and Ryan, M. (1983). Public information persons as mediators between scientists and journalists. *Journalism Quarterly*, 60 (4).

Dunwoody, S. and Ryan, M. (1985). Scientific barriers to the popularization of science in the mass media. *Journal of Communication*, 35 (1).

Dunwoody, S. and Scott, B.T. (1982). Scientists as mass media sources. *Journalism Quarterly*, 59 (1).

DuPont, R. (1981). Coping with controversial research. In P.L. Alberger and V.L. Carter (eds), *Communicating University Research*. Washington, DC: Council for Advancement and Support of Education.

Eron, L.D. (1986). The social responsibility of the scientist. In J.H. Goldstein (ed.), *Reporting Science: The Case of Aggression*. Hillsdale, NJ: Lawrence Erlbaum.

Etzioni, A. and Nunn, C. (1974, Summer). The public appreciation of science in contemporary America. *Daedalus*, 103.

Farago, P. (1976). *Science and the Mass Media*. Oxford: Oxford University Press.

Feyerabend, P.K. (1978). *Science in a Free Society*. London: Verso.

Foucault, M. (1970). *The Order of Things*. New York: Pantheon.

Foucault, M. (1972). *The Archaeology of Knowledge*. New York: Pantheon.

Franklin, J. (1986). Humanizing science through literary writing. In S.M. Friedman, S. Dunwoody and C.L. Rogers (eds), *Scientists and Journalists: Reporting Science as News*. New York: Free Press.

Franklin, J. (1981). Translating the curious languages of research. In P.L. Alberger and V.L. Carter (eds), *Communicating University Research*. Washington, DC: Council for Advancement and Support of Education.

Freimuth, V.S., Greenberg, R.H., DeWitt, J. and Romano, R.M. (1984). Covering cancer: Newspapers and the public interest. *Journal of Communication*, 34 (1).

Friedman, S.M. (1981). Teaching science writing to journalists: Report on a workshop. *Science, Technology & Human Values*, 36, Summer.

Friedman, S.M. (1986a). A case of benign neglect: Coverage of Three Mile Island before the accident. In S.M. Friedman, S. Dunwoody and C.L. Rogers (eds), *Scientists and Journalists: Reporting Science as News*. New York: Free Press.

Friedman, S.M. (1986b). The journalist's world. In S.M. Friedman, S. Dunwoody and C.L. Rogers (eds), *Scientists and Journalists: Reporting Science as News*. New York: Free Press.

Friedman, S.M., Dunwoody, S. and Rogers, C.L. (eds) (1986). *Scientists and Journalists: Reporting Science as News*. New York: Free Press.

Funkhouser, G.R. and Maccoby, N. (1971). Communicating specialized science information to a lay audience. *Journal of Communication*. 27 (1).

Funkhouser, G.R. and Maccoby, N. (1973). Tailoring science writing to the general audience. *Journalism Quarterly*, 50 (2).

Gastel, B. (1983). *Presenting Science to the Public*. Philadelphia: ISI Press.

Gerbner, G., Gross, L., Morgan, M. and Signorielli, N. (1981, May–June). Scientists on the TV screen. *Society*, 18.

Glynn, C. (1985). Science reporters and their editors judge 'sensationalism'. *Newspaper Research Journal*, 6 (3).

Glynn, C. and Tims, A.R. (1980, Winter). Environmental and natural resource issues: Press sensationalism. *45th North American Wildlife and Natural Resource Transaction*.

Glynn, C.G. and Tims, A.R. (1982). Sensationalism in science issues: A case study. *Journalism Quarterly*, 59 (1).

Goldstein, J.H. (1986). Social science, journalism, and public policy. In J.H. Goldstein (ed.), *Reporting Science: The case of Aggression*. Hillsdale, NJ: Lawrence Erlbaum.

Goodell, R. (1977). *The Visible Scientists*. Boston: Little, Brown.

Goodell, R. (1980, November–December). The gene craze. *Columbia Journalism Review*.

Goodell, R. (1981, January–February). TV science: Fun, games, UFOs – and *Cosmos*. *Columbia Journalism Review*.

Goodell, R. (1986). How to kill a controversy: The case of recombinant DNA. In S.M. Friedman, S. Dunwoody and C.L. Rogers (eds), *Scientists and Journalists: Reporting Science as News*. New York: Free Press.

Goodfield, J. (1981). *Reflections on Science and the Media*. Washington, DC: American Association for the Advancement of Science.

Groebel, J. (1986). Determinants of science reporting in Europe. In J.H. Goldstein (ed.), *Reporting Science: The Case of Aggression*. Hillsdale, NJ: Lawrence Erlbaum.

Grouse, L.D. (1981). The Ingelfinger rule. *Journal of the American Medical Association*, 245 (4).

Habermas, J. (1970). Technology and science as 'ideology'. In *Toward a Rational Society: Student Protest, Science, and Politics* (Jeremy J. Shapiro, Trans.). Boston: Beacon Press.

Holmay, K. (1980). *Media Guide*. Washington, DC: American Psychological Association.

Hunsaker, A. (1979). Enjoyment and information gain in science articles. *Journalism Quarterly*, 56 (3).

Jerome, F. (1986a). Gee whiz! Is that all there is? In S.M. Friedman, S. Dunwoody and C.L. Rogers (eds), *Scientists and Journalists: Reporting Science as News*. New York: Free Press.

Jerome, F. (1986b). Prospects of science journalism. In J.H. Goldstein (ed.), *Reporting Science: The Case of Aggression*. Hillsdale, NJ: Lawrence Erlbaum.

Kimura, S. (1985). *Japan's Science Edge: How the Cult of Anti-Science Thought in America Limits US Scientific and Technological Progress*. Lanham, Md.: University Press of America.

Kirsch, J. (1979). On a strategy for using the electronic media to improve public understanding of science and technology. *Science, Technology & Human Values*, 4, Spring.

Krieghbaum, H. (1967). *Science and the Mass Media*. New York: New York University Press.

La Follette, M.C. (1978, April). Observations on science, the media and the public at the 1978 meeting of the AAAS. *Newsletter on Science, Technology, and Human Values* 23.

La Follette, M.C. (1981). On public communication of science and technology. *Science, Technology & Human Values*, 36, Summer.

Lear, J. (1970, Summer). The trouble with science writing. *Columbia Journalism Review*.

Lewontin, R., Rose, S. and Kamin, L. (1984). *Not in our Genes: Biology, Ideology, and Human Nature*. New York: Pantheon.

Marcuse, H. (1964). *One Dimensional Man*. Boston: Beacon Press.

Marx, L. (1983). Are science and society going in the same direction? *Science, Technology and Human Values*, 8 (4).

Mayer, J. (1981). The national importance of communicating university research. In P.L. Alberger and V.L. Carter (eds), *Communicating University Research*. Washington, DC: Council for Advancement and Support of Education.

Mazur, A. (1977). Public confidence in science. *Social Studies of Science*, 7 (1).

Mazur, A. (1981a). Media coverage and public opinion on scientific controversies. *Journal of Communication*, 31 (2).

Mazur, A. (1981b). Opinion poll measurement of American confidence in science. *Science, Technology & Human Values*, 36, Summer.

McBride, G. (1981). Now for the latest news. *Journal of the American Medical Association*, 245 (4).

McCall, R.B. and Stocking, S.H. (1982). Between scientists and public: Communicating psychological research through the mass media. *American Psychologist*, 37 (9).

Metzinger, N. (1974). *Science in the Newspaper*. Washington, DC: American Association for the Advancement of Science.

Miller, J.D. (1986). Reaching the attentive and interested publics for science. In S.M. Friedman, S. Dunwoody and C.L. Rogers (eds), *Scientists and Journalists: Reporting Science as News*. New York: Free Press.

Miller, J.D. and Barrington, T.M. (1981). The acquisition and retention of scientific information. *Journal of Communication*, 31 (2).

Miller, J.D., Prewitt, K. and Pearson, R. (1980). *Attitudes of the US Public Toward Science and Technology*. Chicago: University of Chicago, National Opinion Research Center.

Miller, N.E. (1986a). Foreword. In J.H. Goldstein (ed.), *Reporting Science: The Case of Aggression*. Hillsdale, NJ: Lawrence Erlbaum.

Miller, N.E. (1986b). The scientist's responsibility for public information: A guide to effective communication with the media. In S.M. Friedman, S. Dunwoody and C.L. Rogers (eds), *Scientists and Journalists: Reporting Science as News*. New York: Free Press.

National Science Board. (1983). Public attitudes toward science and technology. In *Science Indicators 1982: Report of the National Science Board 1983*. Washington, DC: National Science Foundation.

Nelkin, D. (1987). *Selling Science: How the Press Covers Science and Technology*. New York: W.H. Freeman.

Novak, M. (1981). Journalism, the academy, and the new class. In P.L. Alberger and V.L. Carter (eds), *Communicating University Research*. Washington, DC: Council for Advancement and Support of Education.

Nunn, C.Z. (1979). Readership and coverage of science and technology in newspapers. *Journalism Quarterly*, 56 (1).

Olean, M.M. (1977). *Communicating with the Public – Via the Media – about Psychology*. Washington, DC: American Psychological Association.

O'Leary, D.S. (1986). Physicians and reporters: Conflicts, commonalities, and collaboration. In S.M. Friedman, S. Dunwoody and C.L. Rogers (eds), *Scientists and Journalists: Reporting Science as News*. New York: Free Press.

Patterson, J. (1982). A Q study of attitudes of young adults about science and science news. *Journalism Quarterly*, 59 (3).

Perlman, D. (1974, Summer). Science and the mass media. *Daedalus*, 103.

Perlman, D. (1981). Informing the public about research: The media. In P.L. Alberger and V.L. Carter (eds), *Communicating University Research*. Washington, DC: Council for Advancement and Support of Education.

Powledge, T.M. (1986). What is 'the media' and why is it saying those terrible things about aggression research? In J.H. Goldstein (ed.), *Reporting Science: The Case of Aggression*. Hillsdale, NJ: Lawrence Erlbaum.

Prewitt, K. (1982). The public and science policy. *Science, Technology & Human Values*, 7 (39).

Prewitt, K. (1983). Scientific illiteracy and democratic theory. *Daedalus*, 112 (2).

Pulford, D.L. (1976). Follow-up study of science news accuracy. *Journalism Quarterly* 53 (3).

Reddick, D.C. (undated). *Literary Style in Science Writing*. New York: Magazine Publishers Association.

Reiss, T.J. (1982). *The Discourse of Modernism*. Ithaca, NY: Cornell University Press.

Relman, A.S. (1979). An open letter to the news media. *The New England Journal of Medicine*, 300 (10).

Relman, A.S. (1981). The Ingelfinger rule. *The New England Journal of Medicine*, 305 (14).

Rensberger, B. (1978). What makes science news? *The Sciences*, 18 (7).

Robinson, T. (1978). Interpreters of science. *New Scientist* 84 (1175).

Rogers, C.L. (1981). Science information for the public: The role of scientific societies. *Science, Technology & Human Values*, 36, Summer.

Russell, C. (1986). The view from the national beat. In S.M. Friedman, S. Dunwoody and C.L. Rogers (eds), *Scientists and Journalists: Reporting Science as News*. New York: Free Press.

Rustrum, R. (1980). A scientist's tithe? *Science*, 207 (4427).

Ryan, M. (1979). Attitudes of scientists and journalists toward media coverage of science news. *Journalism Quarterly*, 56 (1).

Ryan, M. and Dunwoody, S. (1975). Academic and professional training patterns of science writers. *Journalism Quarterly*, 52 (2).

Sagan, C. (1973). *The Cosmic Connection: An Extraterrestrial Perspective*. London: Hodder & Stoughton.

Schneider, S.H. (1986). Both sides of the fence: The scientist as source and author. In S.M. Friedman, S. Dunwoody and C.L. Rogers (eds), *Scientists and Journalists: Reporting Science as News*. New York: Free Press.

Scientists' Institute for Public Information. (1984). Anatomy of a science story. *SIPIscope*, 13 (3).

Scientists' Institute for Public Information. (1986). Media coverage of medical 'break-throughs'. *SIPIscope*, 14 (2).

Shepherd, R.G. (1979). Science news of controversy: The case of marijuana. *Journalism Monographs*, No. 62.

Shils, E. (1974, Summer). Faith, utility and the legitimacy of science. *Daedalus*, 103.

Siwilop, S. (1981). Readership and coverage of science and technology in newspapers and magazines: Report to the Council for the Advancement of Science Writing. In P.L.

Alberger and V.L. Carter (eds), *Communicating University Research*. Washington, DC: Council for Advancement and Support of Education.

Tankard, J.W., Jr. and Ryan, M. (1974). News source perceptions of accuracy of science coverage. *Journalism Quarterly*, 51 (2).

Tavris, C. (1986). How to publicize science: A case study. In J.H. Goldstein (ed.), *Reporting Science: The Case of Aggression*. Hillsdale, NJ: Lawrence Erlbaum.

Tichenor, P.J., Olien, C.N., Harrison, A. and Donohue, G. (1970). Mass communication systems and communication accuracy in science news reporting. *Journalism Quarterly*, 47 (2).

Trachtman, L.E. (1981). The public understanding of science effort: A critique. *Science, Technology & Human Values*, 36, Summer.

Twentieth Century Fund Task Force on the Communication of Scientific Risk. (1984). *Science in the Streets*. New York: Twentieth Century Fund.

Walum, L.R. (1975). Sociology and the mass media: Some major problems and modest proposals. *The American Sociologist*, 10 (1).

Weigel, R.H. and Pappas, J.J. (1981). Social science and the press: A case study and its implications. *The American Psychologist*, 36 (5).

Weinberg, S. (1974, Summer). Reflections of a working scientist. *Daedalus*, 103.

Weiner, J. (1980). Prime time science. *The Sciences*, 20 (7).

Weisskopf, V.F. (1981). The problem of informing people about basic research. In P.L. Alberger and V.L. Carter (eds), *Communicating University Research*. Washington, DC: Council for Advancement and Support of Education.

Welsh, J. (1982). Public attitude toward science is yes, but – *Science*, 215 (4530).

Wenk, E. (1979). Scientists, engineers, and citizens. *Science*, 206 (4420).

West, L.J. (1986). How not to publicize research: the UCLA Violence Center. In J.H. Goldstein (ed.), *Reporting Science: The Case of Aggression*. Hillsdale, NJ: Lawrence Erlbaum.

Wheeler, G.F. (1986). A scientist in TV land. In S.M. Friedman, S. Dunwoody and C.L. Rogers (eds), *Scientists and Journalists: Reporting Science as News*. New York: Free Press.

Zinsser, W. (1980). Science writing and technical writing. In *On writing well*. New York: Harper & Row.

Chapter 13

Mediating science

Promotional strategies, media coverage, public belief and decision making*

D. Miller

Science and scientists are increasingly visible in the media. Science is called upon to adjudicate on the risks of modern living, to provide rational and objective commentary, to promote government policy and undermine it, to further the campaigning ends of pressures groups and safeguard the profits of large corporations. Scientists also appear in the mass media of their own volition, promoting their latest findings, attempting to safeguard public health and sometimes pursuing research funding. In short, science appears in a wide variety of guises in the contemporary mass media for a wide variety of reasons.

This paper will review differing ways of understanding the role of the media in communicating science and will argue that a proper understanding of the media necessitates an approach which locates the media in the context of wider formations of power and influence and of historical processes. The main body of the text examines the relationships between the media and other social institutions, the public and with decision making or 'outcomes' in society. But first let us pause to discuss what it means to 'mediate' science.

Mediation

Communication is essential to the reporting and discussion of science in the public domain. If communications were simple mirror image reflections of the reality they attempt to describe, then they would not be a significant subject of study. In practice communication is a means of 'mediating' science. By mediation we mean that to describe any single piece of science or a body of scientific theory, a selection of what to say or write must be made. The account to be given must of necessity be 'selective'. But this does not mean that the account must be inaccurate or misleading. In describing a particular experiment, for example, the colour of the researcher's hair will usually not be regarded as central to the story. At the most basic level, criteria of relevance will be used. Some form of selection will have to be made from all the possible descriptors available. The selection may also involve an attempt at simplification or transla-

---

*Newly commissioned.

tion depending on the writers' motives for producing the report or on their perception of their audience. We can think here of journalists translating a complex piece of science into a news story, of public health officials presenting scientifically derived information in health education campaigns, or of scientists translating their own or others' work into textbooks or popular science paper-backs. In all these cases we can describe what is happening as a process of mediation.

These types of activity may seem fundamentally different from the business of science proper. But it should be apparent that similar processes are in operation at the heart of the scientific method, not just in terms of writing scientific papers, presenting them at conferences, or submitting grant proposals, but also in the fundamentals of conducting research. Communication and therefore mediation are fundamental to science as they are to all other human endeavours.

The notion of mediation also implies the possibility that communication can be 'distorted', both in the sense of deliberately misleading and in the sense of losing something in translation. But perhaps more important than distortion is that mediation implies agency. Someone does the mediating and does it for particular reasons. One consequence of this is that particular ways of mediating science may be linked to particular interests. For example, Richard Doll has recently argued that the pressures of academic life to secure prestige and research funding can result in the publication of material which might be better left unpublished:

> the pressure to publish to secure funding encourages publication at times when the proper reaction would be to see first if the finding can be confirmed with larger numbers or by another method.
>
> (Doll, 1997: 10)

The point to note about mediation is that it is inescapable in the communica-tion of science, whether at scientific conferences, in expert committees, in scientific journals, in the news, in popular science books, in science fiction, films or other entertainment media (see Collier with Toomey, 1997: Ch. 3 on the process of writing science).

Current commentary on the media and science

The key problem for many commentators on the mediation of science is a lack of public understanding of science. There are a variety of explanations for this 'deficit' model of public understanding, many of which see the public as irrational, emotional or ignorant about science, perhaps because of an intrinsic human inability to understand complex scientific information. Alternatively, some suggest that the public is misinformed. Here the media are charged variously with negative, sensationalist, simplistic or misleading coverage. On occasion the problem is located as a combination of both, as in this comment from gourmet writer Egon Ronay in a review of a Channel 4 documentary on food safety. The programme, he argued:

> misleadingly coats the pill of intimidation, conceals the obsessiveness of doom-merchants and insidiously turns half-baked theories into received wisdom. . . . The television ridden British public, slumped in sofas and vulnerable to prettily presented generalisations, needs to be forewarned to take the diet to be dished out . . . with thousands of grains of salt.
>
> (*The Sunday Times*, 8 March 1992)

A less common approach is to acknowledge that some of the problems of communicating science may be to do with the communicators themselves. One example is an editorial in the *British Medical Journal* by editor Richard Smith, criticising some scientists for being naive in their dealings with journalists and others for simplifying and distorting science to further their own interests in research. Such scientists 'do nothing for the public understanding of science by making statements that can be used to endorse the suggestion that the eradication of genetic disease is something not much more complicated than Lego™' (Smith, 1992: 730).

It is plainly the case that some scientists are better at communicating with the media than others and there clearly are occasions on which the media are responsible for particular types of distortion or parts of the public are misled or misunderstand elements of science. It is well known that the size, scope and length of issues on the media agenda does not mirror their objective severity measured in terms of human misery or death or scientific risk assessment procedures. For example, Figure 13.1 compares British press coverage of BSE with officially confirmed cases of BSE. As can be seen the first major peak in press coverage in 1990 occurred at a time when there were relatively few cases, and the second peak, in 1996, occurred after the peak of cases had passed. But rather than bemoan the disjunction between the media and official assessments, it seems more productive to try to understand why this is the case.

The circuit of mass communication

The mediation of science is a complex phenomenon which involves a large number of contending and co-operating social factors and groups. These include institutions and corporations, media organisations, a range of publics, and policy, cultural and political outcomes. However, the communication of science is often examined from the vantage point of only one part of the 'circuit of communication' (Miller *et al.*, 1998). Thus we find discussions of the coverage of particular issues, examinations of 'lay perspectives' or public opinion, or attempts to evaluate the communication strategies of particular organisations. But we cannot properly understand the actual behaviour of 'experts', the media or the public in isolation. Instead they need to be examined in the context of

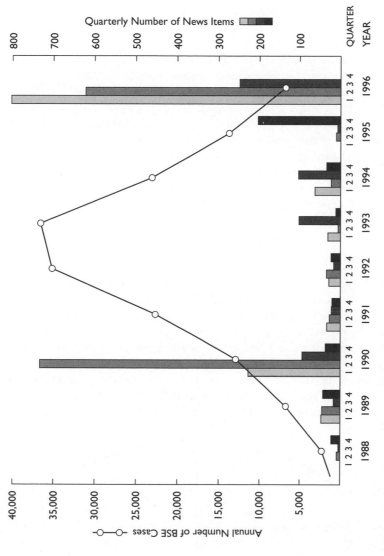

Figure 13.1 Comparison of the press coverage of BSE with officially reported cases.

their interactions with each other. The suggestion in this paper is that we look at the communication of science in a more complex fashion as the product of an interaction between four sets of actors:

1   *Social and political institutions*:   a vast range of organisations in civil society, including government, business, interest groups, universities and scientific research institutes.
2   *The media*:   the press, radio and television news, current affairs and documentary programmes, science programming, talk shows, popular and professional scientific magazines and journals, popular books on science, and women's and men's magazines, which routinely include advice on matters of science and medicine. Fictional forms include novels (including the genre of science fiction), feature films, television and radio plays, drama serials, and soap opera.
3   *The public*:   stratified in terms of class, gender, race/ethnicity, nationality, sexual identity and age as well as by professional and political commitments and social experience.
4   *Decision makers*:   in local, national and supranational government as well as in business organisations, interest groups, universities and scientific institutes.

These four sets of actors can be conceived of as relating to each other in a relatively static and one-dimensional way. For instance, social institutions communicate with the media which reports what they say, with a particular impact on the public, to which decision makers respond. However, if we see the relationship between these analytical types as interactive and dynamic we can begin to understand the way in which issues rise and fall on the public agenda. It is important to see the process of communication as a circuit which is multidirectional in that there can be all sorts of direct relationships between any two of the elements of the circuit (see Figure 13.2).

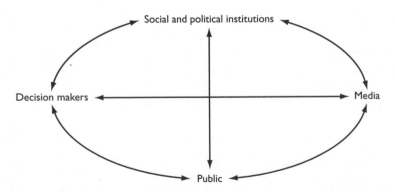

Figure 13.2 The circuit of mass communication.

My argument is first that each of the different elements of the circuit need sustained analysis which is sensitive to variation as well as similarity (e.g. not an assumption that media coverage or public opinion is homogeneous). There is a need to trace the differing pathways between different elements of the circuit. We need to ask not just what is said by science communicators or the media or believed by the public, but why. Examining only part of the circuit directly runs the risk of over- or underplaying the importance of the area studied or of other areas. Thus to examine only public perceptions or the genesis of scientific advice, or the preparation of communication campaigns, misses the interactive and mutually constitutive relations between the various moments of communication. In other words, there is a need to understand the dynamic relations between different elements of the circuit as well as examining the content of the different moments in order to build up a better picture of the circuit of science communication.

Given this model, it becomes easier to explain the rise and fall of scientific issues in the media and on the public and policy-making agenda. The next four sections examine the different elements of the circuit and how they relate to each other.

Social and political institutions

Without sources of information, there would be no news. Social institutions of all types increasingly understand the value of planning media strategies to manage their image in the media and with key publics (Miller, 1998). Equally, the value of keeping an organisation out of the news is also increasingly recognised, particularly in areas of science where there is significant political controversy. In 1997, a leaked briefing document prepared by PR multinational Burson Marstellar for a leading biotechnology firm advised that the best way to gain acceptance for genetically modified foods was by staying 'off the killing fields' of the environment and human health, since the industry 'cannot be expected to prevail in public opposition to adversarial voices on these issues' (Burson Marstellar, 1997: 3–4).

All sorts of organisations now have press offices and engage in public relations activities. Government departments have large information divisions responsible for protecting the image of their department and publishing large amounts of information every day. Research councils, corporate bodies and interest groups also employ PR staff. In addition, in the last 20 years the PR industry has become increasingly significant in attempting to shape the news. Scientific institutes have increasingly turned to the PR industry for help in managing their media profile. For example, the Roslyn Institute hired a PR consultant in 1997 to advise on the presentation of the story of 'Dolly' the cloned sheep. Equally, scientific findings can be promoted by PR companies working for industrial interests, gaining them a higher profile than might otherwise be the case. In 1991, interim non-peer-reviewed findings of the MRC Epidemiology

Unit 'Caerphilly study', which apparently cast doubt on the well-known hypothesis that there is a link between saturated fat consumption and coronary heart disease, were promoted by a PR company working for the Butter Council (Connor, 1991). On the other hand, industry interests can also attempt to sideline research which threatens their interests. John Yudkin, nutritionist and a leading expert on dietary sugars, has written of the attempts by the sugar industry to undermine and discredit his work. He concluded that the public were 'being misled by propaganda designed to promote commercial interests in a way that you thought only existed in bad B films' (Yudkin, 1986: 167; for further material on the PR industry and science/the environment see Nelson, 1989; Rowell, 1996; Stauber and Rampton, 1995).

Social institutions supply information to the media in the form of 'information subsidies' (Gandy, 1982). This means that 'resource-rich' organisations (such as government departments, large corporations and some scientific endeavours) start with an important advantage in the competition for access to the media and decision making.

Presenting and promoting science

One key problem for science communicators attempting to improve public understanding of science is the provisional nature of scientific knowledge. There is a tendency for scientists or presenters of science to represent it as a generator of certainty, in which:

> uncertainties and ambiguities are the result of incompetence of the scientists, or inadequacy of the apparatus, or of the limited tests conducted so far. Residual uncertainties will be eliminated by future tests.
>
> (Collins, 1987: 710)

However, divisions between scientists can make unambiguous statements difficult. In practice, government operates a system of expert advisory committees to distil the best scientific advice. Such committees are subject to a number of limitations. In the first place, prospective 'experts' are, according to one former member, carefully 'vetted' on their 'general views and philosophy of life' in addition to their scientific qualifications (Lacey, 1994). The committees are also the subject of strict secrecy and are attended by a variety of civil servants, whose interventions can be significant. In the case of BSE, the first chair of the advisory committee, Sir Richard Southwood, has publicly acknowledged that some of the contents of their report reflected their judgement of what the ministry would accept, rather than their unvarnished scientific judgement (Miller, in press). Even then, the Ministry of Agriculture delayed the report for seven months while its emphasis was changed (*ibid.*). Furthermore, a number of questions have been raised about the commercial interests of scientists in advisory committees. Many members of expert committees have a financial relationship with relevant business corporations in the form of research grants or consultancies. In some cases, scientists who are actually employed by companies sit on the committees (Abraham, 1995). Furthermore, in recent times, as a result of government policy changes, scientific institutes have become more dependent on commercial funding and many have been transformed into business ventures, with directors of research becoming chief executives (Cannon, 1987; Pain, 1997). These processes decrease the already dwindling number of 'independent' scientists (Miller, in press; Nowotny, 1981).

Moreover, partly because of the limitations of the process of extracting advice, the judgements of advisory committees can be called into question, particularly if appropriately qualified scientists are willing to talk to the media. Thus even where there is genuine agreement among government advisors, unambiguous public statements may be forced to compete with dissenting voices, fostering the impression of ambiguity and uncertainty.

Translating science for public consumption

The process of translating scientific advice into official reports, press releases and health education campaigns is also potentially tricky since it brings all sorts of calculations about communication effectiveness into play. This can work in two ways. First, calculations about what the media or the public might make of particular statements are necessarily involved in science communication, but this can be at the expense of accuracy or of denying uncertainty, as in absolute statements between 1990 and 1995 about the lack of risk from BSE. Second, calculations about what is politically possible can also impinge on government attempts at science communication. One example is the agonising in the Department of Health (and wider in government) in 1985–87 about whether explicit AIDS information was politically as well as medically desirable (Miller et al., 1998).

Such problems are given greater complexity with the involvement of a wide range of different professionals in the production of science-based information. This applies to media relations but can be even more crucial to health education material. For example, in the AIDS campaign a wide range of professional groupings were centrally involved (ministers, administrative civil servants, medical civil servants, information officers, market researchers, advertisers, health educators, expert advisors, etc.). Many of these groupings tended to have opposed conceptions of communication planning and effectiveness, together with differing sensitivities as to what was politically possible. Furthermore, division between professional communicators, who favoured fear arousal campaigns and 'impact' in advertising, often clashed with health educators, who favoured sensitivity and positive alternatives to penetrative sex.

Science communication is sometimes officially stated to be a technical process. In practice, it can involve a complex web of interlocking disputes and alliances, which sometimes result in the communication of messages that as a result of compromises and political interventions are contradictory, vague or contain little useful information and with which none of those involved are satisfied (*ibid.*; see also Farrant and Russell, 1986).

Competition and co-operation in media strategies

Once the message is agreed, there are all sorts of further obstacles to surmount. These include competition with opposing interests as well as co-operation with other interests and the formation of alliances. Science communication strategies may be hampered by conflicting interests inside government, either within or between departments, as well as conflicts within or between scientific disciplines. This is especially the case if such interests 'go public', even in the minimal sense of off-the-record briefings. We can point to the controversy within government over *Salmonella enteritidis* PT4 in 1988/89 or the debates within science over the causation of AIDS or coronary heart disease (Miller and Reilly, 1995). This is not only important in that it indicates conflict in government or science, but also because this will become an added reason for media interest.

The strategies formulated by social institutions for influencing the media and decision making are forced to compete with those of other organisations (whether they be scientific establishments, government departments, business ventures or pressure groups). This is important for two reasons. First, there can be a wide range of information available to the public with which a particular science-based communication strategy has to compete. Furthermore, there are a variety of organisations engaged in communication on science-related issues, which may have diverging reasons for and interests in managing risk (e.g. to protect corporate reputation, increase sales, further campaigning demands, raise research funds or even personal profiles, etc.). This is an inevitable part of our culture, and there is no intrinsic reason why information emanating from scientific establishments or government should be believed above that of competing interests. One implication of this is that scientists themselves (even those not working for industry interests) are players in competition for media space and public sympathy, rather than simply disinterested suppliers of information.

Co-operation and the building of coalitions are also important in that a broad consensus in a particular policy arena makes communication efforts much more likely to succeed. The coalition built around public health interests on AIDS in 1985–1989 is a key example of such co-operation, which was effective in policy terms (Miller *et al.*, 1998).

Media organisations

Much discussion of science communication tends to see the role of the media as a predominantly negative one. The media are dismissed as a homogeneous bloc whose penchant for sensation and irresponsibility are an obstacle to rational science communication. However, it can be suggested that the media are neither uniform nor consistently negative either in relation to the interests of science and scientists or in relation to the public interest. There are a number of key media factors which explain the form taken by particular media outlets.

Political economy of the media

In the first instance, the economics of the media industries is an important influence on how they report the world. The balance between public service media and commercial operations is of prime importance. In recent years, there has been a movement towards the commercialisation of broadcasting in a number of Western countries. In Britain, this has led to a slackening of public service controls on output. One specific result in relation to science programming is that by the mid-1990s the main commercial channel in Britain, ITV, had ceased to broadcast any science-related series. Furthermore, the private ownership of media corporations and the trends towards monopoly of transnational corporations have meant a decline in serious debate about the role of science in the public sphere.

The existence of advertising is an additional factor in newspapers and on commercial television. The content of advertising is determined (within certain limits) by the motive of selling products. This is quite different from a public service motivation and it means that there can often be a contradiction between the messages given about products in advertising and those in editorial coverage. However, given that advertising revenue is what funds commercial television there is a sense in which audiences themselves rather than television programmes 'are the primary commodity. The economics of commercial broadcasting revolves around the exchange of audiences for advertising revenue' (Golding and Murdock, 1991: 20).

So the need to secure large audiences promotes the production of familiar programming and limits the production of innovative, risky or critical programmes. 'Hence', as Golding and Murdock argue, 'the audience's position as a commodity serves to reduce the overall diversity of programming and ensure that it confirms established mores and assumptions far more often than it challenges them' (*ibid*.: 20). This is one factor which tends to mean that mainstream natural science is portrayed relatively favourably in the media. 'Science and medicine still have a unique social authority, as if they somehow bypass social, political, economic and emotional factors: we seem to believe that science is thought with the thinkers removed – as if that were possible' (Karpf, 1993). This tendency means that scientific sources have a very great credibility for the media and in a general sense mainstream science is able to secure very favourable coverage in the media. However, this credibility and prestige can be compromised or undermined by a number of factors, some of which are noted above and others are noted below.

Heterogeneity

Media institutions are not simply the instruments of either government, business, scientists or pressure groups. They have their own interests and agendas. Newspapers are run as a business, but this does not mean that they simply go for the story which will bring in the most readers. Newspapers are carefully targeted at particular social groupings, and stories in the papers will, to some extent, reflect the 'personality' of the paper. Despite recent changes in broadcasting regulation, television and radio do still retain a significant public service ethos. This can mean that some sections of the broadcast media consider their role as an educative one and accordingly their programmes will reflect the dominant trends in medical thinking in relation to diet. With its responsibility for 'minority' programming, Channel 4 is more likely to broadcast contending alternative views on science issues. An analysis of factual and fictional programming on AIDS (between 1983 and 1991) found that the dominant account of AIDS was derived from the medical/scientific orthodoxy, but that there were more spaces to explore alternatives in more 'open' programme formats such as documentaries, films and soap operas, as in the ongoing story line in *Eastenders*, where central character Mark Fowler has known he is HIV-positive since 1990. However, the most limited accounts of AIDS, which gave most credibility to 'hard' sciences such as immunology and virology and downplayed softer disciplines such as epidemiology and social science and the insights of clinicians, were on science programmes such as *Horizon* (Miller *et al.*, 1998: Chapter 5).

Media institutions do pursue readers with a variety of crude and not so crude techniques but there are clear differences in the types of material which appear both within and between media. There are distinctive approaches to some science-related issues in particular newspaper and television outlets. For example, on AIDS and on coronary heart disease (CHD), the papers most likely to take a line critical of the dominant scientific view were particular tabloids and particular right-wing broadsheets. *The Sunday Times* and *The Sun* both criticised the scientific orthodoxy on AIDS between 1989 and 1995. *The Sunday Times* and a wider range of tabloids have also been keen to publicise data which cast doubt on the scientific orthodoxy linking dietary fats to coronary heart disease, as in headlines such as:

Butter 'can slice heart attack risk'

(*Daily Express*, 27 February 1991)

Eat, Drink and be Merry . . . It could Save your Life

(*Daily Mirror*, 23 December 1991)

Fatty food not a Killer

(*Daily Express*, 23 December 1991)

By contrast, such perspectives on both AIDS and CHD tend to be downplayed or 'exposed' as misleading in the liberal broadsheets and tend not to be covered by television news (Miller *et al.*, 1998; Macintyre *et al.*, 1998).

But the overall 'line' of a paper is subject to both change and contest from within. For example, specialist correspondents have a distinctive role on both broadsheet and mid-market tabloid papers. Medical and scientific reporters tend to be very knowledgeable about their areas of responsibility. This can mean both that they adopt an advocate role for key sources in the medical and scientific community and that they can spot news management activities by their sources more quickly than their non-specialist colleagues. Accordingly, their coverage will tend to differ from that of freelancers or of political correspondents, who are drafted in when the story leaves the specialist pages of the paper and becomes a major political issue.

The quasi-advocate role of specialist reporters towards senior sources in the scientific world, official sources in government and their dependence on prestigious medical and scientific journals (*The Lancet, British Medical Journal, Science, Nature*) can mean that they come into conflict with their editorial hierarchy over which stories to cover and how to cover them. Pressure can be exerted on specialists to write up stories which they think are unimportant if they are being carried in other papers. Similarly, where the editorial line of a paper differs from the approach fostered by leading scientific and government sources, specialists can face immense pressure to change the tone and content of what they write. This is especially the case with specialists on right-wing tabloid papers and was a particular issue in relation to AIDS coverage (see Miller and Williams, 1993).

News content and news values

Science tends to make front-page news when scientific advances are made or disputes in science emerge. Furthermore news values favour short-term and dramatic issues over longer-term stories. However, science-related stories rarely become major public issues dominating headlines for days or weeks unless they involve 'matters of state' – that is major political involvement. This can be seen by comparing the profile of coronary heart disease with food safety, remembering that CHD kills many more people each year than food poisoning. Between January 1988 and the end of 1992, BBC television network news broadcast 128 items on food safety, and between 1973 and 1991 food safety stories made the front page of *The Times* and *The Sunday Times* 90 times. By contrast, CHD appeared only 25 times on BBC TV news and on the front page of *The Times* and *The Sunday Times* on only ten occasions (Macintyre *et al.*, 1998).

It is now commonplace for sections of the news media to report on the real and perceived motives of government communication, as in the fixation on 'spin doctors'. Here divisions or excessive secrecy (or the perception of them) within government departments are very important. In the case of patulin in apple juice, secrecy was a key element in the 'news value' of the story. There were a total of 41 items in the British national press on patulin, 30 of which (73 percent) were chiefly about government secrecy. With *salmonella*, the key issue was the perceived division between MAFF and the Department of Health, which became apparent since officials were briefing against each other (Miller and Reilly, 1995).

News values across the media do tend to attach a high importance to controversy, division and secrecy. Plainly this is all rather galling to the prospective science communicator, who may have little control over the wider environment within which they are situated. It can also be argued that the importance attached to such news values inhibits rational discussion of the communication of science. However, the self-interested pursuit of such news values as a means to maximise audiences may sometimes coincide with the public interest in making government or science more transparent, even if in an unintentional, distorted or sensationalist way.

The public

A major problem for critics of the malign influence of the media on science communication, or those who bewail public ignorance or misunderstanding of science, is their assumption that the impact of the media is straightforward and direct. Consumers and especially children and other groups perceived as vulnerable (such as 'housewives') are thought to be particularly at risk from media messages. In much analysis, 'scientific' knowledge is counterposed with public or 'lay' knowledge or belief. More often the terminology used is scientific 'fact' versus public 'perception'. The problem is then located as a lack of public knowledge or understanding. In some versions of the argument this is even claimed to be due to 'human intellectual limitations' (Covello, 1983: 287). Curiously though, scientists, social scientists and risk analysts (or sometimes just 'experts') are not thought to be subject to such limitations. This type of approach, which can be described as the 'deficit' model of public understanding, has been increasingly discredited in recent years (see Davison, 1989, Davison *et al.*, 1989; 1992; Kitzinger 1990; 1993; Macintyre *et al.*, 1998; Miller *et al.*, 1998; Wynne, 1996).

The problem is that people do not passively absorb everything that is beamed from their television set. Instead they interpret and contextualise. Public views are not formed from thin air. Equally, they are not simply dictated by the media or ministerial pronouncements or by lay 'perspectives' or 'cultures'. Judgements are made according to the information available from the media, education, friends and family and other sources and evaluated against previous experience and information. Experience is patterned by class, ethnicity, gender, nationality, region and age as well as by personal experience and evaluated by means of logical processes. Furthermore, in the context of the argument in this chapter about the circuit of mass communication it is misleading to examine the content of public belief to find out *what* people think about science or the degree to which they 'trust' scientists or the government without an analysis of the sources of beliefs and their links with the circulation of information and opinion in society in general and the media in particular.

Media *effects*

The first thing to note about the impact of the media on public beliefs is that there are occasions on which the media have strong effects on public beliefs about the world. Research on AIDS suggests that the government message that HIV is a threat to heterosexuals was widely believed by the public (Kitzinger, 1993; Miller *et al.*, 1998). In the case of the media coverage around *salmonella* in 1988/89 and BSE in 1990, 1996 and 1997, there were sharp changes in public belief and behaviour, resulting in sales of eggs and beef dropping sharply. Similarly, consumption of sugar from the bowl fell and sales of semi-skimmed milk and brown/wholemeal bread rose in the 1980s in response to health advice. However, impacts on belief do not automatically translate into behavioural change, as the case of AIDS shows. Although condom purchases did increase, there were a number of obstacles to condom use which meant that changes in behaviour were difficult to put into practice (*ibid.*).

What these examples and other research show is that people are familiar with scientific advice on risk and safety. This undermines those approaches which stress public ignorance or irrationality. However, familiarity with scientific or medical advice does not straightforwardly lead to its acceptance. To some extent this will relate to whether there are divisions in scientific or political knowledge and whether alternative explanations are widely available in the media, but it will also reflect the knowledge, experience and evaluative processes of members of the public.

The social patterning of media effects

Media information is evaluated and interpreted in the context of previous information and experience. Experience and information vary according to the social stratification of contemporary societies. Class, gender, sexual identity, ethnicity, national identity, occupation and age, together with other demographic factors, can influence the frameworks within which people interpret media messages. In a study of responses to health advice, one element of experience which people used to filter healthy eating advice was their own material circumstances. For working-class respondents health education advice was perceived as 'middle-class'. As one put it:

> We all know what to do and basically would get on with it. . . . I'd love to eat good food all the time, but I have five mouths to feed on one income. . . . That should be recognised by those who are handing out all that advice.
>
> (cited in Macintyre *et al.*, 1998)

Personal *experience*

Another key element that influences the evaluation of media information is personal experience. Research on public responses to food scares found that having heart disease, or knowing someone who had experienced food poisoning, can have a dramatic impact on the evaluation of relevant media information. One group of work mates had all given up eating eggs (and had not returned to them) because a colleague had been seriously ill with food poisoning. A lack of such experience was also often given as reason for not believing dietary advice. Furthermore, alternative information, especially from known and trusted sources, often overwhelmed media accounts of risk. Having a butcher as a relative was a key factor for one young man in ignoring publicity about BSE in 1990:

> I just didn't pay any attention to it at all and now that I think about it, that was definitely because my uncle is a butcher and he said it was a lot of nonsense and that meat was perfectly safe. I assumed he would know if there really was a problem and he wouldn't tell lies.
>
> (cited in Macintyre *et al.*, 1998)

Similarly in research on AIDS, personal contact or acquaintance with gay men, sex workers or intravenous drug users could undermine discriminatory media messages. One hospital doctor related her own experience:

> Before I worked here I always thought I'd know a prostitute on sight, but I don't. No way, and that surprised me. . . . They don't all have dyed blonde hair and short skirts.
>
> (cited in Miller *et al.*, 1998: 199)

However, the influence of personal experience can also vary according to how it is perceived and integrated into other aspects of people's shared understandings in particular contexts. Knowing someone who has experienced coronary heart disease or food poisoning does not necessarily lead to changes in beliefs or behaviour (Macintyre *et al.*, 1998).

The media can make people think about the science-related issues that they report. They can 'set the agenda' for public discussion. Moreover, the media can also influence public understanding, public belief and even behaviour. Importantly, however, people do also interpret, evaluate and make judgements about media information, which affect how much and in what ways they incorporate media messages about science, risk and safety in their beliefs and behaviour.

Analysing the sources of public belief is important because it is a way of linking the elements of the circuit of communication with beliefs. Those approaches which simply examine the content of public belief are, therefore, liable to be limited in their explanatory power. Although polls show trust in government as low, in fact there are times when people (even those who say they distrust the government or the media) do believe what they are told. It is, therefore, misleading to try to redeem public perceptions as rational without an analysis of how and why people make judgements. Trust in government is not a stable or uniform filter through which new information is strained, but varies. It seems likely that it is related to the specifics of the information content and the other sources which make it credible. The extent to which political disputes about risk are at the centre of public debate is important here. We can compare the public response to AIDS and BSE in this context. The significant loss of public trust over BSE was not paralleled in the case of AIDS, where a significant media and policy consensus developed that HIV was a serious threat to hetero-sexuals and where discrimination against so called 'high-risk groups' was discouraged. Both of these messages were widely accepted by the public. Stated trust in government may, therefore not be a reliable indicator of public belief and response. An example from research on food scares might illustrate the point. The respondent started by saying that she did not know much about salmonella but then proceeded to rattle off the official advice about cooking eggs. When asked how she knew, she responded:

> I don't know really, I suppose it just seems like common sense. But . . . I must have got it from somewhere. . . . I suppose I picked up a lot of things from the magazines that I read and there were a lot of people saying things on TV about how to cook eggs. . . . Isn't that funny, I just thought I'd always done that naturally.
>
> (cited in Macintyre *et al.*, 1998)

This example seems to show the way in which – without being aware of it – the media can be deeply implicated in influencing our everyday conceptions of the world. Those approaches which attempt to analyse risk perception in terms of psychological tendencies such as 'optimistic bias' tend to underestimate the significance of mediation in risk communication, concentrating instead on individual psychological processes. There is a need to examine where informa-tion and ideas come from and how these are processed, rather than assuming that events in the world are transparently available to human perception. Equally, some approaches that focus on 'lay perspectives' tend not to examine them in the context of the circulation of information and values in society.

The argument developed here suggests that the media are important in forming, sustaining and changing public opinion, but in the context of the circuit of mass communication, this is not the end of the matter. The next question which arises centres on the role of the media and public opinion in influencing decision making. Considered by itself without any conception of connections with wider formations of power and influence, public opinion is a relatively trivial matter. The public understanding of science is not deemed important simply because it is seen in an abstract way to be 'a good thing' to foster public understanding, but because it is (at least implicitly) assumed to have wider consequences for society and democracy. Yet the links between public opinion and decision making and outcomes in society have been remarkably under-researched. The next section examines some of the key effects which public opinion and the media can have on decision making.

Decision makers

The media have a clear indirect influence on policy making in that they can influence public beliefs and behaviour, to which decision makers have to respond. The clearest examples are the changes in purchasing behaviour consequent on media coverage, such as the effect of the salmonella and BSE crises on egg and beef sales. But we can also think of changes in behaviour over the longer term that have been intentionally prompted by government risk communication, such as the increase in sales of semi-skimmed milk and the decrease in consumption of sugar from the bowl, which were prompted by health education advice on the risks of dietary fats and sugars. Public opinion (or crucially *perceptions* of public opinion) can drive policy and decision making and nudge decision makers or ministers into decisions they would not otherwise have made. But policy makers can ignore public concern on some issues, particularly if opposition is not mobilised (for discussions of the role of the media in health policy see Berridge, 1991; Otten, 1992; Walsh-Childers, 1994; see also Cracknell, 1993).

Risk communicators, scientists, decision makers and other policy actors are members of the general public and consume media representations routinely. As such they can be influenced in the same ways as the rest of us. However, decision makers can also be specifically targeted by both risk communicators and journalists. There is a sense in which much political debate in the media is debate between elites to which the rest of us can listen in if we wish. There are stories in the media that are intended by those who disclose them to reach very small numbers of people, such as senior members of a particular government committee or a particular government minister. Thinking about the media in this way should make it apparent that the media can play an intimate and direct role in policy making. For example, during the early period of the AIDS crisis key clinicians seeing the bulk of new cases of HIV infection used the media to put pressure on policy makers, even though they themselves were on official committees (Miller *et al.*, 1998). The media can also influence policy indirectly by mediating supposed or actual public pressure to decision makers. During the AIDS crisis, tabloid reporting of public opinion did sometimes influence decision makers' assessments of what was possible in policy terms (*ibid.*).

Moreover, policy makers and experts have differing interests in media coverage and impacts work differently in different areas. Proposed cut-backs and redundancies in scientific institutes or government bodies have been put on hold or reversed following news coverage of particular risks. Coverage of issues such as AIDS and the 'flesh-eating bug' had consequences for risk assessment and surveillance personnel at, for example, the Public Health Laboratory Service. Holding on to staff who would otherwise have been made redundant can even be the case when an organisation has done its best to play down the significance of a particular scare, such as in the case of the 'flesh-eating bug'.

On the other hand, scientists working in specialisms which suddenly become big news can welcome the attention and use it to encourage the funding of research. The 'flesh-eating bug' provided such an opportunity for Professor Hugh Pennington, who used it to lobby for research funds, although in this particular case he was unsuccessful.

Impacts on science

This last example is suggestive of some of the kinds of impact which media reporting might have on science. We can point to impacts on the availability of research funds, impacts on the type of research which is done and how it is done and impacts on the standing of the scientist with the public, and perhaps more importantly with her/his peers. Media reporting of apparently new risks may prompt the allocation of specific research funds to new or neglected branches of science or in providing services to cope with public health implications. Usually, but not always, part of the pressure to allocate funds will include advocacy from scientists, perhaps exerted through the media as well as through the normal decision-making apparatus. A clear example of the success of such a tactic was the attempts by leading AIDS clinicians to pressure the government to provide funding for health education and service provision. As one leading doctor put it

> I think that those early media interventions were very effective – not in getting money personally for research or anything – but in getting money put into health education and into services. But it took a hell of a long time.
>
> (cited in Miller *et al.*, 1998: 130)

But appearing in the media can also impact on the standing of scientists or clinicians amongst their peers:

> It is still the case that some scientists look down on colleagues who 'go public'. They give a number of reasons: if a scientist has something to say, he or she should write it up in the proper manner, submit it for peer review and then wait a year for it to be published; a medium as trivial as television is no place for something as important as science; scientists should be self-deprecating and dedicated to their work – they should have neither the time nor the inclination to blow their own trumpets . . . the rewards of a media career can compromise scientific objectivity.
>
> (Shortland and Gregory, 1991: 5)

We can see then that the media and public opinion can have impacts on decision making in the sense of governmental and regulatory policy making, but also in the sense that all organisations, be they corporate organisations, pressure groups or scientific research establishments, have to be aware of the public dimensions of their work. It is at this point that the circuit of communication comes full circle and the public context of an organisation's environment feeds into the planning of promotional strategies and media relations. Such planning will confront and try to incorporate changes in the relationships between the four elements of the circuit of communication brought about by its previous cycles.

The resolution of public issues

Public issues decline when there is some sort of resolution of the perceived problem in the public arena. This does not mean that the problem itself is necessarily addressed, simply that the contradictions which made the story news are resolved. Thus in relation to the salmonella issue in 1988/89, the departure of junior minister Edwina Currie and the compensation granted to producers, together with a reorientation in the media, which blamed consumers rather than producers, killed the story. *Salmonella enteritidis* PT4 poisoning, however, has continued to rise (Miller and Reilly, 1995). By contrast, the first emergence of BSE in 1990 was only partially resolved, with the result that it returned to the public agenda periodically between 1990 and 1995 and then spectacularly in March 1996 and December 1997.

Concluding remarks

The complexity of the interactions between science, industry, pressure groups, government, the media, the public and decision making should make it clear that to simply blame the media is inappropriate. Instead we need to analyse the activities of the groups of actors and the interactions between them that constitute the circuit of mass communication in relation to science.

Whether we like it or not, communicating science will always be bound up with political disputes and struggles over the distribution of resources. There is no neutral or objective way of communicating science, but truth and accuracy ought to be our guide. Furthermore, assumptions and normative commitments can be made explicit and struggled for in the contests over scientific knowledge and decision making. These struggles and contests constitute the key way in which science participates in the public sphere and one of the central mechanisms by which the social distribution of harms and benefits is reproduced, ameliorated or transformed.

References

Abraham, J. (1995). *Science, Politics and the Pharmaceutical Industry: Controversy and Bias in Drug Regulation*, London: UCL Press.

Berridge, V. (1991). 'AIDS, the media and health policy' *Health Education Journal*, 50: 179–85.

Burson Marstellar (1997). *Communications Programmes for Europabio*, Prepared by Burson Marstellar Government and Public Affairs, January.

Cannon, G. (1987). *The Politics of Food*, London: Century.

Collier, J.H. with Toomey, D.M. (1997). *Scientific and Technical Communication: Theory, Practice and Policy*, Thousand Oaks, Calif.: Sage.

Collins, H.M., (1987). 'Certainty and the public understanding of science: science on television'. *Social Studies of Science*, 17: 689–713.

Connor, S. (1991). 'Scientists protest at butter's PR boost', *The Independent on Sunday*, 10 March.

Covello, V. (1983). 'The perception of technological risks: a literature review', *Technological Forecasting and Social Change*, 23: 285–97.

Cracknell, J. (1993). 'Issue arenas, pressure groups and environmental agenda', in A. Hansen (ed.) *The Mass Media and Environmental Issues*, Leicester: Leicester University Press.

Davison, C. (1989). 'Eggs and the sceptical eater', *New Scientist*, 1655 (11 March): 45–9.

Davison, C., Frankel, S. and Davey-Smith, G. (1989). 'Inheriting heart trouble; the relevance of common sense ideas to preventive measures', *Health Education Research: Theory and Practice*, 4: 329–40.

Davison, C., Frankel, S. and Davey Smith, G. (1992). 'The limits of lifestyle: re-assessing "fatalism" in the popular culture of illness prevention', *Social Science and Medicine*, 34 (6): 675–85.

Doll, R. (1997). 'Weak associations in epidemiology', *Radiological Protection Bulletin*, 192 (10 August).

Farrant W. and Russell, J. (1986). 'The politics of health information: *Beating heart disease* as a case study in the production of Health Education Council Publications', Bedford Way Papers No. 28, London: Institute of Education.

Gandy, O. (1982) *Beyond Agenda-Setting: Information Subsidies and Public Policy*, New York: Ablex.

Golding, P. and Murdock, G. (1991). 'Culture, communications and political economy' in J. Curran and M. Gurevitch (eds) *Mass Media and Society*, London: Edward Arnold.

Karpf, A. (1993). 'On medical journalism', *Observer Magazine*, 15 August: 45.

Kitzinger, J. (1990). 'Audience understandings of AIDS media messages: a discussion of methods,' *Sociology of Health & Illness*, 12 (3): 319–35.

Kitzinger, J. (1993). 'Understanding AIDS – media messages and what people know about Acquired Immune Deficiency Syndrome', in J. Eldridge (ed.) *Getting the Message*, London: Routledge, 271–304.

Lacey, R. (1994). *Mad Cow Disease: The History of BSE in Britain*, St Helier, Jersey: Gypsela.

Macintyre, S. (1995). 'The public understanding of science or the scientific understanding of the public? A review of the social context of the new genetics', *Public Understanding of Science*, 4; 223–32.

Macintyre, S., Reilly, J., Miller, D. and Eldridge, J. (1998). 'Food, choice, food scares and health: the role of the media', in A. Murcott (ed.) *The Nation's Diet*, London: Addison Wesley Longman.

Miller, D. (1995). 'Introducing the "gay gene": media and scientific representations', *Public Understanding of Science*, 4: 264–84.

Miller, D. (1998). 'Promotional strategies and media power', in A. Briggs and P. Cobley (eds) *The Media: An Introduction*, London: Longman.

Miller, D. (in press) 'Risk, science and policy: definitional struggles, information management and media', *Social Science and Medicine*, Special issue on Science Speaks to Policy.

Miller, D. and Philo, G. (1995). 'Communicating change in the NHS: A review of health communication campaigns, media coverage of health care issues and the process of public opinion and belief formation', report for the Communication Directorate of the NHS Executive, Leeds.

Miller, D. and Reilly, J. (1995). 'Making an issue of food safety: the media, pressure groups and the public sphere', in D. Maurer and J. Sobal (eds) *Eating Agendas: Food, Eating and Nutrition as Social Problems*, New York: Aldine de Gruyter, 305–36.

Miller, D. and Williams, K. (1993). 'Negotiating HIV/AIDS information: agendas, media strategies and the news', in Glasgow University Media Group, *Getting the Message*, London: Routledge.

Miller, D., Kitzinger, J., Williams, K. and Beharrell, P. (1998). *The Circuit of Mass Communication: Media Strategies, Representation and Audience Reception in the AIDS Crisis*, London: Sage.

Nelson, J. (1989). *Sultans of Sleaze: Public Relations and the Media*, Toronto: Between the Lines.

Nowotny, H. (1981). 'Experts and their expertise: on the changing relationship between experts and their publics', *Bulletin of the Science and Technology Society*, 1: 235–41.

Otten, A. (1992). 'The influence of the mass media on health policy', *Health Affairs*, 11 (4): 111–18.

Pain, S. (1997). 'When the price is wrong', *Guardian Online*, 27 February: 2–3.

Rowell, A. (1996). *Green Backlash: Global Subversion of the Environmental Movement*, London: Routledge.

Shortland M. and Gregory, J. (1991). *Communicating Science: A Handbook*, London: Longman.

Smith, R. (1992). 'Hype from journalists and scientists: an unholy alliance', *British Medical Journal*, 21 March, 304: 730.

Stauber, J.C. and Rampton, S. (1995). *Toxic Sludge is Good for You: Lies, Damn Lies and the Public Relations Industry*, Monroe, Maine: Common Courage.

Walsh-Childers, K. (1994). '"A Death in the Family" – A case study of newspaper influence on health policy development', *Journalism Quarterly*, 71 (4): 820–29.

Wynne, B. (1996). 'Misunderstood misunderstandings: social identities and public uptake of science', in A. Irwin and B. Wynne (eds) *Misunderstanding Science? The Public Reconstruction of Science and Technology*, Cambridge: Cambridge University Press, 19–46.

Yudkin, J. (1986). *Pure, White and Deadly*, London: Penguin.

Chapter 14

The mystique of science in the press*

D. Nelkin

On January 16, 1902, the editor of the *Nation* wrote a critical editorial on the popular appreciation of science. The public conceives of science as a 'variant of the black art', of scientists as wizards and magicians, socially isolated from society. 'The scientist appears akin to the medicine man . . . the multitude thinks of him as a being of quasi-supernatural and romantic powers. . . . There is in all this little resemblance to Huxley's definition of science as simply organized and trained common sense'.[1] To the extent that the public still holds such attitudes, one should not be surprised given the image of science in the press.

Science often appears in the press today as an arcane and incomprehensible subject, far from organized common sense. And scientists still appear to be remote but superior wizards, above ordinary people, culturally isolated from society. Such heroic images are perhaps most apparent in press reports about prestigious scientists, especially Nobel laureates. But the mystique of science as a superior culture is also conveyed in the promotion of science literacy, in the coverage of scientific theories, and even in stories about scientific fraud. The result? Far from enhancing public understanding, such press coverage creates a distance between scientists and the public that, paradoxically, obscures the importance of science and its effect on our daily lives.

The scientist as star

Each year the press devotes increased attention to winners of the Nobel Prize. Most news magazines have doubled their coverage over the past decade; much of this extra space is being used simply for larger headlines and a greater number of photographs. In the accompanying text, the press, with stunning regularity, focuses on the recipient's national affiliations and stellar qualities, using language recycled from reports of the Olympic Games. 'Another strong U.S. show'; 'Americans again this year receive a healthy share of the Nobel prizes'; 'U.S. showed it is doing something right by scoring a near sweep of the 1980

*Chapter 2 in *Selling Science*, W.H. Freeman (1995), pp. 14–30.

Nobel Prize'; 'The winning American style'. These are the headlines one is likely to find in newspapers across the country.

Just as the papers count Olympic medals, so they keep a running count of the Nobel awards: one year 'Americans won eight of eleven'; in another, 'Eight Americans were recognized, tying a record set in 1972'. 'Since 1941', *U.S. News and World Report* announced to its readers in 1980, 'the U.S. has had 126 Nobel winners in science, more than double the number won by second place Britain'. The stories describe nations as rivals somehow competing in a Nobel race for national pride – an image that obfuscates the international cooperation that is supposed to, and often does, characterize scientific endeavors.

Following the style of sports writing or reports of Academy Awards, journalists emphasize the honor, the glory, and the supreme achievement of the prize: 'The most prestigious prizes in the world. . . . They bring instant fame, flooding winners with speaking invitations, job offers, book contracts, and honorary degrees', runs a typical comment. In 1979 *Time* printed a large picture of the gold medal: 'The Nobel Prize Winners are called to Mount Olympus; the recipients have worldwide respect'.

Local or regional papers also cover Nobel winners like sports or movie stars but add a twist, seeking to find a local angle, however remote. Consider Roald Hoffmann, who received the 1981 prize in chemistry. A Rochester, New York, paper mentioned that he was a 'Kodak consultant'. The *New York Daily News* reported that he had graduated from Stuyvesant High School in New York city and printed his picture from the high school yearbook with the caption: 'Another example of an alumnus who has done well'. A journalist on a Seattle newspaper found a local angle in the fact that one of Hoffmann's Ph.D. advisers was a professor at the University of Washington. Columbia University claimed Hoffmann as one of 39 laureates among its former faculty and alumni. In fact, university publications not infrequently provide counts of the prizes of their alumni and faculty as evidence that their institutions are vibrant and vital research centers. A Harvard publication boasts of 'more than twice the number than from any other American university'.

In one important respect, though, reports of Nobel awards differ markedly from sports writing. Coverage of sports stars often includes analyses of their training, their techniques, and the details of their accomplishments. However, except in the *New York Times* and specialized science journals, the coverage of Nobel scientists seldom includes details of the nature of the prizewinner's research or its scientific significance. To the extent that research is noted at all, it appears as an arcane, esoteric, mysterious activity that is beyond the comprehension of normal human beings. 'How many people could identify with Mr Hoffman's lecture subject: "coupling carbenes and carbynes on mono-, di, and tri-nuclear transmission metal centers"?'[2] The presentation of science as arcane is reinforced by photographs of scientists standing before blackboards that are covered with complicated equations.

In their interviews with journalists, scientists themselves reinforce the mystification of science by emphasizing the extraordinary complexity of their work. Physicist Val Fitch describes his research: 'It's really quite arcane'. 'I find it difficult to convey to my family just what it is I've been doing', said physicist James Cronin in an interview with a *Time* reporter in 1980. *Time* cited the words of a member of the Nobel Committee to describe Cronin's work: 'Only an Einstein could say what it means'.[3]

Just as science is described as divorced from normal activity, so the scientist, at least the male scientist, is portrayed in popular newspapers and magazines as socially removed, apart from, and above most normal human preoccupations. Science thus appears to be the activity of lonely geniuses whose success reflects their combination of inspiration and total dedication to their work. One scientist sees 'in a most passive looking object' a 'veritable cauldron of activity' that the rest of us are unaware of. Another 'stumbled' on his find but then spent a year 'probing' for errors.[4] A frequent image is that of scientists spending twelve hours a day, seven days a week, at their work. Reporting on the effect of the prize on Sir Godfrey Hounsfield, one of the 1979 winners in medicine, a journalist from *Time* notes only one change in his life: 'He plans to put a laboratory in his living room'.[5] Another reporter portrays prizewinning scientists as part of 'an inner circle of scientific giants' who talk about science 'the way other people talk about ball games'. Being with them is 'like sitting in a conversation with the angels'.[6]

That a prestigious scientist can behave like ordinary mortals is noted with an air of surprise. The caption of a *New York Times* photograph of Walter Gilbert (the Nobel Prize-winning chemist who gave up his chair at Harvard to run the firm Biogen) notes his managerial skills: '[These] should not be underestimated just because he has a Nobel Prize'.[7] Writing of Nobel physicist Hans Bethe's concern about the buildup of nuclear weapons, a *New York Times* reporter remarks that 'he ultimately places his faith not in technology but in human beings – a remarkable stance for a man who has dedicated his life to the pursuit of science'.[8] The fact that celebrated scientists often teach undergraduate classes or keep office hours is considered a newsworthy point: 'Why would a world-class scientist waste time describing electrons to a fidgety mob of 400 students?'[9]

While successful male scientists appear in the press as above the mundane world and totally absorbed in their work, the few women laureates have a very different image. Stories of female Nobel Prize winners appear not only in the science pages but also in such lifestyle and women's magazines as *Vogue* and *McCall's*, which seldom cover science news.

McCall's described Maria Mayer, who shared the physics prize in 1963 for her theoretical work on the structure of the nucleus, as a 'tiny, shy, touchingly devoted wife and mother', a woman 'who makes people very happy at her home'. Approaching the story in a personal style hard to imagine in the coverage of a male Nobelist, the reporter interviewed Mayer's husband, who observed: 'She was once a terrible flirt but lovely and brighter than any girl I had ever met'. She is, according to this article, 'almost too good to be true'; 'a brilliant scientist, her children were perfectly darling, and she was so darned pretty that it all seemed unfair'. The reporter noted the 'graceful union between science and femininity', but also emphasized the conflict between being a mother and a scientist, the guilt, the opportunities missed by not spending more time at home. Writing about Mayer's work, the journalist remarked that she explains it in a 'startlingly feminine way' because she used the image of onion layers to describe the structure of the atom. The article then goes on to describe Mayer's reputation as 'the faculty's most elegant hostess'.[10]

Science journalists used similar stereotypes in their descriptions. A *Science Digest* article called 'At Home with Maria Mayer' begins: 'The first woman to win a Nobel Prize in science is a scientist and a wife'. It showed a picture of her, not at the blackboard, but at her kitchen stove.[11] Similarly, the *New York Times* headlined its article on Dorothy Hodgkin, who shared the prize for chemistry in 1966: 'British Grandmother Wins the Prize'. And *Time* emphasized her 'domesticity' and 'elegance of appearance'.[12]

The feminist movement did little to dispel such stereotypes. In 1977 Rosalyn Yalow, winner of the prize in medicine, also received extensive coverage in women's magazines. By *Vogue* she was characterized as 'a wonderwoman, remarkable, able to do everything, who works 70 hours a week, who keeps a kosher kitchen, who is a happily married, rather conventional wife and mother'.[13] *Family Health*, a magazine that reaches 5.3 million readers, headlined an article: 'She Cooks, She Cleans, She Wins the Nobel Prize' and introduced Yalow as a 'Bronx housewife'. The journalist expected to meet 'a crisp, efficient, no nonsense type' but discovered that 'she looked as though she would be at home selling brownies for the PTA fund raiser'.[14]

Journalists had more difficulty fitting Barbara McClintock, recipient of the 1983 Nobel Prize in medicine, into this stereotype, and this in itself became news. *Newsweek* called her 'the Greta Garbo of genetics. At 81 she has never married, always preferring to be alone.'[15] This article was published in the section called 'Transition' (along with the obituaries), although an item on McClintock also appeared on the 'Medicine' page. The *New York Times* covered McClintock in a long feature article. Its very first paragraph observed that she is well-known for baking with black walnuts.[16]

The overwhelming message in these popular press accounts is that the successful woman scientist must have the ability to do everything – to be feminine, motherly, and to achieve as well. Far from being insulated and apart from ordinary mortals, women scientists are admired for fitting in and for balancing domestic with professional activities. As a remarkable exception to the usual coverage of scientists in the press, the portraits of female Nobelists only highlight the prevailing image of science as an arcane and superior profession, and point up the lack of attention to its substance.

To complete the image of the esoteric scientist, journalists often convey the need for money and, above all, freedom to sustain science stars. A 1979 *Time* article is a typical example, attributing the prominence of American Nobel Prize winners to the 'heady air of freedom in U.S. academia and the abundant flow of grants. . . . Just do your own thing, the bounteous government seemed to say'.[17] The writer compares this tradition of freedom to the 'rigid' British, the 'ideological' Soviets, and the 'herr doctor' syndrome in Germany and France. Accepting the conventional (but questionable) wisdom among many scientists, he expresses concern that the pressure to apply science to practical ends and to impose 'cumbersome' regulations on experimental procedures will limit future triumphs. This reporter also argues that U.S. science gains by insulation from humanistic pursuits: 'The best minds have not been over-burdened with required studies that are remote from their interests'. Scientists, he suggests, do such specialized and important work that they operate outside a common intellectual or cultural tradition.[18]

Ironically, while treating scientists as somehow removed from the common culture, journalists often turn them into authorities in areas well outside their professional competence. Thus we frequently read of their opinions on nuclear power, the arms race, the prospect for world peace. In 1981, *U.S. News* offered its readers the opinions of past and present American Nobel winners on the question 'What are the greatest challenges facing the U.S. and the world at large and what can be done to meet those challenges?'[19] The answers, of course, varied, but the message underlying the question was clear: science is a superior form of knowledge, and those who have reached its pinnacle have some special insight into every problem.

Science as a resource

The image in the press of the scientist as a superstar of knowledge is matched by another image – that of scientific knowledge as perhaps the most important resource of the nation. This view of science as a national resource is most explicitly conveyed in the recent flood of articles and editorials about the 'crisis' of science education. In 1983, a *New York Times* editorial defined the problem: 'The battle for the future is being waged in the classroom and America is losing. Science and mathematics, once the backbone of education, is now its soft underbelly'. This is not the first time that science literacy has been a news-worthy issue. In 1957, the Soviet launching of Sputnik provoked major concern among scientists, politicians and military leaders about the quality of science education and its bearing on the production of scientific talent and technical skills. The press conveyed this message, and the resulting public concern helped to fuel a national effort to improve science education. The resurgence of the Cold War military mentality in the 1980s, as well as international competition in high technology, has brought renewed interest in science literacy. As commissions and committees deliberate the problem, their reports have become fodder for the press.

The articles on science education present a generally consistent point of view. Because science and technology are increasingly defining our lives, science literacy is becoming a survival skill. But what is science literacy? For the most part, news articles treat it not as understanding of science, but simply as computer literacy, as 'the passport to the electronic universe'. Skill in high-technology fields is portrayed as the definition of competence in a competitive society: 'A Revolution Is Under Way: The Smokestack Industries Are Shrinking, Leaving Millions without Skills to Compete in the Emerging High-Tech Economy'. News articles call resistance to computers 'computerphobia', a problem to be surmounted.[20]

Articles on science education emphasize that our school systems are inadequate to the task of training students for the technological age. A recurring word in the coverage of science education is 'gap', usually referring to a supposed discrepancy between the skills engendered by the educational system and American industry's need for a technically skilled labor force if it is to compete. A headline in the *Milwaukee Journal* reads 'Education Gap Perils Firm'.[21] The *San Jose Mercury* claims that this gap 'has contributed to America's decline as a world leader in technology'.[22] The press throughout the country made much of a statement from a speech on education by Glenn Seaborg, former chairman of the Atomic Energy Commission: 'If the deterioration in U.S. scientific competence is not reversed, I think our economic situation is going to continue to deteriorate and we are not going to recover'.[23]

Accepting reports of the declining quality of science education, journalists propose numerous explanations, usually related to trends in the 1960s. Thus some blame 'the Great Society programs' or the budget constraints that resulted from the shift in national priorities during the late 1960s. Others blame the general 'mentality of the sixties', when students demanded a less structured educational system. A *Business Week* reporter writes that 'during the politically volatile years of the late 1960s, schools shifted their focus from achievement to social relevance and federal funding for science education was the victim. The public programs of the 1970s drained school coffers', leading to low teacher salaries, out-of-date equipment, and especially a shortage of computers.[24]

Many of the reports on the problems in science education come from corporate sources; the press covers such reports with no hint that vested interests may be involved. *Business Week*, for example, quotes a Texas Instruments executive: 'If we don't do something about computer literacy, we will have another kind of haves and have-nots in our society that will be much worse than the black/white division'.[25] Just as computer employment ads promise that 'career minded employees get ahead and stay ahead', so journalists write that science illiteracy is responsible for leaving many people 'behind in the technological dust'.

Following corporate warnings, some suggest that inequities in science education will create a 'two-culture society', a 'gap between the three million professional scientists and engineers and the 224 million others who view technology as an undecipherable and threatening black box'.[26] *Time* published an article in

1982 called 'The Fuzzies Meet the Techs' about the efforts to bridge the 'gulf of mutual incomprehension' between liberal arts students and science students. 'The techs are considered by the fuzzies to be nerds. The techs in turn consider the fuzzies as only marginal in reaching logical conclusions'. Presenting the techs as superior, the article suggests the importance of teaching fuzzies the techs' way of thinking in order 'to overcome technophobia'.[27] It says little about the problem of general illiteracy and the importance of liberal education.

By stressing the gap between fuzzies and techs, between computer haves and have-nots, between the needs of society and the availability of people with technical skills, these reports on science education reinforce the mystification of science. And by idealizing technical professions, they over-simplify both the meaning of science literacy and the actual role of science as a national resource.

The purity of science

One might think that discussion of incidents of fraud in science, which appear in the press with increasing frequency, would undercut the mystique of the purity of science so prevalent in reporting about prestigious scientists and science literacy. But such is not the case. On the contrary, journalists report deviant behavior in a manner that further idealizes science as a pure, dispassionate profession.

Journalistic interest in scientific fraud developed in the late 1970s as part of the post-Watergate preoccupation with corruption in American institutions. Some of the articles on fraud are in fact similar in style to reports of political or business scandals, describing particular acts of fraud, the investigations that revealed the incidents, and the institutional response. Other articles discuss the issue of fraud more analytically, focusing on the causes and extent of fraud and describing particular cases as symptomatic of deeper problems. These two approaches reflect different interpretations; the first suggests that fraud is simply the deviant behavior of individuals, the second that it is a larger phenomenon with underlying causes that are basic to the present organization of science. Yet both convey a mystique about science, idealizing it as a sacrosanct, if vulnerable, profession.

The first type of news report deals with fraudulent behavior in science as a 'scandal', a 'betrayal of trust', a 'sin against science', a 'threat to patients or consumers'. Part of the scandal is the reluctance of research institutions to recognize fraud and the inability of responsible authorities to prevent it. For example, a group of investigative reporters from the *Boston Globe*'s 'spotlight team' wrote up a four-part series of articles on Marc J. Straus, a research physician specializing in lung cancer at University Hospital, who falsified data on his research subjects in order to show the success of his research on cancer therapy.[28] The headlines of the articles focused attention on both the scandalous aspects of his behavior and the institutional failure to take action despite the seriousness of the offense, which involved human subjects: 'Cancer Research

Falsified', 'Boston Project Collapses', 'Doctor under Fire Gets a New Grant'. The articles emphasized that corruption was a deviance from professional norms, an unusual event.

The more analytic articles use individual cases of fraud to criticize current research practices. A *New York Times* reporter, in the article entitled 'The Doctor's World: How Honest is Medical Research?' calls attention to competitive practices in research.[29] The *Christian Science Monitor* sees fraud as part of 'a larger problem', in particular the 'corrosive effect of pressure to publish'.[30] Other journalists have variously attributed the problem to 'the pressure cooker of research', inadequate supervision of younger colleagues, or the fact that most experiments are never replicated because 'you don't get a grant for repeating someone else's work'. Only a few articles in the *New York Times* raised fundamental questions concerning the validity of certain traditional assumptions about science and scientific method. Can scientific honesty be assumed? Is the scientific method adequate? Does the peer review process offer enough protection against fraud? Most reporters avoid these structural issues, rather describing individual cases of malfeasance as stains on the scientific ideal.

Whether journalists define fraud as an individual aberration or a growing problem in the contemporary practice of science, they project a coherent image of scientific ideals. The metaphors typically used to describe fraudulent data are instructive. They 'contaminate', 'tarnish', 'besmirch', 'taint' or 'sully' the reputation of individual scientists, their institutions, and science itself. Faked data must be 'expunged', 'purged', 'withdrawn from the scientific record'. Scientists who learn that one of their colleagues is involved are invariably reported to be 'shocked', 'horrified', 'stunned' or 'reluctant to believe it'. For fraud is a 'sin' as well as a scandal. The culprit has 'fallen' or 'betrayed' the profession. 'When a scientist succumbs to temptation and pays the price, it is always sad'.

Fraudulent acts in most other fields (except perhaps in sport) evoke quite different and less moralistic metaphors. Consumer fraud is a 'ripoff' or a 'crime', hardly a sin. Political scandals are abuses of trust and reported, often cynically, as critiques of political institutions. The bribery scandals in New York city appeared as one more example of the corruption inherent in local politics that the press helps to expose. But science, idealized in the language describing scientific fraud, is portrayed as a profession apart – dispassionate, objective, and with values that remain above those in other fields. A *Newsweek* article states this view clearly: 'A perception of widespread fakery undermines the trust in others' work that is the foundation of science. More than business or law or politics, science rests on the presumption of honesty in a quest for truth. If that presumption comes into question, a backlash against science may not be far away. And that could compromise what is still one of the more objective and honest sources of information in an ever more complicated world'.[31]

The idealization, so evident in the coverage of fraud, has paved the way for the use of science in the press as a neutral source of information for the creation of social policy, and a powerful source of authority in support of popular – if controversial – beliefs.

The authority of scientific theory

Scientific information is often reported in the press, but theories are seldom newsworthy. A notable exception are those theories of behavior that bear on controversial social stereotypes. Thus theories of evolutionary biology and natural selection, when used to explain human differences, have had an active press. The theory of biological determinism attracted considerable news coverage following the controversy over Jensen's claims about the relationship between race and IQ. Its reappearance in the growing field of sociobiology has again attracted the press. The reports on sociobiology have been less concerned with its substance than with its purported applications. In selecting this subject for extensive coverage, journalists are in effect using a controversial theory to legitimize a particular point of view.

Sociobiology is a controversial field devoted to the systematic study of the biological basis of social behavior. Its basic premise is that behavior is shaped primarily by genetic factors, selected over thousands of years for their survival value. Its most vocal proponent, entomologist Edward O. Wilson from Harvard University, contends that genes create predispositions for certain types of behavior and that a full understanding of these genetic constraints is essential to intelligent social policy. He believes that sociobiology is 'a new synthesis', offering a unified theory of human behavior. 'The genes hold culture on a leash', he writes in his book *On Human Nature*. 'The leash is very long but inevitably values will be constrained in accordance with their effects on the human gene pool'.[32]

Wilson's arguments about human behavior, extrapolated from his research on insect behavior, have been widely attacked by other scientists for their apparent justification of racism and sexism, for their lack of scientific support, and for their simplistic presentation of the complex interaction of biological and social influences on human behavior.[33] Yet, ever since the publication of Wilson's first book on the subject, *Sociobiology, A New Synthesis*, was reported as news in the *New York Times* and welcomed as a 'long awaited definitive book,' the press has typically discussed the arguments for sociobiology and the details of particular studies in uncritical, often enthusiastic, terms. Sociobiological concepts subsequently have appeared in articles about the most diverse aspects of human behavior, used, for example, to explain:

- *The differences between male and female behavior.* 'Authorities now say nature not nurture makes him thump and thunder while you rescue lost kittens and crimp'. (*Cosmopolitan*)
- *Human decency.* 'Decency is rooted in gene selfishness to enhance the prospect of survival'. (*New York Times*)

- *Child abuse*: 'The love of a parent has its roots in the fact that the child will reproduce the parent's genes'. (*Family Week*)
- *Machismo*: 'Machismo is biologically based and says in effect: "I have good genes, let me mate."' (*Time*)
- *Intelligence*: 'On the towel rack that we call our anatomy, nature appears to have hung his-and-hers brains'. (*Boston Globe*)
- *Promiscuity*: 'If you get caught fooling around, don't say the devil made you do it. It's your DNA'. (*Playboy*)
- *Selfishness*: 'Built into our genes to insure their individual reproduction'. (*Psychology Today*)
- *Rape*: 'Genetically programed into male behavior'. (*Science Digest*)
- *Obesity*: 'A genetic tendency to stock for a famine that never comes'. (*Science Digest*)
- *Aggression*: 'Men are more genetically aggressive because they are more indispensable'. (*Newsweek*)

The press has been most aroused by sociobiology's controversial implications on the subject of sex differences. Not surprisingly, the most uncritical acceptance of the theory appears in *Playboy*. In a somewhat tongue-in-cheek article, called 'Darwin and the Double Standard,' *Playboy* says the critics of sociobiology are 'burying their head in the sand' and 'refusing to face facts'. The theory, we are told, directly challenges women's demands for equal rights. 'Perhaps [women] are defying biology – it's not nice to fool Mother Nature. Recent scientific theory suggests that there are innate differences between the sexes and that what is right for the gander is wrong for the goose'.[34]

Such efforts to entertain by playing on conventional stereotypes are not confined to *Playboy*. *Time*, for example, begins an article with the question, 'Why do men go to war? Answer: Because the women are watching'. The reporter explains that this conclusion is confirmed by sociobiology: 'Male displays and bravado, from antlers in deer and feather-ruffling in birds, to chest thumping in apes and humans, evolved as a reproductive strategy to impress females'.[35] And *Cosmopolitan*, citing the 'weight of scientific opinion' to legitimize its bias, tells its readers, 'Recent research has established beyond a doubt that males and females are born with a different set of instructions built into their genetic code'.[36]

Cultural stereotypes also attract the press to specific kinds of research. In 1980, two psychologists, Camille Benbow and Julian Stanley, published a research paper in *Science* on the differences between boys and girls in mathematical reasoning. Their study, examining the correlation between Scholastic Aptitude Test scores and classroom work, found that differences in the classroom preparation of boys and girls were not responsible for differences in their later test performance. The *Science* article was careful to qualify the implication of male superiority in mathematics: 'It is probably an expression of a combination of both endogenous and exogenous variables. We recognize, however, that our data are consistent with numerous alternative hypotheses'.[37] But the press was less qualified, writing up the research as a strong confirmation of biological differences and a definitive challenge to the idea that differences in mathematical test scores are caused by social and cultural factors. The news peg was not the research, but its implications.

The authors themselves encouraged this perspective in their interviews with reporters, where they were less cautious than in their scientific writing. Indeed, they used the press to push their ideas as a useful basis for public policy. According to the *New York Times*, they 'urged educators to accept the possibility that something more than social factors may be responsible. . . . You can't brush the differences under the rug and ignore them'.[38] The press was receptive. *Time*, writing of the 'gender factor in math', summarized the findings: 'Males might be naturally abler than females'.[39] *Discover* reported that male superiority is so pronounced that 'to some extent, it must be unborn'.[40] It was left to a few *New York Times* op-ed pieces and to some women's magazines to question the methodology of the research and the limited nature of the evidence.[41]

What is striking about many of the articles on sociobiology is how easily reporters slide from noting a provocative theory to citing it as fact, even when they know that the supporting evidence may be flimsy. A remarkable article called 'A Genetic Defense of the Free Market' that appeared in *Business Week* clearly illustrates this slide. While conceding that 'there is no hard evidence to support the theory', the author writes: 'For better or worse, self-interest is a driving force in the economy because it is engrained in each individual's genes. . . . Government programs that force individuals to be less competitive and less selfish than they are genetically programed to be are preordained to fail'. The application of sociobiology that he calls 'bioeconomics' is controversial, he says; nevertheless, it is 'a powerful defense of Adam Smith's laissez-faire views'.[42]

This journalist and many others writing about sociobiology recognize, indeed rely on, the existence of controversy to enliven the story. Yet most articles convey a point of view by allowing considerable space to sociobiology's advocates and by marginalizing the theory's critics.[43]

In numerous articles, critics of sociobiology are variously dismissed as ideologues, Marxists, feminists or members of the radical left. They are 'few in number but vociferous'; people who are 'unwilling to accept the truth'. To the extent that their views are presented, they are characterized as distorted or isolated. A *Science News* reporter, for example, wrote that 'one runs the risk of misrepresenting the consensus view by focusing, however briefly, on critics and criticism'.[44] *Newsweek* suggested that Wilson was a victim like Galileo: 'The critics are trying to suppress his views because they contradict contemporary orthodoxies'.[45] *Science Digest* compared the criticism of sociobiology to the attack of religious fundamentalism on the theory of evolution – 'Like the theory of evolution, sociobiology is often attacked and misinterpreted'[46] – a comparison that places sociobiology's scientific critics, such as Stephen J. Gould and Richard Lewontin of Harvard University, in the same league as William Jennings Bryan.

The uncritical acceptance, indeed promotion, of sociobiology once again reflects the idealization of science as an ultimate authority, albeit selectively applied. For by its selection of what theories to champion, the press in effect uses the imprimatur of science to support a particular world view. It does so, however, with little attention to the substance of science, its slow accumulative process, and its limits.

Whether they write about prizes, professional problems or scientific theories, newspaper and popular magazine reporters convey a sense of awe about science. The scientist is a star engaged in a highly competitive international race for prizes or prestige. Sometimes the intensity of competition in research can lead scientists to fraudulent behavior, but the image of science remains idealized and unscathed. Even when writing about controversial theories that bear on social policy, the press projects an image of science as an esoteric activity, a separate culture, a profession apart from and above other human endeavors. By avoiding the substance of science and ignoring the process of research, the press ultimately contributes to the obtusion of science and helps to perpetuate the distance between science and the citizen. These effects are highly problematic in an age when science is in fact very much a part of the common culture, integrally tied to public policy and political affairs.

Notes

1 *Nation*, January 16, 1902.
2 *Kansas City Times*, September 17, 1982.
3 *Time*, October 27, 1980.
4 *Newsweek*, October 27, 1979.
5 *Time*, October 22, 1979.
6 *McCall's*, July 1964, p.40.
7 *New York Times*, February 19, 1983.
8 *New York Times*, June 12, 1984.
9 *Binghampton Sunday Press*, March 14, 1982.
10 *McCall's*, July 1964, February 1964, pp.38–40, 124.
11 *Science Digest* 55, February 1964, pp.30–6.
12 *Time*, November 6, 1964.
13 *Vogue*, January 1978, p.174.
14 *Family Health*, June 1978, p.24.
15 *Newsweek*, October 24, 1983.
16 *New York Times*, October 11, 1983.
17 *Time*, October 29, 1979.
18 *Ibid*.
19 *U.S. News and World Report*, April 16, 1981.
20 See, for example, *Time*, December 6, 1982, and the *Christian Science Monitor*, education section, April 15, 1983; also see the local papers catalogued in *Newsbank*.
21 *Milwaukee Journal*, July 11, 1982.
22 *San Jose Mercury*, March 12, 1982.

23 The quotation by Glenn Seaborg appeared in the *Houston Post*, November 17, 1982, and many other newspapers.
24 *Business Week*, March 28, 1983; *Seattle Times*, January 2, 1983.
25 *Business Week* and many newspapers emphasize the problem of obsolete equipment and reinforce this with photographs.
26 Op-ed piece by William McCowan, 'Illiterassee att Wurk', *New York Times*, August 19, 1982, on the 'unlettered underclass'.
27 *Time*, December 6, 1982.
28 *Boston Globe*, June 19, 1980.
29 *New York Times*, August 5, 1980.
30 *Christian Science Monitor*, March 10, 1982.
31 *Newsweek*, February 8, 1982.
32 Edward O. Wilson, *On Human Nature* (Cambridge, Mass.: Harvard University Press, 1980).
33 For a comprehensive review of the criticism and the controversy, see Ullica Segerstrale, 'Colleagues in conflict: an in vivo analysis of the sociobiology controversy', *Biology and Philosophy* 1, 1986, pp.53–87.
34 *Playboy*, August 1978.
35 *Time*, August 1, 1977.
36 *Cosmopolitan*, March 1982.
37 Camille Benbow and Julian Stanley, 'Sex differences in mathematical reasoning: fact or artifact?' *Science* 210, December 12, 1980, pp.1262–4.
38 *New York Times*, December 7, 1980.
39 *Time*, December 15, 1980.
40 Pamela Weintraub, 'The brain: his and hers', *Discover*, April 1981, pp.15–20.
41 See, for example, the *New York Times*, May 30, 1981.
42 *Business Week*, April 10, 1978.
43 See, for example, interviews in the *New York Times*, October 12, 1975, and *People Weekly*, November 19, 1975.
44 *Science News*, November 19, 1975.
45 *Newsweek*, April 12, 1976.
46 *Science Digest*, March 1982.

Author's note: This study was undertaken with the assistance of Christopher Vinger, undergraduate research assistant, and Jeffrey Talbert, graduate research assistant. The research was supported by a grant from the U.S. National Science Foundation, Ethics and Values Studies program. Address all correspondence to Dr. Susanna Hornig Priest, Assistant Professor, Department of Journalism, Texas A&M University, College Station, TX 77843–4111.

Chapter 15

Structuring public debate on biotechnology

Media frames and public response*

S. Hornig Priest

This article reports findings based on the results of a series of twenty-seven focus group discussions exploring how mass media (newspaper) coverage of biotechnology may structure the public's response to that field and what strategies members of the lay (nontechnical) public use to understand this emerging area of research. Biotechnology or bioengineering – the active manipulation of the genetic structure of particular species for agricultural or medical purposes – represents a particularly interesting case for a study of public opinion formation in response to media accounts because it is a relatively new area of research. Researchers did not learn how to isolate and remove a gene from one genetic structure for possible insertion into another until the late 1970s, although the process was well understood by the mid-1980s. Today biotechnology holds the promise of allowing the alteration of food crops and meat animals in desirable directions, of creating new ways to 'manufacture' medicines, and even of identifying and correcting human genetic limitations.

This study builds on two previous studies: one analysing focus group response to mass media accounts of a broad range of science- and technology-related risks (Hornig 1993), and one analysing 18 months of recent newspaper coverage of biotechnology (Hornig and Talbert 1993). The previous focus group study suggested that members of the lay public can be quite sophisticated in the range of issues they see as relevant to the evaluation of a risk, including sociopolitical, economic, regulatory, ethical and communication-related concerns. (This finding is consistent with much of the recent work on the social psychology of risk; see Hornig 1993 for discussion.) Differences between expert and lay publics in the evaluation of particular risks may stem, in these cases, less from public misunderstanding of scientific data than from reliance on a broader 'vocabulary of risk' than the traditional cost–benefit criteria used by risk analysts. However, we felt that because of the relatively recent emergence of biotechnology as an area of research and of mass media reporting of it, this situation may be less true for responses to media coverage about

*Previously published in *Science Communication* (1994), Vol. 16, No. 2, pp. 166–79.

biotechnology than for responses to information about developments of other sorts.

Furthermore, our study of newspaper coverage of biotechnology (Hornig and Talbert 1993) had demonstrated that this reporting is heavily dominated by reliance on industrial and university sources, which emphasize economic considerations and potential benefits almost to the exclusion of other types of concern. This type of issue definition serves distinct political interests (Plein 1991) and is likely to be more influential for newly emerging news agenda items (Brosius and Kepplinger 1992). Given a narrower base of pre-existing knowledge to draw from, and given media coverage heavily weighted toward a narrow range of sub-issues, how would lay publics understand biotechnology? How might limitations on the range of issues included in media coverage limit, in turn, the character of public opinion formation and the terms of public debate? If such a media effect exists anywhere, it ought to exist for a newly emerging, highly technical issue such as biotechnology-based research.

The concepts of *framing* and *schema processing* have been used in a variety of different and sometimes overlapping ways. In this article we distinguish between the two. Framing (Tuchman 1978) refers to the process through which complex issues are reduced to journalistically manageable dimensions in the construction of a news story, resulting in the selective presentation of some sub-themes but not others. We use schema processing (Graber 1988) to refer to the cognitive processing of news information by individual audiences or readers through categorizing an issue or story as being of a particular type previously encountered. Of course, news editors and reporters must also rely on schema processing to settle on an appropriate news frame. Here, framing by institutional sources is likely to be a powerful influence, in turn, on journalists' schemas; at a minimum, it will affect the shape and character of available information. But this particular analysis is concerned primarily with the relationship between news frames and public schemas, rather than the origins of the former.

Kuklinski *et al.* (1991) argue that what they call 'schema theory' is somewhat impoverished as a source of understanding in political psychology, adding little beyond what has already been contributed by a variety of other concepts, including frame and attitude. On the contrary, we believe that these three ideas (schema, frame, attitude) can be usefully distinguished from one another and that our understanding of the way in which mass media information – in this case, information about science – is understood is incomplete without consideration of all three. Schema processing by individual readers or audience members is likely to be a complex activity involving active choice and selective perception, 'fuzzy' and sometimes overlapping categories, and the application of rules that are shaped by the particular social context. Trying to specify the structure of a schema as though it were an object is probably self-defeating, but we found the concept no less useful for these attributes.

Framing, in our view, certainly influences, although would by no means fully determine, schema assignments. That is, we believe that it is through framing, which suggests or invites certain interpretations, that the mass media may have their most powerful effects and that framing effects may be particularly signifi-cant for newly emerging issues. At the same time, we see audiences and readers as active interpreters of mass-mediated information who bring their own know-ledge and experience to the task of understanding a new issue, and the use of schemas based on this knowledge and experience is among the key strategies that readers use to approach the analysis of new issues. Mass media framing and reader schema processing interactively influence one another in ways that appear to be extraordinarily complex – media frames undoubtedly influence the selec-tion of appropriate audience schemas – but we found it useful for our analysis to approach them separately. We also gathered separate data on background attitudes toward science and technology that emerged as powerful predictors of perceptions of risk without being reducible to either frame or schema considerations. Our work reflects a different set of interests than mass media agenda-setting studies typically embody. We are not asking about which issues are seen as important and why, but about how those issues are defined – which themes or attributes are seen as important – and why. We refer to this later on as a 'sub-issue agenda'.

We worked, then, with two research questions in analysing these data, which are stated below in the form of hypotheses:

1   Because of the relative newness and high-technology character of bio-technological issues, we expected that the coverage would strongly structure the general character of the discussions. That is, we expected that the themes explored in the discussions would be different from these explored in our previous focus group research on other issues in directions reflective of the emphases of newspaper coverage of biotechnology (framing).

2   For this reason, and reflecting the recognition that interpretation of news coverage does not take place in a vacuum but depends upon the previous knowledge and experience of the interpreter, we expected that focus group participants would use analogies to other, perhaps unrelated, scientific and technological developments in an attempt to understand biotechnology (schema processing).

The analysis was also designed to explore the differences between the general adult public and university students in terms of their response to science news, since much of our previous research had been done on student groups.

Methods

Eighteen of the twenty-seven focus groups, each consisting of between six and eight members, were composed of undergraduate journalism students at an American university, who received extra course credit for participation in this project. The remaining nine groups contained between four and six adults from the surrounding community. The adult participants were limited to those with no direct personal connection to the university at which the research was being conducted; that is, they were not currently students, faculty or staff at that university. They were paid for their time.[1] One adult group and two student groups considered each one of a series of nine articles that we had chosen as being broadly representative of newspaper coverage of biotechnology, as explained below.

In selecting articles for use in the focus groups, we chose from among 132 articles included in an earlier study (Hornig and Talbert 1993) those that best represented the range of issues and points of view we had prevously found to be characteristic of newspaper coverage of biotechnology. The nine articles used covered both agricultural (five articles) and medical (four articles) biotechnology, and they did so from a point of view emphasizing either industry or the university as spokespersons. They covered developments involving pest-resistant cotton, biosensors, hybrid corn, laboratory mice, tomatoes, potatoes, genetically altered crops generally, and the business potential of biotechnology firms generally. Two outside experts reviewed the articles for evidence of serious technical error; a science-writing specialist holding an M.D. degree reviewed the medicine-related articles, and a Ph.D. agricultural scientist reviewed the agriculture-related articles; they found no major misrepresentations. The original set of 132 articles from which these were chosen consisted of all articles indexed under the keyword *biotechnology* for the period 1 January 1991 through 30 June 1992, in the commercial newspaper index *Newsbank*, which draws its material from small, medium and larger papers throughout the United States.

Each respondent was first asked to complete a sixteen-item questionnaire assessing his or her general attitude toward science and technology; this questionnaire was based on previous research (Hornig 1992) and assessed a variety of beliefs about science (how it is used and controlled, its effects, and cost–benefit considerations) which had proved predictive of risk judgments in the context of that study. Then each group was asked to consider the issue reported in their article (retyped so that publication data were absent and typography was held constant across the nine issues) and asked to arrive at a consensus on whether the development reported could be considered safe for unlimited use, for limited use, or for no use at all. This consensus-building task had been tested in previous research and found to be an effective way of encouraging participants to articulate points they found most persuasive or important. When discussion slowed, a research assistant used neutral probes (for example, 'Does anyone else have any considerations they would like to bring up?') in an attempt to elicit additional responses. When the group seemed to have reached a decision, the assistant would ask group members if they were ready to make their recommendation, record it, and proceed with the next step, completion of a post-discussion questionnaire with standard demographic questions and indication on a seven-point Likert-type scale of how risky each respondent considered the particular technology in question to be. The attitudinal and risk data were analysed quantitatively; the transcript data were analysed both quantitatively and qualitatively.

The coding scheme for the transcripts came from the earlier focus group study of technological risk assessment (Hornig 1993). The unit of analysis was the argument, of which there were nine coded types. Two research assistants coded each transcript; one reviewed the coding and made a final coding decision. The degree of agreement between the two coders was assessed for four of the twenty-seven transcripts (randomly selected). Overall, for these four transcripts, 93 percent of the time the two coders agreed on the category to which each argument should be assigned; other cases of disagreement resulted from differences in perception of where an argument began or ended. The coding categories were derived in the earlier study using a grounded-theory approach in which the particular categories used were not specified *a priori* but allowed to emerge from the data. In that study, twenty-two categories emerged that were later grouped for analysis into the nine groups used here: information issues (concerns about research adequacy) and the sufficiency, validity, and credibility of the information); negative impacts (human health, economic issues, environmental threats, other potential dangers, and statements about the numbers of people or locations affected); benefits ([lack of] availability of alternative technologies or treatments, priority of need, and other potential benefits); implementation issues (awareness issues and safety precautions, including worker training); regulatory issues; ethical considerations; and other (statements that 'no problem exists' plus otherwise unclassified arguments).

Results

We first considered the relationship between responses among students and adults (non-students) using the first ten completed comparable groups to determine whether the balance of the analysis needed to treat these groups separately. There was a statistically significant difference between the students and the adults in the mean level of risk seen (3.611 for students and 2.917 for adults, $t = 2.24$, $p = 0.029$). There was also some variation in the overall level of risk seen for each of these five issues, which ranged from 3.000 to 3.667. However, analysis of variance for the effect of issue discussed and adulthood versus student status on risk judgments using the composite attitudinal score as a covariate indicated that more variance in risk judgments was attributable to attitudinal score ($F = 6.723$, $p = 0.013$) than to either issue ($F = 0.346$, n.s.) or group membership ($F = 2.475$, n.s.). We therefore felt reasonably confident in combining the two sets of transcripts for further analysis.

Table 15.1 compares themes coded from the transcripts for all twenty-seven groups (biotech groups) with results from the earlier focus group research (previous groups) and the biotechnology news study (biotech news) cited above. Examination of this table provides some evidence consistent with the

Table 15.1 Comparison of themes of focus group discussions of a range of science and technology issues, of newspaper coverage of biotechnology, and of focus group discussions of biotechnology (percentage data in all cases)

	Previous Group (N = 361)	Biotech News (N = 600)	Test Article (N = 37)	Biotech Group (N = 608)
Information	27.2	0.0	0.0	32.4
Benefits	13.0	35.2	56.8	12.2
Awareness	11.9	0.5	0.0	2.3
Dangers	11.4	6.2	1.5	18.4
Regulation	10.8	8.2	0.3	11.0
Ethics	9.1	1.3	0.0	6.3
Economics	5.0	47.7	29.7	9.5
Environment	2.2	0.8	0.0	3.1
Other	9.4	0.2	0.0	4.8

framing hypothesis, although the evidence is neither strong nor definitive. Note from Table 15.1 that the range of concerns emerging in focus group discussions of biotechnological news is extremely similar to the range of concerns expressed in focus group discussions of a broad range of other science and technology developments in the earlier study. Contrary to our hypothesis (and our own preliminary results), the emphasis in news coverage on benefits and economic considerations – the traditional grist for the cost–benefit analysis mill – does not seem to have had much, if any, effect on the direction of the focus group discussions. There is some weak evidence, when the data are examined on an issue-by-issue basis, that the increase in economic arguments from 5 percent in the earlier study to 10 percent in this study may result from news framing in economic terms, as those articles most heavily emphasizing economics seemed to engender discussion similarly framed. This does not seem to be the case for the news emphasis on benefits – the percentage here drops to 12 percent from 13 percent, despite the fact that 35 percent of the arguments in biotechnology coverage as a whole and 57 percent of the arguments in the test articles concerned benefits. Nor, conversely, did a relative de-emphasis in news coverage of a range of other concerns appear to depress focus group discussion, with the possible exceptions of public awareness and ethical considerations. Respondents discussed benefits about a third as often as such material appeared in the news stories, and they were about three times as likely to discuss dangers as were the stories. As in the previous study, considerable lay concern but no news coverage at all centered on issues of information and its adequacy.

It is apparent that the range of lay public concerns about biotechnology is substantially broader than the range of concerns reflected in news coverage. Framing effects resulting from the narrowness of the news coverage are not strongly represented in the data, and we make no direct claims about causality. However, overall, discussion of negative impacts, costs and benefits – the traditional vocabulary of risk analysis – accounted for 31.6 percent of the earlier focus group data but 43.2 percent of the biotechnology focus group data. Discussion of other non-information-related issues (public awareness, regulatory, ethical and other issues; see Hornig and Talbert 1993) accounted for 41.2 percent of the earlier focus group data and only 24.4 percent of the biotechnology focus group data. Discussion of information issues (credibility, validity, sufficiency) accounted for roughly the same proportion (27.2 percent vs 32.4 percent) of the data in each case. These data are consistent with an interpretation that asserts that framing and schema processing interact to produce the range of concerns actually represented in the focus group transcripts, since there appears to be an emphasis in the transcripts on cost–benefit considerations reflective of the news coverage, but at the same time, other concerns emerge that are associated with science and technology generally but not heavily represented in the news. Table 15.2 compares the arguments raised in focus group discussions of agricultural versus medical biotechnology, which are almost identical, as was the mean risk perceived to be associated with these two types of issues (3.74 vs 3.77).

Another way of looking at the relationship between media framing and pre-existing cognitive factors is represented by the data in Table 15.3. Here, risk perceived is treated as the dependent variable in an analysis of variance in which the sixteen-question attitudinal scale administered prior to the group discussions is used as a covariate, that is, controlled for statistically. We believe that these general attitudes toward science and technology are a part of the knowledge invoked when biotechnology is understood in a 'scientific development' schema (that is, as new instances of a known phenomenon: the emergence of new scientific knowledge), although the schema is not itself reducible to a set of

Table 15.2 Comparison of arguments raised in focus group discussions centred on news of agricultural versus medical biotechnology (N = 608)

	Agricultural Issue		Medical Issue	
	Number	Percentage	Number	Percentage
Information	99	33	98	32
Benefits	32	11	42	14
Awareness	8	3	6	2
Dangers	58	19	54	18
Regulation	30	10	37	12
Ethics	11	4	27	9
Economics	34	11	24	8
Environment	10	3	9	3
Other	18	6	11	4

Note
Mean risk perceived for agricultural issues was 3.74; for medical issues, 3.77. Chi-square = 12.62; df = 8; n.s.

Table 15.3 Analysis of variance showing relationship between risk perceived (treated as the dependent variable), attitudinal factors (treated as a covariate), agricultural versus medical issue type, student versus adult status, and industry versus university viewpoint

Source of Variation	Sum of Squares	Degress of Freedom	Mean	F	p
Attitude score (covariate)	25.106	1	25.106	15.445	0.000
Main effects	11.133	3	3.711	2.283	0.081
Issue type	0.659	1	0.659	0.405	0.525
Status	3.362	1	3.362	2.068	0.152
Viewpoint	6.272	1	6.272	3.859	0.051
Two-way interactions	16.700	3	5.567	3.425	0.019
Issue type by status	3.541	1	3.541	2.178	0.142
Issue by viewpoint	14.446	1	14.446	8.887	0.003
Status by viewpoint	0.142	1	0.142	0.087	0.768
Three-way interactions	0.483	1	0.483	0.297	0.587
Issue by status by view	0.483	1	0.483	0.297	0.587
Explained	53.422	8	6.678	4.108	0.000
Residual	248.701	153	1.625		
	302.123	161	1.877		

attitudes. The best predictor of risk perceived is these background attitudinal factors rather than any of the aspects of the issues or their coverage used in the analysis. Both viewpoint and the interaction of issue type and viewpoint are statistically significant predictors of perceived risk (that is, article viewpoint predicts risk seen by the reader, both overall and within a particular issue treated separately, in which case the directionality of the relationship between viewpoint and perceived risk may vary from issue to issue). However, these do not explain as much of the variance as the attitudinal covariate (that is, attitudes seem to be an even more important predictor of risk perceived).

Qualitative analysis of the transcript data revealed heavy reliance on reasoning by analogy from issues of quite different types. In almost every group, the discussion centered around comparison and/or contrast with pesticide use, the use of experimental medicines, or the introduction of environmental pollutants. Groups differed in the extent to which they seemed to appreciate the appropriateness of these analogies and focused on contrasts as well as similarities to other types of development, but almost all used them to frame their discussion. (Some of this reliance, again, appears to reflect analogies and emphases of the news articles, although the strength of this relationship is difficult to assess.)

Most commonly, the analogy was to a chemical pesticide or other environmental contaminant:

If this worm is dead and a bird eats the worm, what type of effect is that going to have on the ecological chain in the long run?

How many times have they put pesticides on the market and then pull[ed] them off ten years later?

As long as it doesn't cause pollution . . . then I think they're OK to use.

But then there's always a problem with long term, . . . like NutraSweet®.

Sometimes the introduced substance analogy was implicit:

But this is something that you're introducing into the food supply.

What if it is now poisonous?

Like beef hormones.

Medical biotechnology was interpreted in terms of drug-testing issues:

My mother had cancer and tried a totally experimental drug.

But the problem is deciding on the dosage.

Agricultural biotechnology was understood in terms of older genetic technology as well as pesticide use:

It's just hybridization.

It's like the cross-breeding of a cow.

There were also regulatory analogies:

I wonder if you could refuse this biosensor test like you could a DWI?

FDA regulates this so it's OK; they are almost too careful about testing drugs.

Some analogies came straight from science fiction:

Like the book *Jurassic Park*, it's a scary process.

We can't have anyone have the ability to make half-human mice.

While further, more systematic analysis of the use of analogical reasoning is clearly called for, it seems clear that in the probable absence of specific schemas for understanding biotechnology *per se*, readers and audiences draw from related schemas. Such schemas are likely to contain both points of comparison and points of contrast with issues in biotechnology. Sometimes these related schemas may be appropriate from the point of view of the scientific community; sometimes they may not.

Discussion

Despite the broad range of ethical, regulatory and management (communication and implementation) issues that biotechnology represents, then, lay discussions of news about biotechnology – at least in the United States – are more likely to focus on costs (impacts) and benefits and less likely to focus on other related issues than are discussions of other science and technology issues previously tested. We suspect, but of course cannot prove, that this may be a result of the narrowness of media coverage of biotechnology, as documented in our previous research (Hornig and Talbert 1993), especially since that coverage was shown to be dominated by institutional interests speaking of economic trade-offs and benefits. That is, we believe that narrow media coverage of biotechnology may be framing it in a way that limits the range of discussion of related issues. We conceptualize the media coverage as 'resonating with' – augmenting or diminishing – certain reader concerns, and although our design was not intended to establish cause-and-effect relationships with certainty, we believe that this process deserves further study. At the same time, there is a strong resilience to the lay public's concern with a broader range of the implications of biotechnology than news coverage reflects, such that framing effects observed here are not as strong as we had expected (that is, media emphasis was not a strong predictor of focus group direction).

Biotechnology is consistently conceptualized as a matter of introducing some foreign element, as being in important ways like using or introducing a drug, pesticide or environmental pollutant. The use of this 'foreign element' schema arose in almost all the groups, with students and adults, and in discussions of medical as well as agriculatural biotechnology. Only rarely was the discussion framed in terms of alteration of underlying genetic structure rather than introduction of a substance. And on several of these occasions, science fiction-like scenarios were the result. From a scientific point of view, it may be technically correct that bioengineering involves the introduction of a foreign substance (DNA from another species), but lay over-reliance on this particular type of schema seems to us to limit or distort understanding. A persistent problem that arose in the conduct of this research was that the focus group discussions lagged or stalled to a far greater extent than in our earlier research on other types of risk. We tried to solve this problem by paying more attention to the use of probes but achieved only limited success; it was characteristic of the adult as well as of the student groups, and in the final analysis, it may be another reflection of the inadequacy of both media coverage and public understanding in this area.

On a theoretical level, we believe that these data are consistent with both the assertion that mass media frames influence reader and audience discussions and the assertion that reader schemas actively and independently contribute to the interpretation of news accounts. While this exploratory study was not intended to prove or disprove these assertions, we hope this analysis has illustrated the usefulness of this model for understanding media effects. On a practical level, coverage of the newly emerging, highly technically complex area of biotechnology-based research may productively be thought of as being framed in overly simplistic terms reflecting the priorities of institutional sources, and under these circumstances lay schemas drawn from other developments are less than adequate for the task of grasping and grappling with these new issues. We urge both institutional spokespersons for biotechnology and media professionals to broaden the range of public debate by broadening the media sub-issue agenda in this area, that is, by actively seeking to provide information on dangers as well as benefits and on related ethical, regulatory and other social issues.

Although this study provides only relatively weak and indirect evidence of short-term framing effects, defined as the influence of a media sub-issue agenda on public discussion, we do not believe that this should be taken as evidence that framing is not a useful concept for understanding how science is communicated. Important framing effects here, like other media effects, are likely to be subtle and long-term; individuals' cognitive schemas are likely to be built up over time using information communicated in media frames. In other words, in the long run, the media are likely to be a critically important source of the general background understandings and expectations that readers bring to the interpretation of a new scientific development. The fact that framing effects may be weak in the short run for a given specific issue may reflect the strength and persistence of long-term influences on individual cognition; this finding does not at all rule out the possibility that long-term framing effects may be very important.

What does it mean to suggest, in more general terms, that biotechnology is being framed as a scientific development issue? Could these developments, if presented in some other way, be understood in the context of some other schema? The difficulty of imagining such an alternative may say something about the strength of this framing influence and the primacy of scientific explanation in American culture – its embeddedness in everyday thought. However, we can more readily imagine that in other cultures or other countries biotechnology might be presented and understood in, say, magical or religious terms that would present quite a different constellation of concerns based on radically different schemas. This may help us to think about what might be the implications within the United States (and countries with similar biotechnology industries) of presenting biotechnology as (for example) a business investment decision rather than a scientific development issue. And – perhaps more importantly – we might be better able to ask what political and social dimensions are left out of the assessment process when media frames that are based on the science model fail to focus readers' attention on biotechnology's sociopolitical impact: who gains and who loses when high-technology developments fundamentally alter existing practices in agriculture and medicine?

Note

1 A local civic organization recruited volunteers for the project from among its membership and friends and family of its membership as a fund-raising activity. The participants then donated their pay to the organization. Although there are obvious limits to the use of this sample and the student sample, they came from two relatively homogeneous and yet distinct populations and thus increased our confidence in the generalizability of our results.

References

Brosius, H. and H.M. Kepplinger. 1992. Linear and nonlinear models of agenda setting in television. *Journal of Broadcasting & Electronic Media* 36(1): 5–23.

Graber, D.A. 1988. *Processing the News: How People Tame the Information Tide.* 2nd edn. New York: Longman.

Hornig, S. 1992. Framing risk: audience and reader factors. *Journalism Quarterly* 69(3): 679–90.

Hornig, S. 1993. Reading risk: public response to print media accounts of technological risk. *Public Understanding of Science* 2(2): 95–109.

Hornig, S. and J. Talbert. 1993. Mass media and the ultimate technological fix: newspaper coverage of biotechnology. Discussion Paper No. CBPE 93–4, Center for Biotechnology Policy and Ethics, Texas A&M University, College Station, Texas.

Kuklinski, J.H., R.C. Luskin and J. Bolland. 1991. Where is the schema? Going beyond the 's' word in political psychology. *American Political Science Review* 85(4): 1341–80.

Plein, L.C. 1991. Popularizing biotechnology: the influence of issue definition. *Science, Technology, & Human Values* 16(4): 474–90.

Tuchman, G. 1978. *Making News: A Study in the Social Construction of Reality.* New York: Free Press.

Chapter 16

The interaction of journalists and scientific experts

Cooperation and conflict between two professional cultures*

H. Peter Peters

Introduction

Information on science and technology in the mass media is not new. The form and content, however, of the way in which science and technology are covered have changed considerably over time: the dominant popularization approach, letting the mass media audience share the fruits of successful R&D, has been supplemented in the past two or three decades with the coverage of the less beneficial impacts of science and technology, namely environmental problems and new threats to health, safety, ethics and self-determination (Dröge and Wilkens, 1991). The use of scientific results as a basis and a legitimating resource for political decision making has led to a politicization of many parts of science (Weingart, 1983). The ideology of progress, which for many years had shielded the development of science and technology against fundamental criticism, has eroded, replacing uncritical acceptance of technologies with an approach weighing the costs and benefits of a technology. New social movements, the anti-nuclear movement and the environmental movement, have evolved and promote a more critical look at the impacts of science and technology. Science has proved to be sensitive to that trend and has responded with the development of new methods and disciplines such as risk assessment, technology assessment and environmental monitoring programmes, directing attention to the negative impact of technological progress.

It is no surprise that these changes in the relationship of science and society are reflected in the mass media. Content analyses of German mass media reporting over a period of several decades have shown an increase in coverage of technology and its consequences since the mid-1970s, accompanied by an increase in the relative proportion of statements critical of technology (Kepplinger, 1989; Dröge and Wilkens, 1991). The popularization of science as, for example, promoted by the American Association for the Advancement of Science (*cf.* Etzional, 1972), which in most cases is supportive of science and technology, still exists and has its own special market and legitimate function. The old tradition of scientific experts

*Previously published in *Media, Culture and Society* (1995), Vol. 17, pp. 31–48.

(particularly the health profession) advising and educating the general public by means of mass media is still alive. But the increase in science and technology coverage is mainly due to the rise of another form of coverage focusing on societal problems and conflicts to which science and technology are linked in one way or another: science and technology may be the subject of the problem or conflict; they may be used by one or both sides to support a political stand; or it may be expected that science or technology will find a solution to a problem or resolve the conflict by providing an ultimate answer to the issue. This raises the question of how experts engage in public discussion of these issues and – more specifically – whether they are prepared to interact with the mass media which mediate access to the public.

Scientists in general have a positive attitude towards communicating their research findings to the public. Nowotny (1981) argues that the scientist's role includes the three functions of researcher, teacher and expert (advisor). It seems to be their role as teacher that primarily engenders this positive attitude. In a study of American scientists' motives in consenting to mass media interviews, DiBella *et al.* (1991) found the motive of educating the public to be the most important reason for scientists to agree to being interviewed. Also Krüger (1987) and Peters and Krüger (1985) found that the vast majority (91 percent) of the German scientists they surveyed agreed that there was an obligation on science to engage activity in the transfer of knowledge to the public. The study also produced evidence that this positive attitude towards popularization was linked to the scientist's role as teacher: 76 percent said they considered engagement in science reporting as teaching (*lehre*) in a broader sense.

Besides the intrinsic motivation to share knowledge not only with their fellows but also with a broader public there is much evidence that scientists (and their employers) increasingly also acknowledge the instrumental value of publicity. Such motives ranked lower in the survey of DiBella *et al.* (1991); one might argue, however, that scientists are reluctant to admit that they are motivated by such profane and unscientific reasons as raising funds or exerting political influence and, hence, such motives may be underestimated by surveys. One might also argue that instrumental motives are more likely to be transformed into actual behaviour than an unspecific feeling of science being obliged to educate the public. In any case, surveys by Dunwoody and Ryan (1985), Krüger (1987) and Peters and Krüger (1985) indicate that scientists are well aware of the possible advantages for research funding of media visibility. A large number of other motives may also be considered relevant, such as promotion of a technology or a political stand. Taken together with the increased public relations efforts of research organizations (Nelkin, 1987: 132–53), these survey results clearly indicate that scientists and scientific organizations are increasingly convinced that publicity may help them to achieve their goals. As Nelkin (1984: 63) notes, scientists are sometimes 'sources with a mission'.

Hence, we find a great deal of cooperation between scientists and journalists supported by a large number of very different motives. Scientists write articles for newspapers and magazines, provide scientific photographs, diagrams and even films (e.g. NASA), cooperate readily with TV teams showing up at their laboratories, give interviews to journalists and serve as scientific advisors during the production of TV films on scientific topics.

However, a study of US scientists by Dunwoody and Ryan (1985) also revealed scientific barriers to the popularization of science in the mass media. Scientists as researchers are part of scientific communities, which do not encourage communication across the boundaries of science and in some cases even sanction their members for doing so. It is less the fact *that* a scientist engages in public communication that is controversial than *how* this communication takes place: in many cases it does not conform to norms of scientific publication such as, for example, an impersonal style, high level of accuracy or peer review prior to publication.

There are numerous complaints by scientists who report bad experiences with the mass media. Journalists are, for example, blamed for inaccuracy, a lack of objectivity and an anti-scientific attitude in their coverage. While such experiences do not occur as a rule, they are not rare exceptions. In the surveys of Krüger (1987) and Peters and Krüger (1985), about 17 percent of scientists having had personal contacts with journalists in the past reported 'rather bad' experiences, another 51 percent 'partly good, partly bad' experiences and only 32 percent rated the contacts as 'rather good'. Journalists' experiences with scientific sources have not been studied as systematically so far, but Böhme-Dürr (1992), who polled German science writers, found that they also report many problems experienced with scientists as sources.

A number of problems in scientist–journalist interaction are rooted in cultural differences between the two professions. Scientists are constrained, for example, by the importance of autonomy and the internal review process, while journalists are constrained by their need for audience appeal (Nelkin, 1984: 60–1). Nelkin suggests that the cultural gap between scientists and journalists is particularly evident in communication on risk and uncertainty.

This paper uses the concepts of cultural difference and intercultural communication to elaborate some of the crucial reasons for disagreement and tension during the interaction of scientific experts and journalists in the communication of risk. We use the term 'scientific experts' (or simply 'experts') rather than the word 'scientist' to indicate that our study deals with scientists in their function as experts who apply their knowledge to non-scientific problems.

Expert–journalist interactions as intercultural encounters

Cultural sources of miscommunication and conflict

The concept of 'culture' has been defined in numerous ways (*cf.* e.g. Redder and Rehbein, 1987). For our purpose we adopt a broad concept of culture, including, for example, code systems, knowledge, collective memories, perspectives, relevance structures, stereotypes, conventions, norms, values, roles and scripts which are shared by the members of a certain social group. If communication partners come from different cultures, difficulties during interaction may show up in at least three areas:

1   Difficulties in transmitting 'meaning' increase as cultural differences increase. Hence, miscommunication in the form of mutual misunderstanding is a frequent experience in intercultural encounters. Its sources are different linguistic codes as well as a lack of a shared semantic and pragmatic background.

2   Group stereotypes as part of the respective cultures may cause prejudices and initial (positive or negative) attitudes to be held by the interaction partners. Such prejudices may lead to a biased perception of actual behavioural acts as congruent with the stereotype (particularly if the behavioural acts are somewhat ambiguous and open to different interpretations). In some cases stereotypes may act as self-fulfilling prophecies because responses to behaviour that are perceived as congruent with the stereotype may stimulate exactly the kind of behaviour that is expected, based on the stereotype (Gudykunst et al., 1989).

3   Different conventions, norms, role definitions and definitions of situations, which all form parts of the respective cultures, are confronted during intercultural communication and may cause a mismatch of expectations towards the interaction partner. These may include simple conventions such as order of speakers, use of the first name or surname, turn-taking behaviour, non-verbal cues like loudness of the voice, spatial distance from the conversation partner or line of sight, but also delicate matters of hierarchical position and the rights and duties of interaction partners in given, though differently interpreted, situations.

In trying to analyse the consequences of cultural differences for the interaction of scientists and journalists, three 'cultures' – and not just two – have to be considered. Besides the professional cultures of science and journalism we have to take into account the everyday culture shared by members of both groups but which is of professional importance only to the work of journalists, who constantly have to consider it as the culture of their audience. In their interactions with journalists, scientists are therefore confronted with a professional journalistic culture as well as with everyday culture. Problems of message relevance and comprehensibility dominate in the relation of scientific culture to everyday culture, while stereotypes and pragmatic aspects of how to structure interaction in terms of the social roles of the actors and the goals of interaction are most important in producing tensions between journalistic and scientific cultures.

Differences between scientific and everyday cultures

The problem that scientists experience when talking to lay people is not only that they have to explain their findings in simple language and to find metaphors and models illustrating abstract and unfamiliar concepts, but also that they face an information demand very different from that of their fellow scientists. For the scientific community the relevance of a particular research question and the implications of research results are quite clear. In introducing scientific articles, where scientists usually legitimize their selection of research problems and methodological approaches, they refer to more general research problems that are the core of a scientific community and hardly every challenged. The discussion sections of research articles correspondingly focus on the meaning of the research results for the initially chosen questions. Most of a typical research article is devoted to stating factual claims and proving them. However, typical journalistic accounts of scientific research, particularly if they are designed for a broader audience rather than for the science-interested and scientific-literate audience of science sections and science magazines, address in more detail questions of why the research is performed, who performs it, what its meaning is and what its impact is likely to be. Fahnestock (1986), analysing the 'accommodation' of science to a lay audience, has argued that the type of genre as well as the semantic focus differ between a scientific and a popular article on the same scientific research.

With respect to risk communication, Sharlin (1987) has described different perspectives on risk applied by experts and lay people leading to separate risk constructs. These risk constructs he labels 'macro-risks' (focusing on statistical risk defined by experts) and 'micro-risks' (focusing on the individual fates of possible victims). Sandman (1988) introduces a somewhat related distinction between 'hazard' (as the expert's risk construct) and 'outrage' (as the layman's risk construct). Peters (1992; 1994) has argued that the 'models' used to assess the validity of risk assessments differ between experts and lay people: while experts tend to make assessments and decisions according to a scientific–technical model (Which evidence can be stated? What – technically and economically – is the most efficient option?), lay people are more likely to use a social model (Which interests are involved? What is the distribution of power? What represents a just decision? etc.) for the same purpose. One of the consequences of these cultural differences is a demand for information by experts that differs from that by lay people.

To summarize, differences between scientific culture and everyday culture lead to difficulties in explaining scientific problems, methods and findings to lay people, to a mismatch between what scientists themselves consider important communication topics within their community and what the lay public is interested in, and also to the use of different criteria in assessing the cost–benefit ratio of scientific research. As far as politically sensitive research is concerned, there are also different levels of confidence in science and technology between the two cultures as well as different ways in which opinions are generated and decisions made.

Differences between scientific and journalistic cultures

Surveys (*cf.* Roloff and Hömberg, 1975), as well as analyses based on qualitative evidence (Nelkin, 1987), indicate that science writers among journalists have traditionally felt a close relationship with science. Hence, the intercultural difference may be expected to be smaller if the journalist is a science writer than, for example, if he or she is a journalist dealing with political news or is responsible for coverage of local affairs. However, a small-sample survey among German science writers and scientists (each group consisting of only 30 respondents), confronted with a number of identical questions in the context of genetic engineering, provides evidence that even science writers (nowadays) are quite. sensitive to the economic and political interests of scientists (Kepplinger *et al.*, 1991: 61–5). However, negative stereotypes (at least of experts towards journalists) seem not to be a major source of tension in the interaction between members of the two groups, but problems in 'transmitting meaning' from expert sources to journalists and finally to the mass media audience certainly are important. Many studies reveal that scientists often perceive reporting on science, technology, risk and environmental issues to be inaccurate (*cf.* Bell, 1991; Dunwoody, 1982; Haller, 1987; Moore and Singletary, 1985). A comparison of the criteria used by several groups to assess the quality of environmental reporting showed that 'accuracy' for journalists is a criterion of lesser importance, while for all expert groups studied (industry, government, advocate groups, scientists) accuracy proved to be the most important criterion (Salomone *et al.*, 1990). In their surveys of German scientists, Krüger and Peters (Krüger, 1985; 1987; Peters and Krüger, 1985) found that only 44 percent of the scientists whose work had been reported assessed the coverage as 'generally accurate'. Only 2 percent, on the other hand, rated it as 'generally inaccurate'. The most common experience was coverage that was 'partly accurate, partly inaccurate' (54 percent). These results make it very likely that scientists have difficulties in getting their message accurately (as defined by them) conveyed to journalists. Part of the problem may be due to difficulties in explaining complex scientific matters to non-experts. But the above-mentioned results of Salomone *et al.* indicate that another part of this problem may be rooted in different concepts of message quality embedded in the journalistic and scientific cultures.

To study in more detail culturally based expectations toward the content and form of media articles, the functions, goals and forms of journalism as well as the way journalists and experts should interact, an empirical study of science writers and scientists was designed in ways somewhat similar to an earlier study by Ryan (1979). The aim of this study was to compare beliefs and attitudes towards journalism as held by experts and journalists within the context of risk reporting.

Evidence of cultural differences from a survey

Methodology

Three questions with a total of 38 statements concerning opinions and attitudes towards (1) the functions of journalism in general; (2) the preferred tasks and ways of risk reporting; and (3) expectations concerning interactions between journalists and experts, were included in questionnaires administered to 234 journalists and 448 experts. These journalists and experts were selected by a media analysis. Each scientific expert who (directly or indirectly) was cited by name in an article dealing with risk issues in 22 German print media (newspapers and magazines) between 27 October and 21 December 1993 received a questionnaire by mail. In addition, the authors of the respective articles were surveyed. Response rates were 58 percent (journalists) and 50 percent (experts). The surveys were primarily designed to collect information on, and evaluations of, individual contacts between journalists and experts and to combine them with data gathered by a content analysis of the experts' statements. However, as a separate part of the questionnaire a number of general questions wee also presented identically to interviewees of both groups – experts and journalists. If a journalist or an expert received more than one questionnaire because he or she was involved in more than one interaction leading to a citation, the general part of the questionnaire was nevertheless answered only once.[1]

This sampling procedure implies that our samples are not simple random samples of scientific experts and journalists. The sample of experts is restricted to those who deal with risk issues (broadly defined). About 50 percent of the experts in our sample belong to the medical profession, 40 percent are (natural) scientists from a number of disciplines and 10 percent are social scientists, etc. Experts with frequent contacts with the mass media are over-represented: the chance of being represented in the sample is approximately proportionate to the number of media contacts per year. The same is true for journalists: only those journalists who deal with risk issues and cite scientific experts in their articles are represented in our sample. This leads to the dominance of journalists working for science sections (60 percent), though not always exclusively. However, these properties of the sample are not a disadvantage. The analysis is based on those experts and journalists who actually have mutual contact and on which the transfer of scientific knowledge to the public relies. One should, however, be cautious in generalizing our results to experts and journalists per se.

The differences between experts and journalists

The main functions of journalism

In 12 out of 16 statements concerning the main functions and basic goals of journalism in general there are significant and meaningful differences between journalists and experts (Table 16.1). The greatest difference between both groups concerns the possible function of journalism 'to control political, economic and scientific elites' (statement 1). While experts as well as journalists on the whole agree on the existence of such a function, the acceptance of this statement by experts (as part of the elite to be controlled) is much lower than its acceptance by journalists. The same is true for the statement that it is the task of the media to take the part of the powerless (statement 4). And finally, a difference in the same direction – though much weaker – is also found with respect to the function of investigating and criticizing nuisances (statement 11).

Table 16.1 Functions and tasks of journalism rated by experts and journalists

		Journalists (n = 136) $\bar{X}$	Experts (n = 225) $\bar{X}$	Difference of means	Significance[1]
1	To control political, economic and scientific elites	2.30	1.20	−1.10	***
2	To entertain the audience	1.70	0.82	−0.88	***
3	To educate the public in order to promote correct behaviour	−0.36	0.36	0.72	***
4	To take the part of the powerless	1.27	0.58	−0.69	***
5	To influence the formation of opinions	1.69	1.01	−0.68	***
6	To stimulate interest in science and technology	1.58	2.05	0.47	***
7	To be politically unbiased	0.27	0.71	0.44	*
8	To report in a non-emotional way	2.22	2.66	0.44	***
9	To report objectively	2.41	2.74	0.33	***
10	To orient towards scientific truth	2.07	2.39	0.32	**
11	To investigate and criticize nuisances	2.62	2.31	−0.31	**
12	To educate the public	2.69	2.42	−0.27	**
13	To sensationalize	−2.17	−2.42	−0.25	
14	To exaggerate in order to effect something	−1.53	−1.36	0.17	
15	To speak for the public	0.28	0.36	0.17	
16	To inform the public	2.98	2.92	−0.06	*

[1] Significance levels (two-tailed t-test): *** $p < 0.001$, ** $p < 0.01$, * $p < 0.05$

Note
Acceptance of statements is measured on a rating scale ranging from −3 to +3; statements are sorted according to the absolute difference of means.

Taken together, all three statements make it likely that journalists are more apt to claim a watchdog function of being critical towards those in power than experts are willing to concede it.

While both groups strongly agree on an information function of journalism (statement 16) there are nevertheless some (modest) differences in how that function should be performed. Experts more strongly than journalists require that reporting be politically unbiased (statement 7), non-emotional (statement 8), objective (statement 9), oriented towards the scientific truth (statement 10), and not sensationalized (statement 13). The second largest difference concerns the entertainment function of journalism, which is less accepted by experts than by journalists (statement 2). As a consequence of this less positive attitude towards entertainment one can conclude that entertaining elements in articles primarily designed to inform will probably gain little acceptance from expert sources. To summarize, experts have different expectations from journalists concerning the style of information: they want information displayed more seriously and unpolitically than journalists and more than journalists they want it to address reason rather than senses and emotions.

Preferred tasks and ways of risk reporting

With respect to risk reporting a number of clear-cut differences between experts and journalists are to be observed (see Table 16.2). The most important one concerns reliance on expert authority and an expert-supporting function of the media (statement 17). Journalists on average reject this statement (although surprisingly mildly), while experts on average agree with it. Quite clearly experts welcome coverage best serving their own interests (emphasizing the benefits of scientific research), while journalists express a more or less indifferent attitude towards promoting experts' goals (statement 18). Statements 23 and 28 show that experts, somewhat more strongly than journalists, have a paternalistic attitude towards the audience. They are less prepared than journalists to accept a mature audience. The differences between journalists and experts on this question, however, are not too strong.

Similar patterns to those revealed in the previous section dealing with journalism in general are again found with respect to risk reporting in particular: the critical function of the mass media is accepted more by journalists than by experts (statements 25 and 26); a serious and science-oriented style of risk reporting is required more strongly by experts than by journalists (statements 20, 22, 24 and 27); and experts more than journalists want risk reporting to influence the audience if the exerted influence promotes their own goals (statements 19 and 21).

Expectations concerning contacts between journalists and experts

All mean ratings of the seven statements concerning contacts between journalists and experts show significant differences between both interviewed groups

Table 16.2 Preferred tasks and ways of risk reporting rated by experts and journalists

	Journalists (n = 136) $\bar{X}$	Experts (n = 225) $\bar{X}$	Difference of means	Significance[1]
17 Media should accept expert authority and support experts in their efforts to popularize their findings	−0.73	0.86	1.59	***
18 Media should emphasize the benefits of scientific research	0.18	1.40	1.22	***
19 Media should educate the public in order to promote risk-avoiding behaviour	−0.07	1.05	1.12	***
20 Media should report above all on scientific risk assessments	0.15	1.16	1.01	***
21 Media should contribute to public acceptance (of technologies)	−0.96	−0.03	0.93	***
22 Media should report on risks in a sober and matter-of-fact way	1.33	2.04	0.71	***
23 Media should assume a mature audience and report without educational intentions	1.14	0.58	−0.56	**
24 Media should avoid an emotional style in risk reporting	0.80	1.32	0.52	**
25 Media should be critical of experts and should analyse their interests	2.34	1.82	−0.52	***
26 Media should criticize those causing risks	2.05	1.70	−0.35	*
27 Risk reporting should be entertaining	−0.68	−0.99	−0.31	
28 Media should assume a certain duty of care towards the audience	1.10	1.35	0.25	
29 Media should keep an eye on circulation and audience size in risk reporting	−1.14	−1.24	−0.10	
30 Media should weigh up risks and benefits	1.70	1.63	−0.07	
31 Media should report above all on events that cause damage	0.88	0.93	0.05	

[1] Significance levels (two-tailed t-test): *** $p < 0.001$, ** $p < 0.01$, * $p < 0.05$

Note
Acceptance of statements is measured on a rating scale ranging from −3 to +3; statements are sorted according to the absolute difference of means.

(Table 16.3). The largest difference between experts and journalists is in the rating of the statement about whether journalists should let their interview partners check the articles prior to publication (statement 32). The difference of 3.4 units on a scale of range 6 cannot be explained by minor variations within

Table 16.3 Expectations of journalists and experts concerning source–journalist interactions

	Journalists (n = 136) $\bar{X}$	Experts (n = 225) $\bar{X}$	Difference of means	Significance[1]
32 Journalists should allow interview partners to check the articles prior to publication	−1.22	2.14	3.36	***
33 Experts should restrict themselves to their narrow field of expertise and should refuse to make statements about other fields	−0.72	1.01	1.73	***
34 It is the journalist's task to translate expert statements from scientific jargon into everyday language	2.51	0.94	−1.57	***
35 Journalists should accept expert statements rather than question them	−2.55	−1.09	1.46	***
36 In an interview experts should focus on facts and avoid any evaluations	−1.89	−0.65	1.24	***
37 In an interview experts should use striking formulations that journalists can cite directly	0.85	1.50	0.65	***
38 Journalists should be technically well-prepared when showing up for an interview with an expert	2.63	2.26	−0.37	***

[1] Significance levels (two-tailed t-test): *** $p < 0.001$

Note
Acceptance of statements is measured on a rating scale ranging from −3 to +3; statements are sorted according to the absolute difference of means.

a shared understanding, as might be the case for smaller differences; this remarkable difference indicates clearly contradictory points of view.

The difference in question may be interpreted either narrowly or more broadly. In a narrow sense the opposing views may be seen as reflecting different approaches to accuracy. As mentioned above, for journalists technical accuracy is not among the most important criteria for media coverage, while for experts it is. Experts may look upon checking the article prior to publication as an efficient way of avoiding errors and improving accuracy. From the point of view of journalists, however, this procedure may be judged to be time-consuming, frustrating and useless because according to their criteria it does not lead to an improvement in what is published.

From a broader perspective the demand to check articles by expert sources and its rejection by journalists may be seen as indicating incompatible role definitions. A matter of controversy between experts and journalists may implicitly be that of who, via the mass media, is communicating with the audience, who should have the responsibility and, hence, who should be in command. Experts may perhaps wish to check newspaper articles in which they are cited according to the same logic with which they edit the proofs of articles published in scholarly journals. Journalists, on the other hand, might reject a request to show the manuscript to the expert prior to publication not only because this causes additional work without a pay-off but also because they feel that this would be misinterpreted by the experts as a cue encouraging them to take another – more active – role than that of a 'source'. The large difference in the responses to the statement concerning checking the article prior to publication may well indicate a struggle for control over the communication process.

The narrow explanation is probably valid in many cases, but the responses to a number of the other statements also support the assumption of a struggle for control over the communication process. First, again in this series of questions a critical approach by journalists facing experts is less accepted by experts than by journalists (statement 35). Second, experts are less willing to accept a 'translator' role for journalists than the journalists are themselves (statement 34). Experts more than journalists want their own untranslated words to be used in articles, despite possible conflicts with the norms of their scientific community requiring cautious and reserved formulations (statement 37). Obviously, experts in many cases want to take the translator role on themselves, while journalists assume this role to be theirs. Third, despite their concern for accuracy, experts less than journalists think that the latter should be technically well-prepared when showing up for an interview with an expert (statement 38). This is a surprising result. We would have predicted experts arguing in favour of technically well-trained and -prepared journalists being competent interaction partners and journalists insisting that general knowledge might be sufficient. One possible explanation is that because experts do not want journalists to be in control of the content of their articles, their technical competence is not expected to matter so much.

Differences in the responses to statements 33 and 36 may be explained by the influence of the norms of scientific culture. Within science, speculation is discredited and as an ideal everything must be provable and as accurate and up-to-date as possible. One of the consequences of this norm is that scientists should avoid making statements on matters on which they are not expert. Furthermore, it is part of the scientific culture that science should be value-free. According to the traditional self-understanding of science, evaluations are beyond science and, hence, should be avoided if speaking as a scientist. Both scientific virtues make expert sources difficult ones for journalists. Particularly in the subject field of our study (risk issues), journalists are regularly less interested in the technical details of a problem and much more concerned with the analysis and solution of practical problems which do not respect the established boundaries of academic disciplines. The mean ratings of statements 33 and 36 show that experts and journalists strongly disagree on how strongly scientific values should influence experts' behaviour during interaction with the mass media.

Discussion

A number of scholars have argued that sources and journalists develop a shared culture when interacting with each other (e.g. Chaffee and McLeod, 1968; Scheff, 1967). Analyses of source–journalist relationships (e.g. Cracknell, 1993; Miller, 1978; Sigal, 1973) often support this view and sometimes even describe the relationship of sources and journalists as 'symbiotic'. Dunwoody (1986: 13–14) explicitly challenges this view of the scientist–journalist relationship.She argues that scientists have nothing to gain from interaction with journalists and that as journalists depend on scientists for information, a symbiotic relationship is unlikely to emerge. For the ideal-typical scientist as researcher – governed by the norms of science as described by Merton (1957) – her assumption that scientists have little to gain from public visibility may be valid. However, if one looks at scientists not only as members of scientific communities but also as experts giving advice, as teachers of the public, as proponents of technologies, as managers who have to secure the resources they depend on (money, public acceptance), and as advocates of industrial, governmental or environmental interests, one might very well conclude that even scientists are (increasingly) dependent on publicity. Dunwoody (1986: 14) herself therefore admits that 'the picture is changing'.

Nevertheless, there are other arguments indicating that the common understanding of journalism is not produced by a shared culture of journalists and experts resulting from interaction, as suggested by the co-orientation model. Another explanation is that it corresponds to the wider political culture which is shared by the majority of citizens and political actors. A specific result of our analysis may be interpreted as supportive of the second hypothesis: the more *general* the reference of the items presented (journalism in general – risk reporting – expert–journalist interaction), the smaller are the average absolute mean differences between experts and journalists. Agreement is highest in topics with the *least* relevance for specific interaction. If interaction were the source of a common understanding one would expect agreement to be highest for those aspects most directly concerning source–journalist relations. Furthermore, if congruent beliefs and attitudes were the result of a common culture emerging during interaction, one should expect congruence to increase with the amount of contact with the other group. Ryan (1982), however, shows that this is not always the case.

Our analysis revealed a strong correlation ($r = 0.80$) between the experts' and journalists' mean ratings of the 38 statements and an average mean difference of only 0.7 (on a scale of range 6), indicating a relatively high similarity of the views of both groups. The following discussion of differences must therefore not forget that both groups share a common understanding of journalism –

although somewhat modified by their respective professional frames and individual or organizational interests. The most important differences between experts and journalists are:

- Journalists assign more weight to a critical function of the mass media than experts.
- Journalists accept an entertainment function of the mass media more readily than experts.
- Experts have a more paternalistic attitude towards the mass media audience than journalists.
- Experts and journalists differ in their preferred style of reporting (experts having less understanding of the journalistic need to attract and fascinate readers by means of certain stylistic elements).
- Experts expect the media to support their goals, while journalists have an indifferent attitude towards the experts' goals.
- If supportive of their goals, experts want media to influence the public more than journalists are prepared to.
- Experts and journalists disagree about their respective roles and the extent of control that both sides should exert over the communication process.
- Journalists tolerate (or even expect), more than do scientists, that expert sources will violate narrow scientific norms when interacting with mass media.

These differences may in part be explained by the influences of the respective professional cultures. Journalists consider experts to be passive sources who are used by them to perform the media functions of, for example, informing and entertaining the public and criticizing elites. Sometimes journalists allow experts to control coverage: they may ask them to check the articles prior to publication or even invite them as authors to write articles for science sections themselves. However, the more political and controversial the context, the less likely it is that journalists will accept such an active role for scientists.

Experts, on the other hand, seem to refer to definitions of the situation, scripts and roles they are used to within their culture. Typically these are: (1) interpersonal communication with fellow scientists; (2) the teaching of students; and (3) publication in scholarly journals. All three definitions of the situation are dangerous if applied to the expert–journalist relationship.

When talking to a journalist as if he or she were talking to a fellow scientist, the expert may wrongly assume that a shared background exists including for example, a code, values and relevance structures. If the scientist is successful in imposing this definition of the situation, the journalist may feel obliged to take on the role of a fellow scientist, preventing him or her from asking 'simple' questions in order to secure understanding. As a consequence, the resulting media publication might be inaccurate. In applying this model to the expert–journalist relationship, the expert misses a chance to improve the technical accuracy of the article or – in the case of radio and television interviews – the appropriate understanding by the audience.

Referring to differences in scientific expertise, the scientist may assume that the relationship between academic teacher and student is in some respects similar to that between a scientific source and a journalist. However, the roles of teacher and student include a hierarchical component. If applied to the expert–journalist relationship the journalist may perceive the didacticism of the scientist as arrogant and the expert may interpret the journalist's refusal to accept the role of obedient student in the same way.

Finally, insisting that mass media should operate similarly to scholarly journals would undoubtedly lead to a number of conflicts with journalists. First, while scientists may implicity claim authorship for a publication in which they are cited, journalists regularly insist that they are responsible. The scientist is considered the object of the reporting rather than its author. Our analysis has provided strong evidence that the views of journalists and experts on the amount of control given to each side differ. Second, our study indicates that experts have in mind the style of communication they perform in their scholarly journals as a norm for journalism as well. Scientists' expectations regarding the content and style of mass media outlets are obviously influenced by their scholarly publication norms. These norms, however, often contradict the journalists' crucial professional duty to attract the attention of the audience. Third, experts feel restricted by scientific norms in their public statements that lead them to avoid speculation and (political) evaluation.

In order to reduce the tensions and frustrations encountered during the interaction of experts and journalists, two strategies may be attempted. One would be to reduce the cultural differences between both groups. However, consistently applied, this strategy would lead to a breakdown of the borderline between science and journalism. This solution is probably acceptable neither to journalists nor to scientists, since both professional cultures have evolved for good reasons. A second strategy would be to improve the competence required in communicating with members of another culture (cf. Brislin, 1989). Such improved intercultural communicative competence would not eliminate all the tensions. Value differences between cultures, for example, are not resolved just by being made aware of them. What seems possible by means of intercultural communication training, however, is the better psychological management of frustrations and experiences during contact with other cultures, and a depersonalization of conflicts.

Note

1 The surveys were organized as part of a 'project seminar' for advanced students at the Institute for Communication Research and Journalism of the University of Münster that was directed by the author from 1992 to 1994. The students of this seminar were involved in the design, data gathering and data analysis of the project. I would like to

thank them for their committed cooperation. A small grant from the *Stiftungverband für die Deutsche Wissenschaft* helped to cover the costs of data collection and is gratefully acknowledged.

References

Bell, A. (1991) 'Hot Air: Media, Miscommunication and the Climate Change Issue', pp.259–82 in N. Coupland, H. Giles and J.M. Wiemann (eds), *'Miscommunication' and Problematic Talk*. Newbury Park, Calif.: Sage.

Böhme-Dürr, K. (1992) 'Social and Natural Sciences in German Periodicals', *Communications*, 17(20): 167–76.

Brislin, R. (1989) 'Intercultural Communication Training', pp.441–57 in M.K. Asante and W.B. Gudykunst (eds), *Handbook of International and Intercultural Communication*. Newbury Park, Calif.: Sage.

Chaffee, S.H. and J.M. McLeod (1968) 'Sensitization in Panel Design: A Co-orientational Experiment', *Journalism Quarterly*, 45: 661–9.

Cracknell, J. (1993) 'Issue Arenas, Pressure Groups and Environmental Agendas', pp.3–21 in A. Hansen (ed.), *The Mass Media and Environmental Issues*. Leicester: Leicester University Press.

DiBella, S.M., A.J. Ferri and A.B. Padderud (1991). 'Scientists' Reasons for Consenting to Mass Media Interviews: A National Survey', *Journalism Quarterly*, 68(4): 740–9.

Dröge, F. and A. Wilkens (1991) *Populärer Fortschritt: 150 Jahre Technikberichterstattung in deutschen illustrierten Zeitschriften*. Münster: Verlag Westfälisches Dampfboot.

Dunwoody, S. (1982) 'A Question of Accuracy', *IEEE Transactions on Professional Communication*, PC-25 4: 196–9.

Dunwoody, S. (1986) 'The Scientist as Source', pp.3–15 in S.M. Friedman, S. Dunwoody and C.L. Rogers (eds), *Scientists and Journalists: Reporting Science as News*. New York and London: The Free Press/Macmillan.

Dunwoody, S. and M. Ryan (1985). 'Scientific Barriers to the Popularization of Science in the Mass Media', *Journal of Communication*, 35: 26–42.

Etzional, A. (1972) 'Understanding of Science', *Science*, 177: no. 4047.

Fahnestock, J. (1986) 'Accommodating Science: The Rhetorical Life of Scientific Facts', *Written Communication*, 3(3): 275–96.

Gudykunst, W., S. Ting-Toomey, B.J. Hall and K.L. Schmidt (1989) 'Language and Intergroup Communication,' pp.145–62 in M.K. Asante and W.B. Gudykunst (eds), *Handbook of International and Intercultural Communication*. Newbury Park, Calif.: Sage.

Haller, M. (1987) 'Wie wissenschaftlich ist der Wissenschaftsjournalismus?', *Publizistik*, 32(3): 305–19.

Hömberg, W. (1990) *Das verspätete Ressort: Die Situation des Wissenschaftsjournalismus*. Konstanz: Universitätsverlag Konstanz.

Kepplinger, H.M. (1989) *Künstliche Horizonte: Folge, Darstellung und Akzeptanz von Technik in der Bundesrepublik*. Frankfurt and New York: Campus.

Kepplinger, H.M., S.C. Ehmig and C. Ahlberg (1991) *Gentechnik im Widerstreit: Zum Verhältnis von Wissenschaft und Journalismus*. Frankfurt: Campus.

Krüger, J. (1985) 'Wissenschaftsberichterstattung in aktuellen Massenmedien aus der

Sicht der Wissenschaftler: Ergebnisse einer Befragung der Professoren der Johannes Gutenberg-Universität'. Unpublished master's thesis, Mainz.

Krüger, J. (1987) 'Wissenschaftsberichterstattung in aktuellen Massenmedien aus der Sicht der Wissenschaftler', pp.39–51 in R. Flöhl and J. Fricke (eds), *Moral und Verantwortung in der Wissenschaftsvermittlung: Die Aufgaben von Wissenschaftler und Journalist*. Mainz: von Hase & Köhler.

Merton, R.K. (1957) *Social Theory and Social Structure*. Glencoe, Ill.: Free Press.

Miller, S.H. (1978) 'Reporters and Congressmen: Living in Symbiosis', *Journalism Monographs*, no. 53.

Moore, B. and M. Singletary (1985) 'Scientific Sources' Perceptions of Network News Accuracy', *Journalism Quarterly*, 62: 816–23.

Nelkin, D. (1984) 'Background Paper', pp.21–84 in *Science in the Streets: Report of the Twentieth Century Fund Task Force on the Communication of Scientific Risk*. New York: Priority Press.

Nelkin, D. (1987) *Selling Science: How the Press Covers Science and Technology*. New York: Freeman.

Nowotny, H. (1981). 'Experts and their Expertise: On the Changing Relationship Between Experts and their Public', *Bulletin of Science Technology & Society*, 1(3): 235–41.

Peters, H.P. (1992) 'The Credibility of Information Sources in West Germany after the Chernobyl Disaster', *Public Understanding of Science*, 1(3): 325–43.

Peters, H.P. (1994) 'Mass Media as an Information Channel and Public Arena', *Risk: Health, Safety & Environment*, 5 (Summer): 241–50.

Peters, H.P. and Krüger, J. (1985) *Der Transfer wissenschaftlichen Wissens in die Öffentlichkeit aus der Sicht von Wissenschaftlern. Ergebnisse einer Befragung der wissenschaftlichen Mitarbeiter der Kernforschungsanlage Jülich*, Jülich: Kernforschungsanlage Jülich.

Redder, A. and J. Rehbein (1987) 'Zum Begriff der Kultur', *Osnabrücker Beiträge zur Sprachtheorie*, 38: 7–21.

Roloff, E.K. and W. Hömberg (1975) 'Wissenschaftsjournalisten: Dolmetscher zwischen Forschung und Öffentlichkeit', *Bild der Wissenschaft*, 9(9): 56–60.

Ryan, M. (1979) 'Attitudes of Scientists and Journalists Toward Media Coverage of Science News', *Journalism Quarterly*, 56: 18–26, 53.

Ryan, M. (1982) 'Impact of Personal Contact on Sources' Views of the Press'. *Newspaper Research Journal*, 3(3): 22–9.

Salomone, K.L., M.R. Greenberg, P.M. Sandman and D.B. Sachsman (1990) 'A Question of Quality: How Journalists and News Sources Evaluate Coverage of Environmental Risk', *Journal of Communication*, 40(4): 117–33.

Sandman, P. (1988) 'Hazard Versus Outrage: A Conceptual Frame for Describing Public Perceptions of Risk', pp.163–8 in H. Jungermann, R.E. Kasperson and P.M. Wiedemann (eds), *Themes and Tasks of Risk Communication: Proceedings of the International Workshop on Risk Communication held at the KFA Jülich, 17–21 October 1988*. Jülich: Kernforschungsanlage Jülich.

Scheff, T.J. (1967) 'Toward a Sociological Model of Consensus', *American Sociological Review*, 32: 32–46.

Sharlin, H.I. (1987) 'Macro-Risks, Micro-Risks, and the Media: The EDB Case', pp.183–97 in B.B. Johnson and V.T. Covello (eds), *The Social and Cultural Construction of Risk: Essays on Risk Selection and Perception*. Dordrecht: Reidel.

Sigal, L.V. (1973) *Reporters and Officials: The Organization and Politics of Newsmaking.* Lexington, Mass.: D.C. Heath & Co.

Weingart, P. (1983) 'Verwissenschaftlichung der Gesellschaft: Politisierung der Wissenschaft', *Zeitschrift für Soziologie*, 12(3): 225–41.

Chapter 17

British public affairs media and the coverage of 'Life on Mars?'*

R. Holliman

Introduction

This article aims to provide an overview of how a science issue might be studied, specifically in this case the British public affairs media (PAM) coverage of 'Life on Mars?' (LOM). It summarises the evolution of a science issue within PAM and its subsequent reception by audiences, while illustrating some of the methodologies that can be employed when studying science communication.

Since the Second World War, science has developed beyond all recognition with huge implications for public policy. Some of these scientific breakthroughs include advances in medical science, the invention of the silicon chip, satellite communications, new energy sources, environmental debates, genetics and space exploration. This multi-faceted nature of science and its role in contemporary society, combined with the potential for future progress, has led to calls for greater public accountability. This requires effective science communication.

The postwar period has also seen the media diversify technologically and economically, especially in the form of television and radio. This seems destined to continue with developments in digital broadcasting technology. Throughout this growth the media has become increasingly important as a source of information, education and entertainment. It now has the power to disseminate science communication to a wide variety of audiences, although this is not a linear process. Science communication involves a series of complex interactions that select and shape issues taking them from the laboratory to the living room. To illustrate this process, this article will briefly discuss the production, content and reception of texts with respect to LOM.

Media coverage of LOM was prompted by a 'leaked' research report on a meteorite collected from the Allan Hills, a region of Antarctica, in 1984 (MacKay *et al.* 1996). The rock in question, ALH 84001, is one of twelve confirmed as a Shergotty–Nakhla–Chassigny (SNC) meteorite, i.e. it is believed to come from Mars. The new research was published in *Science* and involved four lines of evidence:

*Newly commissioned.

- Higher levels of indigenous carbonates than in any other SNC meteorite. These have formed into globules at a temperature interpreted by MacKay *et al.* as low enough to sustain life.
- The first organic chemicals to be found in an SNC meteorite, called polycylic aromatic hydrocarbons (PAHs).
- Magnetite and iron sulphide particles, which resemble chemicals formed by some terrestrial bacteria.
- High-resolution scanning electron microscope pictures of structures similar to fossilised nanobacteria. These structures are between 10 and 100 times smaller than any terrestrial equivalents.

Each of these lines of evidence could be explained by non-biological processes. However, the interpretation given by MacKay *et al.* is that 'considered collectively, particularly in view of their spatial distribution, we conclude that they are evidence for life on early Mars' (p.929).

This case study seeks to address the different factors that shaped the PAM coverage. The 'leaking' of the work of MacKay *et al.* led directly to the early publication of this research paper by *Science*. Most of the PAM coverage of LOM occurs within three days of the first announcement, i.e. 6–9 August 1996. This initial coverage is characterised by an emphasis on 'fossil evidence' at the expense of other evidence that both supports and counters the possibility that microbial life-forms ever existed on Mars. Further research on SNC meteorites is also largely ignored, with the emphasis lying on future missions to Mars and the need for further funding to achieve this. This partial representation is, in part, due to the 'leak' of the work of MacKay *et al.*, preventing time for the critical investigation by journalists which press embargoes can allow. While the coverage evolves to include many of these wider issues and further evidence involved, this study found that the audience framed their interpretations from the initial break of the story in August.

Constructing the archive of media coverage

To begin the analysis of LOM an archive was constructed of journal articles and what Fairclough calls 'public affairs media' (PAM). This included clips taken from terrestrial television news bulletins, science documentaries and articles from the national press (Fairclough 1995: p.3). Nine national newspapers were searched: *The Daily Telegraph, Daily Express, Daily Mail, Daily Mirror, Daily Star, The Guardian, The Independent, The Sun,* and *The Times.* This archive had several functions:

- It compiled background information through PAM and relevant journal articles.
- It provided a list of interviewees for production analysis, including journalists who worked on the coverage and scientists involved in meteorite research.

- It provided all the material for content analysis.
- It provided stimulus material for the audience reception work.

Articles were collected when specifically mentioning 'Life on Mars' or ALH 84001. Initial searches were made on the journals *Science*, *Nature*, *New Scientist* and *Scientific American*. In addition, the Times and Guardian Indexes were also searched for 1994–1996 inclusive under the following terms: ALH 84001, aliens, astronomy, meteorites, Mars, NASA, Open University, planetary sciences and space. This led to the following sample periods.

Sample 1 (05/08/96–16/08/96)

Coverage of LOM broke after news of MacKay *et al.*'s research was leaked to an American trade publication called *Space News*, which printed a short paragraph about the research (05/08/96). This was picked up by a BBC science correspondent, leading to a worldwide exclusive on BBC1 (1800, 06/08/96). This research was due to be published ten days later in the journal *Science* (MacKay, Gibson *et al.* 1996). As a result of the story being 'leaked' to the media, the journal lifted the press embargo and NASA brought forward its planned press conference by nine days. This press conference was held at NASA headquarters, Washington DC (07/08/96), involving journalists from across America and beyond and lasted for two and a half hours, including over one and a half hours of questions by journalists. The conference provided detailed scientific information from the research team, with explanations of all lines of evidence given in the paper. Professor Bill Schopf, a palaeontologist independent of the research team, presented arguments about future research that he considered necessary to validate the results. He also provided examples of scientific evidence that countered these findings (e.g. Harvey and McSween 1996).

Sample 2 (30/10/96–05/11/96)

This covers 'The Searching for life in the Solar System and beyond' conference held at the Royal Society (31/10/96). This featured further unpublished research on ALH 84001 along with another SNC meteorite, Elephant Moraine (EET) A79001. Several journalists were invited to publicise the work of British planetary science (Mahood 1996).

Sample 3 (18/12/96–25/12/96)

This sample period was prompted by an article that appeared in *New Scientist* citing two research articles that counter the original NASA evidence (Holmes 1996). The first argues that the temperatures at which the carbonate globules formed were too high for life to survive (Bradley *et al.* 1996). The second article questioned the effectiveness of using PAHs as a bio-marker as these chemicals could be the result of contamination from the Antarctic ice (Becker *et al.* 1997).

Sample 4 (17/03/97-22/03/97)

No press articles were found relating to the 28th Lunar and Planetary Science Conference at Houston, Texas. This conference featured further work carried out on ALH 84001 and EET A79001. There was a large press attendance but no coverage in the British press, although it should be noted that this was the week that the British General Election was announced and therefore different editorial agendas had priority.

Production analysis

Production analysis seeks to analyse the processes and interactions involved in constructing a media text. Interviews were conducted with the Open University press office, and science journalists from television news. This followed a semi-structured questionnaire, including discussion of resource material (including the Internet) and the role of press embargoes. These were taped and transcribed for analysis.

The production of a media text can be seen as a filtering of reality through the selection of issues, agenda setting and practical constraints. Production of science reports involves an interaction begun between two professional cultures: scientists and journalists. This may involve conflict in the aims and motivations of those involved, but the relationship can just as easily be symbiotic. It would be naive to suggest that scientists will not gain experience in dealing with the media throughout their career, and many specialist science journalists are keen to promote the role of science in contemporary society. It should be remembered that LOM received extensive coverage involving many journalists (both specialist science correspondents and general reporters) and experts. The relationships between these two cultures are likely to be as varied and diverse as the number of professionals involved.

Sources

Journalists rely on many different sources of scientific information, including press releases, interest groups and government agencies, and the role of continuing stories. For LOM though, the catalyst was the journal article published in *Science* (MacKay *et al.* 1996).

Scientific journals are a fundamental source of information for journalists. They give credibility to scientific evidence and can provide invaluable background information. Prestigious multi-disciplinary science journals such as *Science*, *Nature*, *The Lancet* and the *British Medical Journal* are respected both within the scientific community and the newsroom and provide much of the 'science' that appears in PAM. The fact that LOM was due to be published in *Science* gave this research credibility. A science correspondent confirms this:

> We're terribly, terribly wary of actually publishing any science, or running any science story unless there is good material in the literature. . . . we tend to rely massively on the journals.
>
> (telephone interview, 20/05/97)

Journal articles can be read and researched in advance of publication by journalists through the system of press embargoes. As LOM was 'leaked' to the press, *Science* decided reluctantly to lift the press embargo to avoid wild speculation, and the chance for journalists to carry out initial background investigation was lost (see 'SCRAMBLE FOR THE FACTS', *The Independent*, 12/08/96: p.18, 'HOW TO HANDLE MARTIAN MANIA', Guardian On-Line, 15/08/96: p.4).

Further important sources can be built up through employing specialist science journalists. This allows for in-depth and on-going analysis of scientific information, and the construction of a reliable list of personal contacts. A codified example of this is the 'Media Resource List', a register where scientists volunteer their names and research interests for journalists seeking background information and interviews (Shortland and Gregory 1991: p.153).

The role of the Internet

The use of Internet resources in news-gathering is still in its infancy. At present, there are no conventions governing its use and it is not covered by broadcasting legislation. NASA used the speed of the Internet to good effect when the LOM research was 'leaked', as a science correspondent again explains:

> It was one of those great things where the Internet actually worked, because the basic pictures were very, very good pictures from the NASA site on the net. . . . I think it was the first time the net actually triumphed you know in terms of getting the stuff quick, it was really, really good.
>
> (telephone interview, 20/05/97)

The journal *Science* also released the paper by faxing it direct to news desks, first appearing on *Newsnight* (06/08/96), and publishing it on the Internet. The editor of *Science* allowed this in an attempt to avoid wild speculation. He argued:

> We wouldn't have chosen to put out the paper . . . but didn't want crazy stories appearing everywhere.
>
> ('HOW TO HANDLE MARTIAN MANIA', Guardian On-Line, 15/08/96: p.4)

How journalists will utilise the Internet in the future remains to be seen. Its speed was certainly an asset in this case, but the problems of providing credibility and the benefits of press embargoes in the long term may well restrict its use to peer-reviewed electronic journals.

Content analysis

Content analysis evaluates the representations of LOM in PAM. It should be seen within the context of both the production and reception of these representations. Within PAM there are different genres for representing LOM. For example, it is covered in the press, television news and science documentaries. Each genre will frame the discourse in different ways according to time and spatial constraints, so coverage will not appear as a homogeneous entity. LOM appeared in all these genres, even though the tabloid press rarely covers science issues. However, when compared with the broadsheet press, the tabloids tend to exploit the more sensationalist elements involved; for example, 'DON'T PANIC – YOU CAN GET 100 MARTIANS ON A SINGLE FULL STOP' (*Daily Mirror*, 08/08/96: p.1).

A coding frame was constructed for each of the articles in the archive. This involved basic information such as the name of the newspaper/programme, date and sample period, page number, format (i.e. news report, feature, letter, editorial, cartoon, news bulletin, science documentary), correspondent, headline, whether there were any pictures used, size of article, experts mentioned (and whether these were direct or secondary citations), evidence cited and the basic themes of the article. Television programmes were audio-taped and transcribed. The archive was then analysed by employing thematic analysis. This involves:

- Assessing the relevant themes, arguments and structure of the coverage.
- Analysing how these themes are portrayed.
- Quantifying the frequency of their appearances.

(Philo 1990: pp.167–8)

The breakdown of the four samples is shown in Figure 17.1. Of the four periods studied, sample 1 clearly provides the vast majority of the press coverage. Samples 2 and 3 provide coverage of the scientific findings to a greater or lesser degree, whereupon the story drops out of the media quickly.

Sample I

Over the ten-day period sample 1 contains a total of 158 press articles and 13 television bulletins. Figure 17.2 shows a further breakdown of press articles in sample 1 over the ten-day period. It becomes apparent that the bulk of the press articles occur on the 08–09/08/96, the days immediately after the NASA press

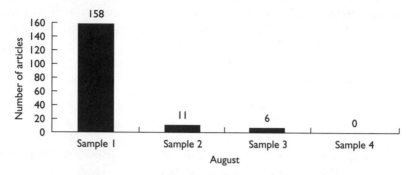

Figure 17.1 Distribution of press articles over the four sample periods

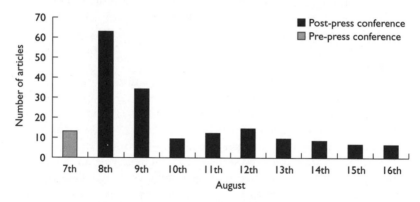

Figure 17.2 Distribution of press coverage in sample I

conference. Due to the 'leaking' of the story though, articles do appear on 07/08/96. The archive was initially split into pre- and post-press conference for further analysis.

Pre- and post-press conference

Pre-press conference coverage contained 13 articles in the press (146 column-inches), with five as front-page stories. Television coverage included seven bulletins with approximately 29 minutes coverage, including 12 minutes on *Newsnight* (06/08/96).

Over the nine days, post-press conference coverage was extensive (1,629 column inches), although much of this coverage appeared directly after the press conference (727 column-inches on 08/08/96), with full-page features, editorials and five papers carrying the story on the front page. Following this, the Sunday broadsheets carried feature articles on Mars but apart from this the coverage tapers off quickly, disappearing initially from the tabloids. Television had a further six bulletins, with approximately 15 minutes coverage, including coverage of the press conference, dropping out of the news on 08/08/96. The vast majority of PAM coverage of LOM appeared over a four-day period (06–09/08/96), before and after the press conference at NASA. It follows then that analysis of this key period is fundamental when evaluating the audience interpretations of LOM.

Sample 2

Coverage appeared in both the television news and press, consisting of eleven items (112 column-inches). No reference to the conference appears in *The Guardian*, *The Sun* or the *Daily Star*. The extract below illustrates the emphasis of sample 2 on the work of British scientists:

> The all-important question of who was the first to find evidence of life on the red planet is also challenged by yesterday's evidence, which puts the British years ahead of the American team.
>
> ('LIFE ON MARS WAS FOUND BY BRITONS AND IT'S
> STILL THERE', *The Daily Telegraph*, 01/11/96: p.1)

New evidence was cited of complex organic chemicals and the fact that due to the geological age of EET A79001, life might still exist. One of the scientists involved, Dr Ian Wright, was quoted in both the press and television coverage:

> We reanalysed grains within the meteorite and the carbon-based material we found had to have been formed by microbial activity. There is no other explanation. This is a smoking gun for life on Mars.
>
> ('BRITISH STUDY STRENGTHENS CLAIMS OF LIFE ON MARS',
> *The Times*, 01/11/96: p.6)

There are references to 'fossil evidence', but these relate to the MacKay *et al.* (1996) paper. The original evidence was also countered in three of the articles, citing the potential for contamination, temperature formation of the carbonates and requirements laid out by Professor Schopf at the original Washington press conference.

Sample 3

Sample 3 comprises six press articles (35 column-inches). The one item on television is a *Newsnight* interview with NASA administrator Dan Goldin (20/12/96) discussing the most important events of 1996. There is no discussion of the new research that contests the MacKay *et al.* interpretation, but it does appear in four of the press articles. Despite citing these same two research articles (Bradley *et al.* 1996; Becker *et al.* 1997), a contradiction emerges. Three of the articles lead with the new research findings, e.g. 'LIFE ON MARS THEORY FACES THE FINAL CURTAIN' (*The Independent*, 19/ 12/96: p.4). One, however, leads with 'TEST BACKS LIFE ON MARS THEORY' (*Daily Express*, 23/12/96: p.4) based on research being carried out at Edinburgh University, which had not been published. This illustrates how the same evidence can be represented very differently following the production process.

The main themes

Coverage of LOM involved several major themes, which are explained below. These are the role of evidence, probability, the desire for future missions to Mars, scepticism (linked to funding and the nature and timing of the August announcement), and the role of experts. Minor themes also appeared. These included 'human stories' such as the British member of the research team, Simon Clemett, and his 'battle with dyslexia', which was covered in seven of the nine newspapers. Cartoons were employed to give a humorous angle to the coverage, while science fiction featured with reference to the H.G. Wells novel *The War of the Worlds* and the film *Independence Day*, released in Britain in August 1996.

Evidence

The crucial element in any science news report is the evidence presented. LOM was dominated in the PAM coverage by the potential that 'fossil evidence' had been found. Despite the press conference and early release of the paper by *Science*, some of the coverage is inaccurate and sensationalist, e.g. 'The discovery of a *six inch fossil* in a meteorite is hugely exciting' (*The Sun*, 08/08/96: p.6, my emphasis). These references to fossil evidence appeared when the story broke:

> Science correspondent: Scientists who have got wind of the new paper are agog. If a *fossil* really has been found in the meteorite from Mars it will revolutionise our understanding of how life began.
> (BBC1, 18:00, 06/08/96, my emphasis)

However, MacKay *et al.*'s paper (1996) was based on several lines of evidence in favour of a biological interpretation, including carbonate globules, PAHs and magnetite crystals. These lines of evidence were largely ignored in the coverage, as was how the scientists confirmed ALH 84001 as an SNC meteorite. Further evidence that countered the MacKay *et al.* interpretation was almost completely ignored until samples 2 and 3. This included a high-temperature theory for the carbonate formation (Bradley *et al.* 1996) and potential for terrestrial contamination (Becker *et al.* 1997). This was despite being cited in the MacKay *et al.*

report and at the Washington press conference. This emphasis on fossil evidence was employed as a substitute for the esoteric and complicated scientific procedures employed. This simplification of the issues, effectively to a single line of evidence, gave the impression that the scientific evidence is not contested.

Probability

The possibility that 'life' might be discovered on Mars has been a catalyst for speculation for centuries, encapsulated by H.G. Wells in the famous phrase from his novel *The War of the Worlds*: 'The chances against anything man-like on Mars are a million to one' (1993: p.9).

Within the coverage of LOM, probability became a metaphor for speculation on the validity of MacKay *et al.*'s research findings. This was most obvious in the stories of betting that appeared in the tabloid press and television news:

> Newscaster: Now it's not official yet, but the bookies at least are worried. The odds against finding intelligent life on Mars have been cut from 500 to just 25–1.
>
> (ITN, 12:30, 07/08/96)

The early coverage in sample 1 also pointed to the potential that if life once existed on Mars it could be ubiquitous in the universe:

> Science correspondent: If it did this could mean the whole universe is teeming with life.
>
> (*Newsnight*, 06/08/96)

This appears again in sample 2 while discussing the findings on EET A79001:

> Interviewee: If you find evidence of life on two planetary bodies from a solar system that are close neighbours, it opens up the door for all kinds of possible speculations about life elsewhere.
>
> (Channel 4 News, 05/11/96)

Future missions to Mars

Further space exploration was discussed at the expense of further investigations on the 12 SNC meteorites already available for further research. Ultimately this emphasis on future missions to Mars was linked to the prospect of colonising Mars:

Newscaster: I suppose the pressure for another mission to Mars is irresistible now?

Interviewee: Absolutely. I think it would be really rejecting our heritage if we were to not follow up on this very interesting result.

(ITN, 12:30, 07/08/96)

Scepticism

The nature and timing of the release of the story raised speculation as to why the article was 'leaked' to the media, lending the story a dramatic impact. Even without this 'leak', MacKay *et al.*'s work would have been published just before Congress was to debate NASA's annual budget. The reasons for this are a matter of speculation, but the end result was extensive media exposure for the question of LOM and an emphasis on NASA's future missions to Mars. This was reflected in the coverage:

> Science correspondent: The discovery has done wonders for the life in outer space enthusiasts, but it will also do wonders for the American space agency NASA. NASA is facing a ferocious budget squeeze. The suggestion of life on Mars will revitalise its future Mars missions.
>
> (BBC1, 13:00, 07/08/96)

The role of the 'expert'

The use of experts gives an argument credibility and authority, and LOM was no exception. What was surprising though was the range and diversity of experts that appeared in the coverage. The use of direct and secondary sources in the LOM coverage was extensive, with a total of 163 different sources in the press coverage of sample 1. These included 78 'scientific experts' and intellectual institutions, three from scientific journals, 16 religious spokespeople, ten philosophers, 25 from the arts (including musicians, film and literature), four politicians, four explorers and 23 miscellaneous. Less than half of those cited were scientists. This is illustrated in Figure 17.3.

Five research institutions were involved in the original research article: Lockheed Martin; the Department of Chemistry, Stanford University; the Johnson Space Centre, NASA; the Savannah River Ecology Laboratory; and the Department of Earth and Planetary Sciences at McGill University. Of these five, NASA was cited in 70 of the articles in the press coverage in sample 1, Stanford University eight times and Lockheed Martin twice. None of the other institutions was mentioned, giving the impression that NASA alone was responsible for the research. This was reflected in the coverage:

> Science correspondent: At a news conference in Washington today the American space agency NASA bathed in the glory of its scientists' findings.
>
> (BBC1, 21:00, 07/08/96)

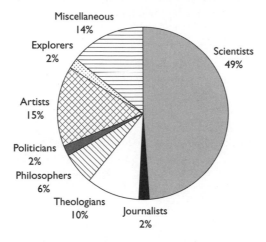

Figure 17.3 Distribution of sources within sample I of LOM press archive

This emphasis on NASA as the sole contributing institution was also reflected where the researchers themselves were concerned. Only once in the whole coverage were all nine scientists involved in the research cited, this being a summary of the findings (*The Daily Telegraph*, 08/08/96: p.4), whereas in the television news coverage, none of the MacKay *et al.* team appeared. Monica Grady, a British meteoriticist studying the meteorites at the Natural History Museum, was the most cited scientist in the coverage. She was quoted 15 times directly (nine times before the press conference) and once as a secondary source. The citations before the press conference centred around comments which first appeared as the story broke on the BBC news. These were quoted directly in seven of the press articles the following day:

> Monica Grady: It is entirely possible that primitive, very, very primitive organisms might have arisen. Now I'm not talking about ammonites or corals or anything like that, I'm talking about incredibly primitive micro-fossils, very, very small organisms. And it would be absolutely fascinating to find these.
>
> (BBC1, 18:00, 06/08/96)

However, the most cited individual was President Bill Clinton, quoted directly ten times and nine times as a secondary source. Many of these citations involved the same quote, taken from a press conference on the White House lawn:

> President Clinton: If this discovery is confirmed it will surely be one of the

most stunning insights into our universe that science has ever uncovered. Its implications are as far reaching and awe inspiring as can be imagined.

(BBC1, 21:00, 07/08/96).

Dan Goldin, NASA administrator, also featured heavily after his comments at the press conference, including ten direct and four secondary citations. His rhetoric was highly emotive:

Dan Goldin: We're now on a doorstep to the heavens. What a time to be alive. Thank you all. I'm so proud of you words can't describe it.

(BBC1, 21:00, 07/08/96)

Conclusion

The content analysis shows that LOM was simplified by many of the journalists involved to emphasise the role of fossil evidence, discussions around the nature and timing of the original announcement and calls for future missions to Mars, while reducing the role of the expert to secondary analysis of the evidence. How then are these representations interpreted by audiences?

Audience reception analysis

Audience reception analysis evaluates the ways in which audiences deconstruct science communication, and in turn what effects, if any, this has on their views of science in society. For the purpose of this research, audiences are seen as heterogeneous, actively deconstructing media messages which are polysemous in their interpretation (Eldridge 1993). Focus group interviews were employed to analyse this reception of LOM (see Morgan 1997 for further discussion of focus group interviews), including twenty-four respondents split into six focus groups, three with scientists and three with non-scientists. Scientists were defined as those with professional scientific qualifications above A-level. Those involved were self-selecting participants, who knew the other respondents in the group before the interview started. This allows for a more relaxed and 'natural' atmosphere with discussion of topics using everyday language (Kitzinger 1994: p.116). The groups included an all-male group, two all-female groups and three mixed-gender groups.

The interviews were based on a semi-structured format and began with a short questionnaire asking the respondents to give information about which media they regularly viewed, and then to write headlines about science and LOM specifically. The aim here was to gain some perspective on individual knowledge before the group interaction began. Respondents were then asked to prepare a news bulletin on LOM. This involved using stimulus material taken from the sample archives and is called the 'news game' methodology (see Philo

1990). This was followed by a general discussion of the LOM story and more general science issues. Groups lasted for approximately one hour and were taped and transcribed. All participants were guaranteed anonymity.

Results

Respondents quickly got to grips with the task of constructing the news bulletin, with all six groups managing to construct a bulletin using the stimulus material. While preparing the bulletin it became apparent that within the non-scientist groups, certain members were seen as having a greater level of scientific knowledge. As a result, they were granted the status of 'pseudo-expert' by the rest of the group and given the opportunity for greater input into the bulletin's construction. This may well have been the result of the groups being self-selecting and members knowing each other before the interview.

The construction, structure, contents and use of stimulus material within these bulletins was strikingly similar when compared with the television news bulletins in sample 1. No group remembered the continuing debates and/or evidence presented in samples 2 and 3. Instead the emphasis was on the initial framing of LOM as it appeared in the PAM coverage in early August. This was also reflected in the group discussion:

> Respondent A: For such a, for such a fantastic thing i.e. Life on Mars, it wasn't really in the media for that long, I didn't even really even hear about it, I just caught it on the news.
>
> (Group 2, 'Scientist')

While respondents did not remember specific names they did remember the main themes of the coverage shown in the content analysis. This compliments earlier research findings using the news game methodology (see Philo 1990: p.175). For example, 'fossil evidence' was mentioned in five of the focus groups:

> *Respondent A:* Fossil, have we mentioned fossil? 'Cos they kept going on about fossil, fossil.
>
> *Respondent B:* I've put this particle contains fossilised bacteria thought to be from a life-form on Mars.
>
> (Group 5, 'Non-scientist')

Further questioning found that respondents were critical of the over-simplification and partial representation of scientific evidence in science communication in general:

> Respondent A: I would say they are just picking on little things and throw little things at you and just sort of pick out one aspect of the story which has got twenty different sort of aspects you could look at.
>
> (Group 4, 'Scientist')

All groups started in the studio with a headline from BBC newsreader Moira Stewart. Respondents then structured the bulletins around arguments 'for and against' the possibilities of LOM. The use of experts follows these arguments put forward in the bulletins. For example:

> Respondent B: You've gotta have conflicting views, 'cos there's always conflicting views isn't there, the British guy is bound to say, yeah it's real and the American's gonna say nah.
>
> (Group 2, 'Scientist')

and

> Respondent B: Professor, just say X, was looking at the fossil evidence, Dr Y has said that the existence of life on Mars may have been quite probable at some stage in the development in the universe. Dr Z is quite dubious about its existence as the fossil may have been blown from another side of the universe.
>
> (Group 4 bulletin, 'Scientist')

Other themes from the coverage also appear. For example, the groups critically discussed the issue of further funding:

> Respondent A: Sceptics have regarded this as another hype for extra funding for NASA, now the space race is slowing down.
>
> (Group 3 bulletin, 'Scientist')

and probability:

> Respondent A: we could have a final one that the odds of finding life on Mars at Ladbrokes have been reduced from a million to one to a thousand to one, or something like that.
>
> (Group 4, 'Scientist')

The science, however, was perceived to be too esoteric and was rarely discussed, and never in a critical light. For example, when asked about how the scientists had discovered ALH 84001 was an SNC meteorite respondents argued that it was 'guesswork', 'because of its colour' 'because it has come through the atmosphere' or 'because they know it didn't come from Earth'. The content analysis proves that this information was excluded in favour of the fossil evidence. The fact that the focus groups also emphasised the role of fossil evidence within the initial framing of the LOM coverage highlights the potential influence of PAM in informing public debate where little information is previously known.

Conclusions

Due to time, spatial and editorial constraints, PAM is selective in its representations of science. The potential discovery of LOM is a dramatic issue that gained extensive coverage between 6 and 9 August 1996, having gained the additional news value resulting from the 'leaking' of the evidence to the media. The content analysis shows that much of the coverage simplified the lines of evidence and counter-evidence, emphasising the most contested element, the fossil-like structures, while appearing to reduce the experts involved to NASA alone. The audience research demonstrates the ability of PAM to frame scientific discourse, which reflects the initial coverage of LOM. This confirms earlier research, which argues that the initial framing of an issue is fundamental to audience interpretations (Eldridge 1993: p.172–3).

However, PAM are not homogeneous, with comprehensive articles appearing in the press, and both *Newsnight* and Channel 4 News continuing to follow the scientific debate surrounding ALH 84001 since the August 1996 furore. Employing specialist science correspondents can only enhance this potential, along with science documentaries such as 'Aliens from Mars' (*Horizon*, BBC2, 11/11/96) and magazine programmes such as *The Sky at Night*, which help to provide a wider perspective on scientific research, providing a counter to the simplistic representations of some PAM. To gain a comprehensive view though requires the audience to follow the coverage over a period of time.

PAM is not the only medium for the communication of science, but it does disseminate information to a wide audience. It may also act as a gatekeeper to further investigation. The relationship between the production, content and reception of messages is far from linear. What we see in the media is not a simple translation of reality. Science communication is shaped by power relations, conventions and structural frameworks. Audiences are not static or passive though, deconstructing information in terms of their environment, the information presented, cultural influences and personal biography. This research confirms that the audience did engage in the issues surrounding LOM, despite lacking expert knowledge of the scientific evidence involved. However, this is heavily influenced by the initial PAM coverage in sample 1, and therefore presents a partial representation of the full complexity of the potential for LOM and the role of SNC meteorites in this debate.

References

Becker, L., D.P. Glavin, *et al.* (1997). 'Polycyclic aromatic hydrocarbons (PAHs) in Antarctic Martian meteorites, carbonaceous condrites and polar ice'. *Geochimica et Cosmochimica Acta* 61(2): 475–81.

Bradley, J.P., R.P. Harvey, *et al.* (1996). 'Magnetite whiskers and platelets in the ALH84001 Martian meteorite: Evidence of vapour phase growth'. *Geochimica et Cosmochimica Acta* 60(24): 5149–55.

Eldridge, J.E.T., (ed.) (1993). *Getting the Message – News, Truth and Power.* London and New York, Routledge.

Fairclough, N. (1995). *Media Discourse.* London, New York, Sydney, Auckland, Edward Arnold.

Harvey, R.P. and H.Y. McSween Jr (1996). 'A possible high-temperature origin for the carbonates in the Martian meteorite ALH84001'. *Nature* 382 (4 July): 49–51.

Holmes, R. (1996). 'Death knell for Martian life'. *New Scientist* 152, No. 2061/2 (21/28 December): 4.

Kitzinger, J. (1994). 'The methodology of focus groups: the importance of interaction between research participants'. *Sociology of Health and Illness* 16(1).

MacKay, D.S., E.K. Gibson Jr, *et al.* (1996). 'Search for past life on Mars: Possible relic biogenic activity on Martian meteorite ALH84001'. *Science* 273 (16 August): 924–30.

Mahood, E. (1996). 'British scientists seek recognition of role in "life on Mars debate."' *Nature* 384 (7 November): 3–4.

Morgan, D.L. (1997). *Focus Groups as Qualitative Research*, 2nd edition. Sage, London.

Philo, G. (1990). *Seeing is Believing.* London and New York, Routledge.

Shortland, M. and J. Gregory (1991). *Communicating Science: A Handbook.* London, Longman.

Wells, H.G. (1993). *The War of the Worlds.* London and Vermont, Everyman.

Index